"Claudio Saunt has written the definit... ...d but seldom understood central episode in American history. In his subtle and exceedingly well documented account, Saunt shows how planters eager for land, southern politicians consolidating their power, and New York bankers launched one of the largest mass deportations in U.S. history. They encountered resourceful Native Americans who deployed all means at their disposal to retain their land. This harrowing account of theft, dispossession, novel bureaucratic capacities, and unimaginable violence drew me in in ways that few history books do. *Unworthy Republic* will make you think in new ways about the history of the United States and will help you understand the roots of some of today's inequalities. It is one of the most important books published on U.S. history in recent years and should be required reading for all Americans."

—Sven Beckert, Laird Bell Professor of History, Harvard University, author of *Empire of Cotton*

"*Unworthy Republic* is a study in power. It describes, in detail, the coming together of money, rhetoric, political ambition, and white-supremacist idealism. Saunt shows his readers the cost of a racial caste system in the United States." —David Treuer, *Foreign Affairs*

"Claudio Saunt . . . offers a damning synthesis of the federal betrayals, mass deportations, and exterminatory violence that defined the 1830s. . . . Lining up his own calculations alongside recent studies of slavery, Saunt casts indigenous expulsion and the domestic slave trade as twinned trails of tears, economic successes rooted in profound moral failures." —Caitlin Fitz, *Atlantic*

"A major achievement. . . . [Saunt] manages to do something truly rare: destroy the illusion that history's course is inevitable and recover the reality of the multiple possibilities that confronted contemporaries."

—Nick Romeo, *Washington Post*

"A powerful and lucid account, weaving together events with the people who experienced them up close. . . . Saunt doesn't try to smooth over the knottier parts of his narrative. . . . He's also aware that the documentary record over-represents the voices of those who left a paper trail. His account acknowledges the diverse experiences within and across Indigenous communities."

—Jennifer Szalai, *New York Times*

"There has been insufficient 'reckoning with the conquest of the continent,' Claudio Saunt relays in this excellent new book. In many accounts of U.S. history, the discussion of the mass deportation of Native nations during the 1830s remains far too brief. Deportation's legacies in law, culture, and community continue to this day and find powerful exploration in this important addition to the field." —Ned Blackhawk (Western Shoshone), professor of history and American studies, Yale University

"A much-needed rendering of a disgraceful episode in American history that has been too long misunderstood." —Peter Cozzens, *Wall Street Journal*

"*Unworthy Republic* offers a much-needed corrective to the American canon, showing how a heavy-handed president, a deadlocked Congress, and a lust for profit combined to construct a shameful national legacy. . . . A riveting story that invites us all to reflect on how we got where we are today."

—Elizabeth Fenn, Distinguished Professor, University of Colorado Boulder, Pulitzer Prize–winning author of *Encounters at the Heart of the World*

"Thoroughly researched and quietly outraged." —Chris Hewitt, *Star Tribune*

"A powerful, moving argument that the state-sponsored expulsion of the 1830s was a horrendous turning point for the Indigenous peoples in the United States. . . . A significant, well-rendered study of a disturbing period in American history." —*Kirkus Reviews*, starred review

"A stark and well-documented case that Native American expulsion was a political choice rather than an inevitable tragedy. This searing account forces a new reckoning with American history." —*Publishers Weekly*, starred review

UNWORTHY REPUBLIC

THE

Dispossession OF
Native Americans

AND THE

Road TO
Indian Territory

~~~

CLAUDIO SAUNT

W. W. NORTON & COMPANY
Independent Publishers Since 1923

For information about permission to reproduce selections from this book, write to
Permissions, W. W. Norton & Company, Inc., 500 Fifth Avenue, New York, NY 10110

For information about special discounts for bulk purchases, please contact
W. W. Norton Special Sales at specialsales@wwnorton.com or 800-233-4830

Manufacturing by Lake Book Manufacturing
Book design by Marysarah Quinn

Library of Congress Cataloging-in-Publication Data

Names: Saunt, Claudio, author.
Title: Unworthy republic : the dispossession of Native Americans and the road to Indian
territory / Claudio Saunt.
Description: First edition. | New York : W. W. Norton & Company, 2020. | Includes
bibliographical references and index.
Identifiers: LCCN 2019050502 | ISBN 9780393609844 (hardcover) |
ISBN 9780393609851 (epub)
Subjects: LCSH: Indian Removal, 1813–1903. | Indians of North America—Government
relations—1789–1869. | United States—History—1815–1861.
Classification: LCC E98.R4 S38 2020 | DDC 323.1197/07309034—dc23
LC record available at https://lccn.loc.gov/2019050502

ISBN 978-0-393-54156-4 pbk.

W. W. Norton & Company, Inc., 500 Fifth Avenue, New York, N.Y. 10110
www.wwnorton.com

W. W. Norton & Company Ltd., 15 Carlisle Street, London W1D 3BS

2 3 4 5 6 7 8 9 0

We have our misfourtine as with other nations on this continent. The Cherokees have bin treated by the American Republic unworthy of the head of a civilized goverment her name will go down to future eyes with scorn and reproach on her head. She will fell it in her legislative halls it never will be eradicated from her history historians will have to write it down on her pages which will go down to the latest posterty.

—JAMES A. FOLSOM, a young Choctaw student
at Miami University of Ohio, to his uncle,
Peter Pitchlynn, October 31, 1831[1]

CONTENTS

SECTION FOUR:

FINANCING DISPOSSESSION

SECTION FIVE:

FROM EXPULSION TO EXTERMINATION

INTRODUCTION

"Words Are Delusive"

~~~

SITUATED IN the hardscrabble red-clay hills of north Georgia, Danielsville had little to recommend it but much to celebrate on July 4, 1836. It was the sixtieth birthday of the American Republic, and nearly one hundred members of the Madison County Company of Volunteers were gathered around a "bountifully furnished" table beneath an awning at Captain Richardson Hancock's plantation. Hancock's dozen or so slaves waited on them. The revelers paid tribute to customary Fourth of July subjects: the government of the United States ("the most equal and best in the world"), patriotism (the "noblest passion"), and the people ("brave, generous and patriotic"). But they also applauded several local heroes, starting with Thomas Chambers, from nearby Gwinnett County, who, just a few days before the festivities, had taken "an Indian's scalp" about a hundred miles south of present-day Atlanta. Inspired by Chambers's feat, A.G. Ware, one of the volunteer soldiers, rose and announced that he was willing to go anywhere at any time "to wreak vengeance on the savage foe of our land." Not to be outdone, Samuel Williford boasted that he would do so without pay. Others followed in the same vein, wishing that the "Indians" would be massacred and promising to "drive" them from the country.[1]

The same week of the Fourth, state militia waded through mud and water and descended on a camp of dispossessed indigenous Americans in southwest Georgia, killing twenty to thirty of the refugees. The fleeing survivors left trails of blood in their wake. U.S. troops force-marched 1,600 native men, women, and children toward steamboats docked at Montgomery, Alabama. The men walked in iron chains. In southern Alabama, soldiers pursued a group of native people into a swamp, where they shot and killed four of them. In Tennessee and North Carolina that summer, U.S. citizens drove indigenous families off their farms with cowhide whips and hickory clubs. The dispossessed took refuge in the dense forests of the Appalachians, where they fought off starvation. In Florida, some four thousand U.S. troops spent the Republic's sixtieth birthday waging war against the region's longtime residents. They had recently shipped 450 native people westward across the Gulf of Mexico and up the Mississippi River. Only three hundred of the destitute deportees survived to reach their destination, a place called Indian Territory.[2]

The summer of 1836 belongs to the decade of "Indian Removal," as the policy was and is still known. Indian Removal is the subject of this book, though I do not use either word except in historical context. "Indian" is for good reason a designation of pride for many native people in the United States today, but when used to describe the diverse individuals and communities who were expelled from their homelands in the nineteenth century, its fanciful and specious associations distort our understanding of the past. Indians were savage and primitive or noble and in touch with nature. They were stoic, brave, cowardly, untrustworthy, honorable, and doomed. The men were not husbands and fathers but "warriors," the women "squaws," "maidens," or "burden bearers." Political leaders were "chiefs," and communities or nations were "tribes." Indians were, in short, different from other people. The label conjures up so many stereotypes that it clouds the mind, making it impossible to see the past clearly. In the context of American history, it evokes tragedy and inevitability, creating a dense fog that obscures the choices that U.S. politicians and their constituents made in the early years of the Republic.

"Removal" is equally unfitting for a story about the state-sponsored expulsion of eighty thousand people. It is "a soft word," said the Massachusetts representative Edward Everett in a debate on the floor of the House in 1830, "and words are delusive." Then and now, it conveys no sense of coercion or violence. The phrase "Indian Removal," coined by proponents of the policy, has all of the problems of its two constituent terms and possesses an additional fault.[3] In the nineteenth century, people removed themselves to new locales or were removed for committing crimes. "Indian Removal," however, was an unusual construction that left unstated who was removing whom. Were Indians doing it to themselves? The phrase is artfully vague.

There are other ways of describing what the United States did to indigenous people in the 1830s. Human rights activists, writing about events in the twenty-first century, speak of "forced migration," but I am not alone in finding the phrase too distant from events on the ground. "Ethnic cleansing," a term of propaganda that became widely used during the Bosnian War in the 1990s, is rightly criticized for being nebulous and even for obscuring violence. "Genocide" elevates a single question above all others: Does the event fit the definition of the crime, as defined by the 1948 United Nations Convention on Genocide? European colonists and their descendants undeniably acted with genocidal intent at certain times and places, but how often and how extensively is a matter of debate.[4] My focus lies elsewhere.

I use three other words to describe U.S. policy in the 1830s. One is "deportation." Deportation is conducted by states, and the term therefore captures the administrative and bureaucratic process that underpinned the federal government's expulsion of native peoples. Since a nation can only deport people who are on its soil—beyond its borders, it must resort to diplomacy or force of arms—"deportation" also points to the U.S.

assault on indigenous sovereignty in the 1830s, when the federal government and several states extended their jurisdiction and authority over
lands not belonging to them. To evoke the underlying violence of the
act, I also refer to the uprooting of Native Americans as an "expulsion."
The word has the advantage of being historically accurate, for it was used
at the time by the policy's opponents and victims. When appropriate, I
use a third term, borrowed from the perpetrators themselves, who on
certain occasions referred to their goal as one of "extermination."[5]

I was inspired to tackle this project when I inherited a cache of letters from my grandfather, who escaped from Hungary to Cleveland,
Ohio, in December 1937. He corresponded with his parents and siblings
in Sátoraljaújhely, in northeastern Hungary, until 1944, when Nazis
deported them to Auschwitz. Reading through the letters, I began to
reconsider the deportation that occurred a little over a century earlier
near my current home in Athens, Georgia. Some of the town's main
streets—Lumpkin, Clayton, Dearing—bear the names of local figures
who played national roles in this earlier deportation. There are several
striking similarities between the expulsion of indigenous peoples in the
1830s and the state-sponsored mass deportations of the twentieth century in Turkey, Greece, Germany, the Soviet Union, and elsewhere. In
both periods, administrators described the inevitable march of "civilization," the "necessity" of deporting populations that could "only with
difficulty assimilate," and the "grandiose" plans that they had devised to
address the situation—arrogant language that masked the brutality and
disarray of their efforts.[6]

"The Indian question" was the U.S. counterpart to Europe's "Jewish
question," two formulations that invited paternalistic measures at best,
expulsion or extermination at worst. "Indians," like Jews, Gypsies, slaves,
and "free negroes," wrote the *Georgia Journal* in 1825, were "a kind of
citizens of an *inferior order*." What was to be done with them? By the
1830s, the expression "the Indian question" was circulating widely in the
United States. About a decade later, "the Jewish question" began appear-

ing regularly in English, though it originated in the late eighteenth century with Russia's invasion of Poland, an event that U.S. citizens in the
1830s frequently compared to the expulsion of the Cherokee Nation.
At least Russia, unlike the United States, was not "exterminating the
population," wrote Robert Campbell of Savannah in 1829.[7] The United
States, the self-described exceptional nation, was not so exceptional in
this instance; it belongs on a woefully long list of states that sponsored
mass deportations. In fact, it was among the first in the modern era to
undertake such an operation.

Rather than systematically comparing and contrasting modern
deportations, however, I am more interested in exploring the deportation that sits at the heart of the American Republic's first century.
This book makes three related arguments. First, it argues that the state-
administered mass expulsion of indigenous people was unprecedented.
At first glance, this assertion may seem foolish. From the moment the
British set foot in North America, they began driving off native residents.
By 1830, the continent's original inhabitants retained only one hundred
thousand of the approximately million square miles in the United States
east of the Mississippi River. Nonetheless, in the long history of dispossession in North America—of the Pequots, Narragansetts, Wampano-
ags, Yamasees, Tuscaroras, Guale, Natchez, and so on—the U.S. policy
of mass expulsion in the 1830s was a first. In previous decades, British,
Spanish, and French colonists had driven out indigenous people by waging war, introducing fatal viruses, destroying the environment, and pros-
elytizing, while this time the United States subjected Native Americans
to a formal state-administered process that produced censuses, property
lists, land plats, expulsion registries, commutation certificates, and the
like, all culminating in a journey, by foot, wagon, or steamboat, to lands
west of the Mississippi.

The U.S.-sponsored expulsion of the 1830s became something of a
model for colonial empires around the world. Though forced resettle-
ment dates to at least the Neo-Assyrian Empire (911–609 B.C.E.), the

massive U.S. undertaking was close at hand, a recent example of what an ambitious state could accomplish with modern administrative tools. Alexis de Tocqueville, who published his famous account of *Democracy in America* in the 1830s, witnessed the "solemn spectacle" of a party of Choctaw families crossing the icy Mississippi River at the outset of the decade. Despite his ambivalence about the policy, he deemed the energy and determination of U.S. expansion a model for French Algeria. Within five years of the French occupation of Algeria in 1830, colonists were referring to the locals as "indigènes," a term formerly reserved for people in the New World. America was "talked about incessantly," French administrators observed.[8]

The U.S.-sponsored expulsion also occupied the minds of Russian officers in the Caucasus in the 1840s. "These Circassians are just like your American Indians," the regional governor reportedly told one American visitor, shortly before Russia deported a half million people. Toward the end of the century, German imperialists in southwest Africa looked to the United States for an example of how to expel local residents in the name of progress, a goal that was widely shared by European administrators who coveted the African continent's vast resources. Notoriously, during the Nazi conquest of Eastern Europe, Hitler equated "indigenous inhabitants" with "Indians" and declared that "the Volga must be our Mississippi."[9]

Those self-serving and unsettling comparisons say as much about the politicians who made them as about the actual policy pursued by the United States in the 1830s. European administrators knew that the United States had expanded relentlessly across the continent but rarely bothered to learn the specifics. Regardless, the comparisons reveal that other imperial states saw something noteworthy and admirable about U.S. policy. When administrators counted, evaluated, deported, and sometimes exterminated people within their borders, the United States— whose meteoric rise was the envy of many—was rarely far from mind.[10]

The second and related point made by this book is that the state-sponsored expulsion of the 1830s was a turning point for indigenous peoples and for the United States. Expulsion was "the worst evil that can befall them," stated Neha Micco to his fellow Creek citizens. It was a "scheme . . . to get rid of them," wrote the great Cherokee leader John Ross. The dispossession of thousands of families was an "act of usurpation . . . unparaleled in history," asserted the Choctaw leader George Colbert. Many white Americans shared the same sentiment. Residents in upstate New York wrote of the "indelible disgrace of our Republic" should indigenous people be expelled. Another group from Portage County, Ohio (just off Lake Erie), insisted that Congress's actions would determine "whether the future Historian of our Country shall applaud their measures, or brand the character of this young and boasting Republic with infamy and disgrace."[11]

Expulsion transformed the geographical relationship between the continent's longtime residents and its newcomers. Though borders, reservations, and neutral grounds had separated the two peoples on maps almost from the outset of colonization, the policy of eliminating every native individual from the region east of the Mississippi—for that was the intent if not the letter of the law in the 1830s—was extraordinary. As one ardent opponent of expulsion observed, Congress authorized "the banishment of Indians from the national limits of the United States, and even from this continent." The Mississippi River, wrote the English Quaker William Howitt, "is the boundary which American cupidity at present sets between itself and Indian extirpation."[12]

The geographical segregation created a westward-moving frontier, and as the United States expanded toward the Pacific over the course of the nineteenth century, the army maintained that frontier by killing native people or concentrating them on marginal lands.[13] The infamous Plains Wars of the second half of the nineteenth century culminated in the massacre at Wounded Knee in 1890. But when the Seventh Cavalry shot and killed over 150 women, children, and men and buried them in a mass grave in South Dakota, they put the final period on a policy established in the 1830s.

This book makes a third crucial point: The expulsion of indigenous people was far from inevitable. This observation should be uncontroversial, for it is a truism that nothing in history is predetermined. Yet we have accepted the argument of the proponents of expulsion, though reversing the moral polarity. They contended that the continent's original inhabitants were too primitive to survive east of the Mississippi, an assertion that the inhabitants themselves vigorously denied. We, by contrast, believe that the continent's newcomers were too avaricious to allow them to remain. (One stream of scholarship calls this clockwork imperialism "settler colonialism.")[14] Statements of inevitability about the past should be greeted as skeptically as predictions about the future.

It is not difficult to imagine an alternative history. Congressmen who were opposed to federal spending, against the expansion of slavery, dedicated to Christianizing native peoples, hostile to Andrew Jackson, or simply reluctant to overturn current policy might have found enough common ground to join together temporarily to block the expulsion of Native Americans. The vagaries of national politics might have delayed further action on the matter for a few years, until the Panic of 1837 slowed the gathering momentum to drive out native peoples. Then the mounting sectional crisis might have brought it to a temporary halt. In the 1850s, indigenous peoples would have still lived on their homelands east of the Mississippi (as indeed several thousand did), with the Civil War looming on the horizon. This counter-scenario would not have reversed centuries of disease and dispossession, but it would have permitted indigenous peoples to weather the dark Antebellum years inside the Republic instead of beyond the line that separated full-fledged states from the subordinate and segregated region called Indian Territory. It would have given them more time to negotiate, delay, compromise, and resist, perhaps allowing for a post–Civil War settlement in which they remained integral to the nation rather than exiled to its westernmost, advancing edge.

A little more than twenty years before Abraham Lincoln depicted slavery as a moral failing and lamented the Civil War's 700,000 dead as the "woe due to those by whom the offense came," a different president condemned the "sickening mass of putrefaction" that was the nation's policy toward indigenous people. "It is among the heinous sins of this nation, for which I believe God will one day bring them to judgement," John Quincy Adams, then serving in the House of Representatives, wrote in his diary in 1841.[15] The rupture between North and South forced white Americans to confront the nation's deep investment in slavery and to emancipate and incorporate four million individuals. They did so unwillingly, and the reconstruction of the nation is in many ways still unfolding. By contrast, there has been no comparable reckoning with the conquest of the continent, little serious reflection on its centrality to the rise of the United States, and minimal sustained engagement with the people who lost their homelands.

The deportations of the twentieth century involved millions of people. Two hundred years ago, the weapons were less destructive and the numbers of dispossessed smaller, but the state was no less remorseless. *Unworthy Republic* tells the story of the road to Indian Territory, one of the first state-sponsored mass expulsions in the modern world.[16]

WHITE SUPREMACY
and
INDIAN TERRITORY

~~~

CHAPTER I

ABORIGINIA

~~~

CAMPED IN eastern Kansas on a surveying expedition, Isaac McCoy reflected proudly on his epiphany eight years earlier in June 1823, when he was struck with the idea of creating an "Indian Canaan" west of the Mississippi River. The plan would consume the rest of his life, at the expense of all else. Seven of his thirteen children would die while he was absent lobbying the federal government on its behalf. "I dare not, for fear of offending my God, neglect my duty even for the sake of Wife or children," he confessed during one trip to Washington City, as the nation's capital was known. Only a near-fatal wagon accident north of Philadelphia would keep the Baptist missionary from witnessing a pivotal congressional debate on his scheme.[1]

McCoy was born in Uniontown, Pennsylvania, in 1784, but five years later his family ventured west, following other colonizers who were moving into present-day Kentucky, Ohio, and Indiana. Floating down the Ohio River, the McCoys passed abandoned and burned-out settlements on the right bank, territory claimed by squatters and speculators but still contested by the original Algonquian and Iroquois owners. The family settled on the opposite side of the river in rural Kentucky. The United States had only recently wrested the land from Shawnee people, and as late as 1795, the leading citizens of nearby Louisville had pooled their money to offer bounties "for every Indian scalp taken in the county." But, compared with the violent region to the north, the indigenous population had dwindled, and confrontations between natives and newcomers had subsided, though not entirely disappeared.[2]

Perhaps inspired by his father, who began sermonizing after the move west, McCoy imagined from a young age that he was destined for great things, though he had no inherited wealth or any formal schooling. As he recalled, he was a serious child who "imbibed an unusual aversion to Dancing" and condemned the frivolous pursuits of his siblings. His only fistfight, he claimed, occurred when other children maligned him as a Methodist, an insult that was intolerable to the young and uncompromising Baptist.[3]

After much agitation and anguish in his teen years, McCoy began preaching, moved to the "strange and wicked place" of Vincennes, Indiana, on the banks of the Wabash River, and took a position as the town jailor. This lowly station did not damage his sense of self-importance. He interpreted a swarm of green flies passing by the jail as a sign of displeasure from God himself. During one illness, he concluded he had a gift for poetry, a conceit that did not subside with the fever, for he later boasted that composing verse was "not so difficult as I had always conceived." In 1817, ailing and burdened by his own mortality, the thirty-three-year-old wrote a 479-page autobiography. He sent the manuscript to his brother-in-law, conceding that it was "astonishing" for someone as little known as himself to pen "extracts" of his life.[4]

McCoy survived the health scare and went on to discover his great calling, saving the Indians. He conducted missionary work among the Miamis, Odawas, Potawatomis, and other native residents in Indiana and Michigan. McCoy's firsthand experience with indigenous westerners gave him a well-founded disdain for the East Coast officials who designed national policy with minimal familiarity with the rest of the continent. Even the Baptist Board of Foreign Missions, the organization that oversaw his work from its Boston headquarters, earned his scorn. Its members, he complained, were "modelling affairs" in the West, though they knew little more of the subject "than they did of the geography of the moon."[5]

The counterpart to McCoy's contempt for easterners was a stubborn insistence that he knew best, despite his exposure to only a small fraction of the diverse indigenous peoples living within the boundaries of the United States and its territories. He dismissed his antagonists as "pious and well-meaning" but "mistaken and obstinate," a good description of McCoy himself. "How grossly mistaken are those writers who would have the world believe that the Indians are quite a virtuous people!" he declared. Native people were impoverished drunks, he insisted, mostly through the fault of "the very filth of civilized society," the white Americans who exploited them at every turn. McCoy had witnessed emaciated mothers digging for roots for their children, men and women surviving for days on boiled weeds alone, and, in the winter, "half-naked" villagers immobilized with frozen arms and legs. From his missionary outpost, he recorded every act of drunken violence and every senseless murder, a bleak catalog of sins that served to confirm his view of human nature. "How depraved must the people be," he exclaimed, "whose general character is drawn by such scandalous vices as we sometimes record in our Journal!"[6]

Even the success stories, the individuals who were "civilized" and "Christianized," were "sheep for the slaughter" or at best "left to the rapacity of noxious vermin." Caught between their "barbarous countrymen" and the remorseless racism of white Americans, they had no place of refuge. They were "hunted like a partridge on the hills," chased with "canine assiduity," and entangled in "a thousand intrigues and miseries." McCoy saw only darkness: "The great mass have become more and more corrupt in morals, have sunk deeper and deeper in wretchedness, and have dwindled down to insignificance or to nothing, like the plant that is shaded to death by the thousands of the surrounding lofty trees of the woods." Native peoples, he declared, will end in "total extermination."[7]

Fortunately, on that June day in 1823, McCoy decided to dedicate his life to a "scheme" for the "national salvation of the Indians" that would transform the U.S. relationship to the continent's longtime inhabitants. The plan was as obvious as it was simple. The United States would concentrate "the perishing tribes in some suitable portion of the country" and guarantee the land to them "*forever.*" Through the dedicated efforts of government agents and missionaries, displaced people in this inland protectorate would be instructed in "morality, literature, and labour," and they would eventually cultivate a flourishing colony. They would become farmers, shopkeepers, teachers and principals, doctors, jurists, sheriffs, statesmen, and ministers, filling almost every conceivable role that existed in civilized society—except for the most powerful political positions, which were reserved for white Americans.[8]

That was not all. One day, indigenous people would be united in "one body politic," McCoy imagined, and constitute "an integral part of the community of the United States." Like the existing states, "Aboriginia," as McCoy called his fanciful creation, would therefore be divided into counties and municipalities, with each tribe making up a separate district or county. At the heart of this Indian Canaan, sixty square miles would be set aside as the seat of government, "uniting the radii of affection of surrounding tribes, and diffusing in return the blessings of science." There, the business of government would unfold and, in McCoy's fervid and buoyant imagination, the diverse tribes would meet around a "central council fire" to smoke the pipe of peace and "mingle gratitude to God with the ascending fumes." Was McCoy too optimistic? He denied it: "I am not enthusiastic, but form my conclusions rationally."[9]

McCoy was not the first to propose a trans-Mississippi reserve for native people, though he was certainly the most zealous. Immediately following the Louisiana Purchase in 1803, Thomas Jefferson drafted a constitutional amendment to give Congress the right to exchange the newly purchased territory for indigenous homelands east of the Mississippi. Though Jefferson abandoned the amendment as unnecessary, he and his immediate successors in the White House encouraged the exchange of lands, contending that the scheme would protect native peoples until they could join the ranks of the civilized. Some isolated native communities accepted offers to decamp in the 1810s and 1820s. Andrew Jackson, still a decade away from the White House, negotiated one such treaty targeting the Cherokees in 1817. (On that occasion, only a few thousand individuals moved west of the Mississippi, largely to escape the constant pressure to conform to the U.S. civilizing policy.) Lewis Cass, then serving as the governor of Michigan Territory, concluded a similar treaty with a community of Delaware people a year later. Territorial cessions, if not actual expulsion, continued apace; in the first two decades of the nineteenth century, the indigenous land base shrank by 600,000 square miles, an area roughly the size of Alaska.[10] Nonetheless, these attempts to convince longtime easterners to move west were piecemeal and sporadic. Jefferson's trans-Mississippi colony of indigenous people remained a distant vision.

Something had to be done. Expecting a sympathetic hearing from the governor of Michigan Territory, McCoy floated his idea first to Lewis Cass, who would later become President Andrew Jackson's secretary of war. The "asylum," located "somewhere in the extensive regions of the west," he explained, would bring uniformity to the unsystematic efforts of the federal government. The benefits were legion: happy Indians, flourishing arts and sciences, and a federal government relieved of a burdensome and hostile population. "Is it practicable?" McCoy asked Cass.[11]

~~~

McCOY FAILED to pose the same question to the people subject to expulsion. In fact, most Native Americans had no desire to leave their homes. By the 1820s, they had been trading with newcomers and living next to them for several generations, and few of them believed, as McCoy insisted, that they could not survive amid people of "other colour." Even between the Great Lakes and the Ohio River (then the nation's Northwest), residents were reluctant to abandon their lands, though the United States had spent three decades waging war against them. In that region between 1800 and 1830, native peoples ceded territory totaling 140,000 square miles, an area the size of Ohio, Indiana, and Illinois combined, and the U.S. population rose from 50,000 to 1.5 million. The numbers, as astonishing as they are, do not capture the magnitude of the loss, which affected every realm of indigenous society, from the mundane to the sacred. Yet the 25,000 native people who continued to reside in the region north of the Ohio wished to stay put. Meehchikilita, a Miami leader, insisted to U.S. officials in 1826 that they wanted to live with white Americans, "like brothers, and sell and exchange our property as we choose." A decade later, under pressure to move west, Potawatomis politely refused. "We are poor," they explained, "but love our little fields in the Country and are not yet willing to abandon them."[12]

Their refusal to depart willingly resulted from an attachment to the land, a skepticism of U.S. claims that expulsion was best for them, and a persistent doubt that Indian Territory was the paradise it was made out to be. Nor did native peoples in the Northwest believe that they were quite as wretched as U.S. officials insisted. In Indiana, John Metoxen, a Stockbridge Mahican missionary, noted that his people were "farmers and macanics," who possessed "considerable farms." "It is my true wish and desire to be settled in some part of the world whare I can Injoy the Blessings of the soil that Gave me Birth," he wrote, "and see my Children and family connection and all nations of people Injoying the same Priviledge with helth." Even some U.S. agents had to admit that the dire reports of imminent extinction were inaccurate. After a tour of indigenous communities in Ohio in 1830, one official commented on the

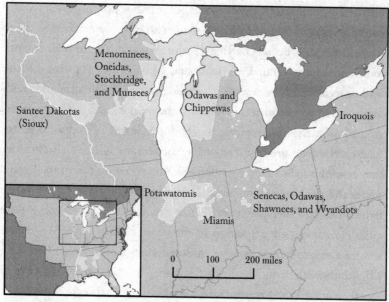

Native nations in the Northwest in 1830
who were potential targets for expulsion.

bumper crop of corn and added, "I . . . can truly say that I have never known them so industrious as they are at present." Another agent, who visited the Wyandot community in northern Ohio, concluded that the residents were thriving. He underscored that it would be "*a cruelty*" to expel them. In some cases, indigenous people compared favorably with their American neighbors. A visitor to Michigan's Upper Peninsula found that the Odawas were "far better" dressed than the U.S. citizens who surrounded them.[13]

The diversity of indigenous peoples—hunters, farmers, beggars, drunks, teetotalers, Catholics, Methodists, animists—belied the simplistic narrative that U.S. officials fed the public. Native Americans in the Northwest lived in wigwams and lean-tos as well as clapboard houses with windows, brick chimneys, and wood flooring—materials that unrepentant U.S. citizens would later cart away as the dispossessed were escorted out of town by state militia. Some native people proved to be as enterprising and opportunistic as their market-savvy neighbors. When white Americans began charting a major thoroughfare through Potawatomi and Miami lands in Indiana and Michigan in the 1820s, native leaders recognized the several economic benefits. The road would facilitate their travel, furnish a market for their game, and stimulate trade. Accordingly, they successfully fought for a degree of control over the road survey to ensure that it passed by their largest villages. (In this way, they resembled the many twentieth-century communities in the United States that lobbied for the placement of highway interchanges.) When federal officials later pressured them to move west, Potawatomis were quite clear about their position in the region. Many white Americans wanted them to remain, asserted a Potawatomi leader named Red Bird. "They hunt with us and we divide the game," he said, "and when we hunt together and get tired we can go to the white men's houses and stay." "We wish to stay among the whites," he concluded, "and we wish to be connected with them, and therefore we will not go."14

To salve their consciences, U.S. citizens maintained that their inability to live together with indigenous people was a law of nature rather than a choice. The purported law justified every act of dispossession, and every act of dispossession furnished yet more proof of nature's inevitable course. Nonetheless, the law did not apply to all areas of the nation, an inconvenient fact that most U.S. citizens chose to ignore. Wyandots in Ohio spoke of the "terms of intimacy" and "ardent friendship" between themselves and U.S. citizens. To their north, Odawas joined with American allies to create the Western Michigan Society to Benefit the Indians, a lobbying group that reflected the shared economic interests of natives and newcomers. "We could not have done without the Indians," recalled one early colonist. "They were our market men and women." Odawas picked cranberries and huckleberries that were consumed in Buffalo and harvested maple sugar that was sold in New York City and Boston. One group of Odawas even successfully bid on a county road contract; others provisioned U.S. troops stationed in Detroit. After ceding territory to the United States, they used the proceeds to purchase land from the General Land Office, a clever way of placing their title on the same solid footing as that of their white neighbors.[15]

There is no need to romanticize the situation in the Northwest before the United States embarked on its determined and deadly campaign to eliminate native residents from the region. Some indigenous people were deeply impoverished. Alcohol consumption was rampant, as McCoy documented religiously—though it is not clear whether Native Americans consumed more than U.S. citizens at the time. Native communities were under heavy pressure to give up their lands. And yet most people insisted on remaining. Like the Wyandots in northern Ohio, they hoped that the U.S. president would "maintain them in the peaceable and quiet possession of that spot for ever."[16]

In the U.S. Southeast, over sixty thousand native people, divided among the Choctaw, Chickasaw, Creek, Cherokee, and Seminole nations, were equally unwilling to abandon their homelands. William Hicks and John Ross, leaders of the Cherokee Nation, called the scheme championed by the federal government a "burlesque," a word that perfectly captures the policy's combination of starry-eyed utopianism and vicious cynicism. (John Ross, who had a masterful command of the English language, skewered his antagonists in the federal government, including Andrew Jackson, on more than one occasion. He once proposed a novel solution to the crisis surrounding their lands: If President Jackson removed white Georgians, he observed, "ere long the difficulties . . . would be amicably adjusted.") Few indigenous Americans were fooled by the boundless promises of the United States. A group of skeptical Chickasaw leaders cast doubt on President Jackson's offer of western land "as long as the grass grows and water runs." Those were "his own words," they gibed, unimpressed with the president's patronizing adoption of indigenous imagery about grass and water. They instead preferred the formal legal expression, "in fee simple," which describes the strongest form of property ownership in the United States. "If we go," asked one prescient Choctaw leader, "how long first will it be when we shall be told to go a little farther?" "You are too near me," the leader imagined U.S. officials would say *after* Choctaw families had crossed the Mississippi River. "The land here is ours," white Americans would once again claim, "and we must have it."[7]

The astonishing resilience and adaptability of native southeasterners made it difficult for federal officials to perpetuate stories of their wretchedness and despair, though eventually U.S. policies would create the very conditions that they were supposedly designed to alleviate. The Seminole people of Florida had weathered a series of invasions in the early nineteenth century—including one launched in 1817 by an impulsive general named Andrew Jackson—but had nonetheless built thriving ranching and farming communities. In 1823, one visitor to the Withlacoochee

Native nations in the South in 1830 who were potential targets for expulsion.

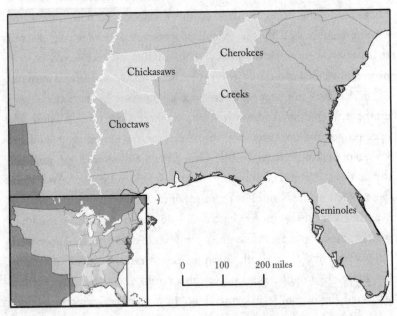

River, west of present-day Orlando, described bountiful fields filled with rice and corn plants. "I am satisfied that no planter in Florida," he wrote, "can boast of so good a crop in proportion to the quantity of land planted." A treaty that same year forced Seminole families onto less fertile lands but did not shake their determination to remain in the region.[18]

In Alabama and Mississippi, many Creek, Choctaw, and Chickasaw families were tightly woven into the regional economy. "Europeans would be surprised to hear that many of these people have large property in slaves and cattle," wrote an admiring British visitor, who noted that a few individuals possessed extensive ranches and upwards of thirty slaves. Cherokee leader James Vann, who owned a stately house that still stands on the site of his former eight-hundred-acre plantation in north Georgia, possessed over one hundred slaves. Said by one acquaintance to be "aristocratic, impetuous, and full of chivalric daring," Vann was unusual in the scale of his possessions but not in the act of slaveholding. Wealthy Cherokee, Creek, Chickasaw, Choctaw, and Seminole citizens, adapting to the ways of white southern elites, were engaging in their own version of African American enslavement. Over 5 percent of the 66,000 residents of those nations were unfree.[19]

Like the majority of their white neighbors, however, most native people sustained themselves without expropriating the labor of others. In rural U.S. households, men worked in the fields, tilling the soil with the help of plows and draft animals, while women tended to gardens, spun yarn and wove cloth, cooked, cleaned, and milked cows. Most indigenous people divided their responsibilities differently. Drawing on traditional subsistence practices as well as foreign technologies, men hunted, but they did so with guns instead of bows and arrows; women farmed with handmade hoes, even while fashioning garments out of European cloth rather than domestically harvested deerskins. The items they acquired in trade—calico blankets, needles, shirt buttons, handkerchiefs, bridles, butcher knives, gunlocks, and the like—are evidence of a hybrid economy.[20]

The ways of living pursued by indigenous Americans and U.S. citizens in the Southeast increasingly overlapped, a trend that John Clark, the governor of Georgia, found alarming, since the longer the two peoples were "suffered to intermix," the more difficult it would become for the state to appropriate native lands. Choctaws were actually "pretty good neighbors," admitted one federal agent, recalling that they sold game to the U.S. outpost in the area. The women, he said, were even willing to work in his fields for a reasonable wage.[21] While U.S. officials would continue to complain about the bonds forming between their citizens and native peoples, they also insisted with growing urgency and dwindling evidence that the two ways of living were fundamentally irreconcilable. In truth, only one thing was truly irreconcilable: native and white ownership of the same land.

~~~

POLITICIANS WHO advocated for the expulsion of native peoples, whatever their deeper motives, often based their public pronouncements on two related and seemingly humanitarian tenets. The indigenous population, they asserted, was suffering an inevitable and rapid decline. That said, they went on to argue magnanimously that the fertile, well-watered, and generally desirable land west of the Mississippi would save native peoples from their tragic demise in the East. Taken together, these assertions ensured the happy convergence of self-interest and philanthropy, permitting U.S. citizens to dispossess native peoples and feel righteous about it. Neither belief was well-founded.

The decline of the native population was an acknowledged "law of nature," according to Thomas Jefferson. It was "a great pity," the Virginia planter and former president wrote, "and indeed a scandal that we let that race of men disappear without preserving scarcely any trace of their history." Indians were dwindling, "dispirited and degraded," agreed Senator John Elliott of Georgia in 1825. Elliott invoked a favorite metaphor: "like a promontory of sand, exposed to the ceaseless encroachments of the ocean, they have been gradually wasting away before the current of white population." (Melting snow often served the same illustrative purpose.) Soon only a few survivors would remain to brood over their misfortunes or to look "in despair on the approaching catastrophe of their impending doom," observed Secretary of War James Barbour a year later. Their imminent extinction—that was the preferred word—was described so frequently that its inevitability became an unquestioned fact, appearing in school readers, daily newspapers, and popular cultural productions such as James Fenimore Cooper's *The Last of the Mohicans* and the hit Broadway play *Metamora*.[22]

What lay behind the regrettable decline of the continent's first inhabitants was something of a mystery, though the subject occupied some of the brightest minds of the time. Jefferson singled out the practice of native women accompanying men in war and hunting. As a result, he observed, "child-bearing becomes extremely inconvenient to them." Thomas Malthus, the minister turned fatalistic population theorist, suggested that the problem was rooted in the inferiority of hunting to agriculture—never mind that indigenous Americans farmed as productively as Malthus's neighbors in Surrey, England. Benjamin Rush, America's leading physician, attributed the primary reason to "the extensive mischief of spirituous liquors." None of the explanations was wholly adequate. "The cause is inherent in the nature of things," concluded the incurious superintendent of Indian Affairs.[23] Regardless of the cause, it was obvious that indigenous and white Americans could not coexist.

As with so many manifest truths, this one was wrong. Since the arrival of the first European colonists, indigenous populations had indeed declined as a result of disease, warfare, and out-migration. They were halved between 1600 and 1700 and then reduced again by a third between 1700 and 1800. "Many different groups of brown people stopped during that time," observed the Cherokees, "and today there are just a few that can be seen." In the Northeast, they lamented, "The Indian people . . . are now just about gone."[24]

And yet by the early nineteenth century, the number of indigenous Americans in the East was on the rise or at least holding steady. That is true for the Southeast as well as for the Northwest and reflects the complex interaction of variables that affect human health, reproduction, and mortality. The imprecise figures that support such a conclusion are admittedly incomplete but inspire more confidence than the opinions of nineteenth-century experts, who usually substantiated their claims with nothing more than their own deeply held sense of indigenous degeneracy. "If any thing is certain," declared William Harper before the South Carolina Society for the Advancement of Learning, it is that "savage and civilized man cannot live together." (In his strolls around Charleston, Harper had apparently seen slaves "possessing Indian hair and features," proving to the wealthy planter that, to save indigenous Americans from extinction, the "benevolent course" was to enslave them.) The few methodical efforts to estimate populations often produced dismal or no results, as one U.S. army survey admitted in the course of collecting "much important matter . . . both Topographical and Statistical" about the Cherokee Nation. Counting people, the engineers explained, was "impossible," since local residents wisely concealed themselves at the approach of the surveying crew.[25]

Nonetheless, most white Americans held an unshakeable belief that native peoples were on the decline. John Ross admitted that in the Cherokee Nation "our population at present is small," but, he added, "it is increasing as rapidly as could be expected." Elias Boudinot, the editor of the *Cherokee Phoenix*, the nation's national newspaper, could barely contain his frustration with the advocates of deportation who circulated specious population numbers. "We repeat again," he remonstrated in 1828, "that the Cherokees are not on the decline in numbers and improvement." Their neighbors to the south, the Creeks, also bitterly objected to the parade of lies that distorted the debate. "To the public thro' newspapers and ingenious pamphlets fabricated by men who style themselves our friends and reformers," Creek leaders told the U.S. Congress, "we are represented as experiencing rapid diminution and decline in population, and to escape which, it is said we are anxious to emigrate to that country so much eulogised by the friends of Indian colonization." "It is due to our Nation," they asserted, "to contradict these statements calculated to mislead the minds of good men."[26]

White Americans who continued to insist on the imminent extinction of their neighbors often held the equally unfounded but stubborn belief that native peoples would find salvation in the West. For a time, the advocates of expulsion argued that refugee camps in the West would be akin to a trans-Mississippi Jamestown or Plymouth Rock, the storied British colonies that had planted the seeds of civilization on the Atlantic Coast two centuries earlier. Aboriginia would animate the minds and harness the energy of dispossessed peoples, lifting them out of dependency and savagery.[27]

In this way, plans for the expulsion of Native Americans resembled another endeavor that targeted nonwhite peoples in the United States. In January 1817, a small group of well-connected reformers based in New Jersey and Washington City had founded the American Colonization Society (ACS), an organization dedicated to the quixotic mission of shipping African Americans to Africa, where the homesteaders were to establish a model colony that would both uplift them and help civilize Africans. In turn, the United States would be rid of its troublesome free black communities and, in the ACS's most ambitious projections, relieved of its enslaved population. The conservative Supreme Court justice Bushrod Washington, the nephew of George Washington, quickly signed on as the organization's first president, lending it an aura of prestige and legitimacy.[28]

The parallels between the colonization of native and enslaved peoples were too obvious to ignore. "The coincidence . . . is very impressive," wrote Isaac McCoy, who was a charter member of the Indiana Auxiliary

American Colonization Society. Just like native peoples, "Africans" had been degraded by white Americans, he observed; colonization would place both groups "on the same footing" with U.S. citizens and give them "the same opportunities of improvement." As an added benefit, as Thomas Jefferson wrote of African American slaves in 1821, "deportation" would free up land for white laborers. In March 1825, Congress even considered colonizing "free people of colour" west of the Rocky Mountains, reviving a proposal that predated the ACS. Together with the relocation of native peoples, the proposal would have turned the continent's demographic distribution into a bizarre manifestation of racial obsession, with "black" people in the far West, "tawny" people in the Midwest, and "white" people in the East.[29]

Despite the conservative leanings of the ACS—it condemned any and all interference with the rights of slave owners—southern planters soon turned vehemently against the organization. The tipping point occurred in 1822, when South Carolina officials arrested and executed thirty-seven African Americans and exiled forty-three others, punishment for an aborted uprising organized by a free black carpenter named Denmark Vesey. How much of the conspiracy existed solely in the imaginations of fearful Carolina planters and how much was real remains a matter of debate. Regardless, after the executions, slave owners demonized the ACS. The organization, they charged, raised the hopes of African Americans, intruded on the power of masters over their slaves, and even fomented rebellion. Following in South Carolina's footsteps, in 1827 Georgia's General Assembly passed a resolution condemning the ACS, adopting the same excessive language it used to discuss Indian affairs. The deportation plan was "wild, fanatical and destructive," it declared, and "ruinous to the prosperity, importance, and political strength of the southern states." Those who interfered in Georgia's "local concerns and domestic relations" were guilty of either "cold-blooded selfishness, or unthinking zeal."[30]

How could the colonization of African Americans be "wild, fanatical and destructive" while that of native peoples was just and humane? Constitutional principles, the favorite recourse of southern politicians, were unhelpful in this instance. Instead, white southerners and their northern allies devised an argument based on proximity. Native peoples imbibed all of the vices of U.S. citizens, they claimed, while slaves absorbed their virtues. In 1825, John Elliott of Georgia laid out the feeble rationalization on the floor of the Senate. Two "independent communities of people" who differed in "color, language, habits and interests cannot long subsist together," he asserted, for the more powerful would always destroy the weaker. He was painting a "somber picture," he admitted, but it was drawn from "real life." By contrast, communities that "subsist together," such as slaves and their southern masters, "increase and better their condition." "In these instances," wrote the owner of over one hundred enslaved people, "the *mutual dependence* which exists, creates, in some sort, a community of interests." In sum, self-interest made it possible for these wealthy planter-politicians to convince themselves that it was best for African American slaves to be held close to their masters and for native peoples to be kept far away. Their expansionist ambitions seemed legitimated by an improbable convergence of the laws of nature. For Elliott and his planter allies, it appeared logical and inevitable, not greedy and self-serving, that the free inhabitants of lands they coveted for cotton production would be summarily exiled and replaced by an unfree labor force. In their minds, both dispossession and enslavement were acts of humanity.[31]

Elliott's argument was preposterous on two accounts. First, although slave owners insisted that the malnourished, poorly clothed, and, by force of law, illiterate people who labored unwillingly on plantations were better off for it, there was no "community of interests." The Denmark Vesey mass executions had powerfully illustrated the point in 1822. Second, just nine years before Elliott's speech, the superintendent of Indian Trade had told Congress that every single case of native "advancement" could be "traced to their contiguity to, and intercourse with the whites."

Elliott, who was no authority on the subject, now told his fellow senators that the exact opposite was true. Later, the Cherokee leader John Ross would pen an incisive response to this favorite argument of the dispossessors. If indigenous people were suffering, it was not because of "the *mere circumstance* of their contiguity of a white population," he said. Rather, it was because of the policies of white men, "when dictated by avarice and cupidity."[32]

At heart, the plan for native salvation in the West was deeply cynical, but white Americans managed to cloak their cynicism in a cheery optimism. James Barbour, the secretary of war, asserted in 1828 that "collocating the Indians on suitable lands west of the Mississippi" would "produce the happiest benefits upon the Indian race." The land was "admirably adapted" to the interests of native peoples, reported Wilson Lumpkin, a leading proponent of expulsion, who represented Georgia in the House of Representatives. It was "fine country," Lewis Cass, the secretary of war in 1832, assured Creek leaders. More broadly, in the words of the House Committee on Indian Affairs, the deportation of native people to the West would allow the United States to atone for "wrongs inevitably incident to the settlement of the country by the white race."[33]

Unfortunately, white Americans knew almost nothing about the land that was to be set aside as Indian Territory. Even the basics remained a mystery. Where exactly would the dispossessed be relocated? "No certainty can be arrived at, until the country is explored," admitted Thomas McKenney, the superintendent of Indian Affairs, in 1826. Ignorance ruled the day. "The question occurs to us, as it does to the Indians," he wrote, "Where is that home? Nobody can answer." Paeans to expulsion stumbled over this most essential of questions. One map from 1828 exhibited both the promise and the peril involved in transporting people to the region. Drafted by William Clark, Meriwether Lewis's companion in the 1803-5 transcontinental journey and now the superintendent of Indian Affairs at St. Louis, it was largely a blank slate, inviting federal officials to project their fantasies onto it. Across the empty space, a War Department employee penciled in who might move where: "Indian Title Extinguished by the Quapaw Treaty of 1818," "Presumed location Kansas under the Treaty of 1825," "Choctaw Lands," and (in pen) "Boundaries proposed for the Cherokees in <u>Red Ink</u>."[34]

One congressman from Ohio summed up the absurdity of the situation. Do advocates of expulsion know anything about the land west of the Mississippi? he asked. "Their answer is, no; we know nothing about these matters, but first adopt the scheme—provide that the Indians must remove West of the Mississippi—let us decide that we will drive them from their lands which we want to occupy; and then, Sir, we will send our agents and commissioners with the Indians, to examine this country."[35]

What little they did know about the region undercut the optimistic picture they painted. The first official report on the area, written by Zebulon Pike in 1806–7, predicted that the land would become an "American Sahara." It was worthless for agriculture but, in Pike's mind, perfect for native peoples. "I believe that there are buffalo, elk, and deer sufficient on the banks of the Arkansas alone, if used without waste," he wrote, "to feed all the savages in the United States territory one century." In 1820, U.S. army explorer Stephen Long confirmed Pike's gloomy assessment. It was "unhabitable" by farmers, he wrote after traversing the region, though "peculiarly adapted as a range for buffaloes, wild goats, and other wild game." Long fixed his description in the American imagination by printing "Great American Desert" across his map, which was soon published and widely distributed. Even the normally exuberant Isaac McCoy admitted that the land left something to be desired, though he still insisted that it was "very good, and well adapted to the purposes of Indian settlement." The greatest defect—"and I am sorry that it is of so serious a character," he confessed—was the lack of timber. A sober assessment by one federal official concluded simply that the region's resources had been "greatly exaggerated."[36]

~~~

McCoy's "great system" to expel native peoples and create a segregated territory in the West departed from established policy.[37] Since
the Washington administration, the United States had pursued the goal
of civilizing native people in place. Federal agents fanned out across
the eastern seaboard, from upstate New York to central Mississippi,
to instruct native peoples how to live right. They told indigenous men to
abandon hunting and take up the plow, and they advised women
to give up hoe farming in favor of producing homespun clothing. These
deeply rooted traditional practices had proven to be reliable methods
of providing sustenance for generations, however, and native peoples
did not welcome guidance from newcomers, whose authority as federal
agents did not impress them. In many instances, only a combination of
bribery, threats, and environmental degradation convinced villagers to
pick up the plow and the loom.

Church groups assisted the federal government by establishing missions to instruct indigenous Americans in English and, more to the
point, in the Bible. Well-meaning but paternalistic benevolent societies
collected donations to support the labors of missionaries, sending goods
that salved the conscience of those who lived on land that had long ago
been taken from native peoples. The Female Aboriginal Relief Society
of Newton, Massachusetts—then as now a center of affluent activists—
shipped a box to Niles, Michigan, filled with twelve women's gowns,
seven pairs of pantaloons, two jackets, four shirts, one comforter, and
thirty yards of white cotton, plus some needles, pins, thimbles, buttons,
and tape for the use of the Potawatomis. The recipients surely appreci-
ated the donations, appraised at $30, but perhaps not as much as they
valued missionary schooling, which many native people embraced, if
only for its practical benefits. Though they had to balance their desire for
literacy with their dislike of the proselytizers who provided the instruction, the Xs they placed on treaties constantly reminded them of the dis-

advantages that they faced in their negotiations with the United States. One group of Potawatomis complained, "We have none in our nation who is capable of attending to our business." It was true, agreed Isaac McCoy. Without a formal education, "They could not compete with our government."[38]

The civilizing plan was ethnocentric and self-serving. In its worst form—as when Thomas Jefferson admitted in a confidential letter that he desired to separate native people from their lands for their own good—it was also paternalistic and cynical. Indeed, the plan to civilize native people could bleed into a desire to erase them. Nonetheless, indigenous Americans understood it as the basis of their relationship with the United States and the governing principle of their treaties, and whether the motives of U.S. officials were nefarious or benevolent, native peoples used and manipulated the civilizing policy for their own ends. The president was their "great father," a term often used by U.S. agents and native peoples alike, and he was therefore obligated to help them. "Be happy, and fear nothing from your Great Father," Superintendent of Indian Affairs McKenney assured a party of Wyandot leaders in 1825. "He is your friend, and will never permit you to be driven away from your lands."[39] In short, the so-called civilization policy was distinct from the political and bureaucratic operation in the 1830s to deport tens of thousands of people.

For three decades, the civilizing plan persisted in various guises. In late 1816, the superintendent of Indian Trade confidently told the chair of the House Committee on Indian Affairs that "an enlarged and liberal policy" would serve to hasten the transition from "a savage to a civilized state." The Creek, Cherokee, and Chickasaw people already excelled at agriculture and wore homespun clothing, he said. (In addition to demonstrating in this instance that women were using spinning wheels and looms, clothing had a charged symbolic value, as it still does today.) Success was not limited to the Southeast. Shawnee and Delaware residents south of the Great Lakes were also "mostly attired as we are" and, judging by their commercial acumen, exhibited a "capacity for the pursuits of civil life." In all cases, the superintendent of Indian Trade concluded, "contiguity" and "intercourse" with whites were the key to success.[40]

Even the staunch racist and segregationist John Calhoun, who served as the secretary of war between 1818 and 1825, had to admit that the civilizing plan was largely successful, if still unfinished. No champion of autonomy and sovereignty when it came to native nations, he nonetheless spoke positively of the "humane & benevolent policy of the Government, which has ever directed a fostering care to the Indians within our limits." "This policy," he stated in 1824, "is as old as the Government itself." The Cherokees were an unqualified success, he wrote, before predicting that "in a short time the advances of the Creeks" would be just as satisfactory. That same year, the House Committee on Indian Affairs felt that it was scarcely worth questioning the value of U.S. policy. "It requires but little research to convince every candid mind that the prospect of civilizing our Indians was never so promising as at this time." Indeed, the progress of civilization "may be more rapid than any can now venture to anticipate." Thomas McKenney, the superintendent of Indian Affairs, expressed similar confidence. "It has ceased to be a matter of doubt among intelligent people that Indians can be Civilized and Christianized," he wrote. "The proofs have multiplied so of late, as to convince the most skeptical."[41]

For state-sponsored expulsion to seem necessary, the prospect of civilizing "our Indians"—said to be never so promising in the mid-1820s—had to yield to the harrowing counterview of "approaching catastrophe" and "impending doom," as the secretary of war James Barbour dramatized it. And the plan had to seem practicable rather than absurdly ambitious. The federal government employed fewer than 11,000 individuals, and the vast majority of them, approximately 8,000, delivered the mail and would be of no use deporting families. Only some 600 worked in Washington City. Likewise, the entire armed forces, responsible for guarding a 1,500-mile western frontier and a 2,500-mile coastline, barely surpassed 11,000 men. Only 6,000 served in the army, with most of the rest in the navy.[42]

There were numerous historical precedents for the wholesale relocation of tens of thousands of people, including the mass deportations of conquered peoples in the Neo-Assyrian Empire in the eighth century B.C.E., north China in the fourth century C.E., Sicily in the thirteen century C.E., and Iran in the seventeenth and eighteenth centuries, to name but a few examples, though these lay far beyond the ken of nineteenth-century Americans. One planter and would-be scholar hazily recalled "only a solitary instance in all ancient history of a whole nation quitting their country and removing to another." "I think it was a province of Gaul," he speculated, "perhaps Belgium."[43]

Better known to U.S. citizens were the forced migrations that took place in Europe over the previous few centuries, such as the expulsion of the Jews from Spain in the fifteenth century, of the Moriscos a hundred years later, and of the Huguenots from France nearly a century after that. The Acadians, French speakers evicted from Nova Scotia by the British in the 1750s, provided one example that occurred especially close to home. Many of these deportees ended up in Louisiana and became known as Cajuns, but the forced migration had not fared well in public memory. "Tradition is fresh and positive among us respecting the guileless, peaceful, and scrupulous character of this injured people," Robert Walsh, a widely read and well-connected public intellectual, wrote in 1819. He was unequivocal about the "miserable vicissitude of their fortunes, and the extreme poignancy of their grief." One of the nation's most renowned historians, David Ramsay, similarly criticized the action and condemned the "severe policy" that Britain pursued against an "unfortunate people."[44]

Robert Campbell, a lawyer from Savannah who was notable for being the sole white Georgian to vocally oppose the deportation of indigenous Americans, stated that "in modern times—in civilized countries—there is no instance of expelling the members of a whole nation from their homes—of driving an entire population from its native country." The policy, he railed, would surpass even the "notoriously disgraceful partition of Poland," when Russia, Prussia, and the Hapsburg Empire had divided the nation among themselves and erased it from the map. In fact, it proved all too easy to find unfavorable comparisons: "the partitioners of Poland," "the invaders of Spain," the "plunderers of India," all instances in which empires stripped "the weak and defenceless of their possessions."[45]

White Americans were not especially keen to model their Republic after the atrocities committed by European tyrants, and they imagined something altogether different for their own state-sponsored deportation. The expulsion of indigenous Americans, if it proceeded, would be a philanthropic enterprise, administered by an army of clerks, census takers, relocation officers, disbursing agents, auditors, and comptrollers. In the words of the secretary of war, it would be a truly "modern" undertaking that spared the weak and embraced "justice and moderation."[46]

From the Capitol Building, situated among Washington City's empty fields and scattered abodes, congressmen began to speak confidently in the late 1820s of launching a massive operation to expel indigenous peoples from their homelands. At the other end of the dirt road called Pennsylvania Avenue, the executive branch drew up ambitious plans. Bellowing bull frogs and the smell of rotting animal carcasses accompanied the planning.[47] In this miasmic environment, the state-sponsored mass expulsion of indigenous people suddenly began to seem both necessary and practical. How did this happen?

CHAPTER 2

THE WHITE PEOPLE OF GEORGIA

~~~

In late August 1825, an eight-thousand-word essay by "Socrates" appeared in the *Georgia Journal*, one of the two newspapers published in the state capital of Milledgeville. In the early years of the Republic, white Americans were fond of writing opinion pieces in the names of famous Greek and Roman philosophers, and this particular disquisition was not unusual, except perhaps for its length. This Socrates set out to address the "great questions" of state sovereignty and slavery, two related subjects that would dominate political discourse in the Antebellum era, but rather than tackling the matter head-on, he spent the entire essay discussing the Creek Nation, which still retained land on the state's western border with Alabama. The author made several points that would have been familiar to readers. Civilized nations enjoyed the right to dispose of the continent as they wished, he wrote, because its native residents were "barbarous and savage." Indeed, it was "philanthropic and just" for colonizers to "rescue the lands from a state of wilderness." In the case of Georgia, he reasoned, because "Indian title" was "permissive" and derived from "mere *custom*," the state could legitimately seize land from Creek people whenever it wished. "Would it force them to join their brother savages beyond the Mississippi?" Socrates asked. "So much the better."[1]

The ardent desire to deport the region's longest-standing residents originated in the fantasy that one day soon the state's politicians and planters would dominate the nation and continent. With the exception of Florida, which was sparsely populated and ridden with swamplands, Georgia was the largest state in the union—larger than even the Empire State of New York—*if* native land title were disregarded. Its ambition appeared to be as limitless as the worldwide demand for cotton. Surveying lands to the west, Georgia senator John Elliott observed that indigenous families owned seventy-seven million acres in the South that "must be very valuable." Most of it would grow cotton, he surmised. But as long as the southern states were inhabited by "savages" who were not enumerated in apportioning representation in Congress, explained one Georgia newspaper, slave owners would be deprived of their rightful political power and remain "tributaries" to the "overbearing aristocracy" of the North. Unlike slaves, indigenous residents were alas not counted by the U.S. Constitution as three-fifths of a person, the cynical device that enhanced white southern political strength. Though one Georgia governor suggested imposing a small tax on Native Americans so that they would be counted in the census, thereby further elevating the white South's political power on the national stage, planter-politicians preferred the more gainful plan to expel them and populate their lands with white people and partially enumerated slave laborers.[2]

Georgia's 240,000 white citizens dreamed of boundless profits and unchecked power over the state's 180,000 African Americans, a cause deeply intertwined with the expulsion of indigenous residents on the state's western and northern borders. Socrates invited his readers to suppose that native peoples remained in their homelands and the U.S. Congress passed a law naturalizing them. Would Georgia be bound to receive them as citizens? "To concede this power to the federal government would be a dangerous tendency," he observed. Indeed, the implications were alarming. "If they make a citizen of an Indian, what hinders them from making a citizen of a *free negro*, and if they can make a citizen of a free negro, what hinders them from *naturalizing* slave negroes?" The time would come, he foresaw, when the North and the South would be forced to confront each other over the limits of federal power to regulate slavery.

In the meantime, Georgia's homegrown philosopher chose to "call things by their proper names." "We the people of Georgia," he declared, meant the "white people of Georgia," and those who objected to this self-evident truth deserved to be "laughed at for their folly." He knew no other citizens of Georgia than "*white people*," he wrote, and wished "to know no others." His evidence for this small-minded but deeply ingrained argument was historical in nature and mostly false. White people, he said, had discovered, conquered, and occupied the continent; they had governed it until the American Revolution; they had declared independence, fought in the war, made peace, and framed and adopted the Constitution. "With all these important transactions," he blundered, "the negroes and Indians had nothing to do," an assertion that was factually wrong. As for those who questioned his logic, Socrates made an emotional appeal to like-minded citizens. "Some *moon struck moralists* may whine about the injustice that the high pretending *white* lovers of liberty are doing to their *sable* fellow creatures of their own species," he scoffed. "Let them whine: but let us be *white people* still."

Since their mastery over people and territory was at stake, planters regarded any defense of indigenous land title as an attack by "Negrophiles" and "Indianites." One Georgian complained in 1819 that the Cherokees were not being relocated fast enough to the "waste public lands over the Mississippi." Others may talk about "civilizing the Indians," he wrote, but "the north is only using it as the means of preventing the growth and consequence of the south." Another editorialist could not suppress his bitterness, even as victory was in sight. "Georgia may forgive but she never can forget the base intent of a certain set of northern men to excite rebellion in the South," he wrote, accusing them of inciting "merciless slaves and Indians." (The accusation not coincidentally echoed the Declaration of Independence, which condemned George III for instigating slave revolts and attacks by "merciless Indian Savages.") Northerners were not motivated by benevolence, he charged, but by jealousy. After native peoples were deported, he calculated, the South and its commercial allies in the North would control the majority of electoral college votes, a fact that "must have struck" northern politicians "with awe, and terror for the future." Planter-politicians were in no mood to compromise. In 1829, the *Columbian Star*, a newspaper published in the small but wealthy slaveholders' enclave of Washington, Georgia, offered native peoples a stark choice: expulsion "to some distant point" or "total extinction." Remaining in Georgia would result in "total annihilation." Socrates even suggested that the state might have to go to war with the United States if the federal government did not cooperate in deporting the region's longstanding residents. If white people were not licensed to do what they wished with Native and African Americans, he threatened, they would have to consider whether to "submit with the smile of slavish acquiescence, or————resort to more efficacious measures."[3]

~~~

FOR ALL of Thomas Jefferson's visionary schemes, for all of the idle speculation on the part of would-be policy experts, and for all of the vicious editorials that angry white southerners published in local newspapers, the state-sponsored, systematic expulsion of indigenous families would not have occurred without a law, passed by Congress and implemented by the executive branch. The scheme was ultimately a piece of legislation, not the inevitable result of some fundamental incompatibility of indigenous and European peoples, as many U.S. citizens wanted to believe. Nor was it the result of an inexorable wave of white colonists that swept westward, washing away everything in its path. In the 1820s, some in Congress even expressed concern that there was too much public land on the market and too little demand. Over the course of the nineteenth century, it would alternately promote and discourage westward expansion.[4]

Everyone, native and nonnative alike, nonetheless recognized that the U.S. population was increasing. Colonists "came to our country few in number, and feeble in strength," recounted Creek leaders, but had since "increased in strength, and in numbers," and "spread over the territory where our fathers formerly walked without restraint." "We are hemmed in within narrow bounds," they observed.[5] The demographic imbalance and the challenges faced by native peoples were undeniable. But how exactly the United States would treat native peoples remained an open question. Within the boundaries of the expanding Republic, would the United States permit indigenous Americans to retain a portion of their homelands? Would it respect, diminish, or eliminate their sovereign rights? Would it extend citizenship to native peoples in good faith? Or would it expel them in entirety?

The once-numerous native populations in the original thirteen states had dwindled—large numbers had even disappeared—and the survivors, numbering 7,000 if Georgia was excluded, lived for the most part on marginal lands. With few exceptions, politicians in the coastal states therefore had little interest in prioritizing the elimination of remnant communities. Actively pursuing the matter could even make for bad politics, since many Native Americans belonged to the same Christian denominations as northern churchgoers. Revisiting the election of 1832, Martin Van Buren, Andrew Jackson's running mate, would estimate that the Jackson–Van Buren ticket lost as many as ten thousand votes in New York alone because of the president's persecution of the Cherokees, turning what would have been a nine-point triumph in the vice president's home state into a more modest four-point victory.[6]

Of the original thirteen states, Georgia alone retained a significant indigenous population. In 1825, Creek and Cherokee peoples numbered well over ten thousand and possessed a quarter of the present-day state, amounting to nearly 15,000 square miles. When it came to the expulsion of indigenous Americans, Georgia and its junior partner, Alabama—which had only recently become a state in 1819—therefore "manifested a feverish feeling on the subject," in the words of one federal agent.[7]

But even in land-hungry Georgia, there was disagreement about the need for native lands. "The people of Georgia," the *Augusta Chronicle* opined in 1830, "have already *too much* land for the purpose of agriculture—far more than they can cultivate—and had they much less, they would cultivate it to far more usefulness and profit, both to themselves and to the state." The newspaper described the environmental degradation that resulted when planters exploited the land, "drawing forth its abundant fruits, without making the slightest return." The land was "gradually impoverished," it wrote, "and at last laid entirely waste and useless, with no other thought, than that plenty more is to be obtained, for little or nothing, from the Indians." The state government, it charged, fostered waste by promising free indigenous lands. Warming to the subject, the newspaper went on to describe Georgia's desolate and barren landscape, scoured as if by a plague of locusts and pocked by abandoned habitations—all the consequence of the cry for more land, "as though we were closely hemmed in within a small and densely populated region." In sum, the state needed "population more than land."[8]

The *Augusta Chronicle* was in the minority but certainly not alone. Eugenius Aristides Nisbet, a state senator from Morgan County, fifty miles east of Atlanta, berated a colleague from the coastal county of Chatham for arguing that Cherokees ought to be expelled "by force." "And what is the necessity of our population in that country?" he asked. "The large land-holders wish the removal," he stated, referring to the state's wealthiest planters, who lived in the Georgia low country. The "gentlemen from the sea coast come to tell us of the necessity," he gibed. Though he was no Cherokee nationalist, Nesbit rejected the right of

Georgians to expropriate Cherokee lands. There was no need. Other Georgians suggested that the expropriation would make a "mere *mockery*" of the state motto: "Justice, Wisdom and Moderation." The "Commoner," one hopeful editorialist imagined, would declare, "I will have nothing to do with this land, obtained, as it has been, by violence, if not by fraud."⁹

In the end, however, Georgia's politicians, defying the values expressed in the state motto, pursued the goal outlined by Governor John Clark in 1821 to replace "all the red for a white population."¹⁰ Determined to remake federal policy in Georgia's image, its politicians drove the national debate, even at the risk of dividing the Union.

No one was more unyielding on the subject than George Troup, who earned the moniker "mad Governor of Georgia" for his extremist rhetoric and saber-rattling ultimatums. Troup had studied Latin and Greek at the College of Princeton (today's Princeton University) alongside fellow Georgians John Forsyth and John Berrien, who would join him in the cause to eliminate native peoples from the eastern half of the United States. They found like-minded classmates at Princeton, for the South's slaveholding elite made up nearly half of Troup's graduating class in 1797. (Before entering college, Troup and Berrien had also attended boarding school together at Erasmus Hall on Long Island.)¹¹ In 1823, after working as a lawyer in Savannah and serving in the House of Representatives, Troup was selected by the Georgia Assembly to be the state's next governor. (The first gubernatorial election by popular vote would not occur until 1825.)

Troup took office in November determined to eliminate the Creek and Cherokee presence from the region. In his campaign to deport thousands of families from Georgia, he used a prose that was bombastic and grandiose, even by nineteenth-century standards. Sometimes referring to himself pompously in the third person ("the Governor of this State," the "Chief Magistrate"), he wrote lengthy and turgid letters to the U.S. president and other officials, invoking "great moral and political truths" to justify the dispossession of the region's longtime residents. He appealed to "indisputable and sacred territorial rights" and insisted that the land was a "birthright"—not belonging to those who had farmed it for generations but to the late-arriving beneficiaries whom Socrates and his compatriots called "the white people of Georgia." Native peoples, Troup asserted, were "simply *occupants*—tenants at will." He pronounced on the "positive obligations" created by contracts entered into by the United States and on the "breach of faith" entailed by violating them— thinking not of treaties with indigenous nations but of the Compact of 1802, an accord between the United States and Georgia in which the federal government agreed to extinguish native title within the state as soon as the lands could be "peaceably obtained." One antagonist, a general in the U.S. Army, compared Troup to a self-important and overbearing "little European despot." By contrast, an admiring nineteenth-century biographer, writing two years before the Civil War erupted, observed of Troup, "Where principle was involved, he was a stranger to the spirit of compromise." Troup's principles, however, were in every instance perfectly aligned with his personal interests.[12]

"Of all the old States," Troup complained to Secretary of War John C. Calhoun in February 1824, "Georgia is the only one whose political organization is incomplete." Its civil polity was "deranged," its militia in a constant state of alert, its natural resources untapped, and its internal improvements suspended, all because it did not yet possess its "vacant territory." That territory was "waste and profitless to the Indians; profitless to the United States; but, in the possession of the rightful owner, a source of strength, of revenue, and of union." How infuriating, then, that early the next year the Cherokees, led by John Ross, followed Troup's letter with one of their own to Congress. It was the "*production and voice of the nation,*" they wrote, "*never again to cede another foot of land.*" Troup blamed U.S. policy for turning indigenous hunters into farmers; the "civilizing plan" was no more than a "great scheme" to fix Creek and Cherokee families on the land, he said, and was "founded in wrong to Georgia."[13] (He was, of course, incorrect. They were farming long before the United States existed.)

Cherokee politicians successfully outmaneuvered Troup, but the Creek Nation proved to be more vulnerable, in part because of the dealings of an influential but dishonest Creek leader, William McIntosh. The son of a British officer and a Creek woman from a distinguished family, McIntosh was equally well-connected in Georgia and the Creek Nation. One of his half-brothers was a Georgia state legislator, another the tax collector for the U.S. Treasury Department in the port of Savannah; his cousin was none other than Governor Troup. McIntosh could not resist the temptation to exploit his position, almost always at the expense of his indigenous relatives. Though the Creek National Council had passed a formal resolution forbidding its citizens from selling lands, McIntosh met with U.S. commissioners in 1825 and ceded the remaining Creek territory in Georgia. Negotiated in secret and consummated with bribes, the Treaty of Indian Springs, as it was called, lacked the signatures of the nation's recognized leaders, with the exception of McIntosh. As a result, the Creek Nation resolved to execute McIntosh for treason, and on the last day of April 1825, some 150 armed men surrounded his plantation house on the Chattahoochee River, set it afire, and shot him dead as he emerged from the flames.[14]

In the history of U.S. relations with native peoples, the Treaty of Indian Springs stands out not for duplicity and fraud—many treaties rested on similarly rotten foundations—but for the fiery political confrontation that it generated. Though the U.S. Senate ratified the treaty shortly before John Quincy Adams took office, the incoming president declined to recognize it and insisted that a new agreement be negotiated with proper Creek authorities. Troup refused to back down and accused the federal government of "fomenting civil war." Acknowledging the validity of Creek grievances was akin to "the servant setting at naught the will of the master, and the master countenancing the servant in defying that will," wrote the slave-owning governor.[15]

It would be comforting if Troup and his political allies were the sole villains in this story, but Georgia's voting citizens—who were, to a person, white men—largely shared the governor's hostility toward their indigenous neighbors. The gubernatorial election of 1825 pitted the incumbent Troup against John Clark, a champion of the state's newer counties that had recently been appropriated from native peoples. As the first Georgia governor's race to be determined by popular vote, the campaign turned into a contest over which candidate hated Indians the most. Clark, a major general, may have actually shot at Indians and "heard the whizzing of a few bullets on the field of battle," opined the Augusta *Constitutionalist*, but Troup, in dispossessing the Creeks, had been even more serviceable to the state.[16]

A memorable campaign slogan encapsulated the election's theme: "Troup and the Treaty," a watchword, it was later claimed, that mothers taught their children "at the first prattle of infancy." Troup "*demanded our rights*," wrote "One of the People" in the pro-Troup *Georgia Journal*. The governor "advised us to *defend our property* with *reason* to the last, and with *arms* when 'argument failed.'" Writing in the *Savannah Republican*, "A Native Georgian" was less restrained. Troup was determined "to maintain at all hazards, the inalienable rights you possess to your slaves and to your Indian territory!" The expectation of unchecked mastery over African and Native Americans had become deeply ingrained during the previous century. But now the state had arrived at a pivotal moment. "Our savage neighbors may be allowed to abide in our bosom; our slaves may be filched from us," fumed the irate "Native Georgian." "Let it be known that you give up the land *only with your lives*—let it be proclaimed that you part with your slaves only after '*you have made a rampart with your bodies*.'"[17] Troup won by 683 votes out of nearly 40,000 cast.

Facing an apparent threat to the Union itself, President Adams hastily arranged for a substitute treaty, signed in 1826 in Washington City by authorized Creek representatives. But even that proved unacceptable to Troup, since it left Creeks with a tiny sliver of land on the western edge of the state. The Treaty of Washington was "a stupendous fraud," charged Troup's Princeton classmate John Forsyth in the U.S. House of Representatives, who insisted that McIntosh's earlier treaty should prevail. John Berrien, the third member of the Princeton triumvirate, denounced the federal government on the floor of the U.S. Senate. "The rights of Georgia," he proclaimed, "have been prostrated" before the "fraud and the insolence of the savages." Until native peoples were expelled, Troup declared, harmony and tranquility between Georgia and the United States could not exist.[18]

More broadly, it was evident to planters that native peoples would not go quietly. In the 1826 Treaty of Washington, Creeks had agreed to cede lands in Georgia, but only on the condition that the United States "guarantee" to them their remaining territory. Likewise, Choctaws, "with great unanimity," refused to give up their stake in Mississippi, wondering why they should seek new lands elsewhere when they lived "in peace" and "in plenty" in their traditional homelands. Chickasaws, also in Mississippi, stated simply, "We have no lands to exchange for any other." The Cherokees not only refused to open negotiations but then denied a request to conduct a survey for a canal through their nation, doing so in a lengthy letter that spelled out their rights under U.S. law. The prospective canal, said Troup with his usual bluster, was to the Union as important as the joining of the oceans across the isthmus of Panama. The expansion of a lucrative southern empire based on unpaid labor remained tantalizingly within sight but out of reach.[19]

To wrest control of the land from native people, southern politicians needed to devise more effective measures. Sometime during the winter of 1826–27, senators and representatives from the southern states met to consider "other means" to expel native peoples. The conspirators were numerous enough to create a crucial subcommittee of three senators, surely selected because they represented the states with the most at stake. John McKinley of Alabama was a fervent supporter of state supremacy and westward expansion. The Creeks owned over 10,000 square miles, or approximately 20 percent, of the land claimed by his state. Thomas Buck Reed of Mississippi, a Princeton graduate, was a political neophyte, but his lack of experience hardly curbed his eagerness for dispossession. The Choctaw and Chickasaw nations owned 25,000 square miles, or about half, of the area claimed by his state. The third committee member, Thomas W. Cobb of Georgia, was a hardline champion of states' rights. The Cherokee and Creek nations owned about 7,000 square miles, or 12 percent, of the 59,000 square miles in his state, a significant amount even after the recent acquisition of Creek lands in the Treaty of Washington. Moreover, Georgia planters were active investors in Alabama and Mississippi cotton lands. Cobb stood poised in the Senate to beat back every chimeric threat to the South's ruling class. The previous year he had joined other extremists in Congress to oppose funding the extension of the Cumberland Road from Wheeling, in what is now West Virginia, to the banks of the Mississippi. Invoking "the great Virginia Prophet" Patrick Henry and foundational constitutional principles, he had sketched out a scenario in which road construction led to emancipation.[20] Together, the three southerners outlined a strategy that became central to the coming national campaign to deport indigenous Americans.

Since it was "extremely improbable" that "negotiation and treaty" would effectively drive native families out of the southern states, the committee set out to devise other "lawful and practicable means" to accomplish "so desirable" an object. McKinley, Reed, and Cobb settled on a simple, and ultimately highly effective, measure. They counseled that the southern states should extend their laws over the "*persons* of the Indians*," italicizing "*persons*" to emphasize that indigenous Americans ought to be treated not as citizens of their own sovereign nations but as members of the states, possessing limited rights. Where possible, southern states should appropriate native lands and assign small, subsistence-sized plots to the dispossessed. The strategy, the three planter-politicians suggested, would have one of two effects: either native peoples would be "speedily induced to remove to the west of the Mississippi," or they would be incorporated into the body politic.[21]

The committee was not serious about the second of these two possibilities, reflecting skepticism among the region's elite that indigenous Americans would "soon lose their distinctive character, language and colour." When the distinguished Georgia politician William Crawford was serving as the secretary of war in 1816, he had proposed a federal policy of encouraging intermarriages between U.S. citizens and native peoples. "It is believed that the principles of humanity in this instance are in harmonious concert with the true interest of the nation," he had written. Crawford had even suggested that the United States should incorporate native peoples before welcoming more European immigrants. By the 1820s, however, most white Americans held "Crawfordism" in contempt. How could marriage "with the vermin-eating Indians" be "*honorable* to the whites?" asked one southern editorialist. In the North, citizens denounced the marriages of two Cherokee students to local women and burned one of the couples in effigy. Speaking in Congress in 1828, Representative John Weems of Maryland thumped a copy of the Bible, asserted that native peoples were the descendants of Abraham and the slave Hagar (plainly confirmed by the observation that "a mixture of the white and the black blood, produced a yellow complexion"), and asserted that "he had seen the mixed breed, and did not like it—he would rather have them a little further off." But what if indigenous peoples nonetheless decided to take their chances in the East, where they still had numerous supporters? If they remained in Georgia, George Troup threatened, they would inevitably sink to the condition of slaves, "a point of degeneracy below which they could not fall."[22]

The committee of three southern senators conceded that its plan was "somewhat bold and daring" but sought to justify it with reference to international law and history, taking pains to demonstrate that native peoples were subject to state jurisdiction. As state subjects, Creeks and Cherokees would fall under the power of the ruling elite, who could do with them as they wished. Moreover, if native peoples resisted state authority, the U.S. Constitution would obligate the federal government to "repress" the "insurrection," just as the same constitutional clause bound it to put down slave rebellions.[23]

The alternative—that the federal government could civilize native peoples and then make them citizens—was so terrifying to the ruling elite that the committee of planter-politicians barely dared to mention it; mere discussion "would admit something like plausibility." The three southern senators shuddered at the consequences of federal authority over citizenship, as would eventually be enshrined in the Fourteenth Amendment. In this nightmarish future, states would be deprived of all power to determine the character, condition, and rights of their inhabitants, "a power which the Southern States *ought* not—*dare* not, resign."[24]

The editor of Milledgeville's *Southern Recorder* added a lengthy and revealing footnote to its reprint of the committee's report. Indians are "a *colored* people," the editor observed. "It will be found that the extension of rights to the *Indians* within a State," he reasoned, "differs from the like extension of rights to the free negroes and slaves within the same *limits, only in the shade of colour* between the two races." The italicized words spelled out the tremendous risk to white supremacy. The South's "coloured population"—whether free, enslaved, African, or indigenous— must remain "mere *inhabitants, (not citizens,)* and peculiarly the subjects of *state municipal regulation.*" As subjects but not citizens, native peoples and African Americans would fall under the same incoherent but deeply oppressive system in which states claimed absolute authority over them but relied on federal power to safeguard the racial hierarchy.[25]

The meeting of southern senators and representatives was extraordinary on several accounts. First, it largely proceeded in secret, beyond the auspices of Congress, and apparently was reported in only a few local newspapers. It is unclear how many national politicians knew that the South had conspired in this way to remake the Republic's relationship with Native Americans. Second, it reveals that southern states were plotting to extend their laws over indigenous peoples and to force them out of the region even before the Cherokees drafted and ratified a constitution in the summer of 1827. The constitution, which enshrined the "sovereignty and jurisdiction" of the Cherokee Nation in the South, became a rallying point for white supremacists in Georgia. Seemingly in response to the document, the Georgia state legislature resolved in December 1827 to extend its jurisdiction over the Cherokee Nation, beginning on June 1, 1830.[26] The 1826–27 meeting of the committee of three, however, shows that the southern states had laid out their strategy well before the ratification of the Cherokee constitution.

Third, and perhaps most importantly, the meeting illustrates that humanitarian concerns did not drive the state-sponsored mass expulsion of indigenous people, as advocates of deportation would later maintain. The three committee members had no association with any of the missionary enterprises, and southern politicians were consistently hostile to social reformers of any sort. "Notions of philanthropy and human[e] policy" were now "fashionable," ridiculed the committee, barely concealing its disdain before mounting a lengthy legal—but not moral— defense of its ruthless strategy.[27]

~~~

WHITE SOUTHERNERS at first gave little thought to the practical details of expelling native families "to the waste public lands over the Mississippi." But the general goal already appeared perfectly achievable to them, even if it seemed unreasonable or fantastical to others.[28] After all, they were used to moving people against their will. In the years leading up to the abolition of the trans-Atlantic slave trade in 1808, the importation of enslaved people into the United States reached an all-time high. Amazingly, in just the final two years of the trade, slavers shipped approximately 55,000 people to North America.[29] It was therefore not so difficult for planters to imagine transporting 60,000 indigenous people, the approximate number living in the South, across the Mississippi.

There were, of course, some differences between the two forced migrations. Africans had been transported overseas, while native peoples would be sent overland, a far more difficult undertaking, given the challenges of traveling over rugged or washed-out roads and bridges. (In the nineteenth century, it was quicker and cheaper to travel by water.) In addition, hundreds of competing firms participated in the vast commercial enterprise that made up the trans-Atlantic slave trade. The expulsion of indigenous Americans, by contrast, would be overseen by a small, inexperienced state bureaucracy. How would a few clerks working out of the War Department in Washington City manage the deportation of 60,000 native people from the South, let alone of 80,000 such people across the entire nation? One final difference complicated the comparison between the transportation of enslaved and native peoples. Since the profit motive drove the Atlantic traffic, cold economic calculation largely determined how well Africans fared on their transoceanic voyages. In the last decade of the slave trade to North America, about 15 percent of the bound captives died during the Middle Passage, a figure that apparently slavers could tolerate. By contrast, the state-sponsored mass expulsion of native peoples would nominally be a humanitarian undertaking, at least as justified to the world. How many deaths would the bureaucrats conducting the operation deem acceptable, and what measures would they need to take to stay below that threshold?[30]

White southerners had another useful comparison at hand. Just as Congress outlawed the Atlantic slave trade beginning in 1808, the domestic slave trade burgeoned. In the 1820s, traffickers deported some 93,000 people from the Atlantic states largely to Alabama, Mississippi, and Louisiana. The following decade, that number would nearly double, to 171,000. Like its trans-Atlantic counterpart, private firms operated this so-called "internal" trade, using balance sheets to determine how well to care for their human prisoners. (Slavers sometimes unceremoniously disposed of dead slaves in "moonlight burials," so as to prevent potential buyers from suspecting that the rest of the coffle was infected with a fatal illness.) The internal trade differed from the trans-Atlantic trade in one significant way, however. It moved people along the same routes that indigenous Americans would follow if they were pushed across the Mississippi. The transportation westwards of African Americans by steamboat and on foot, conspicuous to everyone who traveled in the South in the 1820s, served to make plausible the forced migration of other nonwhite peoples. Eventually, in the midst of the mass deportation of Native Americans, one of the largest firms in the interstate slave trade, Franklin & Armfield, would commission the two-masted brig *Uncas* to transport slaves to lands that six months earlier had supported indigenous families. The vessel was named for the seventeenth-century Pequot leader who appears as the iconic vanishing Indian in James Fenimore Cooper's *The Last of the Mohicans* (1826). "The pale-faces are masters of the earth," Uncas's father concedes over his son's grave.[31]

Despite the suggestive parallels, the interstate slave trade was an imperfect model for deportation. Slave coffles usually contained only thirty to forty people, although larger shipments could include as many as two hundred individuals. Even the largest firms in the nation transported no more than two thousand people a year, a far cry from the 60,000 indigenous southerners who would have to be shipped west. Moreover, the interstate trade benefited from a dedicated infrastructure, including regularly scheduled ships and steamboats, an existing capital market, auctioneers, and holding pens. Traders also had the flexibility to sell off captives along the way, wherever they could turn a profit, and to go where they wanted. If the weather was bad or if roads became impassable, they could head elsewhere, and in fact many set out with no fixed destination.[32] The transportation of thousands of native families to a specific location in uncharted western territory, beyond the reach of established roads and far from supply depots, would present numerous challenges that were both unfamiliar and overwhelming.

If the routes for these westward deportations appeared similar, the motivating desire also seemed intertwined. The coordinated expulsion of native peoples and deployment of unfree laborers satisfied the most intoxicating fantasies of elite white Southerners. To many, the very survival of the southern states seemed tied to the success of these two essential endeavors. The power of white southerners over both native and enslaved peoples depended on narrow readings of the U.S. Constitution's Commerce Clause, which gives Congress the power "to regulate commerce with foreign nations, and among the several states, and with the Indian tribes." The clause would seem to place both the slave trade and indigenous nations under the jurisdiction of the federal government, but southern politicians insisted otherwise. In the first instance, they referred to human trafficking not as trade but as "migration," an innocuous euphemism that helped to skirt troublesome constitutional clauses. Catering to the same interests, when Congress had banned the importation of slaves beginning in 1808, it had cited the Law of Nations, not the seemingly more pertinent Commerce Clause.[33]

As for "Indian tribes," Governor Troup proclaimed, "Georgia must be sovereign upon her own soil," where the United States was "a foreign power." The committee of three southern senators developed a tortured reading of the Articles of Confederation and the Constitution that limited the Commerce Clause. They observed that the Articles of Confederation empowered Congress to regulate trade and manage affairs with native peoples who were "not members of any of the States." That constraint does not exist in the Constitution, but the committee strained to detect it in the infamous three-fifths clause, which excluded "Indians not taxed" from enumeration. If some of them were not taxed, the committee reasoned, presumably others were. "It does not require argument," it happily concluded, "to prove that persons 'taxed' and residing *within* a State, are 'members' of that State" and therefore not subject to federal regulation.[34]

~~~

NORTHERN NEWSPAPERS questioned Troup's "imbecile menaces," pitied his "madness and folly," charged Georgia with "seditious" behavior, and advocated taking "a bold and decisive stand" in favor of "the rights of the Indians." The editor of New York's *Commercial Advertiser*, William Leete Stone, compared Troup with the biblical Ahab, condemned by God for killing his neighbor Naboth and seizing his vineyard, which Naboth had refused to sell. Stone belonged to a group of New York intellectuals and artists who, at least from afar, admired native peoples. Ahab's miserable fate, he wrote, was "righteous retribution for wickedly wresting from Naboth *the inheritance of his fathers*." The parallels with the Creeks were obvious. "The removal by force, or the extermination of this people," Stone charged, "will be a national sin."[35]

One lengthy essay on "Georgia and the Creeks," published originally in August 1825 in a new literary periodical called *The New-York Review*, stood out for its erudition and received widespread attention in the northern press. The piece analyzed the history of Georgia's relations with the Creek Nation, commented on relevant treaties and laws, and cited an array of evidence. But at heart it asked what kind of nation the United States would be. Was the Republic akin to the marauding empires of Europe that invaded the Americas and then debated whether or not the inhabitants were human? Perhaps so. Georgia called for the "extermination" of native peoples, the author charged, and desired to "dispose of thousands of human beings like cattle." Would the United States be responsible for the "smoking, blood-slaked ruins of their huts"? Certainly, the despots of the Old World would take satisfaction. "We might then prate of our regard for justice, of our respect for human rights," wrote the author, "and we should prate in vain."[36]

None of this rhetoric moved the South's well-established white power structure. The region's leaders were accustomed to dismissing the northern reformers while championing lofty constitutional principles that justified their right to hold people in heredity bondage. Rather than engaging with the opposition, they resorted to mockery and sarcasm, a tactic that perhaps did not win many converts but at least rallied Georgia's narrow white male electorate. Many aggrieved citizens resented that Troup had become a figure of ridicule in the North, a target of "doggerel verse" and parody, and that the South's "peculiar institutions" were the subject of "the vilest aspersions." It was infuriating, if predictable, that Troup would be denounced by the "tender hearted and meek mouthed saints of the North, who have so kindly taken every body's business into their homely hands." (In the 1820s, a New England–based campaign against Sunday mail delivery avowed that the very survival of the Republic was at stake, providing white southerners with more evidence of northern sanctimony.)[37]

Northerners were hypocrites, white southerners charged. They had already "literally exterminated" native peoples, stated one "Atticus" with some justification, and now "these very godly given, and grace abounding pinks of piety" demanded that the South accommodate native peoples. It was "rotten hearted hypocrisy," he wrote, that "smells to heaven." Atticus had nothing but contempt for humanitarians. "To our remonstrance," he wrote, they "offer the answer of a whining charity, to our protest they present a long drawn face, to our solemn objections they oppose the overcoming aspect of a snivelling countenance and upraised eyes." Other editorialists shared his scorn. Northerners trafficked in "sentimental trash." Had they forgotten how native peoples "were got rid of in the Northern States?" The *Charleston Courier* found validation in a letter supposedly written by a Danish officer stationed in the West Indies. "Every year," the officer wrote, "we are disgusted by the impertinent cant and whining of certain sentimental travellers, who pour forth their grief at the gradual extinction of the

Indian tribes." He offered a perverse solution: Enslave native peoples for their own good.[38]

It was all too easy to caricature the "zealots and fanatics" of the North, since they were familiar targets of ridicule, but not all opponents of expulsion fit that stereotype. Native peoples, for example, put forward leaders who were acquainted with the halls of Congress and who could quote the Declaration of Independence. "We appeal to the magnanimity of the American Congress, for justice, and the protection of the rights, liberties, and lives of the Cherokee people," one Cherokee delegation led by the tireless John Ross wrote to the U.S. Senate in 1824. Creeks would follow suit five years later in an address to "the citizens of Alabama and Georgia" that was as much prescriptive as descriptive. "You understand how to appreciate free principles, free laws, and institutions," they wrote, "and according to your honest conception of such laws, you will deal out to us all the rights and privileges that we are entitled to, and have been guaranteed to us by the government of the United States."[39]

At almost every turn, indigenous leaders stymied efforts to expel their communities. The Potawatomis and Miamis, told that they "must remove or perish," agreed to cede only a portion of their territory and insisted on reserving numerous tracts for themselves. In Florida, the Seminole leader Hicks declared, "We are unwilling to move" across the Mississippi. "You tell me we will all die here," he said to one U.S. agent. "I think we shall die there too."[40]

The resistance from northern politicians and native peoples placed southern politicians in an awkward position. Despite their constant disparagement of the federal government, they required its assistance to clear the land of native peoples. Only the federal government could locate wasteland for the dispossessed, administrate the population transfer, and pay for it. Since planter-politicians made unlikely and unconvincing champions of indigenous welfare, they needed allies in Congress and a friend in the White House who was as determined as they were to expel native peoples.

It was a stroke of luck then that Isaac McCoy had his epiphany in June 1823. McCoy spoke the language of Protestant reformers and, unlike white southerners, wielded a certain moral authority when he lamented the "perishing Indians."[41] He was also sincere and, when it came to politics, naive. In short, he was the perfect partner for the cynical and self-interested advocates of mass expulsion.

It was also fortunate that the southern slaveholder Andrew Jackson swept into the White House in the election of 1828. Fifteen years earlier, General Jackson had marched through the Creek Nation, torching villages and killing residents. At Tallushatchee, about sixty miles east of present-day Birmingham, his troops burned houses and shot 186 people "like dogs." Lieutenant Richard Keith Call remarked that "half consumed human bodies were seen amidst the smoking ruins." Marching south, Jackson's men killed another three hundred people at Talladega, near the Coosa River. And at the Battle of Horseshoe Bend, the culmination of the U.S.-Creek War, they killed between 800 and 900 more, including some 300 who were shot in the Tallapoosa River as they were desperately trying to swim across.[42] Jackson was a southern war hero.

His opponent, the incumbent president John Quincy Adams of Massachusetts, was everything Jackson was not. The erudite son of the nation's second president, Adams was elite, educated, introspective, and northern. In the election of 1828, nearly 97 percent of voters in Georgia—all white men, it should be underscored—cast their ballot for the aggressive Tennessee planter, leaving a mere 642 votes across the entire state for his opponent. Nationally, Jackson took 56 percent of the vote, a substantial margin of victory, though in a country of thirteen million people he received a total of only 642,806 votes. The "friend of the *people*" had been selected by a tiny fraction of white men.[43]

Americans flocked to Washington City to attend the inauguration, and on March 4, 1829, they gathered by the thousands before the Capitol building's East Portico to witness the transfer of power. An onlooker reported that Jackson emerged from the building to "ten thousand upturned and exultant human faces, radiant with sudden joy." But at least one man in the audience was likely apprehensive and unsmiling. One hundred fifty feet away and directly in front of the president-elect stood Edward Gunter, a Cherokee who was one of John Ross's most loyal allies. Listening to the black-suited Jackson, Gunter may have caught the single sentence in the Tennessean's brief address that mentioned native peoples. "It will be my sincere and constant desire to observe toward the Indian tribes within our limits a just and liberal policy," Jackson declared, "and to give that humane and considerate attention to their rights and their wants which is consistent with the habits of our Government and the feelings of our people."[44]

Nine months later, in his first annual message to Congress in December 1829, the president called for the "voluntary" emigration of native peoples to lands west of the Mississippi. The issue would come to define his presidency. "There was no measure, in the whole course of his administration of which he was more exclusively the author than this," recalled Martin Van Buren, Jackson's secretary of state and then vice president. Congress immediately began drafting bills to answer the president's charge. Isaac McCoy's vision now appeared within reach. McCoy had recently befriended Wilson Lumpkin, an ambitious representative from Georgia who sat on the House Committee on Indian Affairs. The two of them, missionary and slaveholder, carried the fight to Capitol Hill.[45]

THE VIEW
from
WASHINGTON CITY

~~~

CHAPTER 3

THE DEBATE

~~~

IN THE 1830s, it seemed that every crossroads in the United States printed its own newspaper. Hundreds of small but boosterish towns such as Erie, Alabama, Flemingsburg, Kentucky, and Limerick, Maine, supported one and sometimes two papers. Across the nation, approximately 1,300 newspapers served nearly thirteen million people, making one newspaper for every 10,000 Americans, including the 16 percent of the population who were enslaved and by force of law not permitted to learn to read. In this sea of newsprint, self-proclaimed experts, some of whom had never before met a native person, expounded endlessly on "the Indian question." The question was "one of deep concern," commented the Massachusetts *Salem Gazette*. It inspired "flights of fancy, touches of pathos, and streams of eloquence," mocked the *Delaware Gazette and State Journal*. The *Savannah Georgian*, confident that the white people of its home state would carry the day, smirked at the "tea-pot tempest" stirred by "the Indian question."[1]

In indigenous communities, an equally lively but more informed discussion took place at the same time. Unfolding in council meetings, churches, and homes, most of it never appeared in print, and only occasionally did native peoples commit their thoughts to paper, usually with the assistance of a translator and scribe. Fortunately, the Cherokees launched their own newspaper, the *Cherokee Phoenix*, in 1828. Published in the Cherokee capital of New Echota in what is now north Georgia, many of its articles appeared in both English and Cherokee, using the script invented in the second decade of the nineteenth century by Sequoyah, a Cherokee polymath from the Little Tennessee Valley. In Sequoyah's original hand-drawn script, the syllabary consists of eighty-six ornate characters, each one representing a syllable in the Cherokee language; in print, the characters, reduced to eighty-five, are blockier and, in a few instances, resemble uppercase letters from the Roman alphabet. Within a few years of Sequoyah's "transcendant invention," as John Ross called it, an estimated ninety percent of Cherokees were literate. For the first time, they could disseminate print in their own language and use the New Echota press to discuss, debate, and mobilize during the pivotal era of expulsion.[2]

In December 1829, the *Cherokee Phoenix* printed a "Memorial of the Cherokees" to the U.S. Congress, rendering the petition in both Cherokee and English. (Though the Cherokee version appears first on the page, it is not clear which is the original language.) "You are great and renowned," the memorial stated in English; "we are poor in life, and have not the arm and power of the rich." As in this instance, indigenous orators often made themselves out to be supplicants to a more powerful party. The strategy resonated in native communities, since indigenous people were known for their extraordinary generosity, especially compared with the measured compassion of white Americans. "Will you have pity upon us?" the memorial asked.[3]

After establishing the relationship between benefactor and beneficiary, the memorial pivoted to dispute Georgia's assertion that the Cherokees were mere "tenants at will." The state's aggressive actions violated Cherokee treaties with the United States, it stated, and flouted the intercourse law of 1802, which stipulated that indigenous lands could only be conveyed by federal treaty, not by private or state contracts. Unconstitutional and illegal, dispossession would also be "in the highest degree oppressive." "From the people of these United States, who, perhaps, of all men under heaven, are the most religious and free," the English-language memorial concluded, "it cannot be expected."

The Cherokee version differed in significant ways, reflecting the desire of Cherokee politicians to appeal to both the American public and the Cherokee people. In English, the memorial praised "civilized life" and the "christian religion," words dear to the hearts of northern reformers but of less purchase in the Cherokee Nation. In Cherokee, instead of civilization and Christianity, the memorial spoke of "learning," "knowledge of the written word," and acceptance of the "word of God" or "Creator." The English version affirmed the stereotypes held by U.S. politicians, characterizing Cherokees as having been "ignorant and savage." The Cherokee version, by contrast, said simply that they had been hunters. In English, the memorial gently told Congress, "We now make known to you our grievances," while in Cherokee, it protested, "Your people have treated me (us) bad," flatly asserting that U.S. citizens had "cheated" the Cherokees. Perhaps most revealingly, after describing the fate of indigenous peoples in the North, the memorial asked Congress in English, "Shall we, who are remnants, share the same fate?" In Cherokee, this supplication became an accusation: "And still you have no compassion for us—Your intention is to just drive us towards the west, brother."[4]

At the time of the memorial, the Cherokee Nation, significantly reduced from its former extent, stretched from the outer limits of present-day metro Atlanta a hundred miles north to the southern boundary of the Great Smoky Mountains and from western Alabama two hundred miles northeast nearly to Franklin, North Carolina, covering a region of rolling hills, steep mountains, and wide valleys. Messengers carried the memorial from town to town, where local leaders read the Cherokee version in council and, with approval, recorded the names of male residents. "For want of time," according to the *Cherokee Phoenix*, not every person in the nation of roughly eighteen thousand could sign the petition, but the document traveled widely enough to gain over three thousand names, most of them written in the Cherokee syllabary. Cherokee women do not appear among the memorialists. They had spoken against land cessions in the past, if only rarely, since diplomacy was traditionally the realm of men. Their absence on this occasion may reflect the influence of the federal government's civilizing plan. In fact, the 1827 Cherokee constitution borrowed heavily from its U.S. counterpart, and it reflected state laws across the Republic by prohibiting women from voting in national elections.[5]

The bilingual memorial is a striking example of political activism. Even more illuminating are the individual expressions of resolve that memorialists added to the document. One anonymous Cherokee challenged U.S. agents to justify their actions in light of U.S.-Cherokee treaties: "ᎣᎦᏅᏛᏍᎩᏂ ᎤᏂᎬᏫᏳᎯ ᎤᏂᏁᏥᏙᎸ ᏥᎪᏃ ᏓᎫᎵᏂ ᎦᏃᏢᏮ ᏚᎦᏑᎯᏍᏓᏅ." The expression literally means, "We know what the leaders said, or are they going to cover up that we met?" To clarify the expression for Congress, Cherokees paraphrased it as, "We know the treaties existing between us and the United States, and will you pass laws over us?" Another memorialist wrote, "ᎧᏬᏄᎩ ᎠᏁᎯ ᎯᎠ Ꮎ(nah)ᏂᎥ ᏌᏚᏧᏈ ᎠᏂᏍᎦᏯ ᏧᎾᎴᏂᎩᏮ ᎦᏙᎯ ᎤᏂᎨᏳᎯ," meaning "People who live in Kawonugi all of the 1,100 strong men[,] the land they love it." The phrase "the land they love it," which appeared more than once among the signatures, had a particular resonance in the Cherokee Nation, for it signaled a decisive rejection of further land cessions—exactly what white southerners feared most.[6]

With Cherokee assistance, Creek leaders drafted their own English-language memorial to the U.S. Congress around the same time, but without a writing system, they could not circulate it widely to their people. The Creeks quoted a number of treaty articles in their favor, including

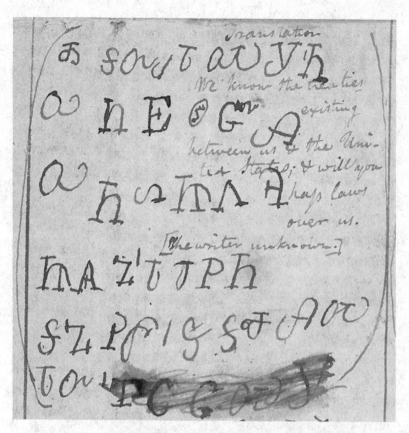

Written by one of the subscribers to the Cherokee memorial, the sentence literally means, "We know what the leaders said, or are they going to cover up that we met?" or, as translated at the time, "We know the treaties existing between us and the United States; and will you pass laws over us."

---

the first Creek-U.S. treaty, signed by George Washington in 1790. They laid bare the hypocrisy of the South's planter-politicians, who, with the help of Isaac McCoy, disguised their plans for mass expulsion as a form of benevolence. "Compulsion in its hideous feathers of inhumanity is not avowed," they observed, "but is indirectly exerted to eject us from the repose and firesides we enjoy in a country to which we have the best of

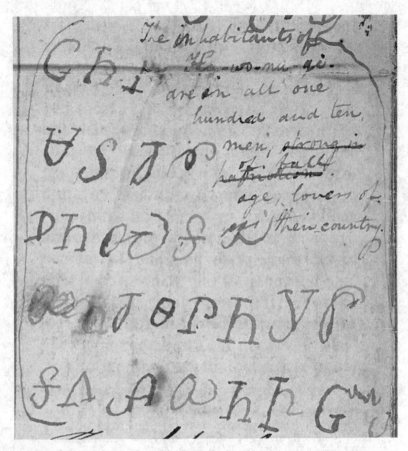

Another subscriber to the Cherokee memorial wrote, "People who live in
Kawonugi all of the 1,100 strong men[,] the land they love it," or as translated at the time, "The inhabitants of Ha-wo-nu-gi are in all one hundred
and ten men, strong in patriotism of full age, lovers of their country."

titles, by provision and solemn guarantees of the United States." Alabama,
they charged, was fattening "on the ruins of our natural and civil rights."
The question, they concluded, was not what was in Alabama's interests or
what the Creeks ought to do—a subject that paternalistic whites never
tired of expounding on—but what was required by Creek-U.S. treaties.[7]

The Speaker of the House, Andrew Stevenson of Richmond, Virginia, dismissed both petitions without discussion, laying them on the table on February 8, 1830. Though disregarded by Congress, the documents served a strategic purpose by rallying northern reformers to the cause. The Cherokee memorial was especially effective. First appearing in the *Cherokee Phoenix*, it was reprinted in newspapers throughout the northern and western states, one of many instances in which the New Echota weekly served as an essential weapon in the fight against deportation. The very existence of the newspaper refuted the rhetoric of savagery and dissipation that, it was said, made expulsion so urgent. One of the nation's leading scientists and most ardent racists, Charles Caldwell, dismissed the ingenious invention of the syllabary as "virtually . . . a Caucasian production." Sequoyah, Caldwell maintained, had "much Caucasian blood in his veins" and was inspired by the alphabet.[8] But the newspaper was undeniably impressive.

On receiving a copy of the first issue of February 21, 1828, the *Commercial Advertiser* of New York observed, "A single sight of such a production is sufficient to overthrow a thousand times all the unprincipled declamation, and unfounded declarations, made by interested white men against the incompetency of all Indians for civilized life." Even Georgia's *Augusta Chronicle* had to admit that it was "handsomely printed." In February 1829, Elias Boudinot, the newspaper's talented editor, lengthened the name to the *Cherokee Phoenix and Indians' Advocate* to reflect its expanded role in speaking for all native peoples against the federal government's policies. Federal officers took note. The superintendent of Indian Affairs, Thomas McKenney, requested a complete run of the publication since its launch, as well as two copies of every future edition.[9]

The *Cherokee Phoenix* defied white southerners who believed that "persons of colour" should not speak for themselves, a conviction that preoccupied the Georgia Assembly and gave rise to several measures, ranging from the ludicrous to the lethal. In 1825, when Creeks insisted that the Treaty of Indian Springs was fraudulent, George Troup commissioned a history of the Creek Nation to prove them wrong "by evidence derived from . . . authentic sources"—in effect writing their history for them. A few years later, in December 1829, the Georgia Assembly was roused to action by the appearance in Savannah of sixty copies of an *Appeal in Four Articles together with a Preamble to the Colored Citizens of the World*, written by David Walker, an African American abolitionist born in North Carolina and living in Boston. One glance at the title, which referred to "colored citizens" and not people, prompted the police to notify the mayor, who in turn informed the governor. In a special session, the state legislature passed an act designed to prevent sailors who were "persons of colour" (exempting "any free American Indian") from "communicating with the coloured people of this State." Anyone circulating written materials that encouraged "insurrection, conspiracy or resistance" would be put to death under the new law. A second act that was passed that same day levied fines on printers who employed slaves or free people of color as typesetters. Alert to the dangers posed by "coloured people" who spoke for themselves, John Berrien, the Georgia-born Princetonian who was now Andrew Jackson's attorney general, advised the president to ship the printing press and typefaces of the *Cherokee Phoenix* across the Mississippi. "I cannot too strongly urge its importance," he wrote.[10]

Well before Boudinot's *Cherokee Phoenix* arose, native peoples had found other ways to reach the American public. A twenty-two-year-old Cherokee scholar named David Brown interrupted his study of Hebrew, Greek, and French at Andover Theological Seminary in 1823 to embark on a speaking tour down the East Coast on behalf of the American Board of Commissioners for Foreign Missions, a New England–based organization dedicated to proselytization. Brown had become an accomplished orator addressing audiences in Salem, Boston, Cambridge, and Newton; now he was impressing overflow crowds as far south as Petersburg, Virginia. The tour was meant to raise money for the American Board, but Brown also used it to cultivate support for indigenous nations and to condemn colonization. It would have been better "had the natives never seen even the shadow of a white man," he told an audience in Boston, citing, among other events, Jackson's slaughter of the Creeks in 1813–14. In subsequent years, his letters appeared occasionally in the press. "How would the Georgians receive a proposition from the Cherokees to exchange the land they now hold, (which originally belonged to the Cherokees) for a tract of country near the Rocky Mountains?" he asked in 1825 in one widely reprinted missive. "Unless force is resorted to, unless the gigantic U. States should fall, sword in hand, upon the innocent babe of the Cherokee Nation," he continued, "the Indian title to this land will remain so long as the sun and moon endure."[11]

There were other speakers too: Elias Boudinot, the editor of the *Cherokee Phoenix*; John Ridge, Boudinot's Cherokee classmate at Cornwall Academy in Connecticut; Red Jacket, the Seneca leader; David Cusick, the Tuscarora historian; and William Apess, the brilliant Pequot Methodist minister. Their advocacy ranged from the cautious to the confrontational, from recounting heartening stories of uplift to laying out damning charges against the United States. Among these political activists, no one was more perceptive and incisive than Apess. His 1829 autobiography, the first by a Native American, recounted a childhood of terrible physical abuse and deprivation, partially caused, he said, by white Americans, who robbed his people of their lands and gave them nothing in return but alcohol. "I believe that there are many good people in the United States, who would not trample upon the rights of the poor," he wrote, "but there are many others who are willing to roll in their coaches upon the tears and blood of the poor and unoffending natives—who are ready at all times to speculate on the indians and cheat them out of their rightful possessions." In a lengthy appendix, he singled out historians for vindicating the colonial conquest and newspaper editors for circulating "every exagerated [*sic*] account of 'Indian cruelty.'"

Apess's self-published autobiography gave a voice to native peoples. In the 1830s, he would speak against the Republic's triumphant national history and expose the contradiction between American values and American treatment of "colored people."[12]

It was more difficult for women to play a public role in the fight over deportation, given the belief in the United States at the time that politics belonged to men. Unable to embark on speaking tours, native women had long made their concerns known in local council meetings, and in one extraordinary case in 1818, in a letter to the federal government. "Our neighboring white people seem to aim at our destruction," wrote the author Peggy Scott Vann Crutchfield, a bilingual Cherokee, who pleaded that without federal protection "we are undone." By the 1820s, however, women's voices were increasingly mediated by Protestant missionaries. Nonetheless, their stories of uplift, told in letters and memoirs, countered the fatalistic narratives disseminated by southern politicians and inspired white women to launch a national petition campaign of their own against deportation.[13]

Native memoirs, letters, and speeches circulated widely in newspapers from Maine to Washington City, but rarely farther south, where many of them were written. Just as white southerners did not care to read the words of African Americans who had escaped from slavery, they did not want to hear indigenous peoples speak for themselves. The reason was clear. Like enslaved African Americans, Native Americans gave compelling testimony about their own oppression. Without their activism, there would have been no debate over expulsion. When the first bill "for the exchange of lands" was introduced to Congress in January 1830, native peoples had already cultivated a fervent opposition.

~~~

WITHIN WEEKS of Jackson's inauguration, his administration began laying the groundwork for what would be the president's signature piece of legislation. After the American Board of Commissioners for Foreign Missions refused to support Jackson's proposal, Superintendent of Indian Affairs Thomas McKenney launched the New York Indian Board for the Emigration, Preservation, and Improvement of the Aborigines of America in July 1829. It was a false-front organization, appearing to be a private initiative but funded by the federal government. The northern headquarters and the inspiring name wrapped slave owners' favorite policy in gauzy humanitarianism. "This sort of machinery," McKenney boasted, "can move the world." It would "silence all opposers."[14]

Isaac McCoy, however, correctly surmised that the organization would amount to no more than "a bag-of-wind." Six months after its creation, the board voted to disband for lack of interest—few northern reformers were willing to lend their names to the charade—though not before Lewis Cass, Isaac McCoy's old correspondent, published a widely read essay endorsing its goals. Cass, who would soon become Jackson's secretary of war, was a former New England schoolteacher who made a political career out of supporting southern planters. His sixty-three-page essay was a morass of distortion and empty speculation. Native peoples were depressed by American "superiority," improvident, habitually indolent, "implacable in their resentments," fatalistic, and "an anomaly upon the face of the earth." It was a wonder that they existed at all. Cass cited the Scottish historian William Robertson and the Swiss lawyer Emerich Vattel but relied mainly on two American authorities, McKenney and "the pious and laborious" Isaac McCoy.[15]

The essay caused a furor, eliciting a number of responses, none more scathing than the lampoon that appeared in Maine's *Bangor Register*. Four years earlier, Cass had published an essay in the same *North American Review* that, his opponents asserted, contradicted his recent effort. In the first essay, he had heaped scorn on native peoples but confessed to being "apprehensive" that the proposal to expel indigenous Americans, "this gigantic plan of public charity," would "exasperate the evils" that white Americans were "anxious to allay." It was "better to do nothing," he had concluded, "than to hazard the risk of increasing their misery."[16]

Now Cass said the opposite. No matter, said the *Register*. "A great many very respectable men are obliged to wind up their opinions every eight days, as they wind up a clock." If an ordinary citizen was entitled to oscillate, so much more was "his Excellency the Governor of Michigan Territory." "If it shows any talent to think well upon one side of a question," the newspaper mocked, "it must be allowed to show just twice as much to think well on both sides." Cass held that the sovereignty of a nation was "to be judged of by the whites," the *Register* observed, and that Indian sovereignty, if permissible, was "only allowable during good behavior." Treaties, in Cass's view, were not binding because Indians were savage, but the evidence of savagery, in the *Register*'s ungenerous summary, was absurd: The Scottish historian Robertson, who never set foot in North America, said that Indians ate bear meat and had no notions of property; the Swiss lawyer Vattel stated that farming, "a decent practice," ought to be encouraged, and therefore Indians "ought to be exterminated"; and Spain and France treated Indians far worse than the United States. It was a caricature of Cass's argument, to be sure, yet not so far from his actual polemic. The *Register*'s editor, Samuel Call, was said to be "a cynical gentleman of considerable sharpness of intellect," but one wonders if some of the sharpness in this instance came from Maine's Penobscot people. Call knew them from his time as a sympathetic state Indian agent in 1824.[17]

Among U.S. citizens, the Jackson administration's most tireless foe was Jeremiah Evarts, the corresponding secretary of the American Board. Evarts was a Yale graduate and former lawyer who had found his calling as a social reformer. Though he had once favored the voluntary removal of indigenous peoples, Native American activists had turned him against the campaign to eliminate nonwhites from the United States. (The famous abolitionist William Lloyd Garrison had experienced a similar conversion at the hands of African American activists, who opened his eyes to the racism behind the American Colonization Society.) Under the name of William Penn, Evarts published twenty-four essays in late 1829 laying out the case against expulsion. The essays extended arguments that Native Americans had been making all along, which is perhaps not a surprise, since Evarts knew David Brown and Elias Boudinot and had traveled through the native South several times. Following the lead of indigenous activists, Evarts wrote about "solemn" treaties, the obligations imposed by the Declaration of Independence, and the improving prospects of Cherokees and other Native Americans, though he did so at greater length and to a larger audience. According to one contemporary, the essays appeared in at least forty newspapers and were read by a half million people in a country of thirteen million.[18]

With Evarts's encouragement, antiremoval petitions began to flood into Congress. They arrived from New York City; Brunswick, Maine; Topsfield, Massachusetts ("I am authorized to state that every individual in this town is in favour of this memorial"); Pittsburgh and Philadelphia; Windham, Connecticut; Champaign, Ohio; and everywhere in between—but not a single one came from any of the slave states. Some were printed, others written in longhand. Signatures ranged in number from two or three to several hundred. One was seven feet long, another fifteen pages. Apologizing for the twenty signatures on his petition, J. Boynton of Philipsburg, Maine, added a handwritten note to his senator: "In consequence of the bad state of travelling there has been but little opportunity of presenting this memorial to the inhabitants of this town, and I feel unwilling to delay longer to forward it." The Senate Committee on Indian Affairs asked to be relieved of the burdensome duty of considering the petitions; it had already made known its firm desire to expel native peoples. A House member from Georgia asserted that the several thousand petitioners "were nothing in comparison with the millions who were silent and satisfied." Compared with "contented majorities," said another, "weak minorities always make the most noise."[19]

The petitions, composed in the evangelical language of northern churches, are predictably parochial and reflect the unquestioned conviction that all the world should be Christian. And yet, drawing in part on the discourse of indigenous activists, the petitions are also deeply radical. It would be "childish" to assert that "the charters of European monarchs or the compacts of neighbouring states with each other can, by imaginary limits, or by lines of latitude and longitude, divest the original inhabitants of their lands," wrote petitioners from New York City. White Americans were "invaders," said residents in Pennsylvania. Petitioners from Brunswick, Maine, insisted that indigenous peoples had a "perfect right, by possession from time immemorial," to their lands. Would the United States "trample . . . treaties in the dust" and sacrifice them "to avarice or ungodly ambition?" asked the residents of North Yarmouth, Maine. "We trust in God," they continued, "that the United States will not fly to reasons of state."[20] The United States would do what was right, the Mainers hoped, rather than what was merely expedient.

One recurring theme in the petitions is the dark stain that expulsion would leave on the reputation of the Republic. It would "stamp our national character with indelible infamy," wrote one group from Lexington, New York. Such acts of "enormous injustice," wrote another group from Pennsylvania, "have rarely been perpetrated by nations calling themselves civilized, and professing to pay a decent respect to their own reputation." A memorial from the officers of Dartmouth College compared U.S. policy to the "bloody conquests of Cortez and Pizarro." "The doctrine that force becomes right," they observed, "has always actuated ambitious and unprincipled conquerors." They were deeply concerned about the reputation of the Republic "in the eyes of the civilized world." Expulsion, petitioners said, was "tyrannical and oppressive," an "unparalleled perfidy," an "atrocious outrage," and a "lasting dishonor."[21]

This last censure from the "ladies" of Pennsylvania was especially notable since women did not traditionally have a place in politics in the United States. Their memorial to the Senate and the House of Representatives belonged to the first-ever women's petition drive, organized by Catherine Beecher, an educator who was born into a family of radical reformers. Encouraged by Evarts and the public protests of Cherokee women, Beecher rallied almost 1,500 women from seven northern states. They recognized the novelty of their petitions but insisted on being heard. Eighteen women from Farmington, Maine, acknowledged that the "delicacy of feeling and modesty of deportment which should ever characterize the female sex" would forbid them from petitioning Congress "on any ordinary occasion," but they rejoiced that they lived in an age that would permit and even encourage them to do so now. They were unduly optimistic. Nevertheless, dispensing with delicacy and modesty, they decried the violation of rights "for which our fathers, fought and bled, and the enjoyment of which so highly distinguishes us as a nation."[22]

Likewise, the "sundry ladies" of Hallowell, Maine, asserted, "We would not ordinarily interfere in the affairs of government, but we must speak on this subject." So too the women of Lewis, New York, who acknowledged that they were "departing from the usual sphere which they occupy." Nonetheless, they continued, the expulsion of indigenous Americans involved "the principles of national faith and honor which they in common with every other member of society are intrusted to preserve inviolate." While many women petitioners invoked the traditional concerns of middle-class white women—the sanctity of the "domestic altar," the well-being of the "feebler sex," and the "endearments of home"—they were no less vehement than men in their condemnation of U.S. policy.[23]

Philanthropists were, in the eyes of slave owners, "meek," "sickly," and "morbid" (meaning soft), no match for the white men of the South and their "fearless, manly exercise of sovereignty." The women's petition campaign was yet another symptom of the effeminacy of the movement, and such gendered criticism found allies among Jacksonians in the North. "FEMALE petitions" were "highly reprehensible," opined the *Pittsburgh Mercury*. Even some Whig papers objected to "pretty creatures" involving themselves in politics. The *New England Review* approvingly quoted John Randolph of Virginia, a congressman famous for his sharp tongue: "The ladies—God bless them—I like to see them any where and every where save in Legislative Hall."[24] Not surprisingly, misogynist comments were picked up and trumpeted by papers in Georgia.

The strutting reached its absurd climax on the floor of the Senate when Missouri's Thomas Hart Benton, raised in central North Carolina and renowned for his buffoonish pomposity, mocked the "benevolent females" and their male allies. When they retreated in defeat, Benton jeered, the women should place "no reliance upon the performances of their delicate little feet," for the men would outrun them. "I would recommend to these ladies," he said, "not to douse their bonnets, and tuck up their coats, for such a race, but to sit down on the way side and wait the coming of the conquerors." Once the real men arrived—the type that John Quincy Adams would later call the "Anglo-Saxon, slaveholding exterminator of Indians"—the women would be secure.[25]

~~~

ANDREW JACKSON'S election and address to Congress implicitly invited U.S. citizens to plunder the homes of the South's longest-standing residents, who, it appeared, were due to be expelled imminently. From the Creek Nation, Neha Micco informed the president that U.S. citizens were stealing their slaves and horses and running them off their land, infringing on rights guaranteed to them by the federal government. In October 1829, Tuskeneah, a Creek leader who was old enough to remember the first U.S.-Creek treaty in 1790, complained that whites stole their property frequently. Without federal protection, he stated, they would be reduced "to a state of penury."[26]

Violence spread through the Cherokee Nation as well, fueled not just by Jackson's inauguration but by the discovery of gold in southern Appalachia in August 1829. Within six months, between one thousand and two thousand intruders were mining the precious metal on native lands. They were "emboldened by indulgence in their trespass," Cherokee leaders complained to Jackson's first secretary of war, John Eaton, and "think it an act of trifling consequence" to drive families from their homes.[27]

The violence threatened to spread and to sharpen internal divisions. In a futile effort to maintain a united front amid deteriorating living conditions, some Creeks beat their neighbors who enlisted to move across the Mississippi, in one instance cutting off the ears of a man and woman. Echoing incidents of frontier violence from the eighteenth century, Creek and Cherokee men attacked the intruders and took their property, acts of repossession from one perspective, theft from another, prompting white Georgians to retaliate. In one particularly vicious assault in the spring of 1830, twenty intruders seized a Cherokee man named Chuwoyee, struck him on the back of the head with a gun, and beat him senseless with clubs and rocks. They threw the incapacitated man over a horse, took him to a camp, and dumped him on the ground, where he remained overnight, exposed to freezing sleet. He died the next morning. Two others escaped, though the assailants stabbed one of them in the chest with a large butcher knife. The marauders threw a fourth Cherokee named Rattling Gourd in jail but released him after the federal government obtained a lawyer for him. In a letter dripping with sarcasm, Cherokee leaders told Jackson, "It cannot be supposed, even tho. our people are Indians (we mean no disrespect) that they can with calmness and submission, witness every act of injustice and plunder by the intruders."[28]

Southern elites were quick to blame outside agitators for the violence. The confrontations were "the first fruits of the 'philanthropic' movements of the North," insisted one Georgia newspaper, a charge that would be leveled with more vehemence the following year, when Nat Turner organized a slave uprising in Southampton County, Virginia. Native peoples were "rude and impudent" as a result of the "Fanatics of the North," the "white savages" who interfered in "local concerns."[29]

Five hundred miles separated Capitol Hill and the Creek and Cherokee nations, but it may as well have been five thousand. No one in Washington City consulted the subjects of the grand scheme proposed by Jackson. In late March 1830, a delegation of Cherokee leaders rented accommodations in Brown's Hotel, halfway between the White House and Congress, but it was Isaac McCoy, rooming in the City Hotel, a block from Jackson's residence, who had gained the administration's attention. "I hope [to] exert a favourable influence on the minds of many," McCoy wrote to his son in late 1829. The zealous missionary-turned-lobbyist had already sent pro-expulsion materials to hundreds of influential people around the country, including scores of newspaper editors and government officials, from the secretary of war down to the chief clerk of the 2nd Auditor's Office. After meeting with President Jackson and Secretary of War John Eaton, he reported that both were "of the spirit of colonizing the Indians." The superintendent of Indian Affairs, Thomas McKenney, was also "very friendly."[30]

The Senate debate on expulsion began on April 6 and lasted for two weeks, exposing sharp fissures between southern slave owners and northern reformers. The freshman senator Theodore Frelinghuysen of New Jersey led the opposition. An active member of the American Board, the American Bible Society, the American Tract Society, the American Sunday School Union, and the American Temperance Union, Frelinghuysen was also a lifelong supporter of the American Colonization Society. Ironically, his zeal for shipping African Americans to Liberia matched his disgust over deporting Native Americans to the West.[31]

In his three-day, six-hour-long speech, Frelinghuysen analyzed treaties, discussed the Law of Nations, and appealed to the conscience of the nation, drawing on the language of his friend Jeremiah Evarts as well as on that of native politicians. Native peoples, he stated, had "extended the olive branch" when the colonies were feeble, but now federal and state governments were using "force and terror" to dislodge indigenous families by extending "grinding, heart-breaking" state laws over them. The United States, he asserted, had violated treaties, disregarded native sovereignty, and abandoned its own values.[32]

George Troup, now representing Georgia in the U.S. Senate, was not well enough to speak on the floor, so the state's other senator, John Forsyth, led the countercharge, surpassing Frelinghuysen's lengthy speech by two full hours. Forsyth suggested that it was not possible for a contract with "a petty dependent tribe of half starved Indians" to be "dignified with the name, and claim the imposing character of, a treaty." He paused to reprimand the deluded "ladies" who had been recruited into service against Georgia. And he asserted that native peoples in the East were "little better than the wandering gypsies of the old world." He reserved special opprobrium for the *Cherokee Phoenix*. The newspaper, he stated, spent funds that could have been better used to feed and clothe "half starved and naked wretches" in the Cherokee Nation, though it is apparent that he was more bothered by the periodical's wide circulation. "It is thus, sir, that the Cherokees have been made so prominent," he complained. Forsyth also objected to the presence of the Cherokee delegation in Washington City and to the circulars, memorials, pamphlets, and essays that they had penned.[33] Adopting a tone that southern orators would hone as the century progressed, he managed to sound both righteous and aggrieved.

Another twenty hours of speeches followed, but in the Senate, the vote on expulsion was a foregone conclusion. The nation was then evenly divided between slave and free states, and the South could always count on the support of a few northern senators, with business and political leanings toward the cotton South. The final vote, on April 24, stood at twenty-eight in favor, nineteen opposed. Four southern senators (two from Delaware and one each from Missouri and Maryland) abandoned the slave bloc and another was absent, but they were outnumbered by the nine from the North who joined their southern colleagues in voting to expel indigenous Americans.

In the House, by contrast, the vote was entirely uncertain. Five of the seven members of the House Committee on Indian Affairs were from slave states, but in the House at large, only 89 of 209 representatives were from the South. A "more important question never came before any legislature," wrote Ambrose Spencer, a representative from New York. "It involves questions of national faith," he declared. Though the debate would not quite determine "the extirpation or preservation of the Indians," as he imagined, it would irrevocably change the lives of some 80,000 people, and the impact would reverberate for generations. A crowd of indigenous Americans stood listening attentively at the entrance to the House chamber for the length of the debate.[34]

At the beginning of the year, Isaac McCoy had met with the House Committee on Indian Affairs, which included his friend and ally Wilson Lumpkin, to champion the case for expulsion. Now it was Lumpkin's turn to push the bill through the House. The Georgia planter had a talent for hiding his extremism beneath a veneer of reason. "Our treatment of the Indians" was "one of our great national sins, and slavery another," the steadfast advocate of expulsion and the owner of nineteen slaves had once said. After meeting with Lumpkin, one missionary was impressed with his reasonableness and concluded that he appeared "like a man of principle and of piety." The Cherokee William Coodey offered a harsher appraisal. Lumpkin, he said, was "a cold blooded hypocrite," who "will say any thing to so serve a purpose whether it be the truth or an untruth."[35]

Lumpkin began his speech as the voice of moderation, conceding that some native peoples were "susceptible of civilization" but insisting that their conditions would improve in the West. He quoted McCoy at length ("one of the most devoted and pious missionaries"), mounted a vigorous defense of his home state ("Georgia, it is true, has slaves; but she did not make them such; she found them upon her hands"), and defended Andrew Jackson ("No man living entertains kinder feelings to the Indians"). Northern reformers were "well paid" hypocrites and "intermeddlers," he charged, out to line their pockets at the expense of native peoples. To save the Indian, he concluded, echoing his friend McCoy, they must be expelled.[36]

The opposition had the better argument. It was easier to contend that treaties were in fact treaties than to assert that they were something less. The chair of the House Committee on Indian Affairs, John Bell of Tennessee, insisted that treaties with native peoples were "a mere device, intended only to operate upon their minds, without any intention of being carried into effect." Henry Storrs of New York countered, "It requires no skill in political science to interpret these treaties." "The plainest man," he continued, "can read your solemn guaranties to these nations, and understand them for himself." Maine's Isaac Bates, imagining a conversation with the president, was more dramatic:

> Sir, they produce to you your treaty with them. Is this your signature and seal? Is this your promise? Will you keep it? If you will not, will you give us back the lands we let you have for it? The President answers, no; and the Congress of the United States answers here is money for your removal.

Jackson, he said, set fire to the city and would not put it out, though he was "its hired patrole and watch."[37]

It was also easier to argue by invoking republican values than by resorting to callousness and derision. The advocates of expulsion mocked those who "indulge" their "tears at the extinction of the Indian race." "The Indians melt away before the white man, like the snow before the sun!" exclaimed Richard Henry Wilde of Georgia. "Well, sir!" he continued. "Would you keep the snow and lose the sun!" By contrast, Henry Storrs of New York called on Andrew Jackson to "vindicate the public faith" of the country, and William Ellsworth of Connecticut reminded congressmen that "the eyes of the world, as well as of this nation, are upon us." "I conjure this House," he concluded, "not to stain the page of our history with national shame, cruelty, and perfidy." House member John Test of Indiana acknowledged that both senators from his state had voted for the bill. He, however, felt "bound in conscience, in honor, and in justice" to speak against it.[38]

Legal coercion, the strategy secretly devised by southern senators and representatives in the winter of 1826–27, lay at the heart of the debate. "We are told," petitioned the Cherokees, "if we do not leave the country, which we dearly love, and betake ourselves to the western wilds, the laws of the state will be extended over us." Creek petitioners spelled out the consequences. Alabama laws were designed to plunder them, "to drag our people to distant tribunals to answer complaints, not before a Jury of peers, or vicinage, but before a Jury of strangers who speak a Language as strange." The object, they concluded, was less to exercise sovereignty than to "expel our Nation from their country."[39]

Congressman Edward Everett of Massachusetts, a renowned orator and onetime Harvard professor, took up this theme on the floor of the House. State laws, Everett asserted, "are the very means on which our agents rely to move the Indians":

> It is the argument first and last on their tongues. The President uses it; the Secretary uses it; the commissioners use it. The States have passed the laws. You cannot live under them. We cannot and shall not protect you from them. We

advise you, as you would save your dear lives from destruction, to go.

Legal force "is the most efficient and formidable that can be applied," he continued. "It is systematic, it is calculated and measured to effect its desired end." Representative Test of Indiana put it more vividly. Native peoples would be negotiating their expulsion "with the horrors of a penitentiary and hard labor staring them in the face, with a rope around their necks, a hangman by their side, and a gallows erected over their heads!"[40]

The debate brought the House to a fever pitch. "I have never witnessed, in any deliberative body, more violence and excitement," wrote one onlooker. The chamber was so evenly divided that Speaker of the House Andrew Stevenson—said by one adversary to be among the "Slaves of the Executive" who were guilty of "subserviency and prostitution"—cast the deciding vote on three pivotal motions. It is unlikely that the bill would have survived without his intervention.[41]

Representatives from Georgia, Alabama, and Mississippi unanimously supported the expulsion of native peoples in order to expand slavery, and almost every other southern member backed the policy for the same reason. They were joined by representatives from New York and New Hampshire, strongholds of the Democratic Party in the North. That was not enough, however, to get the bill through the House. The final vote would hinge on the large delegation of twenty-six House members from Pennsylvania. Though many of them were "the General's friends," wrote Andrew Jackson's future vice president, Martin Van Buren, only four were reliable votes for the pro-expulsion forces. The others lived in dread of giving offence to the large population of Pennsylvania Quakers, who were among the most ardent petitioners against expulsion. To secure a victory, the administration needed to peel off three of the twenty-two members of the delegation who were opposed to the president's key policy initiative.[42]

Jackson resorted to "threats and terrors," said Congressman William Stanbery of Ohio. The administration reminded the House members that the legislation was the president's "favorite measure" and warned them that they would be denounced as "traitors and recreants" if they failed to fall in line. Jackson, they learned, would work to defeat the holdouts at the next election, a threat that was said to be "as terrifying" to some as the guillotine in revolutionary France. One representative who had been browbeaten by Jackson's allies stated that "the *highest authority*" had told him that the bill was "necessary for the preservation of the Indians," a contention that was as much menacing as reassuring.[43]

When the day of the final vote arrived on May 26, two congressmen from Pennsylvania, James Ford and William Ramsey, were missing, and business was suspended while the sergeant-at-arms went searching for them. Ford, a sawmill and gristmill owner from near Pittsburgh, appeared soon afterward, but Ramsey, said to be sick, was not in his lodgings and could not be found. Finally, after more than an hour's delay, said one eyewitness, the fifty-year-old lawyer arrived *"tottering"* into the chamber, "with all the appearance of being very sick." The question, "Shall the bill pass?" was put to the House. The act passed by a margin of 102 to 97, with both Ford and Ramsey switching sides and voting in favor of the legislation. "The prayers of our memorials before the Congress of the United States have not been answered," a despondent John Ross told the Cherokee General Council.[44]

Two hours after the tense vote, a quarrel broke out between Ramsey and South Carolina Representative George McDuffie over the federal tariff. The tariff protected northern industries from foreign competition, but McDuffie, like other planter-politicians, opposed the tax, since it raised the price of the manufactured goods they needed to operate their slave labor camps. Still chafing from his controversial vote, Ramsey accused his southern colleague of depriving the government of income, even while drawing on the Treasury to expel indigenous Americans. When McDuffie called Ramsey "an *ignoramus* and an *old woman*," Ramsey abandoned "all appearance of indisposition" and responded vehemently, leading a witness to speculate that the Pennsylvania congressman had feigned illness in the hope of avoiding the expulsion vote altogether. Ramsey later claimed that he had been cheated in the bargaining for his vote.[45]

Ramsey's theatrics, and the fact that he was one of three to switch sides and secure passage of the bill, made him a target of scorn in Pennsylvania. In Harrisburg, the *Pennsylvania Intelligencer* called out the faithless congressman and the state's other representatives who had voted "to drive the defenceless Indians from their homes." Returning to the subject in mid-June, the newspaper's ire had only grown. Singling out Ramsey once more, it speculated bleakly that for native peoples nothing remained but "extermination." Soon, it predicted, "some blood stained victor" in the Cherokee Nation would close his correspondence to the secretary of war by announcing the final destruction of the Cherokees. "*This morning*," the newspaper imagined the letter stating, "*we found fifteen of them secreted to avoid detection and immediately despatched them.*"[46]

While Jackson pressured and threatened members of Congress to vote for expulsion, there is also a structural explanation for the outcome. The bill, as Martin Van Buren succinctly observed, was a "southern measure," and the South had an undemocratic advantage. As a result of the Constitution's three-fifths clause, slave states wielded an additional twenty-one votes in Congress in 1830.[47] The politics were truly perverse. Planters used the votes accorded to them for owning slaves to make room for more slaves. By a narrow margin of five votes, they succeeded in passing an act designed to open up vast territory for industrial-scale cotton production. Through its passage, hundreds of thousands of fertile acres—the ancestral lands of native peoples—would become part of the empire of slave labor camps that was rapidly expanding across the Lower South.

Beginning with issue of April 23, 1831, *The Liberator's* masthead captured the relationship between the expansion of slavery and the expulsion of native peoples. A planter purchases slaves at an auction, while
"Indian Treaties," highlighted in the inset, lie beneath his feet.

The righteous anger that many people felt for what they called a
"national disgrace" was somewhat undercut by their opponents' insistence that native peoples had long been oppressed and dispossessed in
both the North and the South. The sympathy of northern reformers,
according to one hostile congressman, seemed sudden, shallow, and
hypocritical. "The Indians had nearly disappeared from eleven of the
thirteen old States," he rightly observed, and "heretofore their gradual
disappearance has produced no violent sensation." Another wondered if
the congressmen from Massachusetts, Maine, Connecticut, and New
York who "zealously" spoke against the bill had bothered to examine the discriminatory laws of their own states. The *Georgia Journal*
printed a series of northern laws showing how "the poor Indians—
these inoffensive and oppressed sons of the forest—were treated by the
immaculate puritans and their descendants." In Connecticut, native
peoples were subject to state morality laws; in Rhode Island, they were
constrained by a 9 P.M. curfew, on pain of public whipping; in Massachusetts, bounties were offered for "Indian heads"; in New York, the
state forbade the Senecas and other native nations from trying and
punishing crimes. The allegations were mostly valid; northern states

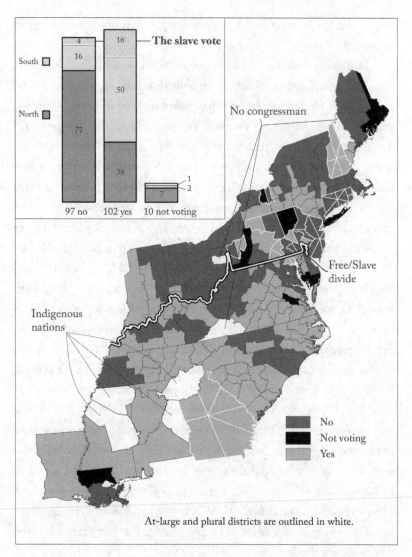

The slave vote

South □
North ■

4
16
77
97 no

16
50
36
102 yes

No congressman

Free/Slave divide

Indigenous nations

1
2
7
10 not voting

No
Not voting
Yes

At-large and plural districts are outlined in white.

Voting by district in the House of Representatives on the "Act to provide for an exchange of lands with the Indians," May 26, 1830. I have subdivided Georgia, New Jersey, Connecticut, and New Hampshire, which had at-large elections. I have also subdivided plural districts with multiple representatives in Maryland, New York, and Pennsylvania. The accompanying bar graph illustrates that the extra representatives accorded to southern states by the three-fifths compromise made the difference in the passage of the bill.

had in fact led the way in the extension of sovereignty over indigenous nations.[48]

Since the Revolution, Americans had struggled with little success to ease the tension between radical republican values and the racial hierarchy in the United States, and they failed once again when Congress voted to expel indigenous peoples. While white southerners cynically dismissed the stirring rhetoric of their opponents, at least a few self-questioning and thoughtful northerners recognized the difficulty they had living up to their ideals. "It is a singular feature in our nature that we often condemn in others what we will do ourselves," one writer, identified only as J.W.B., observed in the *New-Haven Register*. To make the point, the anonymous author imagined a dialogue between "Friend A" and "Public Spirit." Friend A: "Have you heard how the Georgians are driving off the Indians?" Public Spirit: "Yes! and my blood boils with indignation at the deed!" But when the subject turns to the creation of a college in New Haven to educate "colored youth," Public Spirit responds quite differently: "*Colored youth!* what do you mean, *Nigger College* in this place! Why, friend A. have you lost your senses!" "You get a gang of negroes here," Public Spirit protests, "and you would soon find that the value of real estate would fall in this place at least twenty-five percent." This scenario was not fictional, for at a rancorous public meeting, the citizens of New Haven did oppose the creation of such a school, even while they were sending anti-expulsion petitions to Congress. In the dialogue, a resident of Georgia has the last word: "You hypocritical turncoats! . . . When you cease from driving off the blacks from your own cities, then come and tell me of the wickedness of driving off the Indians."[49]

Public spirit also fell short when the subject turned to the treatment of indigenous Americans in the North. In New York, politicians would spend the 1830s dispossessing the Senecas in order to clear the way for canal construction, and in Massachusetts, state leaders faced unrest from the Mashpees of Cape Cod, who in 1833 began protesting centuries of mistreatment. The "Indian's Appeal to the White Men of Massachusetts," a brief statement drafted under the guidance of William Apess, focused attention on the gap between rhetoric and action. "How will the white man of Massachusetts ask favor for the red men of the South," Apess wondered, "while the poor Marshpee red men, his near neighbors, sigh in bondage?" "Will not your white brothers of Georgia tell you to look at home, and clear your own borders of oppression before you trouble them?" he asked. Unlike southern planters, however, Apess wished not to undermine protests over expulsion in the South but to extend them to the North, and he went out of his way to praise the "distinguished" people "who advocate our cause daily." They "are to be prized and valued," he wrote, urging them not to tire in the cause.[50]

The charges of hypocrisy in Congress effectively muddied the debate, and nearly two centuries later, it is still difficult to see clearly through the muck stirred up by southern planter-politicians and their northern allies. The debate can appear as another grim chapter in the centuries-long story of dispossession, in which native peoples would lose no matter what. And yet the charges of hypocrisy, then and now, are largely irrelevant to the political act. Every legislative action is the product of self-serving alliances, principled stands, and distasteful compromises. Those who opposed expulsion were no less right because some of them fundamentally despised Native Americans, acted solely for reasons of party allegiance, or struggled to live up to their lofty ideals closer to home. More to the point, their motivations made no difference to the people being deported. Through all of the mudslinging and rhetorical smokescreens, indigenous Americans stayed focused on the debate's central question: Would the United States disregard its treaties, ignore their appeals, and launch an ambitious and unprecedented plan to deport 80,000 people?

~~~

THE "ACT to provide for an exchange of lands with the Indians residing in any of the states or territories, and for their removal west of the river Mississippi" gave the president the authority to mark off territory "west of the Mississippi" and to exchange it with indigenous people living within the bounds of states or territories for a whole or part of their current lands. Deported families were to receive payment for their improvements and "aid and assistance" during and for one year after expulsion. In an ambiguous sop to secure needed votes, the House proposed an amendment accepted by the Senate: "Nothing in this act contained shall be construed as authorizing or directing the violation of any existing treaty between the United States and any of the Indian tribes." Congress appropriated the absurdly small sum of $500,000 to carry out the provisions of the law.[51]

The act said nothing about how the exchange of lands was to be negotiated. By treaty? By contract? With the threat of violence? Nor did it explain how indigenous lands were to be valued. Improvements were to be appraised, but by whom and with what controls? As for providing "aid and assistance" in moving, the act gave no details about the amount or quality of support, or whether private contractors or the federal government would do the providing. Perhaps most egregiously, it said nothing about the mechanics of transportation, the wagons, ox teams, steamboats, food, tents, clothes and shoes, and medical supplies that would be needed to move thousands of families, including elderly grandparents and young children, across hundreds of miles to the west, over rudimentary roads and uncharted lands. Who would supervise the endeavor? What means would they have at their disposal?[52]

The United States was embarking on a grand scheme with minimal preparation and little good will for the people targeted by the law. Jackson believed he could drive indigenous Americans west by being remorseless and strong-willed, but his confidence quickly gave way to the hard truth that the country's oldest residents were determined to remain in their homelands. Warnings became threats, and threats were soon made at the point of a bayonet. By the mid-1830s, U.S. troops were force-marching people in chains in Alabama and pursuing starving families from camp to camp in Florida. The descent from Aboriginia to exterminatory warfare against desperate families was swift. Within a few years, McCoy's fantasy would become a nightmare.

CHAPTER 4

"FORKED TONGUE
AND SHALLOW HART"

Jackson sent the Secretary of War
To tell the Indians of the law
Walk O jaw bone walk I say
Walk O jaw bone walk away

Eaton tell us go away
Here no longer you can stay
Walk O jaw bone walk I say
Walk O jaw bone walk away

—composed by a Choctaw while
emigrating to the West, 1831–32[1]

WOULD NATIVE peoples simply walk away? Isaac McCoy thought so. "Their emigration cannot be restrained without the employment of an armed force," he claimed. John Eaton, who oversaw Indian affairs from his position as Andrew Jackson's secretary of war, was also hopeful. "It will be *wonderful* if we get through with all the tribes before Congress meets," he wrote shortly after signing the first expulsion treaty with the Chickasaws, "and now I should not be surprised if we did so." But McCoy and Eaton were hardly clear-sighted about the issue. McCoy possessed the zeal of a convert, and Eaton was both boundlessly loyal to Jackson and consistently hostile to indigenous Americans. Eaton had participated in Jackson's campaign against the Creeks in 1813–14 and in the massacre at Horseshoe Bend. In 1817, he had written an admiring biography of his commanding officer, scouring the thesaurus for superlatives. "It is hard to say which is most disgraced," wrote one reviewer, "the hero or the historian."[2]

Those who expressed doubts about the expulsion of native families did not last long in the Jackson administration. Thomas McKenney benefited from years of experience with indigenous Americans, having served as the superintendent of Indian Trade between 1816 and 1822 and as the superintendent of Indian Affairs since 1824. Though he had supported Adams over Jackson in the election of 1828, he survived in office for a time by lending his substantial influence to the passage of the expulsion act. Once he began to question the policy, however, Jackson unceremoniously dismissed him, three months after signing the bill into law. (McKenney received a termination letter while traveling, written by the War Department's chief clerk.) In retrospect, he regretted his role in Jackson's administration. Secretary Eaton, who insisted on reviewing all of McKenney's outgoing correspondence, was "not well-informed on any subject," McKenney said. "It was my misfortune, perhaps, to demure to some of the strange orders that were sent out," he wrote, "the sole tendency of which was to harass, & oppress the Indians." "I *knew* all was wrong," he confessed, "—*deeply* so." The belated stirrings of conscience did not impress one Choctaw, who said McKenney was a "good talker" who worked hard leading native peoples "to slaughter." Jackson also replaced twenty-nine of fifty-six agents and subagents in the Bureau of Indian Affairs in the first years of his presidency.[3] The result was an administration with several zealous officers at the top who had little sympathy for indigenous Americans, and dozens of inexperienced, patronage appointees at the bottom.

To gain leverage over native southerners, Jackson relied heavily on the threat posed to them by state laws, precisely the strategy hatched in the secret meeting of southern congressmen in the winter of 1826–27. In December 1827, the Georgia legislature had resolved that it possessed the right to extend its laws over the Cherokee Nation and "to coerce obedience" from "all descriptions of people," be they "white, red, or black." In 1828, the state passed a law that would, as of June 1830, extend its civil and criminal jurisdiction over the Cherokees and nullify their "laws, usages, and customs." A year later, a second law tightened the noose. One section made it illegal to use "threats, menaces, or other means" to dissuade Cherokees from moving west, on penalty of imprisonment and up to four years of hard labor. Another made it illegal for the Cherokee Nation to deter its citizens from selling lands, on penalty of up to six years of confinement. In December 1830, the state would also forbid the Cherokees from meeting in council or in any legislative or judicial body. Alabama passed its own set of oppressive laws in 1829, and Mississippi followed in January 1830. New York and other northern states had long encroached on the sovereignty of indigenous nations but never so completely and never with the single-minded purpose of driving out native peoples. Remarkably, in 1828, the Ohio Supreme Court had even ruled that the state had no right to interfere in the internal affairs of indigenous nations within its borders.[4]

The first sign that native peoples would not cooperate with their own expulsion arrived soon after the passage of the expulsion act. Jackson hoped to meet Creek, Cherokee, Choctaw, and Chickasaw leaders in Franklin, Tennessee, a small but thriving town about eighteen miles south of Nashville, during the summer of 1830. The Cherokees, rather than accepting the president's invitation, retained William Wirt, the former attorney general under James Monroe and John Quincy Adams, in preparation for filing a lawsuit. Wirt's decision to take the case, Jackson remarked, was "truly wicked." Creek leaders also declined to meet the president, despite U.S. efforts to bribe them to do so.[5] A subset of Choctaw leaders made the journey but agreed only to meet again the following month at Dancing Rabbit Creek, in east-central Mississippi. The Chickasaws alone attended in full, and they regretted it almost immediately.

The Chickasaw delegation of twenty-one leaders arrived in Franklin on August 19. The town's wealth, produced largely by slave laborers who worked the surrounding cotton fields, had funded the construction of a handsome two-story brick courthouse and supported several taverns and businesses.[6] On the outskirts of Franklin, there is a prehistoric ceremonial and trading center with twelve earthen mounds that predate the birth of the United States and its claim of dominion by nearly a thousand years, but no one in the Jackson administration seems to have noticed the irony.

Negotiations opened four days later in Franklin's Presbyterian church, located in the center of town. President Jackson attended, along with Secretary of War John Eaton and John Coffee, another Jackson acolyte and veteran of Horseshoe Bend. (At that massacre sixteen years earlier, it had been Coffee's troops who shot and killed some 300 people as they swam across the Tallapoosa River in a desperate act to escape.) After the president delivered a short address, he retired to his quarters, leaving a written statement for his two commissioners to present to the Chickasaws. The statement was deeply cynical. Jackson hoped only for their happiness, it claimed, and had no intention of forcing them from their lands. But the fact remained, it continued, that they could not live under the laws of the state of Mississippi.[7]

Two days later, when negotiations resumed, the Chickasaws declined to abandon their homelands. The extension of state laws over their nation, they said, was "unparalleled in history" and "an act of usurpation . . . unwarranted by the Constitution of the United States and the treaties that now exist." The object, they rightly concluded, was to "drive us from our homes and take possession of our lands." Their unsparing language challenged Jackson's self-image as the "liberal" "Great Father," though the president was not present to hear the rebuke. "You call us your children, whom you profess to have the highest regard for," they observed, raising doubts even as they said otherwise. "We know you are sincere in your professions," they reassured the absent president, "and it creates in our bosoms the highest feelings of affection towards you, as the great father and protector of your white and red children." And yet, they announced, they wished to bring an end to the paternalistic relationship: "we now conceive that we have now arrived to the age of maturity." They would not cede lands, they concluded, without first appraising the country they would receive in exchange.[8]

Negotiations continued into the evening. The Chickasaws might not receive anything if they hesitated, Eaton and Coffee threatened. "Misery or happiness," stated the two commissioners, "must and will follow on the decision you shall make." Under extraordinary pressure, the Chickasaws yielded and agreed to their expulsion. The next day, a triumphant Jackson reappeared. In the two-story Masonic Hall that still stands in downtown Franklin, Jackson joined Eaton and Coffee in the middle of a square formed by the exhausted and unnerved Chickasaw delegates. Their friendship, Jackson assured, would not be interrupted. It was his "earnest hope" that "the Great Spirit would take care of, bless and preserve them." Writing to his fellow Tennessee planter, the future president James Polk, Jackson was less magnanimous. He proclaimed, "I have in the chickisaw treaty destroyed the serpent."[9]

Two weeks later, Eaton and Coffee arrived at Dancing Rabbit Creek, a clearing near a spring in the eastern part of the Choctaw Nation, where Choctaws had erected a council house for the negotiations. Pursuing the same strategy they had with the Chickasaws, the U.S. commissioners painted a dire picture of Choctaw communities under Mississippi law. "Are you willing to be sued in courts, there to be tried and punished for any offence you may commit? to be subjected to taxes, to work upon roads and attend in musters?" they asked. How would Choctaws survive under laws they could neither read nor understand? And what would they do when the sheriff arrived to arrest them? "Wretchedness and distress will be yours," Eaton and Coffee asserted. To maintain the pretense of free negotiation, they presented a letter from President Jackson implying that for the Choctaws to select between extermination or expulsion remained a "voluntary choice."[10]

Eaton delighted in the paradox of forcing indigenous Americans to leave of their own free will. "Again and again it may be asserted, that there is no disposition entertained by the government to compel those people from their homes," he said, "while on the other hand, no design is had to interfere with the rights of the states." It was a "great injustice" to the administration to assert that it intended to use force, he insisted, for its policy was "calculated to induce . . . a voluntary departure." The phrase perfectly captured the bad faith that underlay the policy. The Choctaw leader George Harkins compared their situation to that of a man surrounded on three sides by a raging fire, with water and a distant shore on the fourth. "Who would say that his plunging into the water was his own voluntary act?" he asked. The "expulsion" of indigenous Americans, he declared, was mandated.[11]

Did anyone believe Eaton and Coffee's cynical statement to the Choctaws that "It is not your lands, but your happiness that we seek to obtain"?[12] No Choctaw responded directly to this incredible assertion— or at least no response appears in the treaty transcript—but on the road to Indian Territory an anonymous deportee revealed his candid opinion of Eaton in "The New Jaw Bone," lyrics he set to a common folk melody. "Secretary Johnny" was a damned dog, he sang:

> *John H Eaton is a pup*
> *With old Nick he'll soon to sup*
> *Withered laurels for his brow*
> *Withered laurels for his brow*
>
> *We hate the fool with all our might*
> *He'd best keep our sight*
> *It is Eaton we do mean*
> *It is Eaton we do mean*

> *At Dancing Rabbit he speak smart*
> *But his forked tongue and shallow hart*
> *Was nough to make old jaw bone shake*
> *Was nough to make old jaw bone quake.*[13]

As the negotiations continued, Choctaws demanded a delegate in Congress and the right for their nation to be admitted to the Union as a state. They also sought school funding of $15,000 per year, full scholarships to educate sixty Choctaw children in "respectable institutions of learning," and a national endowment of $500,000, earning 5 percent interest. These were reasonable requests, given that Choctaw land in Mississippi was worth several million dollars, but Eaton and Coffee rejected guarantees of representation and statehood and agreed only to a portion of the educational funding. As a result, the options before the Choctaws were "truly destressing," wrote one Choctaw negotiator, for they had to submit to state laws and the "attendant train of evils" or face the "privations and sufferings of a reluctant removal." Fearing "extermination," they reluctantly signed a treaty providing for their expulsion.[14]

Even in the northern states, where Isaac McCoy imagined that relocation would be "so obviously advantageous" to the widely scattered and impoverished indigenous communities, native peoples did not always abide by Andrew Jackson's plan for them. Some, such as the four hundred native people living on the Sandusky River in Ohio, were indeed ready to move west. This mixed community of Seneca, Mohawk, Cayuga, and Oneida families had already abandoned homelands farther east once before and were prepared to relocate again in order to escape the influx of American colonizers and the environmental degradation that followed. The "Senecas," as the multiethnic residents were collectively known, lived near two other small indigenous towns, populated by Wyandots and Delawares. Lower Sandusky pressed on their lands, and though it had fewer than three thousand inhabitants, white Ohioans had grand plans for the area, based on the expectation of connecting the north-flowing Sandusky and south-flowing Scioto rivers by canal. The prospective waterway would join Lake Erie to the Ohio River, making it possible to travel eastward by boat from the Great Plains, following the Missouri to the Mississippi, then up the Ohio and Scioto, across the prospective canal to the Sandusky, and through the Great Lakes to the new Erie Canal. Following the Erie Canal to the Hudson, commerce could then reach New York City and the Atlantic Ocean. The circuitous water route would open up the heart of the continent to the millions of consumers on the East Coast and in Europe, quickening the hearts of midwestern politicians and speculators and investing them in the project of native dispossession. (The canal was never built, and Lower Sandusky, which is now known as Fremont, never became "the deposit for all the goods that enter the Western world," as one booster had projected.)[15] The Delawares ceded their land in 1829, even before the passage of the expulsion act. The Senecas followed in 1831. Other native communities in Ohio reluctantly joined the exodus: the Shawnees (1831), the Odawas (1831), and the Wyandots (1832 and 1836), amounting to approximately 3,500 people in all.

The Ohio cessions totaled 482 square miles. Compared with the extensive and valuable native lands in the slave states, the relatively small area at stake in Ohio made it easier for righteous white residents to object to the expulsion. Even so, some clamored for the territory. The Wyandots and Senecas were a "useless, and worse than useless population," wrote a number of U.S. citizens who lived adjacent to them. Residents in other parts of the state disagreed. Expulsion was "insatiable avarice," said a group of Quaker petitioners. Ohioans from Geauga County, just east of Cleveland, underscored that with the expulsion of native peoples "it would be manifest to the world that <u>oppression, in palpable violation of solemn treaties had deprived them of their homes, that their territory had been acquired by means of known and deliberate national perjury.</u>" Remarkably, every Ohio congressman who represented a district with indigenous nations voted against the expulsion act.[16]

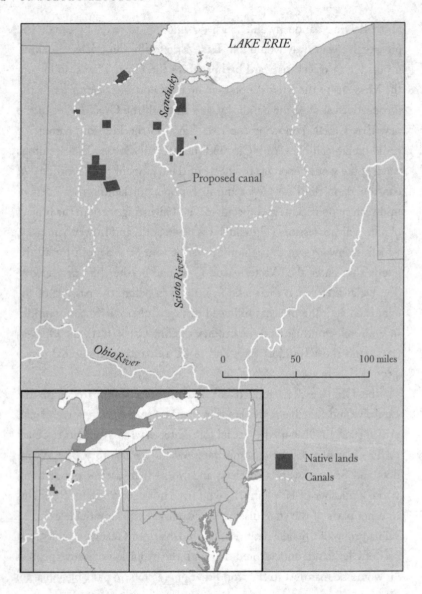

Cessions in Ohio between 1829 and 1836. After 1836, indigenous nations no longer owned lands in the state.

By contrast, the Senecas of New York, who numbered about 2,300, refused to emigrate from their homelands near the head of the Erie Canal, where the city of Buffalo now sits. To mark the occasion of the canal's opening in 1825, Governor DeWitt Clinton had floated down the artificial river from Buffalo to New York on the *Seneca Chief*, continuing a tradition that persists to this day of celebrating American empire with Native American symbols. In 1831, six years after Clinton's ceremonial journey, the Senecas sent three representatives to Andrew Jackson to remind the president that he was "constitutionally bound" to protect them and that treaties were the law of the land and could not be unilaterally repealed.[17]

To bolster their position, the representatives quoted from James Kent's *Commentaries on American Law*, a renowned four-volume treatise that was studied by law students around the country. In his critical assessment of the Roman Empire, Kent observed: "With what little attention *they* [the Romans] were accustomed to listen to the voice of justice and humanity, appears but too plainly from their haughty triumphs, their cunning interpretation of treaties, their continual violation of justice, their cruel rules of war, and the whole series of their wonderful successes, in the steady progress of the conquest of the world."[18] Following the indigenous custom of avoiding direct confrontation, the Senecas left out the references to haughtiness, injustice, and cruelty. Nonetheless, well-schooled and attentive White House lawyers could point out to Jackson himself the full, damning passage.

~~~

WITH THE exception of bayonets and rifles, the United States's most effective weapon in compelling people to move west was state law. In legislating for Native Americans, planter-politicians were doing what they had done unapologetically to African Americans for generations. Both peoples were subject to laws that they had no hand in drafting (as were white women and children), and in Georgia and Alabama both were prohibited from testifying under oath against white people. (In Mississippi, native peoples were allowed to take an oath; Alabama's prohibition was partially removed in 1832.) The reasons given for disallowing testimony by native peoples scarcely concealed the underlying self-interest. Native peoples did not believe in eternal punishment and therefore could not be counted on to tell the truth, said Georgia senator John Forsyth. Their testimony, wrote an editorialist, would jeopardize "the dearest rights of civilized freemen." White Georgians greeted suggestions to revoke the prohibition in the same way they met even the faintest proposals to ameliorate the conditions of slaves—with outrage and alarm. "Indian testimony," according to the state capital's *Federal Union*, would "reconcile the savage to a permanent residence in Georgia," open "all the doors of office," "effect an amalgamation of colors," and "place the lives and property of the whites at the mercy of a relentless and exasperated barbarian."[19] The absurd rhetoric was nonetheless effective; Wilson Lumpkin made it the center of his successful gubernatorial campaign in 1831.

Under state law in the South, free African Americans and native peoples were anomalous and unwelcome. In Mississippi, an 1822 law required every "free negro or mulatto" between the ages of sixteen and fifty to quit the state within ninety days or be sold into slavery for five years. In Alabama, a similar 1832 law prohibited all free persons of color from settling in the state, on penalty of whipping and, if not departing within twenty days, enslavement for one year. In Georgia, free "people of color" who entered the state were bound out as laborers until they could pay a fine of $100, in practice consigning most of them to a life of servitude. The penalties in Georgia for native peoples were less severe, though the underlying commitment to white supremacy was the same. The state passed a law in 1828 that prohibited Creek people from crossing into the state without a permit. Those caught illegally "strolling over the territory of said state" were subject to ten days in prison.[20]

Were Indians not also "people of color"? *"Abstractly,* there is no difference," opined the *Southern Recorder* in 1827, though in the minds of white southerners as well as in the laws themselves there was much confusion about the matter. Most statutes did not define their terms. Mississippi law specifically gave "said persons called Indians, and their descendants" the same rights as free white people but did not define "said persons." Some of them had African ancestry. At what point would they no longer be deemed to be "Indians"? An 1835 Georgia law targeting slaves and free people of color specifically excluded any "American Indian," but it placed the burden of proof on "such person of color," implying that even if native peoples were exempt from this race law, they were subject to others. Moreover, furnishing proof of Indian identity that satisfied white judges and juries was not always easy. In viewing their indigenous neighbors, southern politicians obsessively distinguished between "real Indians" who were "indolent and inefficient" and "hybrid offspring" whose "style of living," said one southern politician, "is pretty much the same as that of our own citizens." The "aristocratical half breeds" who made up the second group were difficult to characterize, for they were a "mongrel breed of people, . . . neither of the white man nor the Cherokee." Some indigenous peoples agreed. John Ross, wrote two of his Cherokee political opponents, was "nearly a white man in color and feelings." Under state law, was Ross an "American Indian" and a person of color? If not, did he enjoy the rights and privileges of white southerners? Even "real Indians" could be difficult to identify, especially when they possessed African ancestry. Lewis Ross, John's brother, described one "Catawba" family living in the Cherokee Nation as belonging to a "motley crew" of "mongrels." He later crossed out "Catawba" and replaced it with "negro."[21]

The occupation of indigenous nations by slave states therefore threatened to reduce native peoples to a condition of servitude. For good reason, the Chickasaws were terrified of losing their "native freedom." In the context of the law forbidding Creeks from entering Georgia, Tuskeneah complained that when they crossed into the state to retrieve property stolen by whites, they were "tied as if they were slaves," severely lashed, and threatened with death should they return. "We have never been slaves," asserted the Creek leader Opothle Yoholo. "We have been born free," he continued, and yet by Alabama laws they were now "condemned to slavery."[22] He did not mean it wholly as a metaphor.

Even if for the moment states refrained from systematically enslaving Native Americans, sheriffs, judges, and juries turned ordinary property and criminal law into instruments of oppression. Sheriffs arrested native people without cause and seized their property for fictional debt. Judges conducted trials in a language that few of the defendants could understand. Juries of white men, who often had a direct vested interest in native displacement, sat in judgment. Most accepted local dogma that the region's oldest residents were vicious savages. Such institutionalized bias, observed one northern newspaper, was "morally absurd and shocking."[23]

The final piece of this system of injustice was the county jail, "a stamp of grinding oppression," in the words of John Ross. Even temporary imprisonment while awaiting trial could turn into a life-threatening ordeal, as it did for Joseph Beanstick, a young Cherokee who was arrested at home and held in Georgia's Carroll County jail during the frigid winter of 1830–31. For four long weeks, Beanstick suffered from the "piercing cold," with no protection other than a cloak and an old saddle blanket. He begged to be taken to the fireplace to warm his frozen limbs but was told by the jailor, "not unless you pay me fifteen dollars." When finally released under a writ of habeas corpus—he was never charged after an arrest that seems to have been without cause—he was severely frostbitten in one foot, with the damage extending up to his knee.[24]

Native peoples repeatedly explained to Andrew Jackson and Secretary of War John Eaton that state laws were designed to oppress them rather than to dispense justice. "Our words and oaths go for naught," stated Neha Micco. Since native peoples could not testify on their own behalf, white Americans could abuse, rob, and even kill them with impunity, just as they could with African Americans. Moreover, indigenous residents had little prospect of even comprehending the laws. Mississippi and Alabama statutes, said the Chickasaw leader Ishtehotopa, "are written in more than a hundred books" that his people could neither read nor understand. "The law if it contains a single provision which can protect the Indian from outrage, or can redress his wrongs when they have been sustained is to this extent unknown to us," Opothle Yoholo stated. "We know it only as an instrument by which we are oppressed," he stressed. Ishtehotopa echoed the same sentiment, telling Andrew Jackson, "We cannot see in the extention of these state laws over us any thing but injustic [*sic*] and oppression." He concluded, "Justice we don't expect, nor can we get."[25]

The answer to such complaints was always the same. Their situation was "unpleasant," acknowledged John Eaton, but nothing could be done. "If a red man contracts a debt," said the secretary of war, "by the laws of the State he is made answerable, and must pay it." "If crime be committed," he continued, "his guilt or innocence must be ascertained before a court, and justice must be done." Justice was blind, Eaton insisted. "The same rules apply to the white as to the red man." One federal agent was more forthcoming, if just as discouraging. He conceded that native peoples were not equal to whites, could not testify in court, had no voice in forming state laws, and could not vote. In short, he said, if they remained in the South they would be "degraded below the meanest vagabond that traverses our country." They would become "drunkards and paupers" and be treated like "dogs." Expulsion was therefore an act of generosity, and if not seized upon, their demise would be their own fault. "I feel conscious of having done my duty to my red children," Andrew Jackson reassured himself, "and if any failure of my good intention arises, it will be attributable to their want of duty to themselves, not to me." A few weeks later, writing to a close friend, he repeated this blame-the-victim sentiment in stronger language: "I have used all the persuasive means in my power; I have exonerated the national character from all imputation, and now leave the poor deluded creeks & cherokees to their fate, and their anihilation."[26]

Since the Jackson administration was prepared to countenance their extermination, native peoples were forced to mount their own defense. On July 15, a month and a half after the United States passed the expulsion act and Georgia extended its laws over the Cherokee Nation, George Tassel shot and killed his friend Cornelius Dougherty in a small Cherokee community about fifty miles north-northeast of modern Atlanta, by one account in a dispute over a woman. Both men were citizens of the Cherokee Nation. Tassel admitted to the crime and faced near-certain execution under Cherokee law. Instead, the Hall County sheriff arrested him and threw him in jail in Gainesville, a north Georgia town located near the Cherokee Nation's gold-mining region. Tassel reportedly begged to be returned to the Cherokee Nation to be tried and shot. But Georgia officials, although indifferent to the actual crime, were eager to assert jurisdiction. As one northern newspaper observed, Tassel might have killed half the Cherokee Nation with the "full consent and approbation" of the state.[27]

Tassel wasted away in the Gainesville jail through August, September, and October. On November 10, Georgia's appellate judges, meeting in the state capital of Milledgeville, affirmed the state's jurisdiction over Tassel and the Cherokees. That same day, the legislature's Committee on the State of the Republic called for the immediate survey of Cherokee lands and the distribution of lands by lottery to the citizens of Georgia. Two weeks later, on November 22, Judge Augustin Clayton presided over Tassel's trial before an all-white jury, drawn from Gainesville's growing population of miners and speculators who hoped to get rich quick from Cherokee gold. Clayton was one of the state's most ardent supporters of states' rights. A slave owner and Athens resident, he enjoyed delivering intemperate screeds from the bench against "intermeddling" northern states and "wandering savages." After a one-day trial, the jury found Tassel guilty, and Judge Clayton sentenced him to be hanged on December 24, 1830.[28]

The trial and sentencing gave the Cherokee Nation an opening to challenge Georgia's assertion of jurisdiction. John Ross had long maintained that the extension of state laws over his nation violated U.S.-Cherokee treaties, federal law, and the U.S. Constitution. William Wirt appealed to the U.S. Supreme Court, which granted a writ of error, agreeing to hear the case in January. Instead of suspending the sentence pending the outcome of the appeal, however, the legislature met in emergency session and resolved to proceed with Tassel's execution. On the morning of December 24, "a vast multitude" of men, women, and children thronged the roads to Gainesville. Tassel, bound hand and foot, was placed atop a coffin in a wagon, transported to an open field south of town, and hanged. Some twenty Cherokees, who had watched the event unfold, retrieved and buried his body.[29]

Tassel's hurried execution ended the Supreme Court appeal, but three days later Wirt filed a second case, *The Cherokee Nation v. The State of Georgia*. Wirt argued that the extension of state laws violated Article 6 of the U.S. Constitution, which stipulates that treaties are the supreme law of the land. In a divided decision handed down on March 18, 1831, the Supreme Court dismissed the case, not on its merits but because the Cherokee Nation did not have standing. The Constitution gives the Supreme Court jurisdiction over cases between the states of the Union and foreign states. But Chief Justice John Marshall, joined by Justice John McLean of Ohio, determined that the Cherokee Nation was a "domestic dependent nation," not a foreign state. Native peoples were in "a state of pupilage," Marshall contended, and their relation to the United States resembled that of "a ward to his guardian."[30] The chief justice's paternalistic metaphor has defined legal relations between the United States and indigenous nations ever since.

Marshall, a towering jurist who had served as chief justice since 1801, was no friend of Jackson's, yet he may have strategically followed the guidance of the president's attorney general in order to reach a decision acceptable to the majority of the court. Attorney General John Berrien and the president shared "certain principles" that were of particular interest to Berrien's home state of Georgia. "I felt it to be my duty not to withhold any assistance which I could give to carry them into effect," Berrien recalled. In the case of *The Cherokee Nation v. The State of Georgia*, he therefore worked privately to persuade the jurists to adopt his views.[31]

In fact, Berrien himself had described a "tutelary relation" between indigenous nations and the United States in one of his official opinions three months before Marshall wrote of "a state of pupilage." Though Marshall did not spell out the implications of the ward-guardian relationship, the metaphor was flexible enough to give some hope to the Cherokees, with whom he sympathized. It was also flexible enough for Justice Henry Baldwin of Pennsylvania and Justice William Johnson of South Carolina to vote with Marshall but issue separate concurring opinions that were emphatically hostile to indigenous sovereignty. They agreed with Berrien that the United States possessed the authority "to make all such regulations as may be necessary for their protection, and for the preservation of the public peace." Justice Baldwin went on to declare that U.S. power was "of the most plenary kind"—that is, absolute— while Justice Johnson argued that indigenous nations "never have been recognized as holding sovereignty over the territory they occupy." The two remaining justices, Smith Thompson of New York and Joseph Story of Massachusetts, dissented, arguing that indigenous nations were fully sovereign.[32] (There were only seven justices at the time, and one was absent during this foundational case.)

Cherokee leaders traveled through their homeland to explain the court's equivocal ruling. John Ross somewhat optimistically announced that Marshall's opinion was "conclusively adverse to the pretended rights" of Georgia. Given a different case in which the Supreme Court had jurisdiction, he speculated, a majority would rule against the state in its extension of sovereignty over the Cherokee Nation. "It is therefore all important," he urged, "that we should yet stand united & firm."[33] The legal challenge was not over.

~~~

WHILE JACKSON and his agents worked to induce native peoples to agree to their own expulsion, the secretary of war and the superintendent of Indian Affairs pored over largely featureless maps to determine where the newly dispossessed would be going. Their second-floor offices stood at opposite ends of the War Department building, a two-story brick structure, situated two hundred yards west of the White House. The Indian Office, occupying one of the building's thirty-two rooms, housed the superintendent, a chief clerk, a recording clerk, a book-keeper, and a messenger. It also contained an impressive display of 130 portraits of indigenous Americans and McKenney's personal collection of "Indian dresses, ornaments, petrafactions," and "minerals." The

Floor plan of the War Department. The building's regular arrangement of rooms conveyed a sense of order, but in truth, the clerks who labored in its offices struggled to determine the most basic facts of how native peoples would be deported and where they would go.

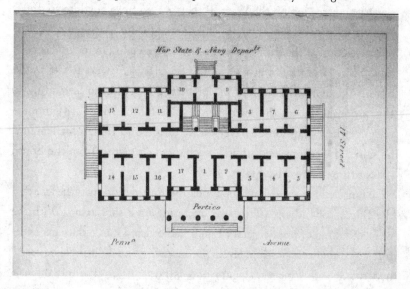

paintings and objects, wrote one sightseer, were "all suited to a place of this sort, where, long after the original owners of this country shall have mingled with the dust of their mountains, the curious will delight to repair, to study the appearance of the native owners of this continent, and indulge in reflections on these scenes which are past."[34] The Indian Office would be a monument to the people it made disappear.

In visiting the War Department, this sightseer was "impressed with the favorable ideas of the system and order with which the affairs of this great people are conducted." Perhaps the uniform arrangement of offices created a sense of regularity, but behind the doors, officers were scrambling to implement the expulsion policy that they had so confidently sold to Congress. Native peoples would be transported somewhere west of the Mississippi, but where exactly? Isaac McCoy suggested that "a medium latitude" would be "least objectionable both to the Indians, and to the Southern and Northern states." One congressman even proposed that native people living in northern and southern states be expelled to their respective regions north and south of 36'30", the line established by the Missouri Compromise that divided slavery and freedom in the West. If they moved from north to south, or vice versa, he observed, it would enlarge the future "power and wealth" of one section at the expense of the other, leading to an inevitable conflict. Years later, the South Carolina secessionist Robert Rhett would bitterly condemn the "ethics of Northern policy" for not attending to this proposal. All of the territory set aside by the Missouri Compromise for the expansion of slavery was "devoted to Indian settlement," he said. "It was expected, thus," he charged, "to wrest from the South two or three more slave States."[35]

Complicating the debate about possible destinations was the fact that the Bureau of Indian Affairs was operating on a shoestring. Within a week of taking office, Secretary Eaton had ordered it to reduce expenditures to the lowest possible level. "Economy in expenditure is desired," he wrote, "—no wine—no cigars—no extravagance." "The Indian business," Eaton complained, "is carried on at more expense to the Government than is necessary." Meanwhile, the War Department was continuing to survey the vast region west of the Mississippi, ascertain the quality of the soil and timber, and report on the navigability of the rivers. But even the most industrious surveyor could not cover sixty thousand square miles in any detail; large exploring parties were expensive and to be avoided if at all possible. Since expulsion was to be on the cheap, the War Department fell back on a reliable ally, appointing Isaac McCoy to visit the region and add his observations to existing reports.[36]

Whether unduly optimistic or excessively bleak, the surveyors' reports all shared the quality of being imprecise. Gradually, consensus emerged in the War Department building that most of the dispossessed would be relocated along the Arkansas and Canadian rivers, which flow east-southeast into the Mississippi and divide present-day Oklahoma into three horizontal sections. Others would be designated for lands to the north, in what would become Kansas. One army officer, visiting lands near the Canadian River, reported, "I saw no place where I believed a settlement could be made to advantage." The region was destitute of water and valuable ores. "The fact is," he concluded, "the whole country is nothing but a barren waste, having no cultivatable lands—no game, no timber." By contrast, McCoy found the region of present-day eastern Kansas to be "exceedingly fertile, with scarcely an exception of any spot." As far west as he traveled, the soil was "almost invariably rich," the streams were first-rate, the salt licks abundant, and the mineral deposits valuable. Despite this rosy appraisal, the region was undeniably suffering from a drought, and fires had destroyed much of the grasses. McCoy's horses began to starve, and one did not survive, belying the missionary's untempered optimism.[37]

Although the War Department's manuscript maps showed steady improvement in detail and accuracy over the course of the 1830s, they still remained frustratingly incomplete. A "general and correct survey" would not be made for many years, conceded one officer, and until then, the federal government depended on maps "fabricated" from the reports of traders and travelers. Secretary of War John Eaton observed that "each tribe should know the precise boundary of his country," and he specified that lines should be surveyed and "plainly marked," a process stymied by the difficulty of matching inaccurate maps to actual terrain. Eaton and his successor Lewis Cass made a habit of repeating "We have no satisfactory information." Knowledge of the country was "imperfect" and "vague and unsatisfactory."[38]

Confusion reigned. Eaton and Coffee had carried a book of treaties with them when they induced the Chickasaws to agree to their expulsion in 1830, but by an oversight, the book did not contain an 1828 Cherokee treaty. That treaty, predating the expulsion act, had set aside land in present-day Oklahoma for early Cherokee migrants. As a result, Eaton and Coffee had inadvertently promised the Chickasaws land that had already been given to the Cherokees. Eaton now proposed two imperfect solutions: move the Cherokees farther north onto Osage land, displacing the Osages to some other still unidentified location, or move the Chickasaws farther south onto Choctaw land, though that was unacceptable to both parties.[39] This comedy of errors was of the government's own making.

To compound the problem, the U.S.-Cherokee treaty of 1828 referred to the Grand River of the Neosho, but no one in Washington City could identify its whereabouts. Few had noticed or cared at the time, but by 1830, when the War Department began plotting maps with distinct boundaries to separate peoples who would be displaced to the West, the matter had become pressing. A frustrated John Eaton rifled through the map files in the War Department to no avail and then instructed Isaac McCoy to locate the missing tributary. McCoy's reconnaissance revealed only one possibility, a small creek that he said nobody would ever use to mark a boundary. In short, the Grand River did not exist, except on the treaty stored in the War Department's Indian Office. The federal government, admitted one officer, was "greatly embarrassed for the want of correct information."[40]

If Cherokee families might be moved north onto Osage lands, or Chickasaw families south onto Choctaw lands, where would Creek peoples reside? McCoy said that Creeks expected to be given the territory between the Arkansas and Canadian rivers—roughly the same area promised to the Cherokees. The early migrants—the allies of William McIntosh, who had been run out of the Creek Nation in 1825—complained that they already had too little land, certainly not enough to give any to the Cherokees. Moreover, if thousands more Creek families arrived from the East, it would lead to their "ultimate ruin and destruction." One War Department map attempted to solve the problem in 1831 by wedging the Creeks north of the Arkansas River, but a year later, a similar map left them off altogether.[41]

This was not the only problem created by bad maps. "I am much

---

Detail of an 1832 map showing the projected locations of dispossessed people.

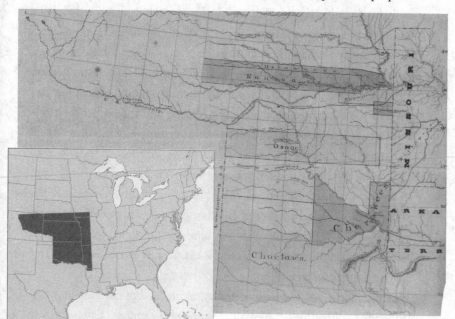

mistaken if the Government acted upon sufficient information in ceding the extensive and immensely valuable territory to the Choctaws, or in the inadequate provision made to the Quapaws," prodded one officer. From his perspective, the Choctaws' allocation was clearly too large, the Quapaws' too small. As for the Winnebagos, did their territory extend all the way to the Mississippi? "Upon examining the map," wrote the commissioner of Indian Affairs, "the department is not able to determine." McCoy drafted a map for the secretary of war without a scale or a meridian line, making it impossible to measure distance or area. Another of his productions was said to be "incorrect" and the accompanying written report even more so. McCoy's errors were not as egregious as the one made by George Vashon, an agent to the Cherokees, who produced a map in which each degree of latitude represented sixty miles, even though the correct distance between degrees of latitude is approximately sixty-nine miles. Such a colossal miscalculation reduced the entire globe, and hence the proposed Indian territories, by roughly 13 percent.[42]

In 1832, Secretary of War Lewis Cass, who had succeeded John Eaton to the office, admitted that the "business of emigration commenced before we had much knowledge of the country." He continued, "The boundaries of some of the grants are confused and contradictory; the extent of the cessions unknown; the quantity of land now at the disposal of the Government, merely conjectural; and the proper locations for most of the tribes who are yet to go, indeterminate." He balanced this embarrassing admission with an authoritative assertion: "The Government must have possession of the necessary facts."[43] But executive desire and force of will could not overcome the messy reality. Over time, the nearly featureless and often error-filled maps housed in the War Department were slowly filled in with neatly bounded polygons, color-coded to represent the destinations of dispossessed people, but consistency and accuracy remained a challenge.

Most native peoples maintained a guarded skepticism about western lands they had never seen, despite the reassurances of their "Great

Father." Persuading them of its bounty, wrote one agent, would take "perseverance and patience," since they were like "spoiled children." The West was as foreign to the Cherokees as Greenland or Africa, said the indigenous intellectual David Brown, an exaggeration that nonetheless conveyed their doubts and fears about moving to unfamiliar lands. A small group of Potawatomis and Odawas, visiting the West with McCoy, reportedly felt as if they were approaching the edge of the world, so distant were they from their Great Lakes homelands. Even if the promised lands were as valuable as claimed, said a clearly skeptical Opothle Yoholo, the Creeks were willing to relinquish the advantage. If, however, their current lands were more valuable, he wondered, "Why should not we the rightful proprietors be suffered to enjoy them?"[44]

It was not enough for the secretary of war to insist that the federal government's assessments of the West were "altogether favorable" or that it was "fine country." After visiting the region, a group of Potawatomis, Odawas, and Chippewas told Andrew Jackson that they felt "deceived," "disappointed," and "dissatisfied." The land was mostly prairie, without enough timber to build wigwams, they said, and "too poor for snakes to live upon." Likewise, two Seminole men who toured the area between the Canadian and Arkansas rivers observed that "it is bad country, where shells cut out the Mocasins." The Choctaw leader Peter Pitchlynn, traveling on an expedition with Isaac McCoy, also found that large parts of the region were "good for nothing" and strewn with "rock and gravel." Nonetheless, he scoffed, McCoy presumptuously insisted that it was "a fine country." A Huron exploring party produced a measured assessment of the lands west of Missouri but emphasized that the scarcity of timber was a significant disadvantage to farmers like themselves. Even worse were the neighboring white Missourians, "the most abandoned, dissolute, and wicked class of people" they had ever encountered. "Missouri is a slave-holding State," they noted, "and slave-holders are seldom very friendly to Indians." They added a fitting parenthetical: "(See Georgia.)"[45]

Native peoples from the East were wary not just of Missouri's white supremacists. There were also the Osages, Kiowas, Quapaws, Wichitas, and Comanches to fear. Eastern Native Americans suspected that the arrival of tens of thousands of newcomers in the Great Plains would stoke conflict. Native westerners, said two Seminole visitors, were "Bad Indians" who would "destroy" them. They were "warlike," wrote the Chickasaw leader Levi Colbert. Peter Pitchlynn found them to be "wild in the extreme." Pitchlynn, in a chance encounter with Charles Dickens on an Ohio River steamboat, would later surprise and impress the English author with his erudition, dignified manners, and "remarkable" handsomeness. The educated and worldly Choctaw leader could not help but feel somewhat contemptuous of his "long separated brothers" in the West. Likewise, John Ross, meeting a delegation of indigenous westerners in Washington City, would marvel at their painted, mostly unclothed bodies and "primitive state."[46]

The reports of early migrants to the West were not encouraging. Neha Micco learned from fellow Creeks that western lands were indeed fertile but that the region was sickly. "From all accounts that we have received," he said, "it is a grave yard." Early migrants spoke of years of "sorrows," exclaiming "Our load is too heavy to bear!" Along the Red River, separating what are now the states of Texas and Oklahoma, 60 of 455 Quapaws had starved to death in 1827. One federal agent described the horrific scene: "Young women were discovered in the agonies of death, with a child tugging at the breast, and another child lying dead on the other side." Many of the survivors took refuge with Cherokee migrants, with whom they shared their struggles. A few years later, when Pawnees were struck with a "monstrous" epidemic, people died so fast that the living gave up burying the bodies. Corpses floated down the Platte River, washed up on the sand bars, and rotted in the brush surrounding Pawnee villages. Some were dragged off and devoured by dogs and wolves.[47]

Among the several exploring parties charged with selecting a suitable territory under the 1830 expulsion treaty was a group of Chickasaw men. On returning, they reported to President Jackson that they had found only enough land for the Choctaws. "Some of our people are dissatisfied and wish to remain at their old homes and think that injustice has been done them," wrote Ishtehotopa. Levi Colbert, an enterprising and influential Chickasaw leader, gently suggested to the president that perhaps the disagreement between his people and the federal government was "but an honest difference of opinion in the way to happiness." While many Chickasaw families believed that they would fare better in Mississippi "in the bosom of our white brothers," Jackson supposed that they would find more success in the West. As for Colbert, he observed that in the "wild distant regions of the west" they would be situated far away from their commercial partners. Wouldn't Mississippi laws be better than "all the evils of the west[?]" he wondered. Colbert, who was not formally educated but who spoke some French and "tolerable" English in addition to his native Chickasaw language, prepared his own children for the possibility of living in Mississippi by sending them to school in Cotton Gin Port, a rude town in the northeastern corner of the state that served as the symbolic and real gateway between the Chickasaw Nation and the United States.[48]

Because the 1830 treaty was conditional on the Chickasaws finding a suitable location in the West, John Coffee negotiated a second expulsion treaty in 1832, without the conditional clause. The Treaty of Pontotoc, as it was known, prompted a remarkable fourteen-page letter of protest from Levi Colbert to Andrew Jackson. Sixty-one Chickasaw men, none of them literate, signed the letter by placing an "X" by their names. The memorial objected to Coffee's attempts to bribe them. "When Genl Coffee attempts to buy my honesty," Colbert stated, "he must have a pile of money high as my head; then I will keep my honesty still." It accused Coffee of "long continued abuse and menace" during the negotiations. And it singled out and objected to specific treaty clauses.[49]

The memorial is most extraordinary, however, for characterizing the United States from Colbert's viewpoint. The Chickasaw leader was under no illusions. "I had not lived and cast my senses, as you know, along the whiteman's march, with my eyes shut," he said. "I saw the white man's march, was to take my country. I prepared my mind and the mind of my Nation for it." Was the "spirit of liberality and equality which distinguishes the United States from all the Empires," he asked, merely a "jealousy and defence of their own particular rights, an unwillingness to be oppressed themselves?" Or was it "a high respect for the rights of others, an unwillingness, that any man high or low should be wronged"? The answer hinged on U.S. policy toward the continent's original residents.[50]

~~~

WITH THE Choctaw treaty in hand, the United States prepared to deport between fifteen and twenty thousand people from their Mississippi homelands. Advocates of expulsion blithely or naively assured the public that the process would be efficient, though Secretary Eaton admitted in private after the passage of the act that he did not yet have a plan in place. A few months later, he downplayed his predicament by stating that to supervise expulsion demanded "no great labor, or high mental powers." It was principally an accounting job, he said, demanding "cautious attention" to appropriations and expenses. The arrogance was palpable. "There is a set of men about the Executive that wish to be thought that they possess all the knowledge and all the efficiency," said one army officer who was posted in the West. "They think too well of themselves."[51]

In an early strategic decision taken in December 1830, Jackson elected to place the logistics of deportation under the authority of the Commissary General of Subsistence. The president wanted someone close to him to be in charge, and this War Department office had been occupied by his friend George Gibson since 1818. The commissary general, responsible for provisioning the army, was foremost a glorified accountant. The "Regulations of the Subsistence Department" described his ordinary duties: "He will make all estimates of expenditures for his department, regulate the transmission of funds to his assistants, receive their returns and accounts, and adjust them for settlement." Gibson, who was renowned for his probity and punctiliousness, excelled at the job. His system of provisioning, wrote one acquaintance, "was always in order, and its operations were as regular as the habits of its chief."[52]

Nonetheless, deporting fifteen to twenty thousand Choctaw people was outside Gibson's realm of expertise. Until Jackson appointed him to supervise the project, almost all of Gibson's correspondence with field officers—always written with exactitude and formality—involved the forwarding of quarterly accounts to Washington City, and the remainder addressed matters such as how to obtain fresh beef for U.S. troops stationed at far-flung posts. He had never provisioned more than 12,000 soldiers in a single year, never attended to the elderly, infirm, and young, never managed hostile and uncooperative people, and never supplied families moving at an unpredictable pace through unfamiliar territory.[53] No matter his attention to detail and adherence to regulations, women could not be forced to postpone labor and childbirth, toddlers could not be commanded to walk faster, the sick could not be made to recuperate more rapidly, and the dead could not be ordered to bury themselves.

Surveying the vast undertaking, the Massachusetts congressman Edward Everett exclaimed, "Whoever heard of such a thing before? Whoever read of such a project? Ten or fifteen thousand families, to be rooted up, and carried hundreds, aye, a thousand miles into the wilderness! . . . It is an experiment on human life and human happiness of perilous novelty." The Choctaws would be the first unwilling subjects. "We are preparing every thing," the secretary of war assured one Choctaw leader. "Wagons will be in readiness," he claimed, "and abundant Depots of provisions will be placed at different points, ready when notice is had, that your people are prepared to depart." Careful planning would ensure that operations unfolded with "promptitude and energy," asserted the assistant commissary general. Their confidence was misplaced. Nearly a hundred Choctaw women and children, belonging to one of the first groups to be dispossessed and deported, were already starving in Indian Territory.[54] The experiment was underway.

SECTION THREE

THE BEST LAID PLANS

~~~

CHAPTER 5

THE PLAN OF OPERATIONS

On my way to the Arkansas
God damn the white mans laws
O come and go along with me
O come and go along with me.

At Memphis Town we took a dram
And once more damned old Uncle Sam
The die is cast and we are undone
The die is cast and we are undone

—composed by a Choctaw while
emigrating to the West, 1831–32[1]

FROM GEORGE Gibson's boarding room in the house of Henry Huntt, President Jackson's personal physician, it was a short walk across the South Lawn of the White House to the commissary general's office, which occupied five rooms on the second floor of a brick tenement building at 17th and G streets, just across the street from the War Department. The commute was perhaps slightly longer for Gibson's five clerks, who crossed ditches, passed over stretches of weeds and rocks, and cut through empty fields, before climbing the stairs to report for work. The capital city's grandiose but still unrealized design reflected the ambitions of the expanding nation, even if some visitors were unimpressed. "Its seven theoretical avenues may be traced," scoffed a British tourist, "but all except Pennsylvania Avenue are bare and forlorn." Only a "few mean houses," the sheds of the navy yard, and three or four "villas" relieved the eye "in this space intended to be so busy and magnificent."[2]

The city must have made a different impression on native peoples. In the first fifty years of the Republic, one hundred seventy-four delegations from at least fifty-five different indigenous nations traveled hundreds of miles on horseback, by stagecoach, on steamboats, and occasionally by train to meet with the U.S. president and Congress. In the single month of February 1831, the capital hosted delegations of Cherokees, Creeks, Quapaws, Iroquois, Ho-Chunks (Winnebagos), Menominees, and Stockbridges. Gibson's clerks perhaps spotted them at "public tables" throughout the city or drinking at the "very fine parlour at Gadsby's," a well-known tavern in Alexandria preferred by Menominee leaders.[3] These polyglot delegates from across the eastern half of the continent could not have failed to notice the contrast between their hometowns and the U.S. capital. Indigenous villages were composed of a few dozen log cabins or even less permanent constructions made of wattle, mud, bark, hides, or mats, depending on the region. There were no grand avenues, no brick buildings, and no bureaucrats. The commissary general's office connected these two deeply intertwined but fundamentally distinct worlds.

The officers and clerks in the commissary general's office labored under a fantastical vision of a "systematic plan of operations" that was simple and efficient and offered "complete accountability." White people had "made all nature subservient to them," crowed one officer. (The audience for this preposterous claim was the Creek leader Opothle Yoholo, who predicted that "white people also had their limit of prosperity" and that they would become extinct as "the nature of all things" sank away to ruin.) The clerks' yellowed collars and cuffs and their daily trek past rotting carcasses through Washington's empty fields did not dispel their fantasy of perfect mastery. Yes, deportation was "of a multifarious and complicated nature," Gibson conceded. But that simply meant that the commissary general required "great assiduity"—the Bartleby-like diligence he prized so highly—on the part of the clerks in his office.[4]

Their daily labors were mundane. The copying clerk did nothing but copy letters, a full-time job in the era before photostatic reproductions. (Across the street in the Indian Office, the copying clerk was two to five months behind schedule.) The chief clerk folded and endorsed papers, retrieved files as needed, and assisted in preparing reports and estimates. The bookkeeper, whose work was "unremitting," kept all accounts. As the operation expanded into indigenous lands, clerks marched in the vanguard, whether in Washington offices or in remote outposts. In the Chickasaw Nation, they would soon be working six hours a day "in the best and most speedy manner" to sell off the land of the deported. There were never enough of them. The supervising officer in Mississippi asked for two more clerks and a good draftsman. "A bungler I would not want in office," he declared. Without "competent and industrious" clerks, another officer admitted, "we could not get along with our business." In the late 1830s, a federal commissioner in the Cherokee Nation suggested that the two clerks working under him were insufficient to copy the "great number of books, registers, etc." They were both "expert penmen," he said, but had "a heavy work" before them. Even the addition of two more clerks would not meet the challenge of duplicating the four payment register books (each five hundred pages), the judgement and spoliation books, the valuing books, and the vouchers, all of which swelled the labor "to an immense amount." When no additional clerks materialized and paperwork continued to pile up, some officers threatened to resign; others relied on their wives to assist in copying letters.[5]

The implements employed by Gibson's army of scriveners were commonplace, though specific to the task: inkstands, steel pens, pen wipers, blotting paper, paperweights, pen racks and holders, pencil sharpeners, rulers, copying brushes, sealing wax, penknives, hones, pencils, erasers, blotters, leather-bound ledgers, letter books, and loose-leaf paper. With these tools, they produced hundreds of volumes, including "Weekly Reports of Letters Addressed and Referred to the Commissary General of Subsistence," "Docket of Claims (Choctaws)," "Miscellaneous Records Concerning Contracts (Creeks)," "Decisions on Claims of Attorneys Against the Cherokee Nation," "General Abstract of Valuations and Spoliations Allowed and of Balances Due," "Ledger Recording Debts of Indians," and so on, some cross-referenced with each other, others in triplicate, organized once by name, a second time by date, and a third time by account number. On the final page of four volumes of letters sent by the commissary general, an elated clerk wrote, "Finis—!!!"—a joyful exclamation, tempered by the fact that somewhere there was always another stack of letters to copy.[6]

Their Sisyphean labor was a testament to the administrative ambitions of the Republic. The scale of the effort can perhaps be grasped by measuring the subset of "Settled Indian Accounts and Claims" that date to the decade of deportation in the 1830s and belong to the Office of the Second Auditor in the Treasury Department. If stacked atop the Statue of Liberty's pedestal, they would surpass the height of her torch. The entire series of accounts and claims, covering the century between 1794 and 1894, would rise nearly twice as high as the Empire State Building.[7] The paperwork was indeed monumental.

And consequential. It is not an exaggeration to say that Gibson and his clerks made life-and-death decisions. "Where medical aid shall become indispensable, you can procure it," Gibson's assistant J.H. Hook wrote to an officer supervising the deportation of the Choctaws. But the commissary general's frequent admonitions against unnecessary expenditures discouraged officers from allocating funds to medical care. Medicines should only be purchased "when actually required or danger from sickness is apprehended," advised Gibson. Officers were forbidden from acquiring full medicine chests and employing doctors, except in individual instances of illness or in case of epidemic. For the employment of a physician, warned the commissary general, there "must be the most satisfactory evidence of the necessity." J.T. Sprague filed an invoice to be reimbursed for $35 for medicine he deemed necessary to keep native people "from perishing upon the road when sick." The invoice was rejected and returned with an explanation: "The expenditure mentioned seems to have been irregular and the authority or propriety of having made it is not known." The auditor left his initials and job title: "J.W.—Clerk."[8]

~~~

IT IS impossible to know if George Gibson was motivated by a soldierly sense of duty or by his own personal history. Indigenous Americans had played a key role earlier in his life, in a single far-reaching event. In 1791, when Gibson was sixteen, his father marched into Ohio country with Arthur St. Clair's army to conquer the region's native peoples. Gibson's father never returned, one of 630 soldiers who perished in a stunning victory in western Ohio for the Northwest Confederacy. Young Gibson left home and his impoverished mother a few years later, worked in a mercantile firm in Baltimore, made several ocean trips to the West and East Indies, and served in the War of 1812. After the war, he received the commission of quartermaster general and supplied Andrew Jackson in the Tennessean's foray against Seminole families in 1817. The two officers became lifelong friends. In 1818, Gibson was appointed the first Commissary General of Subsistence, a new office created to provision the army more efficiently. At one point during the expulsion of indigenous Americans, he conceded that regulations sometimes had to be bent in the interest of justice, writing, "It will not do to reason too closely where humanity has a claim to be heard," but he did not live by this tenet. On just about every occasion, he resorted to his twin obsessions: rule following and frugality.[9]

Gibson's desire for unwavering compliance with regulations both trivial and significant reflected nineteenth-century military culture. He instructed officers who were in the field dispossessing, corralling, and conducting families hundreds of miles west to fold their papers uniformly, "of the size of half a sheet of letter paper, folded three times." They were to keep a detailed record of "numbers, deaths, births, etc." so that the War Department would know "every fact" connected with deportation. The "muster roll," Gibson's military term for the list of deportees, was in his eyes "the very point upon which hinges the whole system." Officers should draw up these rolls "with a view to entire correctness," with each person enumerated and classified. Likewise, they should number each "detachment" of deportees and also every wagon. They should prepare a second register recording all temporary employees and noting when their service began and ended. Officers were not to issue feed to Indian ponies. ("It is not warranted by the regulations," explained Gibson's assistant.) Nor were they to purchase sugar, tea, or coffee for the deportees, or transport people in wagons or on horses, except for those too young or too infirm to travel by foot. Woe to the subordinate, such as J.B. Clark, who lost Gibson's instructions. "It placed me in a very unpleasant situation," confessed Clark from his posting in Fort Smith, Arkansas.[10]

It was fortunate for Gibson that his two obsessions aligned with each other. In the deportation of native peoples, every expense had to be diligently invoiced and sent to Washington City, where the commissary general scrutinized the records, returning flawed accounts to the agent and forwarding acceptable ones to the Treasury Department's second auditor. The second auditor, in turn, reviewed the accounts again, rejecting some and sending others to the second comptroller for final approval. One army office explained that the United States had improved on the "rigid economy" and strict accountability practiced by European militaries. "It is probable a more perfect system of accountability is nowhere to be found than in our little army," he boasted. "It takes years to understand it," he claimed, and it required "martial law to enforce it."[11]

Over time, Gibson relaxed the standards somewhat, recognizing that many of the people employed in expelling native peoples were not in the military, but he continued to scour accounts for the slightest errors, right down to the smallest fraction. J.P. Taylor's bill for harnesses should have been $66.25, not $65, an error in favor of the government but nonetheless unacceptable. S.V.R. Ryan's bill for corn should have been $7.1875, not $8.63. George Gaines should have submitted a per diem for fifteen instead of sixteen days, a common error that Gibson attributed to an ambiguity of language. "The word *inclusive*, as applied to time," Gibson explained, "is, in some instances, used to express both the date of commencement and of termination, whilst, in other cases, it embraces but one." There "ought to be uniformity in the meaning of the word," he insisted. For the same reason, he objected to the use of "from" and "to." "They sometimes mean neither day, and sometimes both days, inclusive," he observed, deciding that "Commencing on, and ending on, are better." Rarely did an inferior officer receive the praise accorded to Jacob Brown, who shared Gibson's fixation with "waste and extravagance." "It gives me pleasure to say, that the examination of your accounts has proved highly satisfactory," Gibson wrote. "The disbursements," he continued, "have been made as strictly in conformity to the Regulations and instructions, as, I believe, was agreeable to a due regard for public interest."[12]

Public interest, in this case, meant saving money, even at the expense of the families who were being expelled from their homes. Gibson feared that some deportees were receiving more than their daily allotment of rations. To guard against that "imposition," he instructed officers to keep meticulous records. "Too much care and vigilance . . . cannot be practiced," he wrote. A "strictly economical and prudent course" would result in "great saving to the United States." He advised one officer to look into every expense "and lop it off or lesson it, if either can be done without detriment." "The object," he explained, "is to bring to your mind the necessity for a strictly economical course." Other officers received similar injunctions. "I would impress upon you the necessity for a great degree of care and economy in the administration of your Agency." "You are urged to use 'the most rigid economy.'" "Let nothing that takes the money of the public needlessly exist a moment." "Wherever money is expended by you, or others, the greatest practicable exactitude will be expected." This last instruction apparently did not satisfy Gibson's boundless desire for cost savings, so he closed the letter with a stronger statement: "There is one all important thing I will draw your attention to. I mean economy."[13]

While Gibson had the advantage of preaching austerity from a distance, his subordinates were in the unfortunate position, year after year, of dealing face-to-face with dispossessed and desperate families. William Armstrong, conducting a party of Choctaw families in 1832, declared that he was making "every exertion to emigrate on the most economical plan." But on the day that one of the deportees broke a leg and had to be abandoned on the road, his frustration boiled over. They had no medicine and no doctor, he complained. "Where there are two thousand Indians," he protested, "at least a physician could have been employed." Three years later, John Page also assured Gibson that he would "incur as little expense as possible" while supervising the expulsion of over five hundred Creek people, but he found that he had to spend more than anticipated to keep infants and the elderly from freezing to death during the brutal winter. Someone in the commissary general's office circled the "enormous" cost of this particular deportation, "$60 a head." Page was incensed at Gibson's disapproval. "I never did witness or experience anything to equal the scenes of the trip in my life and hope it will never be my lot to do it again," he wrote. "Many persons pronounced it murder in the highest degree for me to move Indians or compell them to march in such severe weather when they were dying Every day with the influenza," he continued, "but I am well Convinced it was the only thing that Kept them alive not withstanding their Exposure." Perhaps no officer was as forthright as A.M.M. Upshaw, who conducted a group of Chickasaw families in 1838. On reaching the Mississippi River, he told them that they would have to leave their possessions behind. They objected. "We are moved out of our own money," they told him. "This is our property.

We want it. It is valuable to us." "Will you make us burn or throw our property in the river?" they asked. "Under these circumstances," Upshaw challenged the secretary of war, "what could I say?" "I tell you what I did say," he vented: "Put your baggage in the boat." "If I was wrong," he stated, "it was in not obeying the Regulations." "Feelings of kindness and justice," he declared, "compelled me to take the course I did."[14]

Upshaw was the rare officer who recognized the incongruity between strict regulations and practical justice. U.S. policy, Gibson insisted, was to expel people "with every regard to the principles of humanity." Since there was no conflict between policy and principle, he saw no reason not to act "consistent with the laws." And, yet, he did in fact bend the rules— or at least interpret them loosely—when he thought it would speed up expulsion, as when he suggested to the secretary of war that annuities owed to native peoples be paid out exclusively in the West. "With respect to the legality of such a measure or its consistency with Treaty obligations, I offer no opinion," he wrote. His greatest pride was not that he had acted with justice or compassion but that no act of embezzlement had taken place under his watch and that "the most laudable exertions" had been made "to economize in the expenditure of public funds."[15]

While it is usually admirable for public servants to economize and follow regulations, in the context of deporting eighty thousand people from their homes, the commissary general's insistence on austerity and compliance seems like a bizarre inversion of priorities. In a long exchange with William Clark, the superintendent of Indian Affairs at St. Louis, Gibson was put on the defensive. "If, at times, I seemed to require a great deal, it was because much was required of me," he explained. "There are regulations, and instructions, by which to be guided, of a character quite as rigid as those in the military service," he continued, "and they are unfortunate, as you know, in their application to a people, the reverse of order, system, or regularity." "Yet," he insisted, "these regulations must be carried into effect."[16] Gibson and his clerks buried themselves in the minutiae of office work, taking satisfaction in properly folded reports, accurate accounting to the fraction of a penny, and the systematized processing of invoices, all the while shielding their eyes from the full scope and impact of the extraordinary human operation that they were directing from afar. They never commented on the fact that they were conducting a degrading, dangerous, and irreversible experiment with the lives of other people.

Thomas McKenney stated in 1828 that the reports of the second auditor itemized expenses "almost down to the nail that is driven in an Indians coffin." What was once morbid hyperbole became workaday reality during the Jackson administration, as epitomized by one ordinary item that passed through the commissary general's office. A single receipt from 1836, located in box 257 of the Treasury Department's massive collection of "Settled Indian Accounts," gives some sense of both the petty drudgery of the clerical work and the tragic arc of the huge project that it sustained. The receipt recorded a payment to William Spickernagle in Memphis, Tennessee, for "making two coffins and digging two graves for an Indian man and woman. $10 Each."[17]

~~~

THE CHOCTAW expulsion, the first to take place under the legislation of May 1830, was meant to be a test case for future operations. It was unfortunate, then, that the federal agent in the Choctaw Nation, William Ward, was often too drunk to read or write and sometimes so incapacitated that he had to order his "negro servant" to open his mail for him. Witnesses described the "confused and impaired" agent futilely hunting through stacks of papers in search of official correspondence. Needless to say, Ward was incapable of conducting business of any kind, though that apparently did not prevent him, in the assessment of two federal officers, from being "arbitrary, tyrannical, and insulting." One acquaintance concluded that the Indian agent had "soured" against "all mankind."[18]

The Indian Office had entrusted Ward with what turned out to be a key responsibility in the summer of 1831. Under the fourteenth article of the Treaty of Dancing Rabbit Creek (1830), Choctaws who signaled their intention to become Mississippi citizens became entitled to a plot of land in the state. After residing on the land for five years, they were to receive full title. The article, federal negotiators believed, would be largely inconsequential, since they envisioned that only about two hundred people would take advantage of the concession.[19] Ward's job was to record their names.

To the astonishment of authorities, Choctaws registered by the thousands; it appeared that perhaps half wished to stay on their homelands in Mississippi, jeopardizing the westward expansion of the empire of slave labor camps. Ward did everything he could to deter them. If he was "to suffer all the Indians to register who wished to do so," he declared, "the policy of the government would be thwarted and disappointed." He browbeat Choctaws who tried to enroll, and he told "emigrating agents," responsible for deporting families, to whip those who did not abandon their lands. When Tishomah appeared before Ward, the agent lied that he had received instructions to stop registering people. When Pahlabbee and his neighbors did the same, Ward bullied and threatened them. They were unmoved, for they "had made up their minds to stay." Many others arrived at Ward's agency, in the eastern part of the Choctaw Nation, bearing hundreds of sticks made of split cane, a traditional way of counting and keeping records. The long sticks represented parents who, by the terms of the treaty, would receive 640 acres, the short ones denoted children ten and over who would receive 320 acres, and the still shorter ones designated children under ten who would receive 160 acres. Ahtonamustubbee and Cheshahoma gave Ward a large bundle of some three hundred sticks that Ward threw away, pronouncing that "there were too many of them." Mingohoma arrived with two hundred sticks, neatly bundled by family, but Ward insisted that he and his community must go west. The Choctaw leader retorted that he understood the treaty and their rights, but Ward swept the sticks off the table and refused to record their names. A crowd outside debated what to do next. Give up and move west? Remain on their farms and hope that the federal government would preserve their rights? [20]

Under Ward's drunken supervision, the registration book, containing the names of a fortunate few who had escaped the agent's tirades, became an object of abuse. It was thrown about the agency, the stitching came apart, and the pages began falling out. One night, it was left out in the sleet, frozen solid, and thawed the next day before a fire. A visitor recalled tearing off a part of the cover to clean his straight razor. Another saw Ward record names on loose slips of paper, which the addled and ill-willed agent promptly lost. A related book, recording the names of orphans who were due lands, was "so torn and mutilated as to be of no service." [21]

"These white folks," said one Choctaw, were "monsters." He saw no place to escape them and for that reason decided to stay in Mississippi. By the fall of 1831, however, thousands of others had reached a different conclusion and become resigned to expulsion. [22] At the corner of 17th and G streets, the commissary general's clerks inked their pens and opened their letter books.

~~~

SITUATED ON the forested plains along the Red River, about five miles from the then U.S.-Mexico border in what is now southeastern Oklahoma, Cantonment Towson was so remote that the U.S. Army had abandoned it a little over a year before it was reopened in November 1830 to oversee expelled Choctaws. Heading nearly due west from the Choctaw Nation, Cantonment Towson was about 375 miles away, but the journey by land or by river was far longer and far more circuitous. Two routes suggested themselves to the War Department. The easier would be by steamboat from Vicksburg, down the Mississippi, and up the Red River to the Great Raft, an enormous natural logjam of uprooted trees that blocked the river in northwestern Louisiana. From there, the deportees could walk the remaining one hundred miles to Cantonment Towson. Steamboats could only ply western rivers in the late winter or spring, however, when snowmelt and rain filled the waterways. If dispossessed families arrived in the West at that point in the year, they would not have enough time to clear fields and plant crops. When their government-supplied rations came to an end twelve months later, with no corn to harvest, they would face starvation. The other possibility was to travel by wagon and arrive at Cantonment Towson in late November, leaving time to prepare for a spring planting. Unfortunately, roads were dismal or nonexistent.[23] The secretary of war chose the first of these options, then changed his mind, settling on a combination of the two. Most of the dispossessed, he decided, would travel by steamboat north from Vicksburg or south from Memphis to Arkansas Post, near the mouth of the Arkansas River, and then upriver or overland to Little Rock. From there, the refugees would be obliged to walk the remaining 230 miles to their final destination on the Red River.

The change of route was not the only sign of disarray in 1831. The commissary general did not learn that he was responsible for operations east of the Mississippi until July, only about four months before Choctaws began assembling. Nor did he receive accurate counts of how many Choctaw people were actually intending to head west in the first year of the government's experiment, with estimates ranging from 5,000 to 8,000. (Because so many elected to stay, the actual number turned out to be closer to 4,000.) Nonetheless, his office sent out an impressively elaborate series of orders: Deposit barrels of carefully packed pork, bacon, and flour at "proper intervals" along the way; repair buildings to store the provisions; purchase oxen, horses, and wagons; send tents to Vicksburg to shelter women, children, and the decrepit; remit government funds to Little Rock; inspect and repair roads as necessary; build several bridges. While the authoritative instructions sounded effective, they did not make the remote operation any less chaotic. Only ten days before the refugees reached the Mississippi, J.B. Clark, appointed to oversee deportation on the western side of the river, learned that they would be congregating at four separate places, forcing him to scramble to redistribute supplies. He doubted the practicality of the government's operation and twice asked to be relieved. "No one can form a proper estimate of the difficulties that will attend the removal by land, and subsistence on the route, who has not been in this country," he wrote from Little Rock.[24]

The four thousand children, women, and men who walked to the Mississippi in November 1831 left behind their land, houses, corncribs, farming implements, orchards, and livestock. Though the treaty set aside some compensation for the loss of land, approximately 95 percent of the dispossessed received nothing. The treaty also provided for selling Choctaw cattle and returning the proceeds to the deportees, but William Ward colluded with a friend to purchase the livestock for "almost nothing."[25] The treaty offered no compensation for the improvements or personal property that had to be abandoned.

As the dispossessed reached Memphis and Vicksburg, a ferocious winter storm, the worst in fifty years, descended on the eastern half of the continent. The temperature dropped below zero, and the Ohio, Tennessee, and Missouri rivers froze over. By coincidence, the French aristocrat Alexis de Tocqueville and his companion Gustave de Beaumont arrived in Memphis at the same time as a party of Choctaws. An old woman, said to be more than a hundred years old and near death, was among the refugees, they wrote. She boarded a steamboat and sat along with the rest of the party on the open deck, braving the punishing temperatures with only a small wool blanket, barely large enough to cover her shoulders. Tocqueville asked one of the deportees why the Choctaws were leaving their country. "To be free," the man said somberly.[26]

For white Americans, the steamboats that ferried goods and slaves, and now native peoples, up western rivers were potent symbols of empire and progress. White westerners brushed aside the victims. "So much the worse for the conquered," they exclaimed; "so much the worse for those who perish in the steamboats!" They were willing to concede present-day Oklahoma to native peoples in part because steamboats could not navigate the region's shallow rivers in the summer and fall.[27]

For indigenous Americans, by contrast, the boats represented dispossession and death, both as heralds of U.S. expansion and as floating prisons. It was a "disgusting sight" to see refugees on the crowded steamboats, wrote one U.S. agent, who complained that the unwilling passengers left "their evacuations in every direction through the whole range of the cabins and decks." A more sympathetic officer noted that

---

Gustave de Beaumont's sketch of a Choctaw party boarding a steamboat at Memphis on December 24, 1831. The caption reads, "Departure of Indians (Choctaw tribe) crossing the Mississippi under the direction of the government of the United States to go to Arkansas."

Beaumont's sketch aboard the steamboat *Louisville*, which carried a party of Choctaws from Memphis to Arkansas Post.

"their native modesty" discouraged them from sharing a single bath-
room. One Choctaw observed diplomatically that the mode of travel did
not "well agree" with them, since they found "confinement" on board
to be "peculiarly irksome." Their dislike of river travel stemmed from
practical concerns. Voyages could last a month or longer, depending on
the distance covered, and the cramped quarters bred disease, as would
become clear the following year. Even short trips could be deadly. When
boilers burst, hundreds might die in an instant. One group of Shawnees
and Senecas from Ohio refused to board the vessels for fear of being
"scalded to death, 'like the white man cleans his hog.'"[28]

In late November and early December 1831, steamboats from Vicksburg and Memphis converged on Arkansas Post with some 2,500 of the
refugees. Perched on a precipitous and eroding bank on the Arkansas

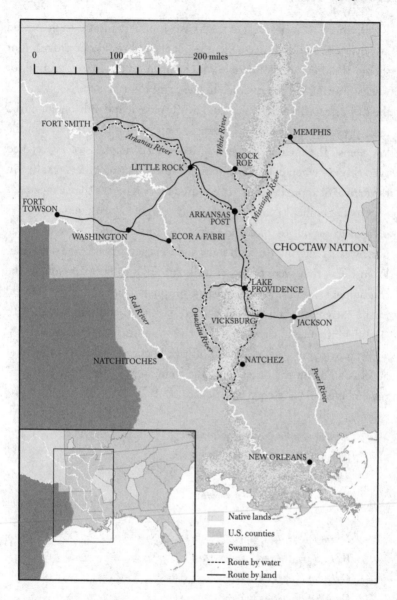

Despite Commissary General Gibson's best efforts, the operation to deport Choctaws in 1831–32 ended in disarray. Multiple detachments were stranded, provisions arrived late or not at all, and scarce tents and inadequate clothing offered little protection against the bitter winter weather.

River, thirty-six miles west of the Mississippi, Arkansas Post possessed just over one hundred permanent residents and could not provision or shelter the thousands of people who camped on the frozen ground for weeks, waiting for the river ice to clear and the water to rise. Many of the dispossessed were shoeless and nearly naked, and only one hundred tents provided scant protection from temperatures that hovered in the low teens. The inadequate government-issued supplies were stretched even thinner when poor coordination and conflicting orders resulted in the arrival of approximately six hundred more refugees than expected.[29]

On December 13, one party of 524 refugees at Arkansas Post was obliged to set out by foot and wagon for Little Rock, 90 miles to the northwest. Trudging through snow and ice, they arrived nine days later. From there, they were forced to walk 230 miles to Fort Towson, as the cantonment was now known, on a hastily prepared road that was "horrid in the extreme." The road was choked with mud and punctuated with "indifferently made" causeways that lay two to three feet under water.[30]

Approximately two thousand other Choctaws remained camped at Arkansas Post in the bitter cold. The composer of "The New Jawbone" remembered the wretched experience:

> The damnest time we ever saw
> Was at the Post of Arkansas
> The meanest place in all the world
> The meanest place in all the world.

> Seventy sleeps there we laid
> While it snow'd and upon us hail'd
> O the hard times we did see
> O the hard times we did see

> It snow'd it hail'd I do you tell
> I thought it twould pelt us all to hell

O the hard times we did see
O the hard times we did see.[31]

When the Arkansas River finally became navigable in early January, they boarded steamboats for Little Rock. Some four hundred of the refugees eventually proceeded on to Fort Smith by steamboat, but the vast majority followed the arduous road to Fort Towson.[32]

Rather than joining their relatives at Arkansas Post, two other parties embarked on government-contracted steamboats from Vicksburg and traveled 100 miles south to the Red River, followed it to the Ouachita, and ascended for 200 miles to Ecor a Fabri, a high bluff that was about 160 miles due east of Fort Towson, their final destination. In the punishing weather, the walk overland was deadly. One of the parties, leaving Vicksburg with 564 people, lost 34 individuals along the way.[33]

Despite Gibson's best efforts to economize, deporting people proved to be expensive—unexpectedly so, at least in view of the untroubled projections of the policy's advocates. The original appropriation to deport eighty thousand people was a mere $500,000, a wildly unrealistic and misleading sum. The actual expense, claimed Massachusetts congressman Edward Everett, would be "five times five millions"—a figure that sounds hyperbolic but in fact proved too low. An optimistic accounting produced by the commissary general's office in the fall of 1831, before the operation started, estimated the price of transporting seven thousand Choctaws by land to be $65,000, including over $22,000 for wagons, oxen and yokes, tents and axes; $4,500 for teamsters; and $28,000 for rations. By reselling the surplus property after the conclusion of the deportation, it was hoped that $15,000 could be recuperated, bringing the per capita expense down from $9 to $7. The actual cost turned out to be three times higher, around $25 per person.[34]

The uncertainty of the early estimates, which varied considerably, may have been one reason that the secretary of war encouraged native

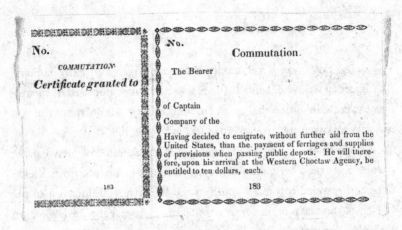

A blank commutation certificate, good for $10 on arriving at Fort Towson.

peoples to transport themselves to the West at a fixed cost per head, known as a "commutation." The other reason was certainly to minimize the logistical challenge of taking charge of so many people. "What amount will silence murmur, and induce cordial departure?" wondered the secretary of war, who ordered William Ward to "ascertain the lowest sum that they will individually be willing to take." Initially, commutation was set at $10, though one agent admitted that the sum was "quite insufficient to move them to their new homes."[35]

In 1831, about a thousand Choctaws traveled west in this way. Though few could afford to transport themselves to Fort Towson, several entrepreneurial and wealthy Choctaws, seeing an opportunity to profit from the commutation payments, organized and paid for the migrants. Greenwood LeFlore, the most notorious of these speculators, was a wealthy Choctaw slave owner with considerable French ancestry who favored expulsion for everyone but himself. Accused by one acquaintance of selling their native land "in a precipitate manner," LeFlore was reviled by many of his fellow Choctaws, who described him as an unscrupulous "tyrant" and disgraced despot. For LeFlore's services in deporting his compatriots, the secretary of war offered to "compensate" him in secret so as not to "excite the jealousy" of the dispossessed. "We dreaded to confront Greenwood LeFlore," recalled one Choctaw, so relentlessly did he press them to move. (LeFlore himself remained in Mississippi, where he commissioned the largest plantation house ever constructed in Carroll County, a mansion he furnished with gilded Louis XIV furniture and named Malmaison, after one of Napoleon's chateaus. He died in 1865, just as his four hundred slaves were emancipated.)[36]

Commutation only added confusion to the government's already bungled operation, turning what was intended to be one or two streams into a multichannel current of refugees. By December 1831, this tangled river of shivering exiles seeped along varying routes from the Mississippi to Fort Towson. One group of three hundred struck out on its own from Vicksburg, intending to travel on foot to Ecor a Fabri, where they would meet their relatives. The route had the advantage of avoiding steamboats altogether but at the cost of traversing fifty miles of swamp in heavy sleet. The refugees—entire families, including the elderly and toddlers—were shoeless, and many wore only cotton tunics in the freezing temperatures. The scene was too much for Joseph Kerr, whose farm they passed in Lake Providence, Louisiana, just before reaching the swamp. He gave them permission to enter his field and harvest its frozen pumpkins, which the starving refugees devoured raw. In a scathing letter to Secretary of War Lewis Cass, who had replaced John Eaton in August 1831, Kerr condemned the federal government's meanness. "Blame is due somewhere," he charged, "and to a great extent." (Kerr had a long history of irreverence. Years earlier, he was often seen shouting imprecations at a team of oxen named Jesus and Christ.) Two weeks later, the refugees were still trudging through the swamp and had run out of food entirely. When federal officers rescued them six days later, one hundred of their horses were found frozen upright in the mud. As many as thirty-five of the three hundred people who entered the swamp may have died there. Kerr's letter was forwarded to Commissary

General Gibson, who predictably defended himself and his operation: "all was done for them which, consistent with the laws, the dictates of humanity could have urged."[37]

~~~

WHILE CHOCTAWS wended their way west in the winter of 1831–32, federal emigration officers began preparing to deport the Senecas of Sandusky, Ohio. In January 1831, U.S. citizens had petitioned Congress to expel the "useless" Senecas, who signed an expulsion treaty a month later. Since the Senecas were reluctant to relocate, an eager subagent named Henry Brish, a recent arrival from Maryland, decided to compel their departure by auctioning their property. He posted broadsides in surrounding towns to advertise the event.[38]

Scores of U.S. citizens attended the auction. Benjamin Pettinger bought a brass kettle, a colt, an ax, and a grindstone. Francis Bernard purchased a churn and an oven. William Fuller acquired a hoe, an iron kettle, and two augers. But Brish himself was the single largest bidder, auctioning dozens of items to himself, including a pair of skates, several horses, a wagon, and a frying pan. The total sum of this fire sale was $2,587. The dispossessed received the proceeds, plus an additional $6,000 for their improvements, including their houses, stables, farms, and apple and peach orchards. As the Senecas filed out of town, their white neighbors rushed in to dismantle their lodgings, carrying away windows and doors, disassembling and carting off brick and stone chimneys, and prying up and hauling away flooring and fencing. Some simply moved into the freshly vacated houses.[39]

The complete list of auctioned property is as disturbing as it is revealing, for it documents the liquidation of the mundane objects that made up the daily lives of the deported families. Each family faced the difficult decision of what to bring and what to relinquish, not knowing which items they would need during the journey or on their arrival in the West.

Lewis Tall Chief decided to leave behind a brass kettle, an iron kettle, a tin bucket, a hoe, a coffee pot, a cow, a heifer, a small dun mare, a young colt, and some old tinware, items that sold for $59.98. Coffee House surrendered three brass kettles, a skillet, an oven, a knife, a tin pail and dipper, and two axes, for which he received $11.74. Mrs. Hard Hickory relinquished a shovel and tongs, two clevises (for connecting draft animals to a plow or cart), a tin pan, stirrups, two hoes, three "squaw axes," some scrap iron, two brass kettles, a hoe, two tin cups, two colts, and a cow, amounting to $42.20. Even then, Brish would complain that the Senecas carried an "immense quantity of baggage," a burden that would prove difficult to bear during the journey west.[40]

The refugees, 340 in all, were joined by 58 Delaware people from a neighboring village. With wagons overloaded with adzes, augers, saws, bedding and household goods, and even sacks of peach stones and seeds, they struck out for the West on November 5, 1831, covering only four to five miles a day through incessant rain and severe cold, the same winter storm that was lashing Choctaw deportees farther south. After splitting into two groups, one party of 232 boarded flatboats at Dayton and followed the Miami and Erie Canal to Cincinnati on the Ohio, where they took a steamboat to St. Louis. They arrived without incident on November 16. The party camped seven miles outside of the city for a few days, while Brish purchased more supplies. As opportunistic as ever, he also hired three of his friends to assist in administering the deportation, blaming the "extremely dissipated habits" and "blood-thirsty disposition" of the Senecas for his own mismanagement and nepotism.[41]

In early December, the party struck out across Missouri on foot in the dead of winter. The meager path out of St. Louis took the refugees thirty miles northwest, where they crossed the Missouri River and entered St. Charles, a rough frontier town of land speculators and slave owners who had recently moved to the former French settlement. There, one woman died, and Brish abandoned fourteen others, who were too ill to continue. He pushed the refugees onward another five miles north-

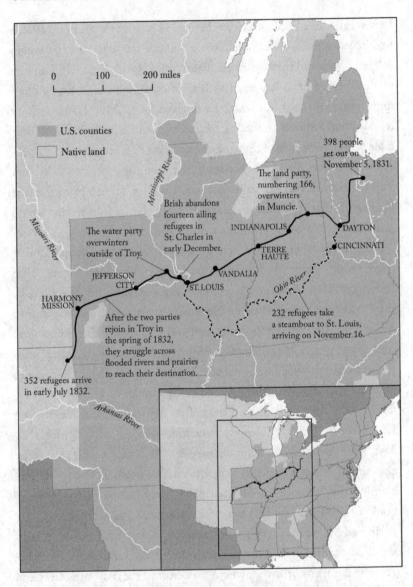

0   100   200 miles

U.S. counties

Native land

Mississippi River

Missouri River

398 people set out on November 5, 1831.

The land party, numbering 166, overwinters in Muncie.

Brish abandons fourteen ailing refugees in St. Charles in early December.

The water party overwinters outside of Troy.

INDIANAPOLIS

DAYTON

CINCINNATI

TERRE HAUTE

VANDALIA

JEFFERSON CITY

ST. LOUIS

HARMONY MISSION

Ohio River

After the two parties rejoin in Troy in the spring of 1832, they struggle across flooded rivers and prairies to reach their destination.

232 refugees take a steamboat to St. Louis, arriving on November 16.

352 refugees arrive in early July 1832.

Arkansas River

The Senecas and Delawares of Sandusky endured eight months on the road. Of the 398 people who departed on November 5, 1831, at least thirty died before reaching Indian Territory.

west to the little village of Troy, but the bitter cold made it impossible to proceed any farther. By now, the children were suffering with frozen feet and hands, most of the refugees were sick, and several were near death. In mid-December, a frustrated Brish decided to establish a winter camp on the Cuivre River, just outside of Troy.[42]

The second group, numbering 166 people, was still in Ohio, intending to travel the 350 miles west to St. Louis by foot. As they crossed into Indiana, these families were inexplicably abandoned by federal agents, who insisted that the refugees would "live well on the way," since they were good hunters. By early December, however, the freezing weather had brought them to a standstill in the plains just northeast of Muncie, Indiana. Many in the party were sick, and two children had already died. Eighteen of their horses, struck with distemper, had perished, and the remaining were unfit for the journey. In this bleak situation, two desperate families turned back to their Ohio homelands. Those who remained sent a note to their relatives, now camped in Troy. In the spring, they said, "what then remains of us will set out with all diligence, to meet you beyond the Mississippi."[43]

In May 1832, when they finally reached Troy, they found six of their relatives near death and another sixteen seriously ill. Measles had broken out, striking nearly half of the camp. Anxious to complete his mission rapidly and at minimum cost, Brish loaded the sick and dying into wagons and set off on the three-hundred-mile trek to their final destination, the northeastern corner of present-day Oklahoma. He left no time for recuperation, a decision he later regretted. "I charge myself with cruelty in forcing these unfortunate people on at a time when a few days' delay might have prevented some deaths, and rendered the sickness of others more light," he confessed. The refugees begged him to hire more wagons to assist the ailing; with the commissary general's repeated warnings to economize in his ear, he refused. The rivers were flush with spring rain, and each crossing was a trial, sometimes demanding the construction of bridges, at other times forcing a long wait until the waters fell. Oxen became mired in the muddy riverbanks, and flooded prairies turned into quagmires. The teams labored to pull their loads through the muck and had to be doubled to make any progress, leaving behind half the carts and later returning to retrieve them, a procedure that was repeated mile after mile. Brish complained, "The difficulty in crossing wet bottom prairies can scarcely be imagined."[44]

Near Harmony Mission in western Missouri, two hundred miles into the trip, the Senecas buried a woman, and several children lingered near death. A new plague arrived. "Immense swarms" of flies descended on the horses and oxen, forcing the refugees to limit travel to nighttime. Nine more people—four adults and five children—died during this final leg of the journey. By the time the Senecas and their Delaware companions reached their allotted lands in early July, eight months after their departure, at least thirty people had lost their lives, a mortality rate approaching 10 percent.[45]

In Little Rock, a federal officer carefully scrutinized the muster roll for the refugees, newly arrived in Indian Territory, and noticed that none of the same names appeared on the treaty that the commissary general's office had forwarded him. There had been a mistake. One of the clerks had confused the Senecas of Sandusky with the Senecas of Lewiston and forwarded the wrong treaty, a symptom of the disarray that enveloped the operation from start to finish.[46]

~~~

COULD THE government learn lessons from the first deportations of Choctaw and Seneca families? If the Senecas who went by land suffered, wrote a patronage appointee named John McElvain, "it is their own fault." They should have moved by water, he scolded. As for the Choctaws, they had been taught a "suffering lesson," judged F.W. Armstrong, another patronage appointee, for they had departed too late in the season. He objected to their sense of entitlement. "As it now is," he wrote, "the Indians really seem to think, that they have nothing to do, on their part, but wait to be moved by some operation of the Government."[47]

Secretary of War Lewis Cass drew more utilitarian lessons from the first year of deporting families and concluded that "a more systematic plan of operations" needed to be devised. To that end, he issued a lengthy set of "Regulations Concerning the Removal of the Indians." According to the new regulations, no one except those too young or too infirm to travel by foot would be transported in wagons or on horses. Baggage was not to exceed thirty pounds per person. No wooden furniture or heavy utensils would be hauled. Wagons were to be limited to one for every fifty people. (How a single wagon could carry 1,500 pounds of baggage as well as twenty or so elderly, young, or sick people was not explained.) In a characteristic statement of deniability that would ward off future expenditures, Cass stipulated that the United States would not be liable for any accidents.[48]

The new measures also included guidelines for purchasing provisions. The War Department had long ago concluded from hard-won experience during the War of 1812 that private contracting, in which contractors deliver and distribute provisions, was ineffective and even deadly. Since profit depended on the difference between the price of the contract and the cost of the goods, contractors, as one general observed, "palm upon the troops the coarsest and cheapest provisions." He contended that the army had lost more men to bad provisions than to enemy fire. Nonetheless, because the system was less expensive than the alternative in which the commissary general purchased goods on the open market in regions with few provisions, the secretary of war strongly encouraged agents to procure by contract. The results were predictable. "The salted pork and damn poor beef / Is nough to make the Devil a thief," sang the Choctaw composer of "The New Jawbone."[49]

The secretary of war directed the commissary general to prepare the "necessary forms" to ensure the "uniform" implementation of the new rules, and he instructed subordinates that the forms were to be "strictly adhered to." Accounts and vouchers were to be transmitted immediately at the close of each quarter, abstracts of expenditures were to be submitted monthly, and every purchase was to have a duplicate voucher. All communications from field officers were to be headed in precisely the same way: "Emigration of Indians, Commissary General of Subsistence, Washington City."[30]

In brief, the new secretary of war's regulations focused single-mindedly on economy and uniformity, reiterating the twin priorities that Jackson's commissary general had stressed from the outset. The tightened system, Gibson applauded, was "every way improved" and would effect "a degree of pecuniary accountability and efficiency not exceeded in any other department of Government." The tremendous suffering of the refugees during the first year of operations went unmentioned, though the commissary general's office had repeatedly if perfunctorily instructed its field agents to be kind to the refugees. Some field agents had occasionally expressed sympathy for the plight of the dispossessed, but few of them voiced serious reservations about their work. "Our poor emigrants," lamented one officer, with a mixture of concern and condescension.[31] As the enormous and disturbing operation entered its second year, the government's bureaucrats proceeded as if they were working in a mechanized and predictable world, without sudden winter storms and unforeseen epidemic diseases and, most of all, without people who stubbornly and frustratingly refused to abide by the War Department's expectations.

CHAPTER 6

THE CHOLERA TIMES

~~~

WHILE THE commissary general labored over plans to launch a second year of Choctaw deportations, across the street on the second floor of the War Department building, Secretary Lewis Cass was supervising military operations against the Sauk and Meskwaki (or Fox) people on the Wisconsin and Mississippi rivers. The Sauks' central town, Saukenuk, was situated on the Rock River, a few miles above its junction with the Mississippi, not far from present-day Davenport, Iowa. Surrounded on three sides by a brush palisade, it was organized around a large square and contained more than one hundred wood and bark longhouses that extended fifty or sixty feet, each capable of lodging as many as sixty people. North of the town, the villagers cultivated eight hundred acres of corn, beans, and squash. To the alarm of federal officials, their population, including that of the surrounding villages, exceeded six thousand people and was expanding.[1]

The "three sisters"—corn, beans, and squash—conjure stereotypes of an idyllic, unspoiled America, but in fact lead mining was the fastest-growing industry in Sauk, Meskwaki, and neighboring Ho-Chunk (Winnebago) communities. Long before the arrival of Europeans, native peoples had mined lead sulfide, using the metallic blue-black crystals for religious purposes and to produce paint pigment. Archaeologists have recovered 265 pounds of the material from Mound City, the eighteen-hundred-year-old ceremonial center on the Scioto River in Ohio. By the nineteenth century, the ore had acquired an additional use in manufacturing ammunition, and the U.S. economy, by offering access to national markets, had transformed the occasional native industry into a profit-seeking enterprise. Indigenous women, the traditional miners in the region, seized the opportunity. At one "lead house" on the Mississippi River, ten to fifteen Sauk canoes arrived daily, each carrying two thousand pounds of the metal. "I was kept from morning to night weighing and paying in goods," recalled the store owner. By one estimate, native residents mined as much as 800,000 pounds of lead in the summer of 1826. Colonists swarmed into the region to participate in the lead rush, founding towns such as Galena (named for lead sulfide), Mineral Point, Hardscrabble, and New Diggings. The newcomers, who erected shanties and sod huts that compared poorly with the comfortable lodgings of the Sauks, lived in uneasy proximity to the region's longtime landowners.[2] Inevitably, their arrival sparked conflict.

By December 1828, U.S. citizens were moving into Sauk houses and displacing the residents, and in 1831, the Sauks finally abandoned their villages and crossed the Mississippi. A year later, however, about one thousand of them returned, creating a tense standoff. The seasoned commander of the army's Western Department, Edmund Gaines, was then recovering from influenza and rheumatism in Memphis, Tennessee. Since Gaines had spoken out against the president's favored policy of expelling native peoples, the Jackson administration was happy to pass over him and give command to General Henry Atkinson, a North Carolinian with scant battle experience and little tactical sense. On May 5, 1832, the army's commanding general in Washington City ordered

Atkinson, with the assistance of Colonels Zachary Taylor and William S. Harney, to "drive the Sac's and Foxes over the Mississippi."[3]

Nine days later, a company of drunken Illinois rangers attacked the Sauks and were routed, despite their sizable numerical advantage, marking the start of the U.S.-Sauk War. The conflict is often called the Black Hawk War, after the Sauk leader who rallied people to the cause. An example must be made of the Sauks, Secretary of War Cass declared, "the effect of which will be lasting." The *Galenian* urged the governor to "carry on a war of extermination until there shall be no Indian (with his scalp on) left in the northern part of Illinois." Galenians, it boasted, were "ready to exterminate the whole race of the hostile Indians."[4]

With an army of 450 regulars and between 2,000 and 3,000 volunteers, including a twenty-three-year-old greenhorn named Abraham Lincoln, Atkinson pursued the Sauks without success for a month. By mid-June, the ongoing war was becoming an embarrassment for President Jackson, and he ordered reinforcements under General Winfield Scott to move west from New York to Fort Armstrong, an outpost on Rock Island in the Mississippi River, south of Galena and close to the main Sauk town of Saukenuk. The Sauks "must be chastised," Jackson scolded, "and a speedy & honorable termination put to this war, which will hereafter deter others from the like unprovoked hostilities by Indians on our frontier."[5] The mission did not go as planned.

~~~

VIBRIO CHOLERAE had not yet arrived in North America when George Gibson began planning the route for the second round of Choctaw deportations. The comma-shaped bacteria first appeared on the continent on Grosse Ile, on the St. Lawrence River east of Quebec City, in the late spring of 1832, shortly before Andrew Jackson ordered troops to Fort Armstrong to confront Sauk villagers. The disease had journeyed from India, by way of Afghanistan, Russia, Germany, and Britain, killing tens of thousands of people along the way. From Grosse Ile, infected persons carried the microbes up the St. Lawrence, through Lake Ontario to Buffalo. There, General Winfield Scott, his staff, and fifteen companies of artillery and infantry boarded the steamboats *Sheldon Thompson* and *Henry Clay*, bound west through Lakes Erie, Huron, and Michigan for Fort Dearborn in Chicago. From Fort Dearborn, they would march overland to Fort Armstrong to do battle with Black Hawk and the Sauk people. The expedition embarked on July 3, but one day later a soldier aboard the *Henry Clay* suddenly sickened, dying that same night. Officers ordered his body thrown into the Detroit River.[6]

V. cholerae prefers warm brackish waters, where it attaches to zooplankton and phytoplankton. If ingested by a human, it can pass through stomach acid intact and colonize the upper small intestine, where it produces a toxin that the body flushes out with watery vomit and a voluminous and distinctive rice-water diarrhea. Infected individuals may lose several quarts of fluid and rapidly become dehydrated. Blood pressure collapses, eyes recede in the skull, skin becomes shriveled and pallid, and victims go into shock. About half of those who are severely infected will die, some within a few hours after the onset of symptoms. "You remember Sergeant Hoyl," wrote one of Scott's officers. "He was well at 9 o'clock in the morning—he was at the bottom of Lake Michigan at 7 o'clock in the afternoon!" Food and water that are contaminated with the victim's copious effusions introduce the microbe to its next host.[7]

By July 16, cholera had killed thirty-four soldiers from the *Henry Clay*, and many others had deserted and died on the road, reducing the detachment of 370 troops to 68. Meanwhile, the microbe spread to the *Sheldon Thompson* on the way to Chicago, and General Scott's men threw twenty-one corpses into Lake Michigan. The contaminated bodies washed up on Chicago's shoreline. By July 19, of the 190 enlisted men on the *Sheldon Thompson*, 62 had died and 51 were ill. At the time, most people believed that the disease arose from lax morals, excessive anxiety, or atmospheric peculiarities, but General Scott was the rare "contagionist" who held that it could be transmitted between individuals. By posting notices in Chicago newspapers and writing open letters warning of the deadly contagion, he attempted to erect a "paper barrier" around the city. Such warnings proved ineffective, however, and mounted rangers soon carried the bacteria nearly 200 miles west to Fort Armstrong. In the space of a week, cholera struck 146 troops at the outpost and killed 26. Twenty more were expected to die. Scott was mortified. Without engaging in battle, he had "brought disease and death" upon his soldiers.[8]

Just as Scott's diminished forces were arriving, General Atkinson's army of volunteers and regulars managed to defeat the Sauks in battle. Devastation reigned. In late July, soldiers pursued the surviving families west toward the Mississippi, passing corpses on the trail, the victims of starvation, disease, and gunshot wounds. They captured an elderly Sauk man, "extracted some information from him," and "coolly put him to death." On August 2, federal troops and state militia pinned the largest group of survivors against the east bank of the Mississippi River and began "the work of death," as one scout put it. They killed at least 260 Sauks, with some 200 escaping across the river. Ho-Chunks, Menominees, Dakotas, and Potawatomis, settling old scores and currying favor with the United States, hunted down survivors, bringing in emaciated villagers and their starving children.[9]

Because the federal government claimed that the Sauks had ceded their eastern lands in a disputed treaty in 1804, the villagers were not formally subject to the 1830 "Act to provide for an exchange of lands with the Indians." Nonetheless, U.S. citizens recognized that there was an uncomfortable connection between the federal policy to expel Native Americans and the mobilization of federal troops against the Sauks. What if the Sauks' disaffection spread? Would the United States exterminate all native peoples who refused to relocate? A Washington newspaper concluded that every "dispassionate man" would now see the necessity of the "immediate removal of the Indians beyond the sphere of our settlements." In the patriotic afterglow of victory, one skeptic insisted that the U.S.-Sauk War had its origins "in the injustice of the whites" and the "ignorance of the Indians." "But," he stated sharply, "there are no historians among the Indians."[10]

Winfield Scott, Zachary Taylor, and William Harney would soon be sent from Sauk country south to Georgia and Florida to fight other deep-rooted families. In the meantime, a different vector connected the military mobilization on the upper Mississippi with the federal operation to deport people in the South. In late August, General Scott released several Sauk prisoners from confinement at Fort Armstrong, hours before cholera erupted in the barracks. The freed prisoners carried *V. cholerae* into indigenous communities in the West. How many native people died is unknown, though the chilly fall weather and dispersed populations surely lessened the toll.[11] (*V. cholerae* becomes dormant in cold temperatures.) Deserters from Fort Armstrong also dispersed the microbe far and wide as they fled into the countryside. Steamboats stood ready to carry the disease farther down the Mississippi to the riverport cities of Memphis and Vicksburg, where thousands of Choctaw refugees would soon converge.

~~~

THOUGH U.S. officials had not learned many lessons from the disastrous first year of deportations, they conceded that Arkansas Post was a poor staging ground, since supplies and wood were scarce on the river bluff. Instead of congregating there, Commissary General Gibson determined that this time Choctaw deportees would march to Memphis or Vicksburg, on the east bank of the Mississippi. There they would board steamboats destined for Rock Roe, a landing about one hundred miles up the White River, in east-central Arkansas. From Rock Roe, some of the dispossessed would walk over two hundred miles west to Fort Smith, on the border of Arkansas and Indian Territory, while others would turn south-southwest at Little Rock, heading to Fort Towson, a journey of 350 miles.[12]

Operations began in October 1832, just as cholera was descending the Mississippi and Ohio rivers. In Mississippi, a recent state law had invited U.S. citizens to settle on Choctaw lands, so many dispossessed families were desperate to escape the army of squatters and speculators that had invaded their nation. As thousands of Choctaws assembled at staging areas for the trek west, federal Indian agents raced to load wagons and break camp in a futile effort to beat *V. cholerae* to Memphis and Vicksburg. Each steamboat descending the Mississippi was a cause for alarm. On the journey downriver, seven people died on the *Express*, two on the *Constitution*, and five on the *Freedom*. Meanwhile, over two thousand refugees were converging on Memphis. Francis W. Armstrong, the federal officer conducting the detachment, wrote to Gibson on October 21, "I fear that we are to encounter the cholera with our Indians." A week later, the dreaded disease struck the refugees at Memphis.[13]

A separate group of Choctaws headed for Vicksburg. Numbering seventeen hundred, they set off from the eastern part of the nation in early October and encountered difficulties almost immediately. Rains clogged the road with mud and turned low-lying areas into swamp, and dysentery spread through the crowded and unsanitary camps. Within a week—during which four babies were born and a child died—word reached the train of refugees that cholera was in Vicksburg. As they approached the northern edge of the city, they encountered people fleeing the epidemic. The wagon drivers threatened to desert, and one frightened federal agent was dismissed and admonished "to forebear the expression of his fears." It was imperative not to alarm the refugees. On November 8, cholera entered their camp.[14]

Most of the refugees at Memphis and Vicksburg went to Rock Roe by steamboat. Plying the Mississippi and White rivers, the transports called at deserted woodyards to fuel their boilers. The workers, afraid of making contact with the diseased deportees, had abandoned their posts. "Scarce a boat landed without burying some person," wrote a federal agent. Over a thousand people who were camped outside Mem-

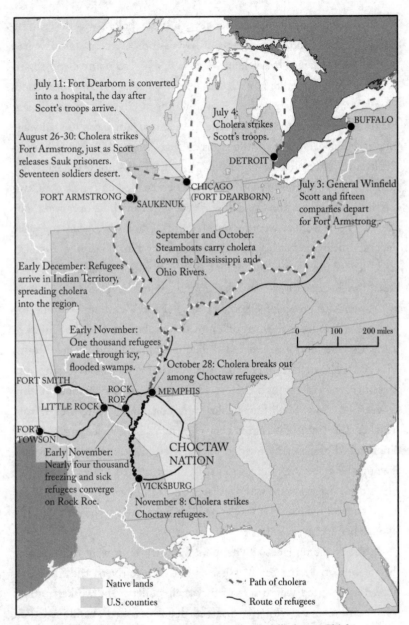

July 11: Fort Dearborn is converted into a hospital, the day after Scott's troops arrive.

July 4: Cholera strikes Scott's troops.

August 26-30: Cholera strikes Fort Armstrong, just as Scott releases Sauk prisoners. Seventeen soldiers desert.

July 3: General Winfield Scott and fifteen companies depart for Fort Armstrong.

FORT ARMSTRONG

CHICAGO (FORT DEARBORN)

SAUKENUK

DETROIT

BUFFALO

September and October: Steamboats carry cholera down the Mississippi and Ohio Rivers.

Early December: Refugees arrive in Indian Territory, spreading cholera into the region.

Early November: One thousand refugees wade through icy, flooded swamps.

October 28: Cholera breaks out among Choctaw refugees.

FORT SMITH

ROCK ROE

MEMPHIS

LITTLE ROCK

FORT TOWSON

CHOCTAW NATION

Early November: Nearly four thousand freezing and sick refugees converge on Rock Roe.

VICKSBURG

November 8: Cholera strikes Choctaw refugees.

0   100   200 miles

Native lands

U.S. counties

Path of cholera

Route of refugees

As cholera moved down the Mississippi in the fall of 1832, Chicka-saw deportees converged on Memphis and Vicksburg.

phis refused to board the contaminated vessels, and instead chose to set out on foot. Taking what happened to be the lesser of two evils, they followed a newly constructed military road. But their new route was plagued with problems, since it passed through low-lying lands that were frequently flooded. In the first twenty miles alone, the road crossed Mill Seat Bayou, Blackfish Bayou, Shell Lake, Biven's Lake, and Beaver Lake before arriving at Despair Swamp. Even outside of the normal spring floods, travelers struggled to traverse the unusual landscape. The terrain harbored a confusion of lakes, bayous, cypress swamps, and marshy grounds covered with huge gum, sycamore, oak, and hickory trees. The occasional canebrake, a dense field of woody stalks rising twenty to thirty feet high, was impassable. Some low-lying areas regularly held fifteen to twenty feet of standing water. After a week of wading through knee to waist-deep water, at least seven Choctaws had died from cholera or exposure, and the families had covered only forty of the ninety miles to their destination.[15]

Because no Choctaw left a full account of this dismal period, we must rely on the writings of unsympathetic federal agents for descriptions of the "*cholera times.*" One federal officer complained that the Choctaws were "perfectly inefficient" and willing to work only when compelled. On one occasion, he recounted, he and his assistant were obliged to dismount to lift a dying man in the final stages of cholera into a cart. More than fifty refugees stood by, he wrote, for "sheer want of energy." It seems not to have occurred to him that the Choctaws feared catching the disease. "Having received assistance once," he remarked, "they would not bury their own dead afterward without asking help." On another occasion, a thirty-year-old lieutenant faulted the refugees for refusing to abandon an elderly but still healthy man named Etotahoma. The beloved leader was "old, lame, and captious," complained the officer, and had delayed the party considerably.[16]

The same officer, Jefferson Van Horne, composed a vivid account of his own suffering from *V. cholerae* northwest of Vicksburg. Attacked by the microbe, he retired to a nearby cabin, where his frightened host removed a floorboard, leaving a hole through which Van Horne vomited and defecated. After a day of "constant purging and vomiting," Van Horne took a large dose of opium and calomel, a toxic purgative. Near midnight, as the violent attack continued, his host evicted him, explaining that he had a large family whose lives were at stake. After begging in vain to remain in the cabin by the fireside, Van Horne rolled himself in a blanket and stumbled into the cold, walking three quarters of a mile over frost-covered ground to his tent. "My suffering for two or three days exceeded any thing I ever experienced," he wrote.[17] How many Choctaws went through similar struggles without the benefit of a warm cabin or even a canvas tent is unknown.

West of the Mississippi, the deportees were under the authority of Francis W. Armstrong of Tennessee, a patronage employee who had obtained his position because he "talked loudly" in support of Jackson during the election campaign of 1828. It also helped that his brother was a veteran of the 1813–14 U.S.-Creek War and, more to the point, "a pet of the President." One disgruntled and recently dismissed federal agent observed that Armstrong and his fellow officers "were worse than useless." Yet Armstrong did possess one distinguishing qualification for the job: When efficiency demanded it, he could be uncompromising. The refugees had been "spoiled" the year before, he asserted. By one account, it particularly irked him that in 1831 the Choctaws had been permitted to carry their hominy mortars, the stone grinders that were essential to processing corn, their staple food. Armstrong would allow no such indulgence. When the steamboats stopped for wood, he stationed a guard to beat the refugees back from the shore, though they were desperate to relieve themselves on land, away from the overcrowded and filthy transports. The draconian measure "largely economised both time and means," approved one officer, but it also may have unintentionally contributed to the spread of *V. cholerae*. At Rock Roe, Armstrong refused to distribute blankets to the refugees, leaving them "naked, wet and cold." He was a "tyrant and cruel," said one antagonist. Armstrong was clear in his defense: His detractor was "outrageous in favour of the poor Indians."[18]

The road west from Rock Roe offered no relief. The daily log of one group of seven hundred refugees catalogs the toll. On November 14, the day they departed the encampment, several came down with cholera, and a child died. The next day, three more caught the disease. On November 16, during a march of eleven miles, another child died. The party walked eighteen miles the next day, and two more became ill. When the weather turned cold, the refugees continued through torrential rain. Over the next week, eight new cases of cholera appeared, and measles erupted. Four more people died. On December 8, after nearly a month on the road and after six deaths, they arrived at Fort Towson.[19]

The overall death toll remains unknown. Hundreds became ill, but the winter weather may have spared refugees the worst of the epidemic. One group of 455 aboard the steamboat *Reindeer* incurred fourteen deaths on the way to Rock Roe, a mortality rate of 3 percent. Another group of 1,200 "suffered dreadfully with the Cholera." A federal officer reported that the "woods are filled with the graves of its victims." Armstrong approached the crisis by insisting to those at risk that all was well. "We have been obliged to keep every thing to ourselves, and to browbeat the idea of the disease," he confessed, "although death was hourly among us, and the road lined with the sick." "Fortunately, they are a people what will walk to the last," he wrote to the commissary general, "or I do not know how we could get on." One thing kept the refugees going. Approaching Fort Towson after hundreds of miles on foot, the Choctaws changed into their finest clothes to greet their friends and family members who had made the journey the year before.[20] For the survivors, the reunification was a moment of joy in a season of suffering.

During his trip to Indian Territory in October 1832, Isaac McCoy had seen only promise; in his rapturous imagination, native peoples were following "the path for their deliverance." But his optimism was unwarranted. In the spring of 1833, only a few months after the arrival of the cholera-ridden Choctaws, those who had journeyed west the year before ran out of food. The first migrants had arrived too late in the season to clear fields and plant crops, and now, as the weather warmed, their twelve months of government-supplied provisions had come to an end. They scavenged for carrion and retrieved and ate the carcass of a diseased cow that was putrefying in the spring heat. The disbursing agent, a young West Point graduate named Gabriel J. Rains, suggested that he could give them condemned pork. The Choctaws had refused it once before as a part of their rations, but now, he correctly surmised, they would be glad to have it. The meat, which was six or seven years old, was not putrid or spoiled, he hastened to add, "except by age and salt." In distant Washington City, the commissary general's office noted that the starvation of the dispossessed was "much to be lamented," but these bureaucrats lacked the power and motivation to do anything, beyond issuing condemned pork.[21]

The situation turned from bad to worse as the summer began. In the first week of June 1833, a catastrophic flood of the Arkansas River destroyed the Choctaws' newly established corn fields, swept away their recently built houses, and destroyed the government corncribs. Cholera and malaria took hold in the stagnant water, and when F.W. Armstrong visited that fall, he was shocked to see so many dead and dying people. "Will the Government suffer them to die for want of a little medicine," he asked the commissioner of Indian Affairs. The usually frugal officer volunteered to purchase the medical supplies himself, if the federal government would not approve the expense. A few months later, he all but begged the War Department to provide for the starving families. George Gibson held firm. "This is a disagreeable state of things," Gibson wrote, "and I wish there were any way in which to remedy it." He had no authority to issue more than a year of rations to the Choctaws, he explained, closing the letter with a bit of moralizing: "I wish that everything may be done to influence them to self-reliance, and not to a dependence on the bounty of the Government." The disbursing agent Gabriel Rains reassured the commissary general that those who were not cultivating crops would be "let to starve."[22]

By one estimate, about 20 percent of the Choctaws in the West died in the fall of 1833. The death toll among Creeks who had migrated appeared to parallel this precipitous decline. Most Creeks still remained in their eastern homelands, but about 3,000 had moved west in small parties over the previous few years. Of these, there were only 2,459 survivors by the end of 1833. According to one officer, after the flood not more than a quarter of the Creek children born between 1830 and 1833 were still alive.[23]

~~~

To THE north, three indigenous communities were also on the move during the cholera times. The Shawnees of Wapakoneta, the Odawas, and a mixed band of Senecas and Shawnees from Lewistown—numbering eight hundred in all—were expelled from their homelands in western Ohio in September 1832. The operation was chaotic from the outset. The secretary of war insisted for months that "the plan of removal" by steamboat was "unalterable," even as the Shawnees refused to consider traveling by any means but horseback. Elderly women were especially resolute, maintaining that they would prefer to die in Ohio and be buried with their relatives rather than board a steamboat. They were clear-sighted about the matter. "It will [be] but a short time before we leave this world at any rate," they said; "let us avert from our heads as much unnecessary pain and sorrow as possible." Andrew Jackson finally relented—a rare example of Old Hickory bowing under the relentless pressure of elderly Shawnee women—but his belated decision delayed the day of departure. Likewise, though the dispossessed had requested smallpox vaccinations, the medicine arrived late and was apparently useless. The federal government also failed to deliver promised blankets, rifles, and money on time.[24]

By one account, the supervising officer James Gardiner was "swelled like a toad" with pride in his government position, though his name was "a jest upon the road." An alcoholic, he once fell drunk from his horse and was carted home sprawled atop a wagonload of corn. The disbursing officer John F. Lane was perhaps more sober, but his self-restraint extended only so far, for he was said to be involved in "a settled plan of extortion" to profit from the operation, even inventing the position of "Disbursing Assistant's Clerk" for his younger brother. Lane, a vain young man of twenty-two years, became an object of derision when he made a "flowery" speech to the Shawnees, urging them to follow the War Department's route west rather than their preferred, more direct route. By the U.S. route, he advertised, "they would get to see several fine towns, fine houses and farms on the road, as well as many white people." The Shawnee leaders returned to the conference the next day and proceeded with formal greetings and pipe-smoking. Wayweleapy, a Shawnee elder renowned for his stately speeches, then stood up and turned to Lane: "My friend, we, the chiefs, are old men. . . . Tell the President, we don't do business with boys." Natives and newcomers alike erupted in laughter, a humiliating moment for Lane that momentarily eased the Shawnees' frustration with the callow West Point graduate, who neither spoke their language nor knew anything about them.[25]

The Shawnees' departure could not take place before the Feast of the Dead, customarily performed before abandoning a village to memorialize and perpetuate the memory of deceased relatives. Told to hurry up—they were in danger of "offending" the president, who "was paying large sums of money every day for their comfort and convenience in moveing to their new homes"—they ignored the request. They would be ready after their "religious duty" was performed, and not before. Federal officers bided their time by distributing blankets, guns, and tents, and auctioning the property of the dispossessed to U.S. citizens. Meanwhile, the Shawnees and Senecas secured the release of a relative who was imprisoned in the state penitentiary.[26] Finally, in late September 1832, they set out from Ohio on their journey west.

The refugees soon became an object of curiosity for U.S. citizens, who visited the nightly camps to sell alcohol and to gawk at their "tawney brethren." The peddlers of alcohol were "miserable and mean wretches," complained Gardiner, who blamed them for bringing "disorder, mutiny, and distraction" into the camps. At a time when the American Temperance Society was the single largest reform organization in the nation, these men were easy to condemn, but the spectators who gathered merely to lay eyes on Indians one final time were in their own way also shameless. They were sightseers rather than witnesses, there to celebrate the disappearance of the region's native residents. On one occasion, one of the refugees participated in a ruse to drive off the visitors by delivering a loud speech in his indigenous language, which was mock-translated as a threat that armed warriors would soon take up positions in the camp. The crowd quickly dispersed.[27]

By the time the refugees crossed into Indiana, barely a week into the journey, Lane, in his role as disbursing agent, had already exhausted the limited government funds, leaving the operation without means to purchase food, supplies, and fodder. In a letter to Cass, Gardiner underscored the absurd and bitter irony of the situation, reporting that over the past month the expulsion had been supported by money "<u>borrowed from the Indians themselves</u>." Meanwhile, Gardiner's clerk and nephew confessed—in a letter not seen by Cass—that the federal agents had been living better than ever. Throughout the fall, he had found the weather beautiful, the views "romantic" and "sublime"—and the tavern bills "immoderately, extravagantly high."[28]

In early October, as they headed past Indianapolis, word reached the refugees that cholera had appeared in St. Louis, the busy river port on the Mississippi that then boasted a population of six thousand. "Keep cool" and "trust in Providence," advised the St. Louis *Republican*, assuring its readers that mortality was confined to "persons of intemperate habits" and "people of color." About two hundred individuals, or 3 percent of city residents, would die from the disease. As residents fled the city, federal officials prevented them from entering the refugee encampments for fear of contamination.[29] Skirting to the north of the deserted river port and its cholera-infested streets, the Odawas and Shawnees of Wapakoneta crossed the Mississippi near the city of Alton, Illinois. From there, they would march due west to their destination in Kansas. Meanwhile, the Shawnees and Senecas of Lewistown circled St. Louis to the south and then set out southwest, heading for the northeastern corner of what would become Oklahoma.

It is not clear when *V. cholerae* struck the Odawas and Shawnees of Wapakoneta. Though several of their children had died reportedly from cholera, dysentery, and other illnesses before reaching the Mississippi, the true causes of death are uncertain. On November 5, a few days after crossing the great river, an Odawa was found sick by the roadside, in terrible pain and begging for water. He survived at least until the next day, but four others died shortly after. One federal agent denied that the microbe was circulating among the deportees, but like his fellow officers, he had scant medical knowledge and just as little reason to identify the disease when he saw it, given the panic that would ensue. As the train of refugees crossed through Missouri, fearful residents slammed their doors, peeking out windows to catch a glimpse of the weary travelers. It was now late November, and the weather turned to snow and ice, mercifully halting the spread of *V. cholerae* but producing its own hardships. Setting up camp after dark in frigid temperatures, the shivering refugees struggled to find a spot to stretch their tents over the snow and build a fire. The children "wept bitterly" in the frigid weather, wrote one officer, and some of them nearly froze to death.[30]

The Shawnees of Wapakoneta and Odawas arrived in eastern Kansas seventy days after their departure from Ohio, while the Shawnees and Senecas of Lewistown arrived in northeastern Indian Territory (now

Oklahoma) two weeks later. The road had been filled with obstacles. The United States failed to deliver supplies on time. Peddlers plied the refugees with alcohol along the way. The disbursing officer ran out of funds. Cholera struck at least a part of the group. And the weather turned dangerously cold. Despite the difficulties, there were moments of relief, if not pleasure. On one occasion, a refugee took out a fiddle, and a mixed crowd of white men, Senecas, and Shawnees danced together, a scene that was repeated more than once. On another, the refugees stayed up late telling amusing stories. The assistant conductor went to bed that night "laughing a good deal" at "Indian wit," which, he noted, "was indeed good."[31]

When the operation was over, officers reported that they had successfully completed their assignment, but the numbers tell a different story. Some 808 people had departed Ohio in late September, but only 626 arrived at their destination, an attrition rate of over 20 percent. Though the sources indicate that a few had died on the road, there is no record of what happened to the vast majority of the 182 people who had disappeared. One officer explained the discrepancy by referring vaguely to "various changes made during the route."[32] Whether the missing people died or slipped away is unknown.

~~~

THE CHOLERA times posed no great challenge to the fiction that native peoples were leaving their homes voluntarily. Many Americans in the East were too busy speculating in indigenous lands to care much about what had happened to the original residents. As far as their curiosity and conscience prompted them to wonder, they told themselves that the United States had embarked on a humanitarian enterprise to remove Indians. How and where the Indians were sent did not much trouble them. As for the U.S.-Sauk War of 1832, many U.S. citizens thought that the attacks waged by Sauk partisans justified calls for their extermination. One U.S. Indian agent detailed the atrocities. Sauks reportedly cut out the hearts and severed the limbs of U.S. soldiers on the battlefield, and they mutilated American citizens "beyond the reach of modest description." White women were "hung by their feet," wrote the agent, and "the most revolting acts of outrage and indecency practiced upon their bodies," while the children were "literally chopped to pieces." The United States, he concluded, should expel the Sauks "with every indignity"; it should "spew them out of its mouth."[33]

There was, however, another challenge to the expulsion of indigenous Americans that proved to be more difficult for U.S. citizens to reconcile with their self-image. While the Sauk leader Black Hawk went to war, his Cherokee counterpart John Ross went to court. Black Hawk was a generation older than Ross, but their distinct approaches resulted largely from their upbringing, not their age. Ross grew up surrounded by English speakers and, aided by private tutors, learned to read and write in English as a young boy. While Ross was mastering cursive script, Black Hawk killed his first man and triumphantly returned to his father with the scalp. As a result of these contrasting childhoods, Black Hawk knew far more about warfare than Ross did but had little understanding of U.S. politics. The differences between the two men only continued to widen. Ross visited Washington City and participated in negotiations with the U.S. president for the first time in 1816, when he was all of twenty-six years old; Black Hawk would not do so until the close of the U.S.-Sauk War of 1832, when he was in his mid-sixties. Even after the eye-opening trip, he would continue to refer to U.S. army officers as "war chiefs," as his words were translated into English. When the expulsion crisis approached, it is not surprising that Black Hawk consulted with a prophet, while Ross retained a lawyer. The Sauk leader—said to be "of undoubted bravery" but "ferocious, cruel and vengeful"—was in many ways a more comforting figure to white Americans, who expected their Indians to sport a Mohawk, wear earrings, and pick up a tomahawk when angry. By contrast, Ross, dressed neatly in a waistcoat, tailcoat, and bow tie, waged what his fellow Cherokee John Ridge called

Black Hawk in 1837 at age
seventy, a year before his death.

John Ross in 1835 at age
forty-five.

"intellectual warfare."[34] For the U.S. government, Ross would prove the
more formidable opponent.

After the equivocal decision in *The Cherokee Nation v. The State of
Georgia*, Ross and William Wirt sought out another case that might
resolve the question of the Cherokee Nation's relationship to the state.
They were handed one by the Georgia Guard, a band of some forty
men organized by the state in 1830 to patrol the Cherokee Nation. The
Guard resembled a paramilitary organization more than a police force,
as Elias Boudinot, the editor of the *Cherokee Phoenix*, observed, for it
operated with little legal restraint. In the summer of 1831, the Guard
arrested eleven missionaries for violating a state law that required white
people residing within the Cherokee Nation to take an oath to sup-

port and defend the constitution and laws of Georgia. The missionaries were tried and convicted in a state superior court and sentenced to four years of hard labor at the state penitentiary. All but two of them, Samuel Worcester and Elizur Butler, pledged not to violate the law again and accepted a pardon from the governor, who was eager to forestall a legal challenge to state authority over the Cherokees. The two holdouts, guided by Ross and Wirt, appealed to the U.S. Supreme Court. Since the "domestic dependent nation" that Ross governed was not a party to *Worcester v. Georgia*, as the case is known, the Supreme Court had clear jurisdiction. The court would finally determine whether the extension of state sovereignty over the Cherokee Nation violated the U.S. Constitution, U.S.-Cherokee treaties, and U.S. law.[35]

Wirt and his law partner John Sergeant argued the case before the court in late February 1832. The Cherokees, Sergeant asserted, were "a State—a community." "Within their territory," he continued, "they possess the powers of self-government." Moreover, their rights were guaranteed by treaties, which remained the "Supreme law of the Land" and were superior to the laws of Georgia. The assertion that the treaties were somehow not treaties was "without the slightest foundation." Sergeant's argument was not particularly original, for the Cherokees had made it often on the pages of the *Cherokee Phoenix* and had presented it to Congress in two separate memorials in 1830. Sergeant concluded by quoting Chief Justice John Marshall's own language from *The Cherokee Nation v. The State of Georgia*. "Indian tribes," Marshall had said, were "domestic, dependent nations" and in "a state of pupilage." Their relation with the United States, he had declared, resembled "that of a ward to a guardian."[36] But what sovereign rights did they retain as "domestic, dependent nations"? Knowing that Marshall was sympathetic to the Cherokees' cause, Sergeant now invited the chief justice to elaborate on the paternalistic metaphor he had formulated in the previous year.

Writing for the majority, Marshall handed down the decision on March 3, 1832. "The Indian nations," he allowed, "had always been considered as distinct, independent political communities, retaining their original natural rights, as the undisputed possessors of the soil, from time immemorial." They were the "weaker power," he admitted, but in associating themselves with the stronger, they had not surrendered their independence. Rather, the Cherokee Nation occupied its own territory in which the laws of Georgia had no force, and Georgia citizens had no right to enter without permission from the Cherokees themselves. Georgia's laws targeting the Cherokees, he declared, were "repugnant to the constitution, laws, and treaties of the United States."[37]

Cherokees greeted the decision with jubilation. "It was trumpeted forth among the Indians," reported one federal agent, who was dismayed by the "rejoicing, yelling and whooping in every direction." "It is glorious news," celebrated Elias Boudinot from Boston, where he was on a speaking tour with John Ridge. "The question is for ever settled as to who is right and who is wrong," he wrote, observing that the struggle was now between the federal government and the State of Georgia. Ridge, for his part, described the victory as a rebirth. "Since the decision of the Supreme Court," he wrote, "I feel greatly revived—a new man and I feel independent."[38]

Worcester v. Georgia represented a complete legal victory for the Cherokees, but the consequences were far from clear. "We shall see how strong the links are to the chain that connect [*sic*] the states to the Federal Union," Ridge observed. Two days after Marshall handed down his stunning decision, John Quincy Adams, four years past his presidency and now serving as a representative from Massachusetts, introduced a petition to the House from the citizens of New York City asking Congress to "enforce the observance of the laws of the Union" and "vindicate the constitutional authority of the Federal Government" by protecting the Cherokee Nation. The memorial touched off a fiery debate. Representative Augustin Clayton of Georgia, who as a state judge two years earlier had sentenced the Cherokee George Tassel to death, took the floor to proclaim that Marshall's decision would not be executed "till Georgia was made a howling wilderness." His state, he warned, "only wanted the application of a match to blow the Union into ten thousand fragments." Would the House provide the spark, he asked, that would "rend the Union to pieces?"[39]

Clayton's attack on New York's memorial was a thinly veiled defense of the prerogatives of slaveholders. He outlined for his fellow representatives the horrors that Cherokee independence brought to the Deep South. A white man had rented a horse from the Cherokees, he recounted, and accidentally traveled farther than agreed. The Cherokees accused him of theft, suspended him from the limb of a tree, and whipped him fifty times as he begged for mercy. "The savages," Clayton charged, "were perfectly inexorable." Without the extension of Georgia sovereignty, he warned, such incidents would multiply.[40]

In fact, the events surrounding Clayton's anecdote were quite different. The accused horse thief had been put on trial before a jury of Cherokees in the Cherokee Nation and convicted and punished according to Cherokee law. Summary judgment and arbitrary punishment were hallmarks of Clayton's home state, not the Cherokee Nation. The "dreadfully savage" Thomas Stevens, for example, severely flogged John Brown on numerous occasions. The crime? Stevens, a white planter who had recently purchased Brown and separated the young boy from his parents, objected that his new slave labored indifferently in the cotton fields. On one occasion, Stevens nearly beat Brown to death for not running fast enough to retrieve a key. Brown was saved when a neighboring planter rode up and announced that a "drove of negroes" had arrived from Virginia, prompting Stevens to drop his whip and hurry off to have "the pick of them." On another, as Brown was kneeling to fix a broken plow, Stevens kicked him between the eyes with all his might, breaking his nose, dislocating one eye, and permanently damaging his vision. The slave owner "became so savage to me," recalled Brown, "I used to dread to see him coming." Perhaps even more horrifying were the medical experiments that a neighboring doctor was permitted to perform on Brown. They included exposure to extreme temperatures (to measure the effect of heatstroke), bloodletting (purpose unknown), inci-

sions (to determine the depth of skin pigmentation), and other proce-
dures, "which," Brown painfully acknowledged, "I cannot dwell upon."[41]

Clayton and his fellow planters did not concern themselves with
such crimes, however, because the extension of Georgia sovereignty, in
their minds, ensured the rights of white people to rule over others, not
the rights of their would-be inferiors. *Worcester v. Georgia* had become a
proxy for white supremacy. As John Ross and other Cherokees anxiously
looked on, the slave society that had grown up around them and that had
corrupted their own communities—for they too now had plantations—
denounced the Worcester decision as passionately as it defended slavery. Not far from the site of Brown's brutal treatment, the white men
of Jones County in central Georgia resolved that the court's decision
jeopardized "the perpetuity of the Union"—a dire threat that would be
heard repeatedly in coming years. Similar declarations rang throughout
the state. Marshall's opinion was "a palpable and dangerous invasion of
rights," said the white men of Taliaferro County, seventy-five miles east
of Atlanta. "Georgia," they asserted, "has ever had the right to subject
every class of her population to her laws." In Burke County, just south
of Augusta, white men resolved to defend their "rights and interests"
against the Supreme Court's "arbitrary assumptions of power." And in
Gwinnett County, bordering the Cherokee Nation, the aggrieved citizens complained that northerners were intermeddling with their "*local
concerns*" by slandering them on the subject of two "troublesome" populations, Indians and slaves. Marshall's decision was "not binding on the
people of Georgia," they said, vowing to support state authorities "to
repel all invasions on their Jurisdiction."[42]

Ross was besieged by advice from would-be allies who urged him to
sign a treaty agreeing to expulsion. The Cherokees' situation had become
"perilous," reported one federal agent, who delighted that the longtime
inhabitants would soon be compelled to move west. A few had already
registered to be deported, and the United States recruited white volunteers to surround their temporary encampment to prevent them from

escaping before the departure. One letter arrived from Supreme Court justice John McLean, who had joined the majority in *Worcester v. Georgia*. Motivated, he claimed, by "a deep solicitude" for the Cherokees' prosperity, he counseled them to move west. It was true that the 1802 Trade and Intercourse Act forbade U.S. citizens from crossing into Indian territory, he wrote, but since Cherokee lands were held in common, individual Cherokees could not sue for trespass. Nor could the nation as a whole take legal action. As *The Cherokee Nation v. The State of Georgia* had made clear in 1831, it had no standing as a foreign state before the Supreme Court. "The cases are very few where the Courts of the United States can take jurisdiction, in the assertion of any rights which you may claim," Justice McLean explained. "You can judge, how inadequate a remedy must be for your nation, which is limited to a very few cases, involving individual rights, and prosecuted at a heavy expense." Whatever his motivation, McLean's legal point was true enough, for it was widely held that the Bill of Rights limited the actions of only the federal government, not the individual states. Most jurists agreed that Georgia was free to oppress African Americans and Native Americans with impunity.[43]

Elisha Chester, Worcester's one-time attorney in Georgia, also offered his unwanted counsel to Ross, warning that the "evils . . . are hourly increasing." Chester insisted to the Cherokee leader that there was "not the remotest prospect of relief" for his people in their present location. But he was hardly a disinterested observer. The attorney, after working on behalf of the Cherokee Nation, had unscrupulously accepted employment as a special agent for the United States. He advised Secretary of War Cass to give no relief to the Cherokees from the "pressing evils" that surrounded them.[44]

In the fall of 1832, the Cherokees' troubles multiplied further. After the legislature authorized the appropriation of Cherokee lands in December 1831, surveyors had run chains in every direction in the Cherokee Nation, crisscrossing family farms and bisecting native villages. They completed the surveys in September 1832. For a nominal fee, any state citizen could now purchase a chance to own a piece of the Cherokee homeland, as long as he or she was white and not a resident of the Cherokee Nation. Finally, with great fanfare state officials drew lottery tickets at random from great revolving drums and announced the names of 53,000 lucky winners. This horde of fortunate stub holders lost no time in rushing into the nation to stake their claims, driving off the native residents by lash if necessary.[45] The state would distribute over 4.28 million acres of Cherokee land this way.

As the fate of *Worcester v. Georgia* hung in the balance in late 1832, Georgia politicians received a gift. The Nullification movement in South Carolina reached a climax, propelled by a series of alarming events that had brought slaveholders to the barricades. In January 1831, William Lloyd Garrison had launched his abolitionist newspaper *The Liberator*. Eight months later, Nat Turner had organized a slave uprising in Southampton County, Virginia. Soon afterward, the Virginia legislature had taken up the question of abolition. And Congress was once again debating whether or not to fund the American Colonization Society. Slavery itself seemed to be under attack, galvanizing South Carolina politicians to insist on their right to nullify national laws that might challenge their hegemony. The immediate cause of their protest was a federal tariff, but the true value of nullification was not in the savings on tax-free pig iron, roofing slates, and woolen goods—though the financial benefits would be significant—but in the peace of mind that they were the unquestioned masters over their human property, the more than two million slaves, valued at nearly $700 million, who were laboring in the South. With the right of nullification, the region's "domestick institutions," as John C. Calhoun put it, would remain forever safe from "Colonization and other schemes" dreamed up by fanatics in the North.[46]

If Georgia joined South Carolina in nullification, thereby fusing the movements against *Worcester v. Georgia* and the federal tariff, the integrity of the Union would be in danger. Quietly, politicians worked behind the scenes to separate the states' two causes. Stephen Van Rensselaer, president of the Missionary Society of the Dutch Reformed Church and one of New York City's wealthiest men, appealed directly to the American Board of Commissioners for Foreign Missions, urging Worcester and Butler's home organization to concede the legal battle to Georgia. Simultaneously, Georgia's governor expressed his keen desire to issue a pardon to the two missionaries. The campaign was a success. In February 1833, the missionaries capitulated, writing to Governor Lumpkin that they would accept a pardon, and Georgia, in turn, rejected South Carolina's invitation to join the Nullification movement.[47]

By the spring of 1833, it had become clear that Jackson would not enforce the Supreme Court's decision. In response, Boudinot, Ridge, and several other native leaders despaired of the Cherokees' future in the East and began urging their people to sign a treaty with the United States. Although they were (and still are) accused of having betrayed the nation, their capitulation reveals less about their personal integrity than it does about the unremitting persecution that the nation faced. Ross, however, held firm. "Let us still patiently endure our oppressions," he exhorted, "and place our trust under the guidance of a Benignant Providence."[48]

~~~

IN A public meeting in late March 1832, the citizens of Columbus, Georgia, appointed a committee of men of "distinguished character and moderation" to draft a statement of opposition to *Worcester v. Georgia*. "It is, indeed, felicitous that, upon a question embracing the vital interests of Georgia, her citizens are speaking as with one voice," wrote the *Columbus Enquirer*, for "the spirit of the times requires united counsels and united movements." Founded only four years earlier, Columbus sat at the fall line of the Chattahoochee River, the northernmost point of navigation for steamboats coming upstream from Apalachicola and the Gulf of Mexico. The city's boosters projected that it would come to dominate interior trade, though their high hopes would later be dashed by the arrival of railroads, which carried cotton directly to the Atlantic Coast, bypassing the river port. By the time of Marshall's decision, Columbus boasted a population of 1,800, about 40 percent of whom were enslaved. "Well done, Columbus!" exclaimed the local newspaper; "Four years ago a howling wilderness; now a handsome town." The river had not yet become polluted with sewage and runoff from cotton plantations, and in the spring, Creek families still fished for shad in its waters, using nets fashioned out of strips of bark. Creeks regularly visited by the hundreds and sometimes thousands, doubling the town's population, but, recalled an early resident, they were not permitted to stay overnight on the Georgia side of the river. No southern inland town had progressed with "more rapidity," crowed one Columbus denizen. Nonetheless, its eminent residents were hardly distinguished by national standards, and the committee to draft the statement on *Worcester v. Georgia* was composed of small-town businessmen and local politicians who possessed unbounded ambition and parochial views. It is not surprising that Eli Shorter was among them.[49]

"Among the proud intellects of Georgia, . . . none was more commanding, none more transparent, none more vigorous and subtle in analysis, than that of the Hon. Eli S. Shorter," wrote an admiring biographer. Born in Georgia in 1792, Shorter was orphaned and left penniless at age five. Educated at the expense of his older brother, Shorter became a lawyer, enriched himself by specializing in debt collection, ran successfully for state superior court, and resigned in a sex scandal. He did not stay down; instead, he "cast off difficulty as a lion shakes the dew from his mane." This overblown image—Shorter's own—was "worthy of Napoleon," wrote his biographer.[50]

Whatever his qualities, a working sense of irony was not among them. The committee's statement on *Worcester v. Georgia* began by underscoring that "the dearest interest and most sacred right of freemen"— that is, self-government—was at stake. The Supreme Court ought to be respected, it continued, except when its decisions deprived states of "the power of making laws for their own government." In such cases, it was "the duty of the people" to "protect and defend" their sovereignty. The choice before the citizens of Georgia was stark—submit as slaves, or resist and defend their freedom. They had inherited their freedom from their fathers, the committee proclaimed; they would just as surely bequeath it to their children. It seems not to have occurred to Shorter and his fellow committee members that, in defense of self-government, native peoples had the stronger claim. Where *their* fathers had "formerly walked without restraint," Creeks petitioned Congress, they were now "hemmed in" and "condemned to slavery."[51]

In his frequent high-minded and self-pitying protestations, Shorter often failed to see the irony. The tariff that triggered the Nullification crisis, he charged, was a "system of oppression and plunder." To surrender, the owner of seventeen slaves wrote, would be to "meekly *submit* our necks to the galling yoke of our oppressors." A few years later, he objected to permitting native peoples to testify when their own interests were at stake, though he took for granted his own right to do so. How could Native Americans be trusted, he asked. It galled him that the federal government accepted "the *bare-naked* statements of Indians." "What have we done which is to deprive us of the protection of the laws of our country?" he pleaded, suggesting to Secretary of War Cass that "We may have the misfortune of bearing your deep-rooted prejudices." Creeks of course had asked the same question many times. In Shorter's prose, imitation was not a form of flattery. In all sincerity, or with complete cynicism, the colonizer and slaveholder insisted that he was "scrupulously regardful of the rights of others."[52]

In brief, Shorter's sense of entitlement and aggrievement, like that of most elite white southerners, knew no bounds. He felt particularly entitled to the native lands that lay across the Chattahoochee River from his Columbus residence and especially aggrieved that Creek families still lived on them. Casting an eye on the rich soils of the Creek Nation, he and other ambitious Georgians set about dispossessing the region's longtime residents.

FINANCING
DISPOSSESSION

~~~

CHAPTER 7

THE FINANCIERS

~~~

"I HAVE been all my life a slave to bad habits, which have hung around me as heavy as millstones," Eli Shorter confessed in June 1830. Shorter was an inveterate gambler, and although he had recently given up cards, he admitted that his fingers "itched" whenever he saw a playing deck. Instead of yielding to the temptation, he looked for other places to wager his money, finding one in December 1830, when Georgia's state legislature chartered the Farmers Bank of Chattahoochee. The bank, which would be only the second in Columbus, Georgia, set off a scramble among investors to control the board. Though founded only two years earlier, no other southern city possessed "more real capital and business capacity" or contained "a more enterprising population," boasted the *Columbus Enquirer*. Its trade for the moment was "divided into various channels," the newspaper admitted, but "the causes which produce the diversion will soon be removed."[1]

The causes lived across the Chattahoochee River. As one early Columbus resident put it, a "strip of Indian territory sixty miles wide," widely known for its "fertility and beauty," separated Columbus from "white civilization." It was only a matter of time, however, before the residents would be expelled and the town reaped the benefits. With such bright prospects ahead, when the Farmers Bank of Chattahoochee opened its subscription books, throngs of eager investors crowded the doors. Shorter, who had raised $20,000 from Beers, Booth & St. John, a Philadelphia mercantile firm with extensive experience dealing in southern cotton, won the day. The firm became the single largest stock-holder, followed by Shorter, who ventured $16,400 of his own money. In November 1831, Shorter became the bank's first president.[2]

Across the river from the Farmers Bank, conditions were deteriorating rapidly in the Creek Nation. Neha Micco wrote directly to Andrew Jackson to complain about "white people" moving onto Creek lands without permission, "infringing on our rights guaranteed to us by the U.S. Government." And the influx was no mere trickle; between 1,500 and 5,000 newcomers had intruded on Creek lands by 1831. Without either formal title or legal right, they nonetheless had the ability to steal Creek property with impunity, since native people were not allowed to testify in Alabama state court. Wielding axes and compasses, they marked off tracts for themselves, dispossessing entire families of their homes and enclosing fields that had long been cultivated by indigenous farmers. County sheriffs, accompanied by state militia and armed volunteers, arrested Creeks who fought back. Those Creeks who enlisted with the federal government to be relocated were in turn targeted by their own people, who seized their property and in some instances threatened their lives. Sandy Grayson, one of the first to enroll to move west, was victimized by both sides. The Creek Nation confiscated sixteen of his cattle, and the circuit court in Shelby County ruled that he owed $305 to an Alabama merchant. Grayson maintained that the debt was fraudulent.[3]

As conditions worsened, Neha Micco beseeched Andrew Jackson and his administration for help. The answer from Jackson's first secretary of war, John Eaton, was predictable. Nothing could be done. "You are within the limits of Alabama, which is an independent State," Eaton wrote in May 1831, "and which is not answerable to your great father for the exercise of her jurisdiction over the people who reside within her limits." The administration's legalistic argument did not impress the Creeks, since it treated states' rights as an inviolable principle rather than what it was, a political claim, brandished when expedient. "We admit that we do not comprehend this subject," Creek leaders wrote. "It is too deep for our understandings." They were incredulous rather than confused. As they rightly observed, they had made treaties with the United States before Alabama existed, when the federal government was the only power with which to negotiate. "If we have not been solemnly guaranteed that our possessions were sound and should not be wrested from us," they stated, "inform us what is the meaning of the language to which we have attached so much value."[4]

The abdication of federal authority was "like a clap of thunder upon me," Tuskeneah, a prominent and elderly Creek leader, wrote to the president in May 1831. The flood of intruders had dispossessed Creeks, he said, and when the starving refugees crossed into Georgia to poach cattle and hogs, whites hunted them as if they were deer. Georgians had recently pursued seventeen people through the woods and shot them, "and nothing thought of more than if they had been so many wild Hogs." Tuskeneah closed his letter with a statement that was at once a supplication and an assertion of seniority:

> All I want is peace and be protected in what belongs to ~~my~~
> the Red people, and have been Solemnly guaranteed to them
> by your Government. With everey Respect I have the Honor
> to be your unfortunate old Brother.[5]

For the citizens of Columbus, the dire situation in the Creek Nation created both a humanitarian crisis and an opportunity. In a petition to the governor of Georgia, they described the "intense suffering" among their indigenous neighbors, averring that they had "never seen greater misery and want." Many native people were "in a state of starvation" and survived only by begging from door to door in Columbus's streets. The Jackson administration, which had helped to generate the problem by silently encouraging the colonizers, was asked to provide a solution. Now would be "an auspicious time" to enroll emigrants, the petitioners observed. One witness wrote that it was "beyond description distressing" to hear the "incessant cry of the emaciated creatures . . . , *bread! bread!*" But there was a bright side to this dark picture of human misery. "Government could now succeed in sending off a large part of them," he exclaimed, "as they would doubtless consent to emigrate for the purpose of preserving life." It was an opportune coincidence: "the policy of removing the Indians to the westward might be partially effected, while at the same time the cause of humanity would be subserved."[6]

The federal government showed no interest in relieving the starving families in the East. Once the precedent was established, Secretary of War Eaton predicted, native peoples would "make no exertions for their own relief." President Jackson "regrets the misery" and "would most cheerfully afford them relief," the War Department explained, "but there are no funds at his disposal that can be applied, where they are, for such an object." With starvation pressing in on them, Creek leaders met with Eaton's replacement, Lewis Cass, in Washington City in March 1832. "No one will compel you to go," Cass had promised; "no force will be applied." But hunger was force enough, and the Creek delegation signed a treaty that required indigenous peoples either to move west or to register for allotments in Alabama. Those who chose to remain in Alabama would have to accept individual title to their lands.[7]

To facilitate the anticipated invasion and seizure of Creek lands, Columbus's citizens began constructing a bridge across the Chatta-hoochee River just a few weeks before the signing of the treaty.[8] Speculators marshalled financial capital for the onslaught; slave traders readied their forced laborers for the march. Commanding the capital of the

Farmers Bank of Chattahoochee, Shorter prepared to sweep into the Creek Nation.

~~~

THE IMPORTANCE of landed property and the practice of defining it varied widely among indigenous Americans. Some communities with state structures and taxes, as in central Mexico, erected cairns or drove in stakes to mark boundaries, while others with looser tributary systems defined their territories using natural features such as rivers, and still others who hunted and foraged relied on custom and memory to define boundaries with their neighbors. Surveying—mapping and measuring land—existed in Mesoamerica but apparently not elsewhere, at least according to surviving evidence. French, Spanish, and English colonists each brought to the Americas their own distinct ways of measuring land and defining ownership. By the nineteenth century, however, the United States had reduced the multiplicity of indigenous and colonial practices to a single system that divided the surface of the globe into six-mile-by-six-mile squares called townships, which were further divided into thirty-six sections each. In theory, the subdivisions of each section, or aliquots, were endless. For example, "the northeast corner of the northwest corner of Township 10 north, on Range 10 east, in section 15" describes a plot of the proverbial forty acres. The system, which is still in use, has the advantage of precision and infinite divisibility. For speculators, it was a boon to moneymaking, because it divided the surface of the Earth into a standard unit that could be graded by quality, listed in ledgers (W½, Sec. 2, T14, R27; S½, Sec. 19, T15, R26; NE¼, Sec. 33, T17, R25, and so on), and bought and sold by bankers in New York and Boston who had never set foot on the land itself.[9]

By the terms of both the Choctaw treaty of 1830 and the Creek treaty of 1832, each head of a family was entitled to a reserve of land, which he or she could sell or, if intending to become a state citizen, hold for five years, after which the title became permanent. The Choctaw treaty allotted a full section of 640 acres to each head of a family, plus 320 acres for every unmarried child over ten years of age and 160 acres for every child under ten years of age. Under the later and less generous Creek treaty, each Creek head of a family was entitled to 320 acres. Reserves were to contain the improvements of each family—houses, corncribs, cultivated fields, and the like—and were to be bounded by the grid system, which surveyors imposed on indigenous lands immediately after the signing of the treaties, oblivious to streams, swamps, forests, villages, and everything else that distinguishes the surface of the Earth from a piece of paper.

The federal government's deep desire for regularity did not allow any room for complexity. It should have been obvious at the outset that indigenous families had not located their houses in concert with an abstract grid that was anchored to the globe by invisible lines of longitude that were arbitrarily defined a thousand years after native peoples began farming in the region. When the federal government's well-ordered fantasy came into conflict with the real world, as it did immediately, U.S. agents asked for guidance. What was to be done when two Choctaws lived within the same section? Would one of the individuals be entitled to a "float"—that is, a section of his or her choice lying elsewhere in the Choctaw Nation? If so, who was to be given preference? What if a reserve fell on a fractional section, as when a river cut through the grid? Could the fractional section be supplemented with the adjoining fraction?

Such practical and immediate problems fell to yet another part of the growing—though still quite small—bureaucracy in Washington City. The Commissioner of the General Land Office, who oversaw the surveying of "public lands," made up answers on the fly. When two people lived in the same section, he decided, it was permissible to subdivide adjacent sections, so that each received a half of each section, as long as the reserve was given "as *square* a form as practicable." When two families lived within the smallest legal subdivision of a section (forty acres), they would have to make arrangements among themselves for one of them to move elsewhere. As for fractional sections, supplements were permitted but again taking care "to give the entire reserve a square form."[10]

The attention to squares satisfied two desires. One was to force indigenous farmers to accept a quantity of subprime land, since almost every unnaturally square reserve would contain some terrain that could not be farmed productively. In turn, some prime cotton land would remain beyond the reserve and become available to U.S. citizens, who would move into the region, it was assumed, and eventually displace the original residents. The second desire was born of a more general interest in uniformity and marketability. Property boundaries that followed a twisting river or prairie might have more accurately defined some indigenous farms. But organic contours were difficult to describe and map and, if adopted by U.S. citizens, would have led to conflicting claims, clouded land titles, and endless court battles. A grid-like division of the Earth was more in keeping with the Jeffersonian vision of a seamless parcel map of privately owned tracts.[11]

No amount of patching could hide the mismatch between the diverse settlement patterns of native farmers in the South and the government's totalizing fantasy. Native peoples lived in villages and communally farmed nearby river bottomlands; or resided in houses adjoining their fields, which sensibly followed the contours of the terrain rather than a geometric grid; or worked multiple fields in different locations to take advantage of microclimates and soil patterns. None of these practices fit the General Land Office's vision. In the summer of 1833, George Martin, the hapless surveyor assigned to the Choctaw Nation, sent a series of questions to Secretary of War Cass, asking for clarification. When settlements overlapped, what method should be used to determine who had the prior claim? When a child's land adjoined the parent's, did the sides have to conjoin, or could the reserves meet at the corners? When a house was in one section and the field in another, could the reserve

The rectangular survey system laid over the Creek Nation in eastern Alabama, west of the Chattahoochee River.

contain a part of each section? If a residence sat on worthless land, could the reserve include terrain across the section line? The questions multiplied by the day. When the time came to allot the reserves, Martin wrote and distributed a circular: "TO THOSE WHO CLAIM RESERVATIONS UNDER THE TREATY OF DANCING RABIT CREEK." The misspelled title was the least of Martin's problems. The circular began with a lengthy complaint about the government's imperfect records, ambiguous instructions, and unreasonable expectations. Only afterward did the circular make a futile attempt to list every settlement pattern that might be encountered and explain how land would be allotted in each case.[12]

As the federal government puzzled over these dilemmas, the U.S. attorney general began rendering opinions that were impressively legalistic and comically makeshift. One example: "Where the reservation exceeds a section, the excess beyond the section containing the dwelling house, ought to be so taken from a contiguous section, as to include the other improvements, if any, possessed by the grantee, at the date of the treaty." "And if those improvements are on different sections," the attorney general continued, "I think the excess ought to be taken from that section within which the greatest portion of the improvements shall have fallen." There was yet one more possibility to be considered: "If the grantee had no improvements in his possession at the date of the treaty except such as shall have fallen within the section containing his dwelling house, then I am of the opinion, that he may locate the excess beyond that section, in any contiguous section not otherwise appropriated." Allocating lands according to the set of byzantine and improvised rules devised by the federal government would have been difficult in the best of circumstances. When residents had little motivation to cooperate, implementing such a system was nearly impossible. The Choctaw Samuel Cobb revealed his disdain for the process. Questioned by a U.S. agent about a list of his neighbors, he retorted that it was "not part of his business to tell about them." He would answer when "he thinks a question is right," he said, but would not "when he thinks it wrong."[13]

The federal government faced a second and related problem, also born of its desire to enumerate and standardize. For the purposes of distributing rations, stockpiling supplies, assessing military threats, and the like, it desired a complete count of the people it was deporting from the South. With the exception of a few Indians who paid taxes, however, the decennial U.S. Census excluded Native Americans and would not enumerate them in their entirety until 1890. The War Department therefore ordered the taking of special censuses. But counting people turned out to be as difficult as dividing up the surface of the Earth.

In the Creek Nation, the War Department sent out two diligent officers, Enoch Parsons and Thomas Abbott, to complete the task. Charged with listing the heads of families and the number of males and females in each, they quickly found that what constituted a head and what constituted a family was not easily determined. If a man had several wives who lived in separate households, they asked the secretary of war, was each wife to be considered a family head and thereby entitled to a reserve? What if a white man had married a Creek woman? Was he a family head, and should there be any effort to determine if the man was acting in bad faith solely to obtain title to indigenous lands? After all, marriages of convenience were a serious problem, according to Neha Micco. The white men in such relationships "annoy us much," he said, "and are particularly disliked by all our people." What about a Creek man who had a black slave for a wife? Was this a family? And, adding further confusion, what about a man of African and native descent who had "a negro slave for a wife"?[14]

The questions betrayed two preconceptions at work within the government: men rather than women ought to be counted as heads of families, and race determined citizenship. In the Creek Nation neither presumption held sway. "The question of 'What is an Indian family?'

naturally precedes the question 'Who is the Head of such family?'" the Chickasaw leader Ishtehotopa King lectured Andrew Jackson. The answer could only be determined with reference to native "Customs and manners of life," he continued, explaining to the president that in the Chickasaw Nation (as well as among the Creeks and most other native peoples in the South), the wife presided over the family and owned all the property. The Creeks were in fact in the midst of a rapid social transformation, but it was still the case that many families were matrilocal—men moved into the households of their wives—and that they were far less fixated on race than were U.S. citizens. The situation on the ground was indeed puzzling to Parsons and Abbott. Although the printed census form had no column for slaves, some Creeks owned more than one. And yet there were also a number of free black families that seemed to be "in Every way Identifyed with these people, and the only differance in the coler." Parsons was especially confused by a family of two young Creek orphans, who were living in the care of a "negro woman" who belonged to them. "Very many such cases has presented themselves," he wrote.[15]

The divergence between the government's ambitions and its limited capabilities was nowhere more obvious than when Abbott encountered two individuals with the same name living in the same town. U.S. Census takers regularly faced similar situations and thought little of it, but in this instance the federal government had to distribute resources to people with identical names in communities that were, to its army of clerks, unknowable. There were no street addresses, no surnames, no dates of birth, and no familiar family groupings. Abbott concocted a ridiculous solution. "With all the solemnity attendant on the ceremony," he explained, perhaps in self-jest, he "caused the individual publicly and by the proper authority, to be named anew." There is no record of what local residents thought of this farce. At a minimum, it was, as they said of the U.S. citizens surveying their lands, "strange conduct."[16]

In the Creek Nation alone, an area the size of New Jersey was at stake, over eight thousand square miles of some of the most valuable farmland in the world. To mark the section lines in the Creek Nation, surveyors walked about sixteen thousand miles—the equivalent of trekking from New York City to Tierra del Fuego and back again—pulling a sixty-six-foot steel chain end over end more than 1.2 million times as they cut through forests and trespassed on native farms. Meanwhile, Parsons and Abbott enumerated some 22,000 Creeks who lived in more than 6,000 households. U.S. officials also undertook surveys in the Choctaw Nation (approximately 20,000 inhabitants and nearly 17,000 square miles of land) and the Chickasaw Nation (over 6,000 inhabitants and 10,000 square miles of land).[17]

~~~

As THE president of the Farmers Bank of Chattahoochee, Shorter commanded $120,000 in financial capital, an immense sum in Columbus, the thriving frontier town of 1,800 residents. The bank's capitalization, which seems inconsequential today, placed it in the top third of corporations chartered between 1820 and 1836. Nonetheless, that sum amounted to only a small fraction of the money necessary to transform the Creek Nation from a patchwork of indigenous farms to a matrix of slave labor camps. At $1.25 per acre, approximately $2.7 million would be needed to purchase the reserves that had been allotted to individual Creek families. It would require even more to populate the new holdings with some 58,000 enslaved workers, valued at roughly $32 million. Choctaw and Chickasaw lands would demand similar infusions of money.[18] Who would furnish such enormous sums of capital?

Joseph Davis Beers, known to his family as Davis but to Wall Street as J.D., was said to be "a clever man" who was "quick as a steel trap" and "as affable as a good prince." His career rose along with Wall Street itself, which in the early nineteenth century was just emerging as the center of American finance. The son of a well-known publisher of almanacs, Beers was raised in Connecticut, operated a general store for a time, and then moved to Manhattan, where, as his father warned, "all manner of Vice and wickedness rains [*sic*]." His modest grocery store on the East River in lower Manhattan was "not so pleasing" next to the better-capitalized competition, he wrote in 1812, but he managed to save enough to open a small banking house at 39 Wall Street a few years later. By hard work and good fortune, he eventually became a man of "great wealth," joined the New York elite at Trinity Church, supported a dissolute grandson who squandered tens of thousands of dollars living in Paris, and at age seventy-nine married his third wife, thirty-four years his junior, who, according to family members, "became the best customer at Tiffany's."[19]

Beers's firm initially traded in unglamorous goods such as hams, pickled pork, and mattress feathers, but it was southern cotton, notoriously volatile in price but irresistibly profitable in boom times, that shaped his investment strategies. Beers, along with other cotton brokers, made money by advancing funds to planters in exchange for the right to sell the incoming crop on commission. Like many investors, he kept a utilitarian distance from the source of his profits, the several million unpaid workers confined to the privately owned slave labor camps of the rural South. During one visit to Charleston, Beers liberally tipped the enslaved people who waited on him, perhaps as a salve to his conscience, while his wife Mary (his first) spent her time reading the New Testament and going to church. When a rare snow and ice storm hit the city, the New Yorkers lamented the suffering of the fifteen thousand slaves who lived there and who made up the majority of the population. "The poor Negroes," Mary wrote, "it would make your heart ache to see them barefoot and naked." Some of them were almost frozen to death, she observed, remarking on their forbearance and silent suffering and expressing a desire to purchase and free the young girl who was waiting on her. "I have found it necessary to put all my patience in practice" not to complain about their condition, she added. She found solace in reading William Wilberforce. This was a remarkable statement for the wife of a cotton broker, for Wilberforce, who had recently died, was a devout Christian like Mary but also a renowned abolitionist, whose central message was unmistakably clear. Slavery, Wilberforce wrote, was "a system of the grossest injustice, of the most heathenish irreligion and immorality, of the most unprecedented degradation, and unrelenting cruelty."[20]

When Mary and J.D. coauthored letters to their daughter and son-in-law during the trip, they, like so many wealthy northern visitors, were critical but slightly envious of the planters who "don't think of labour at all." "Oh you don't know how these people are waited on," Mary exclaimed, underscoring that the work "is all done by slaves." Meanwhile, J.D. was working day and night, visiting his clients' plantations on the Ashley River, where the largest slave labor camps in South Carolina were located. He "makes it another Wall Street," wrote Mary. In New Orleans, they marveled that their hostess owned thirteen house slaves, each one worth $1,000, and the guests were amazed that she was offered $400 "for a little Girl 4 years old."[21]

Later in 1835, after returning from the South, Beers joined New York's business leaders at City Hall Park in lower Manhattan to preside over a public meeting that drafted a resolution condemning abolitionist and antislavery societies for precipitating "violence and disunion." Deeply invested in the slave economy, the bankers and merchants cobbled together a tepid condemnation of the institution and a convoluted but determined defense of planters. They deplored the existence of slavery, they stated, but denied that it was "necessarily immoral and criminal." Not all slaveholders were "equally guilty," they argued, distinguishing those who had inherited their slaves from those who had acquired them by "voluntary conduct." The resolution became increasingly feeble as it plodded toward an unconvincing conclusion. The relation between slave owners and slaves, they reasoned, may exist "without the fault of either parties, and against the will of both, and may impose on each peculiar obligations."[22] This clumsy sleight of hand—condemning slavery but not the practice of slaveholding—was a familiar trick of southern planters, and it is not surprising that New York bankers and merchants, whose capital fueled the slave economy, employed it as well.

Their talent for abstracting the profits from the source turned out to be indispensable when they turned their attention to the millions of acres of native land in the South. Although New York and Boston were among the centers of anti-expulsion activism in the 1830s, when the opportunity arose to invest in the dispossession of native peoples, Wall Street and State Street financiers seized it, apparently unmoved by the popular protests against federal policy. These men were the North's equivalent of the southern planters. While one practiced slavery and the other investment banking, both groups were equally indifferent to the fate of indigenous Americans and the slaves who would replace them.

In the aftermath of forced uprooting, one anonymous Choctaw wrote in verse about the experience, capturing the bitter sentiments of many of the victims. The subject was dispossession. White Americans had a dream, the author wrote,

> *A day dream, bright as new dollars,*
> *And aye the dream was about dollars!*
> *Not about Indians as you know,*
> *But about them t'would do to blow.*[23]

In the coming years, as Beers pored over lists of thousands of tracts he had purchased from indigenous farmers—sec. 23, T2, R4; sec 27, T2,

Joseph D. Beers.

R4; sec. 28, T2, R4; sec. 13, T3, R4, and so on—not once in any of his surviving correspondence would he mention the original owners, even in passing. About them, "t'would do to blow."

~~~

THE IMMENSE sum of capital needed to dispossess native peoples and transform their lands followed two streams, fed by a network of financiers stretching from New York to London. The first supplied Mississippi's and Alabama's banking sectors, which were expanding rapidly in order to finance the purchase of land, slaves, mules, plows, and seed. The second flowed into several joint-stock companies that were formed to dispossess indigenous farmers of their reserves. Beers invested in both streams.

Two days before annexing Choctaw and Chickasaw territory in February 1830, the Mississippi General Assembly voted to "give impulse and vigour to agricultural labour, activity to commercial enterprise, and increased value to our lands"—in other words, to fund the transformation of its new acquisition—by chartering a bank and issuing $2 million in bonds to provide it with working capital. Beers partnered with several of the nation's leading financiers to purchase the entire issue and sold at least $388,000 of the Mississippi bonds in London.[24]

Likewise, in Alabama, the talk in the state capital was incessantly of "cotton, negroes, land and money." In three separate acts in November and December 1832, the Assembly issued $3.5 million in bonds on behalf of the Bank of the State of Alabama. In a letter to Beers, the governor, the state treasurer, and the bank president explained that "Indian titles to extensive tracts of land" had recently been extinguished and that agriculture and commerce would increase proportionally. The agent who was commissioned to sell the bonds appended his own commentary. With the addition of Creek and Choctaw country, he projected, cotton exports from Mobile would rise 20 percent each of the next five years and reach 135 million pounds by 1838 (an absurdly optimistic 27 percent of U.S. production). If the Cherokees were also expelled, he offered, cotton exports would rise to even greater heights.[25]

Alabama officials had their eyes on European investors as well as Wall Street bankers. In a letter to Baring Brothers of London, they appealed directly to the "monied men of your country." "Like all new states," they wrote, "monied men are scarce amongst us—and capital much in demand." In the end, J.D. Beers and Co. and its London partner Thomas Wilson and Co. purchased the entire offering, closing Alabama's first-ever multimillion-dollar bond sale and first-ever bond sale in Europe. One London stockbroker wrote enthusiastically of the investment opportunity to a financier who placed U.S. securities with private investors in Spain and Germany. In Britain, investors bought the bonds for 4 percent to 10 percent above par in 1833, in effect financing the transformation from indigenous farms to cotton plantations in Alabama.[26]

While financiers purchased Alabama and Mississippi bonds to profit generally from the transformation of native territory and the economic expansion that would follow, they invested in joint-stock companies with the more specific goal of speculating directly in indigenous lands. For J.D. Beers, the opportunity to invest arrived in a letter from David Hubbard, an Alabama planter, manufacturer, politician, and habitual schemer. Hubbard had a lead on 240 square miles of land to be purchased from Chickasaws for $1.56 per acre. "Our sections have been on the most valuable cotton lands in the U.S.," he boasted, predicting that the price would soon rise "with a rapidity unknown in the settlement of other new lands." All that was lacking was capital to close the deal. It will be "the best speculation ever offered you," he told Beers, tempting him with the possibility of realizing "enormous profits." Do not hesitate, he urged, since other speculators were already buying up the land, and wealthy planters from Georgia and South Carolina were "pouring in upon us" to obtain property. In March 1835, immediately after returning with his wife from their trip through the South, Beers joined with six other investors to form the New York and Mississippi Land Company.[27]

Beers's firm was one of several similar ventures established on Wall Street and State Street. The companies had utilitarian names that often described the origins of their financial capital and the target of their investment. Besides the New York and Mississippi Land Company, there was the Boston and Mississippi Cotton Land Company; the Boston and New York Chickasaw Land Company; the New York, Mississippi, and Arkansas Land Company; the American Land Company; the Chickasaw Land Company; the Apalachicola Land Company; and the Florida Peninsula Land Company. (The last two firms focused on Seminole lands in Florida.) The company boards were composed of distinguished bankers, creating a dense network of investors that touched most of New York's and Boston's financial institutions. The board of the Boston and Mississippi Cotton Land Company, to give one example, consisted of the presidents of the Fulton Bank, the Merchants' Bank, and the Mercantile Marine Insurance Company. Those same men also

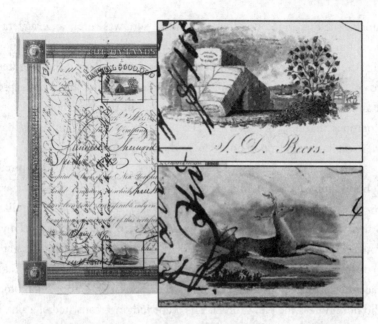

Stock certificate in the New York and Mississippi Land Company, showing two details. The certificate's artwork made the investment more palat-
able to northern financiers by depicting neither slaves nor native peoples.
Instead, the top illustration pictures a stack of cotton bales awaiting ship-
ment, while in the background, a horse turns a screw press, a device that
pressed cotton into bales. The bottom illustration shows a leaping stag.

held offices as directors of the Ocean Insurance Company, the Manu-
facturers' Insurance Company, the Tremont Fire and Marine Insurance
Company, and the Suffolk Bank.[28]

The land companies served as vehicles for pooling capital, the better
to squeeze out competition and efficiently separate the dispossessed from
their lands. Capitalized at $130,000, the New York and Mississippi Land
Company promptly increased its stock to $332,000 and then to $500,000.
The American Land Company and the Louisiana, Mississippi, Arkansas,
and Missouri Land Company were each capitalized at $1,000,000. Agents
of one firm reportedly traversed the South in search of subscribers to a

stock issue of $4,000,000. That gargantuan sum was surely an exaggera-
tion, but the reason given for the subscription was accurate: to monopo-
lize the country "at the Cost of the poor Aborigines." To put these figures
in context, as measured by capitalization, the New York and Mississippi
Land Company ranked in the top 10 percent of the four thousand corporations chartered between 1820 and 1836. The two land companies that
were capitalized at $1,000,000 were in the top 4 percent.[29]

In March 1835, the New York and Mississippi Land Company hired
John Bolton, a trusted financier, to relocate to Mississippi to oversee
its investments. After heading south and then completing a fatiguing
journey through rain and flooded swamps, Bolton finally arrived at Pontotoc, located in what is now northern Mississippi. Populated by get-
rich-quick speculators, attorneys, and merchants, the boomtown had
recently sprung up around a tavern in the Chickasaw Nation. Pontotoc
did not impress the New Yorker. His crude lodgings consisted of a small
log cabin with a wooden chimney, furnished with a box for a table and
a straw mattress for a bed. The corn bread, butter, milk, and bacon were
admittedly tasty, but the coffee, he complained, was "rather bitter." Plus,
as he wrote in June, the weather was "really <u>Hot</u>."[30]

The lands, however, were spectacular. Hubbard's wife, whom Bolton
had met in Alabama, promised "<u>immense profits</u>," and he could see why.
The country, he reported, would settle rapidly with "the rich Planter with
his gang of negroes down to those who depend on the labor of themselves and families." Soon, Bolton predicted, the area would outproduce
the best cotton lands elsewhere. Struck by the "deep rich black" soil,
he wrote that he had "never seen so large a body of superior land." The
hardwood trees, a sign of the region's fertility, were enormous, including ancient oaks with trunks five feet in diameter. Bolton not only called
for more capital to be invested in the operation; he also doubled his own
initial investment of $10,000.[31]

Though Creeks, Choctaws, and Chickasaws each farmed different physiographic regions—river valleys, upland hills, and open prairie

lands—they were unsurprisingly alike in preferring fertile lands that were also desirable to speculators and planters from the United States. In fact, there are striking long-term continuities in settlement patterns that span centuries and transcend cultures. One region stood out to the intruders, the Black Prairie, a stretch of dark, fertile soil that arced through the Creek, Choctaw, and Chickasaw nations. Bolton noticed that it was littered with oyster shells, and he found one large enough to hold nearly a quart of water, a fossilized remnant of the ancient Cretaceous and Paleo-

The richest agricultural lands in the South, the Black Prairie, passed through Creek, Choctaw, and Chickasaw lands.

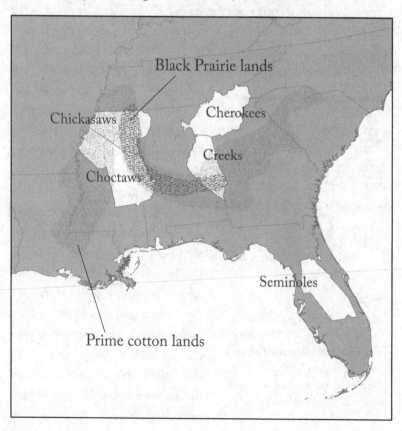

gene ocean that covered the region between 23 and 145 million years ago.[32] The soil's high calcium content would turn out to be a boon for planters, since cotton takes up the nutrient in especially large quantities.

It was not just geography that drew planters to the native South. They had spent the previous decades exhausting the lands in Georgia and the Carolinas, as they themselves acknowledged. They could now "exchange the cultivation of poor or worn out lands, for the fresh and fertile soil" in Mississippi. Native country, Hubbard assured Beers, was "sought for by the cotton planters from the worn out lands of Georgia and Carolina, with great avidity." When the time came to flip the lands, speculators made the same pitch. "It is confidently recommended to the growers of Cotton, to abandon their worn out lands," Eli Shorter advertised in the pages of the *Columbus Enquirer,* "and timely to secure themselves homes, before this last desirable scope of new country is taken up and settled."[33]

There is ample evidence that native peoples exhausted soils with the cultivation of corn, but three factors differentiated them from their neighbors in the United States. The first simply had to do with numbers. Because there were fewer indigenous Americans, they placed less pressure on the land. Second, most native farmers did not dedicate themselves to the intensive growing of cotton. Unlike peaches and apples, which native peoples eagerly cultivated, cotton belonged to a global market in which individuals strove to produce as much of the crop as possible, using slave labor as needed, to sell the harvest at the highest market price—all for the purpose of buying

"Important to Cotton Planters." This detail shows eighteen of the 385 tracts, amounting to over 192 square miles, that Eli Shorter advertised for sale in the *Columbus Enquirer* in April 1835. The rectangular survey system made it easy to identify and list the tracts.

more land and more slaves. The practice, needless to say, was not kind to the land or to the enslaved people. It was also risky. International price fluctuations could leave farmers holding a worthless crop that, no matter how bountiful, could not feed a family. Moreover, monocrop agriculture places families at the mercy of drought, pestilence, and natural disaster. Only extremely foolhardy or avaricious indigenous farmers would wager their fortunes on such a crop. Third, what were wastelands to planters in the United States were valuable resources to native farmers. Forests and prairies, edge zones between croplands and woods, and old fields provided habitat for game animals and hosted blackberries, mulberries, persimmons, and other useful plants. Natural harvests made up a significant portion of the annual diet in indigenous nations, as the Choctaw names for summer months reveal: *hash bihi* ("mulberry month"), *hash bissa* ("blackberry month"), and *hash kafi* ("sassafras month"). The Black Prairie lands produced wild strawberries in the summer and, after indigenous residents burned the grasses in the fall, brought forth a proliferation of mushrooms. (Unable to resist the strawberries, Bolton overindulged on one occasion and suffered from a "slight bilious affliction.")[34] Whereas indigenous farmers had preserved this varied landscape, planters from the United States set their slaves to work clearing, plowing, and sowing it with cottonseed.

The conversion of the Black Prairie to monocrop agriculture and the dispossession of its longtime residents did not trouble the speculators. "The dawn of civilization now beams on its horizon," toasted one gathering of bankers and politicians in Natchez, Mississippi. They were less optimistic about the fate of native peoples, though they suggested that everyone could be a winner in this best of all possible dispossessions. "If capable of civilization," they hedged, "how glorious the destiny which awaits our Indians in their new home." The prospect of profits overwhelmed all else. Land in the Chickasaw Nation, declared one enthusiast to an out-of-state investor, was "the best cotton Estate in the World." From his post in Pontotoc, John Bolton thrilled to the sight of a North Carolina planter passing by with 1,500 slaves bound for native territory. After selling their Carolina lands, the slave owner boasted, planters would soon arrive with 10,000 more unfree laborers.[35]

~~~

WHILE SPECULATORS and planters eagerly anticipated the sun rising over endless cotton fields worked by tens of thousands of slaves, native peoples delayed the arrival of this perverse vision of civilization. As the Choctaw poet observed, the business of speculation was unexpectedly "uphill." He mocked the slave-owning proselytizers of freedom who were dispossessing indigenous Americans. By being "dead slow to go," he wrote, "Indians" struck a "sad blow" to the "liberty" of colonizers. In fact, the Choctaws and Creeks, by the terms of their treaties, did not have to go at all. (The Chickasaws, by contrast, were required to sell their allotments.) Thousands of Choctaw and Creek farmers declared that they intended to remain in their eastern homelands and become state citizens. From the Creek Nation, Neha Micco offered one explanation for the decision of native peoples to stay in the South. Their "aged fathers and mothers" beseeched them "to remain upon the land that gave us birth, where the bones of their kindred are buried," he said, "so that when they die they may mingle their ashes together." "Our people yet abhor the idea of leaving all that is dear to them—the graves of their relations," confirmed Opothle Yoholo. One cynical Georgian scoffed at the sentiment. Creeks were represented as saying that "they would die among the tombs of their fathers, and that they would lay down at the corner fences, and manure the ground with their bodies," he wrote, skeptical that any of it was true.[36] But the attachment to place and to ancestors was genuine and widespread in indigenous communities.

There were also practical reasons why Choctaw and Creek families were willing to become state citizens in Mississippi and Alabama. For one, they were familiar with the land and knew when the fish ran, where the best soils were located, where to hunt, and which plants to utilize for medicine, food, fiber, and dye, knowledge that was essential to their survival. A partial list of botanical remains found in a single Creek town—diligently recovered by archaeologists—gives a sense of the wide variety of plants that native peoples used and depended on:

> maize
> manna grass
> goosefoot/chenopot (wild type)
> smartweed
> knotweed
> pokeweed
> purslane
> spurge
> false mallow
> honey locust pod
> maypops
> blackberry/raspberry
> sedge
> hickory nuts
> beech nuts[37]

Today, few Americans can distinguish the plants on this list, but in the early nineteenth century, native peoples knew them well and had multiple uses for each.

The risks posed by relinquishing the land and rendering useless the accumulated multigenerational expertise in its flora and fauna were enormous. One study has determined that, of the 739 culturally significant plants used by Cherokees—Virginia pine, sand hickory, Aztec tobacco, dwarf ginseng, American spikenard, hoary mountain mint, and so on—more than 30 percent were not found in Indian Territory. River cane, to take but one example, exists in far smaller quantities in

Oklahoma, where it reaches its westernmost extent, than it does in the Southeast. Native southerners used it widely for housing, fencing, forage, constructing animal and fish traps, grinding flour from the seeds, crafting furniture, weaving mats and baskets, fabricating musical instruments, building rafts, and treating various ailments. Before the arrival of European firearms, they also employed it to make weapons and armor. In the West, indigenous Americans would be forced to rebuild their lives without this all-important construction material.[38]

In addition to their well-founded fears of starving in the West (as would in fact come to pass), native peoples were concerned about the journey itself. A mortality rate of between 3 percent and 10 percent looked very different from the commissary general's office at 17th and G streets than it did from the town square of Ottissee, in the Creek Nation, where the 389 residents debated whether the uncertain prospects of a better life in the West outweighed the possibility that dozens of them would perish next month on the road. The risk of dying or watching a child or parent die during a weeks-long march through hostile U.S. settlements toward an unknown destination tempered their desire to escape their troubles in the South.

Finally, they considered the political and legal consequences of moving. Would their rights to the land become more secure if they moved, as the secretary of war and other government officials assured them? Indigenous leaders remained skeptical. "We never can get a country there with a title as strong as the one we have to this," observed the Choctaw Peter Pitchlynn. Creek leaders were equally dubious that their "white brethren" could "give assurances more distinct and positive" than those they had already received and trusted for the current lands. Did another form of contract exist, more powerful than a treaty, that would somehow give them an unbreakable title to their territory in the West? If so, they did not know what it was. John Ross made this point repeatedly, remarking that there was "no safety" in moving west.[39]

Attacking the competence of indigenous leaders turned out to be easier than undermining their sensible arguments. Native peoples, U.S. officials insisted, could not be trusted to reason through the situation. They were like "children" who had inherited a deadly mansion, wrote the superintendent of Indian Affairs Thomas McKenney in one labored analogy (composed before Jackson fired him). For their own good they had to be made to leave. As children, they needed "to be nursed, and counselled, and directed as such." Self-styled experts who pretended to "superior understanding and intelligence" on the subject, the *Cherokee Phoenix* derided, never tired of offering them paternalistic advice that was obviously colored by the federal government's ultimate goal: "to get rid of them, that others may seize and divide their property." Creek leaders reached the same conclusion. They "slowly and reluctantly" decided that the guidance offered by their "white friends" was "founded in mistake," they said diplomatically, that U.S. officials had underestimated the consequences of moving west and overestimated the costs of staying in place.[40]

Four years into the federal government's scheme to rid the region east of the Mississippi River of native people, the fantasy of willing migrants and orderly deportations could no longer be sustained. The promises of uplift and salvation that had cloaked the political debates in 1830 were now a distant memory, and even Isaac McCoy, who never ceased lobbying on behalf of his utopian colony in the West, had to admit that, as the decade progressed, people were "astonishingly indifferent to the subject of Indian reform." The expectation of U.S. officials that native peoples would voluntarily leave their homelands was giving way to frustration and anger, and they blamed their failures not on their own unrealistic and misinformed policies but on the victims, who, as one agent asserted, were "blind to their own interest."[41]

For native peoples, several years of U.S.-sponsored mass deportation had only confirmed their suspicions. Western lands were not as splendid as promised, the United States would not fulfill the various treaty articles compensating them for the enormous land cessions in the East, and the deportation operations were poorly organized and often lethal. Deportees who trudged through freezing swamps and survived cholera epidemics only to arrive in a country where malaria was endemic and the promised rations were badly spoiled made poor advocates for U.S. policy. Watching from afar, Cherokees were certain that the "government and government agents intended to fool and disappoint" them and that the United States desired to send them west to "do as they pleased" with them. "They are laughing at our calamities," Cherokees said. One Cherokee summarized the deal offered by U.S. agents enrolling people for deportation: "Let me give you money to allow me to kill you!"[42]

Into this standoff between frustrated War Department officials and determined and distrustful native families stepped Wall Street financiers. "INDIAN affairs!" exclaimed Joseph Baldwin, an Alabama lawyer, who recalled the 1830s with a mixture of disapproval and merriment. The "very mention is suggestive of the poetry of theft—the romance of a wild and weird larceny!" Indigenous Americans, he said, were swindled "by the nation," conducted to the Mississippi River, stripped "to the flap," and bid "God speed as they went howling into the Western wilderness." It was the decade of the "Rag Empire," of "credit without capital, and enterprise without honesty." Baldwin diagnosed "a sort of financial biology," in which people were mesmerized by speculative fever. "Let the public believe that a smutted rag is money, it is money," he wrote.[43]

Lured by the promise of "Virgin lands," cheap slave labor, and easy credit, U.S. citizens rushed into the Choctaw, Chickasaw, and Creek nations in such numbers that the roads disintegrated under the traffic. Native property bought for $1.25 per acre soon sold for $30 or $40 per acre. Prices "rose like smoke," leaving indigenous residents in the middle of the flames. "We have for the last six months lived in fire," said Neha Micco, shortly after speculators began moving into the Creek Nation.[44] The South's longtime residents soon found themselves engulfed in an expanding firestorm of fraud, deceit, and violence.

CHAPTER 8

"A COMBINATION OF
DESIGNING SPECULATORS"

~~~

NEW YORKERS considered J.D. Beers to be one of Manhattan's eminent residents, a "high-toned Episcopalian" and talented businessman who owned some of the city's most valuable real estate, including three properties on Union Square and a lot in midtown that would later become the site of Radio City Music Hall. He was, said a family member, "a consistent Christian in his walk and conversation." Likewise, in Columbus, Georgia, Eli Shorter, despite a somewhat checkered past, enjoyed a "distinguished" reputation as a local dignitary and member of the bar. A fellow lawyer called him "a man of a century."

In the Creek Nation, however, residents despised these two outsiders. Beers and Shorter were among the most rapacious of the "merciless horde" that haunted Opothle Yoholo's homeland. "The homes which have been rendered valuable by the labor of our hands," the Creek leader protested, "are torn from us by a combination of designing speculators," who were "so fierce" that no one could pass by them and so relentless in their pursuit of Creek lands that it was as if they were possessed by demons. "The helpless widow and orphan, the aged and infirm father," he continued, "are alike the victims of their cupidity." Opothle Yoholo drew his imagery from a passage in the Book of Mark that is often read as an anticolonial parable in which colonizers are akin to demons. In the Creek leader's retelling, the United States resembled imperial Rome and its occupying army the Roman legion. He was not alone in finding that the speculative fever of the late 1830s resembled a sort of diabolical possession, for some U.S. citizens attributed the overheated market to "mesmeric influence." The speculators were "ravenous," said one U.S. official, "carrying every thing before them" and "devouring the carcass."[2]

There was indeed something ghoulish about the speculators who rushed to possess native farms before the hearths had cooled and who preyed on starving families during their final desperate months in the South. They stole not only fields, houses, and corncribs but also, as Opothle Yoholo stated, the dead. "Beneath the soil which we inhabit," he said, "lie the pail remnants of what heretofore composed the bodies of our fathers and of our children our wives and our kindred." One elderly Creek man who had lost his land said with "great bitterness" that "he would stay and die here and then the whites might have his skull for a water cup." This was no dark fantasy, for a phrenologist had recently visited his village, dug up a number of corpses, and carried off the skulls. Several Choctaw, Creek, and Seminole crania ended up in Philadelphia in the collection of the renowned scientist Samuel George Morton, who used the skulls to argue that the "Caucasian race" was superior to all others. If the speculators were not possessed by demons, they were at least consumed by greed. The Chickasaw leader James Colbert had a word for them: "capitalists."[3]

The methods of dispossession employed by speculators differed from nation to nation but were all equally devastating. In the case of the Choctaws, the Treaty of Dancing Rabbit Creek described multiple classes of people entitled to reserves of land: Choctaws wishing to become Mississippi citizens; their children older than ten; their children younger than ten; the "Chiefs" of the Choctaw Nation; individuals who cultivated more than fifty acres; those who cultivated between thirty and fifty

acres, twenty and thirty acres, twelve and twenty acres, and two and
twelve acres; "certain individuals" (Colonel Robert Cole, John Pitchlynn, Ofehoma, and so on); captains; and, last and least, orphans. The
number of classes, though unwieldly, was apparently insufficient, and a
day after the two sides signed the treaty, they agreed to a supplement,
setting aside reserves for still more individuals. Astoundingly, despite its
detailed enumeration of classes, exceptions, and set-asides, the hastily
negotiated treaty did not clearly account for the land not allotted to individuals, the Choctaws' national domain, which amounted to ten million
acres and represented one third of the present-day state of Mississippi.
The General Land Office would undoubtedly auction this territory, but
what would be done with the proceeds? Subsequent treaties with the
Senecas, Shawnees, and Odawas in Ohio and the Chickasaws in Mississippi explicitly stated that native peoples would receive the funds, after
deducting for various expenses. The Treaty of Dancing Rabbit Creek,
the first to be concluded after the passage of the expulsion act, contained
no such stipulation. Not until 1886, fifty years after the fact, would the
Supreme Court rule that the proceeds from the land sales belonged to
the Choctaw Nation.[4]

The United States ignored most of the treaty's obligations, though
not the one that truly mattered to its citizens, the cession of Choctaw
lands and expulsion of the longtime residents. By the government's own
admission, 1,585 Choctaw families, entitled to between two and three
million acres, attempted to select reserves and become citizens of Mississippi, but thanks to the incompetence and ill will of the U.S. agent
William Ward, only 143 received land, accounting for just over 140,241
acres. Under the treaty's other categories, Choctaws who were entitled
to 578,960 acres received only 193,860 acres.[5]

Speculators swarmed into the region. No piece of property remained
beyond their grasp, not even the herds of cattle belonging to Choctaw
farmers. Speculators conspired to purchase the livestock for "almost
nothing," colluding with Ward, who left his son in charge of the opera-

tion. "His sun as hee informed me is a wild Boy," said one acquaintance, "but the Col says hee supposes hee will answer the purpose." When Choctaws received certificates of valuation for their animals, the intruders speculated in those too. Other schemers fought to possess the people themselves, part of a ploy to provide legal services to the dispossessed in exchange for their land. One such operation "collected the Indians" on multiple occasions to catalog the people "belonging" to it. When a dispute arose over who was "entitled" to which families, one schemer "agreed to settle for his thirty two and the others settled for theirs." Still other speculators purchased reserves directly from Choctaws for a $5 or $10 advance, promising to pay the balance, an additional $1,000 or $2,000, after the president approved the deeds, as required by treaty. By the time the Choctaws sought payment, however, speculators had bought and sold the deeds half a dozen times, and the original purchasers, indebted to the Choctaw owners, had long since disappeared.[6]

The greatest prize in this frenzy was the Choctaw national domain, an area the size of Massachusetts. Over the course of its first four decades, the Republic had devised a systematic and methodical procedure, overseen by the General Land Office, for auctioning public lands. Members of the federal government's small but aspiring bureaucracy, designated as "registers," oversaw the process from local agencies. Choctaw sales would take place in Mount Salus, Chocchuma, and Columbus, Mississippi, three insignificant crossroads that became hives of activity when the land offices were open for business. On auction day, the public crier announced the townships for sale, speculators shouted out their bids, and the winners reported to a window to file their applications. The register placed the paperwork in a box and, consulting a table of maps, placed an "S" on the corresponding tracts to signify that they had been sold. Later, the receiver accepted payment, wrote out receipts, and recorded the sum in a leather-bound volume.[7]

As with so much of the federal government's operation to expel native peoples, the practice was quite different from the stipulated procedure.

Applications disappeared, maps were marked in the wrong location, and sales and payment records did not correspond. Some of the errors resulted from incompetence or carelessness. The receiver at one office was usually drunk and incapacitated, while at another he was severely ill and unable to complete his paperwork. But many other errors were the product of deceit. "Fraudulent persons" gained access to the register's maps and marked lands as sold in order to purchase the tracts at a later date during "private entry" sales, when there were no competing bidders. To thwart this particular scheme, the register at Chocchuma constructed a "confined desk," but speculators continued to mark up the maps surreptitiously. Still other speculators bid on land, declined to complete the payment, and then, after the sale was forfeited, purchased the same tract at a lower price in private entry sales.[8]

The hordes of speculators devoured the majority of lands using a simpler, time-tested strategy. They colluded with one another. When the auctions opened in Mississippi in October 1833, Robert J. Walker, an ambitious lawyer and future U.S. senator, gathered speculators in a tavern a few yards from the land office and persuaded them to form the Chocchuma Land Company. Prices dropped by 30 percent the day after, the result of the lack of competing bids. Walker claimed that it was "a source of inexpressible gratification" to him that by artificially lowering prices he was protecting common white men, the sturdy farmers who had "moistened with their blood the soil of Mississippi" when defending the state against the "exulting savage." It was true, he admitted, that in the course of his altruistic activities, he had also acquired a "considerable body of land" for himself, but, he maintained, he had no interest in profits—an assertion belied by his lifelong pursuit of wealth. Other partners were more candid. One company member and congressman boasted that he had arrived in Chocchuma without a dollar and left with $40,000 to $50,000. The company as a whole purchased at least 376 square miles, a little under 1 percent of the state.[9]

Across the Choctaw Nation, families fended off the marauders as best as they could, but behind each lone intruder stood a vast array of state power, beginning with local sheriffs and ending with the U.S. Army and its commander in chief, the president of the United States. Many Choctaws farmed their land under the mistaken assumption that the Indian agent William Ward had done his job, recording their names and establishing their title as required by treaty. Instead, the General Land Office auctioned their land to white farmers and planters, who arrived whip in hand to claim the property. Mingo Homa's experience was not unusual. His community of two hundred people registered with Ward, but in 1833, U.S. agents ordered them to move west. "They said they would catch the children," Mingo Homa recalled, "tie their legs together like pigs, and haul them off in waggons, and drive the grown people after them." The families fled into the swamps, and a band of white men seized and imprisoned Mingo Homa. After he escaped, the Choctaws returned to their lands, only to be driven off a few years later.[10]

In 1837, in an effort to conciliate Choctaws and whitewash its own failures, the federal government would create the first of several commissions to investigate Ward's dereliction of duty and compensate the dispossessed with scrip, good for purchasing public lands in Alabama, Mississippi, Louisiana, and Arkansas. The scrip generated its own corrupt market. "By judicious management," wrote one speculator, "a large amount of it, may be had at from 25 to 50 cents in the dollar." Eventually, he surmised, the scrip could be converted into cash at 95 cents to the dollar. He would double or even triple his money.[11]

In the end, the scrip did little to make amends for the massive land theft. Nonetheless, federal commissioners interviewed hundreds of Choctaws and recorded numerous, harrowing stories of dispossession. The dispossessed, surrounded by a hostile, foreign population, faced two choices: seek refuge with other Choctaws on marginal lands in Mississippi or begin the dangerous journey west, perhaps penniless and alone. Immaka, a sixty-five-year-old woman, lived with her three grown children until a white man built a house near her and plowed a field right up to her front door. After he pried the boards off her house while she was living in it, she fled to "an old waste house" and survived on a small crop of corn. Oakalarcheehubbee, described as "an old grey headed man having but one eye," stayed at home until Hiram Walker drove him out with a whip. Walker then put his fifteen slaves to work on the land. Illenowah, fifty years old, was living with his wife and three children when a white man named McCarty built a house next to him and pushed him off. Okshowenah, said to be "an old and infirm" woman, was a widow at the time of the treaty. All but one of her children had moved west, but she remained in the Choctaw Nation until a man plowed around her house and fenced her in. She fled, and in 1838 was preparing to move west. "I hardly expect she will get there," said one relative, who commented, "She is remarkably old."[12]

Dispossession could come at any moment. Elitubbee lived with his wife and eight children in the Choctaw Nation until 1835, when he returned from hunting to find that a white woman had moved into his house with her two children and plowed his land. Likewise, Abotaya, out hunting with his wife and mother-in-law, came home to find a man named Gibson in his house. So too Shokaio, an elderly widow. While she was hunting with her son, a white man dismantled her house and used the wood to make a stable and corncrib. Chepaka also returned home, in this instance from a visit to his father, and discovered that John Pyus had turned his residence into a stable. The invaders showed no mercy. Hiyocachee, ill and dying, moved nearby to be under the care of friends and family. Meanwhile, a white man took his land, dispossessing his soon-to-be widow. Ahlahubbee was visiting relatives when a white man moved into his house, leaving his "deeply distressed" family members with nothing more than the clothes on their backs. They built a house nearby but were turned out of that too. Ahlahubbee seemed "fit to cry," said one witness.[13]

After riding past Peter Pitchlynn's old stomp ground in Mississippi in August 1834, one of Pitchlynn's relatives was thrown into "deep reflection." The land was "as natural as ever," he wrote, but the stomp ground, once a ceremonial and social center that was full of song and dance, was now deserted. "I see no pleasing countenance of a Choctaw or any to be seen only now and then here and yonder in places," he observed. The patchwork of native farms had been replaced by cotton plantations, the Choctaw people by white planters and their slaves. "There is a great alteration in this part of the world since you left," Pitchlynn learned from a different correspondent. "Was you back here you wou'd be a stranger in your native land."[14]

~~~

IN THE Chickasaw Nation, where native residents did not have the option of remaining in Mississippi, speculators had two ways to purchase lands. They could buy directly from Chickasaws, who each received a temporary allotment of anywhere from one to four sections, depending on the size of the family (a section equaled one square mile). Or they could bid on "the residue of the Chickasaw country"—the lands not allotted—at one of the General Land Office auctions. The government agreed that it would invest the proceeds of the auctions on behalf of the Chickasaw Nation, after deducting the expenses for surveying and selling the lands and deporting the inhabitants.[15]

In the case of allotted lands, as James Colbert observed, speculators used "every stratagem" they could devise to prey on the Chickasaws' "ignorance," but their success depended less on ingenuity than on ruthlessness. In more than one way, the exchange of money for lands was skewed to favor investors. The impending expulsion obligated Chickasaws to sell quickly, within a few months' time, and many did not fully understand the details of the treaty that controlled the sales. Most could not read the contracts they signed or comprehend legal jargon written in English. Moreover, they had no recourse when speculators disregarded laws, since the U.S. agent to the Chickasaws, Benjamin Reynolds, was happy to overlook the violations for a price. Colbert explained that the speculators paid "no more attention to the treaty than if it was a blank piece of paper." In league with opportunistic "half breeds" (as Colbert said), speculators demanded that Chickasaws sell on the spot by signing a blank deed in exchange for a $5 or $10 advance. Reynolds, who had established a mutually profitable relationship with the land companies, often compelled native farmers to sell if they seemed hesitant. Either he deemed them incompetent and then disposed of their allotments for a fractional price, or he pronounced them to be "cholera cases," shutting them out of sales altogether and making them "sweat," until they agreed to a cut-rate price. Reynolds, said one critic, was "very <u>poor</u>"

Contract between a Chickasaw woman named Fickhiyea and Thomas Niles, who speculated widely in native land. Fickhiyea sold 640 acres of Black Prairie land at the minimum price of $1.25 per acre, for a total of $800. This particular contract was never confirmed by the president.

when appointed U.S. agent and "immensely rich" when he left office. The proceeds of collusion can be measured in slaves. Reynolds owned two people in 1830 and twenty-one a decade later.[16]

By the calculations of the federal government, individual Chickasaws sold 3,546 square miles for a total of $3.8 million, an average price of $1.73 per acre, but the official accounting assumes that farmers received full payment rather than only the initial advance of $5 or $10. Moreover, the transactions usually involved paper money, whose exchange value fluctuated widely according to the health of the issuing bank and the national economy. (Until the United States moved to a single national currency in the 1860s, most business was conducted in regional banknotes.) When U.S. financial markets crashed in 1837, Chickasaws were left holding paper that was close to worthless. "They are incessant in their demands for specie," complained Beers's partner David Hubbard from Pontotoc. It was "so annoying to me," he continued, "that I shall leave here shortly untill these poor creatures are moving west."[17]

Apart from the individual sales, the General Land Office began auctioning 6,745 square miles of "residue" Chickasaw land in 1836. In Pon-

---

One of the depreciated bills from a bank capitalized by J.D. Beers, who sold the related state bonds in London. The bill's artwork, featuring a stereotypical and insulting image of an Indian, encapsulates the relationship between dispossession, cupidity, and white supremacy.

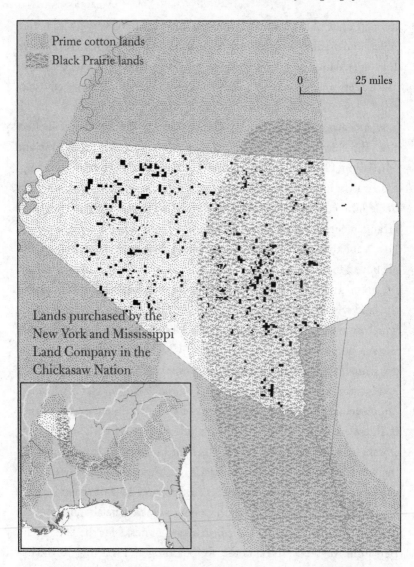

Prime cotton lands
Black Prairie lands

0   25 miles

Lands purchased by the
New York and Mississippi
Land Company in the
Chickasaw Nation

The New York and Mississippi Land Company purchased 600
square miles of prime cotton lands in the Chickasaw Nation.

totoc, the site of the auctions, strangers crowded into every house within miles, and planters fought to purchase sections from the land companies. It is "speculation run mad," said one amazed participant. Since Chickasaw leaders were aware that buyers had colluded at the Choctaw land auctions, they insisted on a treaty article requiring the president to "use his best endeavours to prevent such combinations." The article was ineffective. The New York and Mississippi Land Company and the Boston and Mississippi Cotton Land Company had "a mutual good understanding" that was, said Richard Bolton, "essential to the interests of both." His uncle John counseled "caution and silence" so as not to reveal the illegal arrangement, but no one was fooled. One disgusted observer described how "capitalists and companies" combined to create a monopsony (a single buyer) to force deportees to sell their lands well below market value.[18]

In the Treasury Department, an army of accountants dutifully tallied the land sales and just as dutifully deducted the expenses of deportation, which amounted to an astounding $1.2 million, or fully thirty percent of the $4,000,000 that was credited to the Chickasaw Nation. The federal government billed the Chickasaws for the census ($725), the certifying and locating of reservations ($25,735), and the dozens of clerks who were "employed in the various departments of the government on Chickasaw business" ($35,717). It billed them for 59½ pounds of nails for building storehouses on July 8, 1837; for Lieutenant G. Morris's expenses traveling from Washington City to Fort Coffee, Arkansas, in May 1837; for camping equipment for U.S. officers engaged in Chickasaw deportation; for dressing the wounds of a Chickasaw named Uneichubby; and for postage. It billed them for the construction of desks for the U.S. agent, Benjamin Reynolds, in Pontotoc; for boarding and washing Reynolds's horses and those of his servant; and for every newspaper advertisement announcing the sale of Chickasaw lands.[19]

But that was not all. The federal government billed them for quills, stationery, twelve thousand slips of parchment for the General Land Office, a bookcase, the printing of regulations and blank forms, the construction of a pigeonhole case for the second auditor's office, and the building of a mahogany bookcase for the office of the secretary of the Treasury. Since someone had to meticulously record and sum up all of these expenses, clerks from the treasurer's office, first comptroller's office, second comptroller's office, General Land Office, Indian Office, register's office, and second auditor's office also billed the Chickasaws for their "services" and "extra services."[20]

In addition, bookkeepers added itemized surveying costs to the ledger of expenses. The General Land Office billed Chickasaws right down to the chain and link (66 feet and 66 hundredths of a foot, respectively), with the price ranging from $3.50 to $5.00 per mile walked. Three examples of the more than one hundred surveying invoices will suffice to illustrate the government's commitment to passing on the expenses of deportation to the victims:

SURVEYOR	MILES	CHAINS	LINKS	COST
Abraham F. Rees	318	78	16	$1,275.91
Olsimus Kindrick	326	71	35	$1,307.56
Volney Peel	240	66	22	$842.89

Between 1833 and 1841, the General Land Office charged the Chickasaw Nation a total of $114,324.[21]

For all of the scrupulous attention to accounting, the Chickasaw Nation later identified over $600,000 of suspicious or fraudulent charges—a massive sum that in today's dollars would employ an army of nearly 8,000 laborers for a full year. The charges ranged from the negligible, an unwarranted $2.75 for stationery, to the indefensible. John Bell, the president of the Agricultural Bank of Mississippi, for example, received $20,000 of Chickasaw funds for reasons unknown. Simeon Buckner, a steamboat owner, received $77,401 for transporting

5,338 people, when in fact no more than 1,500 traveled by water. Perhaps most egregious was the expense to feed 2,464 more people than were deported. The Chickasaws suspected that the federal government had continued billing them for rations even after the supposed recipients had died, including the 800 individuals carried off by smallpox soon after arriving in the West.[22]

The Chickasaw funds that were not embezzled or drained away by armies of clerks were subjected to a separate assault. Soon after Chicka-saw leaders had signed the Treaty of Pontotoc of 1832, they objected vociferously to the article that placed national funds in trust with the United States. "We wanted this money in our own power," they insisted. "The investment of any part of the proceeds of the reserved lands," they declared, "was and now is object to." Levi Colbert condemned the U.S. agent's paternalism: "he says my nation got no sense, I tell him, if my people make a bad bargan it will be our loss, not the government, he says he knows best for us."[23] Colbert was right to be wary. For the federal government, what was best for deported families turned out to be secondary to what was best for bankers.

Using the trust fund that accumulated from land sales, the secretary of the Treasury purchased over $2.5 million in state bonds, including $1.3 million in Alabama bonds alone. In another era, the investments would have been conservative and unobjectionable, but in the late 1830s, the market was flooded with state bonds that were rapidly depreciating. The purchases seem to have been timed to prop up ailing financiers and ill-conceived state-sponsored projects. Alabama bank president B.M. Lowe wrote to the secretary of the Treasury, "I beg to add that you would greatly oblige the Institution I represent, as well as the community where it is located by taking the $250,000 now." The secretary obliged by purchasing the bank's bonds. In similar straits, J.D. Beers expressed his desire to the commissioner of Indian Affairs that the Treasury immediately purchase the Alabama bonds he had underwritten. "Under the circumstances I should esteem it a favor." A few weeks later, he described

A copy of an Alabama bond sold to the Chickasaw Nation. Holders detached and returned the coupons on the lower half of the sheet to collect the interest. The penciled note states, "105 per 100," or 5% above par.

"this pressing time for cash" and outlined for the secretary of the Treasury a plan to infuse New York (and his own bank) with "a large sum" of specie, if Wall Street financiers "should get a share of government business." The Treasury obliged by purchasing $65,000 in bonds from him at a 4.5 percent premium, though they were selling at a 5 percent discount in London. Likewise, Robert J. Ward, director of the Bank of Kentucky, used his personal connections to Andrew Jackson's advisor Francis Preston Blair to secure funding for his struggling financial institution. He was "anxious" to sell $350,000 in municipal bonds "for the benefit of the Chickasaw Indians," he explained to his fellow Kentuckian. "You will confer a great favor on your native state by making the arrangement," he appealed.[24] The Treasury Department purchased $150,000 in Kentucky bonds.

Other politically connected favorites benefited through a special arrangement between the Alabama state bank in Decatur and the Treasury Department. Hard money was scarce in the South, especially after Andrew Jackson's specie circular of July 1836 required that all public lands (including native lands) be purchased with gold or silver. The Decatur branch saw an opportunity when the Treasury Department bought $500,000 of Alabama state bonds using the Chickasaw national fund and deposited the specie in Decatur. At the request of the bank president, the secretary of the Treasury permitted speculators to borrow specie certificates representing the Chickasaw gold and use the paper to purchase Chickasaw land at the public auctions in Pontotoc, about 140 miles to the west. The General Land Office then redeposited the certificates in the Decatur bank, where speculators borrowed again from the replenished pot to purchase still more land. In theory, the scheme might have benefited deportees—more buyers meant more bidding and higher prices for their land—but in practice, it served mostly to give a "decided advantage" to a subset of speculators, as one rival complained. The major investors colluded with each other and by "force of capital" eliminated stray competition, permitting the purchase of the best lands, worth $10 or $20 per acre, for close to the minimum price of $1.25 per acre. "There has never been a sale in the United States perhaps," one speculator celebrated, "when those who had money, have done better with it."[25]

The details of this fleecing, complicated as they are, ought not to distract from the bitter irony that lay behind the Treasury secretary's mahogany desk, the second auditor's pigeonhole case, and the Chickasaw specie in the vaults of the Decatur bank. The United States made Chickasaws finance their own dispossession and pay for their own deportation.

~~~

NOWHERE DID the speculators destroy as many families as in the Creek Nation. "On one side," observed a federal officer, there was "wealth" and "active capital"; on the other, he continued, there was "squalid poverty and deep distress." The first wave of invaders staked claims, even if illegal for the moment, to valuable cotton land in eastern Alabama. They built houses, constructed mills, cut down timber, and plowed fields. Nathaniel Greyer seized twenty-four acres from "an old helpless Indian woman." A Mr. Logan avoided the hard work of farming, even on someone else's already-cleared land, and instead dedicated himself to stealing Creek horses and cattle. Ignoring the native residents, occupiers trespassed on long-established farms, plowing fields and raising fences. "In many instances," reported Neha Micco and Tuskeneahhaw, "we are entirely fenced up."[26]

The second wave of invaders consisted of speculators, eager to purchase Creek reserves for a fraction of the market value. Sometimes they enlisted the help of local sheriffs, who seized Creeks and imprisoned and tortured them, until they surrendered their land for a pittance. On other occasions, they torched Creek houses, driving off the residents with firebrands. A federal marshal who tried to intervene was nearly blown up in a booby-trapped house. Speculators especially were drawn to dying or dead individuals, since it was relatively easy to seize control of their reserves, sometimes by coaxing young orphans to sign an "indenture," written in legalese, that conveyed their rights to the land. The indenture was accompanied by an oath, in which subscribing witnesses—"highly respectable citizens"—swore that the orphaned children, "by making their marks," were acting voluntarily. This bit of theater left the survivors to starve. Creeks, Opothle Yoholo complained, were "helpless sheep among devouring wolves."[27]

As for the living, speculators devised one particularly effective ploy. It hinged on the fact that many certifying agents were corrupt and had a direct interest in the transactions that they were charged with validating. At little cost, a shrewd speculator could hire a dishonest and desperate Creek to impersonate a neighbor before the certifying agent. "In this way," explained Opothle Yoholo, "a few hundred dollars and four or five Indians could sell all the land in the Creek purchase." Eli Shorter, accused of running such a scheme, claimed that it was difficult to differentiate Creek names. Even the most honest of men, he insisted, "can scarcely avoid, in some instances, getting hold of the wrong Indians," though elsewhere he reportedly admitted that "it made no difference with him whether he had the right Indian or not." When Creek farmers protested that their land had been sold by imposters, judges told them to bring "white proof," since courts did not permit "colored persons" to testify against whites.[28]

Sometimes speculators did not bother to employ impersonators and instead hunted down the legitimate Creek landowners as if they were "malefactors or wild beasts," harassing them until they signed away their homes. One speculator pursued Irfulgar all the way to the Cherokee Nation, where he finally coerced the tired and despairing refugee to sell his property for a quarter of the value. Takhigehielo lost her land closer to home, after a seemingly friendly neighbor invited her to share his fresh peaches. Then, in exchange for three handkerchiefs and some flour, he made her mark a piece of paper. It was of course a deed, though she "knew nothing of the object of it." Another woman was cheated of her land with the assistance of her nephew, who received five "little pieces" of "the meanest kind of calico" for his efforts. A third woman, named Suhly, sold her land only after speculators threatened to kill her. She signed a deed and walked away in tears.[29]

As the "harvest" came to an end, wrote one speculator, they "rogued it and whored it among the Indians" in a final frenzy to consume the remains of the nation. The federal government, concerned that fraudulent contracts would lead to lengthy legal battles and delay the deportation of Creek families, threatened to halt the certification process. Facing the termination of sales, Shorter urged his partners onward. "Give up the beautiful Miss Jenny for the present" and "lay aside" poetry, he chided one associate. "Swear off from the society of ladies for one month," he scolded another. The "great struggle," he declared, "should be for the *most valuable* lands." "Every man," he exhorted, "should now be at his post." Shorter and his partners gathered the desperate Creeks in camps on the side of the road, drilled them in the procedure of deceiving the certifying agent, and promised to pay them $10 for every contract. No matter if these sellers were not the true holders of the land: "*Stealing* is the order of the day." "Hurrah boys!" Shorter's partner exclaimed. "Let's steal all we can."[30]

In April 1835, Andrew Jackson suspended the certification of sales, and the speculators turned their attention from Creek lands to the Creek people themselves. Devising yet another scheme to take advantage of the dispossession of the South's indigenous residents, they lobbied the federal government to privatize deportation. They relished the idea of profiting from both Creek lands and the deportation itself, and the ever-parsimonious commissary general George Gibson desired to save money. In September 1835, the federal government awarded a no-bid contract to John W.A. Sanford and Company to feed, transport, and provide medical care to the deportees. "We can make a hansame amount to compensate us for our time" and "trouble," John Sanford, a Georgia businessman and politician, explained to Gibson. The contract, he assured, "is much less than the government has ever be able to emigrate these people for." Promising to square the circle by making deportation both cheap and trouble-free, Sanford insisted that he could complete the operation "with full justice to both the Government, and the Indians."[31]

Creeks were furious. The company's partners were the very people who had stolen their lands. They "would die," they said, before agreeing to place themselves under the control of men who "would abuse them." In a letter to President Jackson, Opothle Yoholo denounced the "company of speculating contractors." But both George Gibson and Lewis Cass defended the privatization. "The more capital and force," Gibson ventured, "the greater will be the efficiency of the company in the removal of the Creek Indians." Cass lectured Creeks that outsourcing would be "more economical" for the United States. With dubious logic, he insisted that it "is therefore better for the government and cannot be worse for you."[32]

Between December 1835 and February 1836, John W.A. Sanford and Company transported approximately five hundred Creeks west. With the future of the contract resting on this trial run, the outfit made every effort to ensure a smooth operation. As luck would have it, decent weather and good health ensured that only two people died during the journey. But because other Creeks were unwilling to place themselves under the control of speculators, the company's ambitious plans remained unrealized.[33]

In Alabama, Creeks survived by eating bark off trees and consuming rotten animal carcasses. "There was no garbage that they would not greedily devour," wrote one witness. He commented that starving families, so desperate as to consider eating their own dead, felt forced to take "from those who have to spare," the well-fed residents of surrounding U.S. settlements. The most wretched of the dispossessed—hungry, homeless, and drunk—could be seen staggering about, with bloodshot eyes and "clotted and bloody garments." "I talk to them but they have nothing to Eat," said Opothle Yoholo. "What can I do," he protested; "they must Eat, they cannot live on air."[34]

Armed white men patrolled the area surrounding Columbus, allegedly to defend the town from bands of starving Creeks, who were, in Eli Shorter's words, "insolent, arbitrary, and warlike." But more than one person believed that the patrols were a "contemptible" farce, as one federal official charged, designed by speculators to drive off the desperate families living across the Chattahoochee River.[35] The conflict between starving refugees and avaricious colonizers would soon come to a head.

~~~

THE FANTASY of an expulsion that was both a blessing to the victims and a source of profit to U.S. citizens, that was at once altruistic and self-serving, did not die easily. Despite four years of disappointment, Commissary General George Gibson could still dream in 1835 of creating a system of transportation that extended to the western margins of the United States and that made every detail of the operation "perfectly intelligible" to his subordinates working at 17th and G streets. Gibson's dogged optimism, shared with many of his clerks, reflected an unquestioned confidence in the superiority of the United States over the uncivilized and inferior peoples within its borders. If Native Americans often seemed "uncertain in their movements, slow & vacillating," then his hardworking office staff simply needed to redouble its efforts. Given their upbringing, training, and general loyalty to President Jackson, few were ready to concede as yet that Native Americans had their own desires and goals.[36]

Joseph W. Harris remained among George Gibson's most dedicated and tireless of field officers, even after presiding over a calamitous deportation that would have demoralized most sensible people. In March 1834, the young West Point graduate had set out down the Tennessee River, escorting 457 Cherokee women, men, and children who had decided to escape the increasingly dangerous conditions in their homeland. They floated down the river on flatboats for nine days. At Waterloo, Ala-

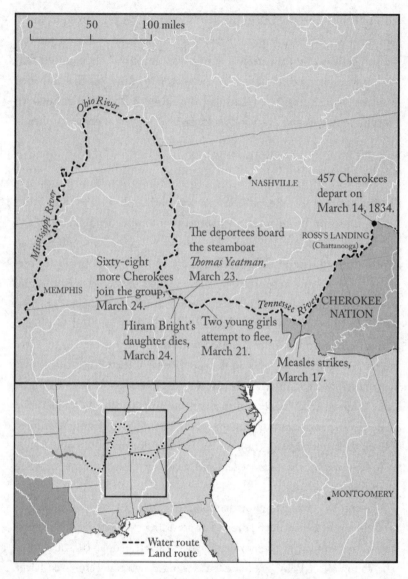

0   50   100 miles

Ohio River

Mississippi River

NASHVILLE

457 Cherokees
depart on
March 14, 1834.

ROSS'S LANDING
(Chattanooga)

The deportees board
the steamboat
Thomas Yeatman,
March 23.

Sixty-eight
more Cherokees
join the group,
March 24.

MEMPHIS

Tennessee River   CHEROKEE
NATION

Hiram Bright's
daughter dies,
March 24.

Two young girls
attempt to flee,
March 21.

Measles strikes,
March 17.

MONTGOMERY

- - - - Water route
———— Land route

March 14 to March 31, 1834. The first two weeks of the journey west for Joseph Harris's detachment of Cherokee refugees.

bama, in the northeastern corner of the state, they boarded the steamboat *Thomas Yeatman*, joining sixty-eight other deportees who had been stranded at the river port. Since the *Yeatman* could accommodate only 180 people in comfort, the captain lashed two of the flatboats to the steamer. This unwieldy vessel, akin to a floating refugee camp, transported its passengers to the Ohio River, where it added a keelboat. It then proceeded down the Mississippi to the mouth of the White River in southeast Arkansas. There, on March 31, the detachment encountered two hundred Cherokees who were transporting themselves west at their own expense. The refugees in this second group were ailing, and Harris agreed to take twelve or thirteen of the sickest aboard the *Yeatman*. They were perhaps the source of the contagion that soon began to destroy the officer's charges.[37]

At first, the deaths mounted gradually from a variety of causes, as Harris reported in his journal:

> APRIL 5: "buried here the girl child of Oasconish a Cherokee"
> APRIL 6: "Stephen Spaniard's girl child died this morning of measles"
> APRIL 7: "Bear Paw's boy child died this morning of dysentery"
> APRIL 9: "Henson's child died today of the worms"
> APRIL 10: "Richardson's child died this morning."[38]

It was impossible to preserve "a proper police amongst these people," Harris complained, and the *Yeatman* had therefore "become impregnated with a foul atmosphere." On April 11, the detachment reached Cadron Creek, about fifty-five miles above Little Rock, and began setting up camp in preparation for the two-hundred-mile march west to Fort Gibson, in what is now eastern Oklahoma. The next day, Thigh Hare was seized with "violent spasms of cramps & watery discharges," obvious symptoms of cholera. He died that night.[39]

The makeshift camp quickly became contaminated with *V. cholerae*.

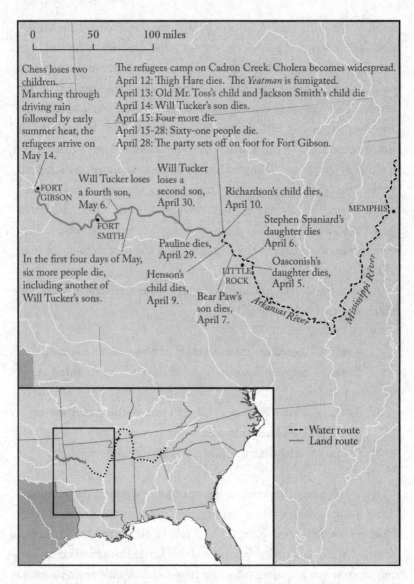

0   50   100 miles

Chess loses two children.
Marching through driving rain followed by early summer heat, the refugees arrive on May 14.

The refugees camp on Cadron Creek. Cholera becomes widespread.
April 12: Thigh Hare dies. The *Yeatman* is fumigated.
April 13: Old Mr. Toss's child and Jackson Smith's child die
April 14: Will Tucker's son dies.
April 15: Four more die.
April 15–28: Sixty-one people die.
April 28: The party sets off on foot for Fort Gibson.

FORT GIBSON

Will Tucker loses a fourth son, May 6.

Will Tucker loses a second son, April 30.

Richardson's child dies, April 10.

MEMPHIS

FORT SMITH

Stephen Spaniard's daughter dies April 6.

In the first four days of May, six more people die, including another of Will Tucker's sons.

Pauline dies, April 29.

Henson's child dies, April 9.

LITTLE ROCK

Oasconish's daughter dies, April 5.

Bear Paw's son dies, April 7.

Arkansas River

Mississippi River

- - - Water route
—— Land route

April 1 to May 14, 1834. The final six weeks of the journey west for Joseph Harris's detachment of Cherokee refugees.

Five or six people died almost without warning, and children began to succumb daily. The microbe wiped out entire families. In the space of two days, Black Fox lost his wife and three children. Will Tucker lost four sons. Over one three-day period that began on April 17, twenty-three people died. Harris desperately sent for medicine and tried to hire wagons, but his efforts failed since no teamsters dared to approach the diseased camp. A local doctor who risked tending to the sick caught the microbe himself and died after a brief but agonizing sickness. "His was one of the most painful deaths I have witnessed," wrote Harris.[40]

On April 28, Harris ordered the refugees to break camp and set off on foot on the seventeen-day journey to Fort Gibson. By the time they reached their destination, two full months after departing their eastern homeland, eighty-one of Harris's charges, or about one out of every six people, had died, including at least forty-five children who were under ten years old. At Fort Gibson, Harris filled out paperwork for the War Department and then returned east "by easy journeys." "From my Experience," the officer wrote with characteristic reserve, "I would say that humanity forbade the further transportation of the Cherokees by water."[41]

Somehow Harris was not discouraged, and he turned his attention to the expulsion of the Seminoles from Florida. This next deportation, if modeled after the "plan of operations" that he drafted in 1835, would be more efficient. "These papers have been drawn up by me in consequence of my belief in the necessity of a speedy adoption of some systematic plan," he explained. He excused the length of the thirty-one-page document, declaring that he wished to describe "the very minutiae" of the operation.[42] Like so much of the paperwork that had preceded it, Harris's plan had the virtue of being precise and methodical, with the single defect that it was divorced from reality.

Harris's "plan of operations" to force several thousand Seminole people from their homes and ship them to the farthest reaches of the United States envisioned a system that ran like clockwork. On a fixed day, the refugees, directed to be "prompt and <u>punctual</u>," were to collect themselves in camps at Tampa Bay, where they would be divided into companies of five hundred and carefully enumerated, recording the age, color, and sex of each person. "Too much accuracy cannot be observed with regard to the Muster Rolls," Harris instructed. From Tampa Bay, the first division of refugees would be placed on transports and ferried west along the Gulf Coast to Balize, a port at the mouth of the Mississippi River. Once there, they would not set foot on land. Instead, steamboats would pull alongside to collect each company, allowing six square feet of deck space per person. Heading up the Mississippi and then ascending the White River, the steamboats would "travel industriously & without stoppage." As a measure of protection against the spread of cholera and other deadly diseases, the vessels would be "thoroughly policed" and fumigated daily with chloride and lime. After this orderly trip upriver, the refugees would debark in central Arkansas to begin a 250-mile march overland to their final destination on the western border of the United States. Sentinels would rigorously patrol each camp, especially monitoring use of the pit latrine. "The Indians," wrote Harris, "should be required to use it, and <u>it only</u>." In the morning, the refugees were expected to break camp punctually. With such exacting precision, it was a "mere matter of calculation" that the first division of Seminoles would arrive at its destination the night of March 4—assuming, of course, that the weather did not interfere, the refugees cooperated, the companies remained in perfect health, food supplies arrived as scheduled, steamboats were supplied with adequate water and wood and had no mechanical problems, and rivers remained high and clear of snags. Meanwhile, the transports would return to Tampa Bay to receive the second division, exactly on February 3, and the model operation would repeat itself.[43]

Harris especially recommended constant and forceful supervision of the deportees. "The observance of an uniform system of police is all important," the former West Point cadet wrote in a section dedicated to the subject. The police were to exhibit "a general good will and a manly regard for the welfare of their charge," without "descending to vulgar familiarity." The "laws" necessary to maintain sanitation, keep the peace, and issue rations were to be clearly explained to the dispossessed, who were to be made to understand the "propriety & certainty of their execution."[44]

Well-meaning and thoughtful within its narrow limitations, Harris's plan was among the last of the zealous and unworkable schemes to deport people devised by the commissary general's office. In November 1835, a few months after Harris laid out his finely wrought proposal, George Gibson admitted that "active operations of the year have not been productive of such results as might have been anticipated." A party of Odawas from Maumee, Ohio, at the west end of Lake Erie, had positively refused to relocate, after learning that the lands west of the Mississippi were "hard and flinty" and the region "sickly." The Seminoles still would not agree to move, despite a large and intimidating military presence in their homelands, and the Creeks had departed in "a very insignificant body." As for the Cherokees, only a few families had journeyed west as yet. No matter how "strenuous" Gibson's efforts, native peoples were not cooperating.[45]

Six years had passed since the "Act to provide for an exchange of lands with the Indians." Over sixty thousand people remained to be deported from the East. Speculators, planters, and politicians were increasingly impatient. Lobbyists stalked the halls of Congress, offering a share of the profits if their speculations in indigenous lands remained secure.[46] And planter-politicians eagerly anticipated the slave empire they would build after expelling native residents. Altruism would have to yield place to swiftness and self-interest. The act of expulsion would soon devolve into a war of extermination.

FROM EXPULSION
to
EXTERMINATION

~~~

CHAPTER 9

1836: THE SOUTHERN
WORLD AT WAR

~~~

THE HUNTERS initially thought their dogs had picked up the track of a fugitive slave. The U.S. population in Tallahassee and the surrounding area had nearly doubled in the 1830s, and by the end of the decade, there were over seven thousand unfree people in the county, owned by approximately three hundred thirty families. These households obliged their unpaid workforce to labor in cotton fields. In addition, local masters sometimes rented out the enslaved to work for the Tallahassee Railroad Company, which transported bales of cotton on horse-drawn carriages over unstable rails to St. Marks, the closest port lying thirty miles away. It was not uncommon for slaves to run away. As the hunters closed in, however, they discovered that the fugitive was in fact Native American—and therefore not worth sparing. They raised their rifles, took aim, and shot. As they approached the wounded man, his identity became clearer. He was about nineteen years old and appeared to be a Creek villager, who must have fled across south Georgia in a desperate attempt to find refuge in the Florida Panhandle. One hunter drew a knife, pulled the man's hair taut, and cut off his scalp.[1]

The descent into this abyss of violence was swift, with the steepest slide occurring in 1836, during the final year of Andrew Jackson's presidency. Increasingly, leaders twisted the benevolent, if hypocritical, rhetoric of the first half of the decade to justify the exterminatory violence of the second. There was of course ample precedent, both recent and long past, for waging war against the continent's native inhabitants, and on some occasions colonists had seemed intent on eliminating native peoples entirely.[2] Since 1810, in the space of only twenty-five years, the United States had launched the War of 1812 (fought in part against Tecumseh's alliance), the First U.S.-Creek War of 1813–14, the First U.S.-Seminole War of 1817–18, and the U.S.-Sauk War of 1832. And yet, despite the deep-seated racism and long history of conflict with native peoples, at no time before the mid-1830s did the United States devise a policy and wage a multifront war to eliminate native peoples east of the Mississippi.

The difference between deportation and extermination was never as clear as U.S. officials liked to believe. The putative benevolent goal of moving indigenous Americans to the nation's outermost margins became the excuse to expel them by force of arms or to kill them. In 1830, many "distinguished individuals," as Congressman Wilson Lumpkin of Georgia had observed, shared the belief that expulsion was the only hope of saving native peoples from "ruin and extermination." Three years later, in 1833, now-Governor Lumpkin reasserted the likelihood of "speedy extermination" if indigenous Americans remained in their homelands. Five years after that, Lumpkin, sitting in the Senate in 1838, would suggest that his earlier predictions were coming true. He turned to the question of responsibility. Since native peoples refused to move, he stated, the "evil" that would inevitably result would be "chargeable" to them. The Georgia senator was speaking specifically about his Cherokee antagonist John Ross, in this instance.[3] But across the South in the second half of the decade, U.S. soldiers, state militia, and white vigilantes felt justified in killing indigenous Americans. In so doing, they were merely substantiating what Jacksonian experts had predicted all along: Native peoples who remained in the East would be exterminated.

As the pressure to depart mounted, native peoples despaired. "White folks" now appeared so relentless and inescapable, wrote a relative of Peter Pitchlynn's, that he compared the difficulties faced by native peoples to biblical plagues. Colonizers would breed "difficulties of every description in order to prevail in geting the indians to move out of the country." Considering how native peoples had been treated by the United States, he concluded, "I can never be convinced to believe that they can ever have land that they can say is theirs forever or own it as long as they exist as a nation."[4]

In Georgia, the plague besetting the Cherokees did not involve infestations of lice or rivers of blood. Instead, it centered around the winners of the land lotteries that had distributed Cherokee territory to the state's white population. In a memorial to Congress in May 1834, John Ross and four other Cherokee representatives laid the blame for the intruders squarely at Andrew Jackson's feet. The power of the presidency, they wrote, "has been exerted on the side of their oppressors, and is cooperating with them in the work of destruction." They gave two examples. First, Jackson insisted on distributing Cherokee annuities—the money that the United States owed to the Cherokee Nation for selling lands— to individual Cherokees rather than to the government of the Cherokee Nation. This duplicitous policy was designed "to reduce them to poverty and despair," they wrote, "and to extort from their wretchedness a concession of their guaranteed rights." Second, they charged, the United States was employing "unfit persons" who were laboring to make Cherokee lives "intolerably wretched."[5]

They had in mind Benjamin F. Currey, a patronage appointee from Jackson's home state of Tennessee, whose sole qualification for the position of Indian agent was his work as a minor political operative in Nashville. Appointed in 1831 when he was only thirty-one, Currey was ill-tempered, unprincipled, tactless, and zealous. He arrested Cherokees who worked against him, proposed employing secret agents (a suggestion wisely rejected by the secretary of war), bribed the principal attorney for the Cherokee Nation, and asked for U.S. troops and the power to declare martial law (also rejected). In early 1834, he organized a paramilitary band of mounted and armed men to round up Cherokees who had enrolled to move west. The band threatened to whip one man a hundred times if he did not reveal the locations of his children and to shoot another if he spoke with a friend. Women from one family fought back, and in the struggle a guard bit off one of their fingers. Ross described Currey with a single word: "demonical."[6]

Currey found a like-minded ally in John F. Schermerhorn, a native of Schenectady, New York, graduate of Andover Seminary, and minister in the Reformed Dutch Church. Schermerhorn had expressed the desire to become a "foreign missionary" and had even imagined being "cruelly martyred" in the service of carrying the Gospel "to the poor heathen"; but instead of risking that gruesome fate, he settled down with his wife in 1816 in the comfortable surroundings of a rural parish in the Bible-reading "burned over district" of upstate New York, twenty miles from his birthplace. The enterprising Schermerhorn was not content as a mere "country Clergyman," however. In 1813, he had met Jackson during a trip down the Ohio and Mississippi, and he used the connection to enter national politics. In 1824, he campaigned hard to elect Jackson during the general's failed bid for the presidency, reminding his would-be patron that "your old friend John F. Schermerhorn" would "never forget your kindness & attention" during their river journey. In 1826, Schermerhorn transitioned into church administration, participating in a bitter doctrinal debate, whose metaphorical assaults "in the dark" he compared to "Indian warfare." That was the closest he ever came to martyrdom.[7]

After Jackson's election in 1828, Schermerhorn began corresponding with the president and Secretary of War Lewis Cass in the hope of marrying his political ambitions with his religious zeal. In 1831, he penned a flattering letter to the president, claiming that Old Hickory's administration would be viewed by future generations "as second only to that of the Father of his country."[8] A year later, Jackson appointed him Indian Commissioner to the West, a position earned largely by cultivating his personal acquaintance with the president.

Like Isaac McCoy, Schermerhorn lent the administration's policy of expulsion an aura of pious benevolence, though Schermerhorn, contrary to his Baptist counterpart, was ruthless and devious. He also felt the times demanded extreme measures—perhaps because he, along with many other evangelicals, expected the final Apocalypse to arrive within the next few decades. At a minimum, the Gospel had to be preached "to all the nations" and the "Jews converted to Christianity," an injunction that could partially be fulfilled by isolating and segregating native peoples in the West, where they could be more effectively supervised and Christianized. Perhaps, Schermerhorn hoped, he could even benefit personally during the apocalyptic times by governing the territory he was actively creating.[9]

Schermerhorn had the extraordinary trait of being disliked by just about everyone he met. He was "bigoted and opinionated," said one government clerk, who even less charitably claimed that a "more designing, malignant, vindictive, illiberal man lives not upon the earth." Missionaries accused Schermerhorn of hypocrisy and duplicity and rued that he was a minister, and a federal agent charged that he "prostituted the dignity of his station." Even Isaac McCoy disliked the man, finding him officious, or more insultingly, an "Old Simpleton."[10]

The targets of Schermerhorn's machinations were equally scornful. The Seneca leader Maris Pierce referred to him sarcastically as that "certain notorious minister who preaches General Jackson's *humane* policy for the removal of the Indians." The Cherokees, playing on his name, called him "Sginuhyona," meaning "Devil Horn." As usual, John Ross offered the most exact characterization. Referring to the French minister who interfered in U.S. policy in the 1790s and attempted to undermine both President Washington and Secretary of State John Adams, Ross said that Schermerhorn was "a Genet in clerical robes, with a military guard."[11]

Astoundingly, the New Yorker participated in treaty discussions with twenty different nations in the 1830s, including the Osages, Quapaws, Miamis, Chippewas, Odawas, and Potawatomis. His two most explosive negotiations took place with the Seminoles and Cherokees. Since the 1820s, U.S. officials had worked to confine Seminole families "to the most limited boundary that could sustain them," in the words of Charleston-born James Gadsden, a Yale graduate, Florida planter, and treaty commissioner. (Gadsden went on to be a railroad entrepreneur and expansionist who negotiated the massive Gadsden Purchase from Mexico, as well as a secessionist who viewed slavery as "a social blessing.") The strategy impoverished Seminole families and pushed them southward into unfit territory while using the treaty-making process to cover the real intent, which was to starve them out of the region. "19/20 of their whole country," said the Florida governor, "is by far the poorest and most miserable region I have ever beheld." Gadsden reaped the harvest in 1832, when he met Seminoles to negotiate a treaty for their deportation. By then, many Seminoles were "half-starved" and surviving on nothing but roots and the fruit of the cabbage palm tree. The resulting Treaty of Payne's Landing provided for the Seminoles' deportation to the West, *if*, after visiting the region, they were satisfied with the "character" of the country.[12]

From the outset, the treaty was mired in controversy. One army officer charged that its "hard and unconscionable terms" were "extorted" from individuals who were "in distress." The Senate did not ratify the document for two years, long after some of its articles were supposed to have been enacted. This prompted Florida governor and past secretary of war John Eaton to wonder if the treaty was even valid, but Jackson's attorney general decided that it was. Seminoles asserted that it was a "White man's treaty" and that its terms were in violation of the 1823

Treaty of Moultrie Creek, which guaranteed the Seminoles possession of their land for a period of twenty years. "The title of the Seminoles to any part of this country has been disputed by those only who know nothing of that treaty," agreed Major Ethan Allen Hitchcock. Hitchcock, the erudite and principled grandson of a Revolutionary War hero, was "out of his element in this vulgar atmosphere," observed one officer stationed in Florida, who claimed that the major confined himself to his quarters to study Kant's *Metaphysics of Morals* and "other abstruse works." But Hitchcock was merely stating what the Seminoles knew to be true. The twenty years since the Treaty of Moultrie Creek had not yet expired, asserted Holata Micco, echoing other Seminole leaders. "I never gave my consent to go west," he said; "the "whites may say so, but I never gave my consent.""[13]

Schermerhorn, though not involved in the 1832 negotiations, put Gadsden's disputed treaty into operation by persuading or coercing a Seminole delegation in the West to agree that the land was satisfactory. Members of the delegation insisted that the minister "made" or "forced" them to assent, while Seminoles back in their eastern homelands denied that the delegation had the authority to act on their behalf. Despite the protests, Schermerhorn celebrated his accomplishment. Hitchcock, by contrast, observed that the consequences would be "written in blood."[14]

Schermerhorn boasted of a second vexed achievement three years later. By the fall of 1834, several prominent Cherokees had reluctantly determined that it was time to conclude an expulsion treaty, with or without the support of John Ross and the Cherokee government. The "Treaty Party," as the group became known, included Major Ridge, John Ridge, and Elias Boudinot, who, pressured by Ross, had resigned from the *Cherokee Phoenix* in August 1832. Ross's own brother Andrew joined them. They had no praise for the "compulsive measures of the States," the faithless pledges of the federal government, and the "unrelenting prejudices" of U.S. citizens against their "language and color." Rather, those manifest injustices led them to conclude that Cherokee families could no longer survive in the South. Cherokees were depressed and degraded "in the kindling of the wood," observed John Ridge, referring to the extension of state laws over their homelands. When the dismantling of the Cherokee Nation was complete, he wondered, what would become of them "in the heated furnace?" Removal, he concluded, "can now alone save them from ruin."[15]

Ross remained unruffled in the face of this internal opposition, and he maneuvered to co-opt his adversaries. Every "course calculated to produce strife among the people from partyism," he wrote to John Ridge, "should be discarded." "Our country and our people," he urged, "should be our motto." But Currey and Schermerhorn, showing no respect for due process or representative government, exploited the political division. In August 1835, they ordered the Georgia Guard to seize control of the *Cherokee Phoenix*. The publication was "prostituted" to "party politics," Currey maintained. Two months later, the two men had the Georgia Guard cross into Tennessee to arrest Ross and a visitor, the New York–born actor and playwright John Howard Payne. The State of Georgia, which did not give a cause for the arrest or file charges, released the prisoners within a few days. Then in late December, while Ross was away in Washington City, Schermerhorn called a meeting in New Echota, the onetime capital of the Cherokee Nation, now in north Georgia. No more than a hundred Cherokees attended, but Schermerhorn used the occasion to settle the now-infamous Treaty of New Echota, which provided for the final expulsion of the Cherokees from their homelands. Twenty men signed the document, including Major and John Ridge, Elias Boudinot, and Andrew Ross. They insisted that they had rescued the Cherokee Nation; they were "patriots" rather than traitors. And yet, as the principal chief underscored, the Treaty Party was composed of self-appointed Cherokee leaders, with no formal authority. Schermerhorn, with Benjamin Currey assisting, had concluded a decisive treaty not with the Cherokee Nation but with a group of usurpers.[16]

~~~

ON DECEMBER 28, 1835, one day before twenty Cherokees signed the Treaty of New Echota, a young man named Osceola and several of his companions ambushed the U.S. agent Wiley Thompson at Fort King, in north-central Florida, killing Thompson and four others and scalping and mutilating the bodies. Joseph Harris, the author of the aspirational "plan of operations," had the displeasure of reporting to the War Department that its officer had been "cruelly murdered." The victors reportedly made humorous speeches to Thompson's scalp, imitating his gestures and haughty manner of lecturing them.[17]

That same day, Seminoles and their black allies, positioned behind scrub palmettos and pine trees, surprised a column of 109 U.S. troops, who were marching through the barrens between Tampa Bay's Fort Brooke, the staging ground for the deportation of Seminole families, and Fort King. The sharpshooters destroyed half the column with a single volley. A break in the firefight allowed the beleaguered troops to chop down trees and construct a makeshift barricade, but the ambushers regrouped and picked off the remaining men. One hundred eighty Seminoles had annihilated two entire companies of the U.S. Army. By one report, the return of Captain George Washington Gardiner's dog, unaccompanied, first alerted the garrison at Fort Brooke that something had gone wrong. Soon after, one of the three surviving soldiers crawled into the fort. Shot in the shoulder, thigh, temple, arm, and back, he was said to have covered sixty miles on his hands and knees, a journey that took three days. When a burial detail finally reached the site of the battle two months later, they picked through the broken cartridge boxes and belts and dead oxen and horses in search of decomposing bodies. They dug two mass graves to inter the remains of ninety-eight enlisted men. Separately, they buried the eight officers, including Francis Dade, the commanding major whose rotting corpse was identified by his vest and infantry buttons. The remarkable Seminole victory is today commonly known as the Dade Massacre.[18]

Four days later, General Duncan Clinch, still unaware of Dade's defeat, set out with 250 troops and 700 mounted militia from Fort Drane, located conveniently on the general's sugar plantation south of present-day Gainesville. Marching south, he expected to locate and route the Seminole partisans on the Withlacoochee, but on reaching the river seventy miles north of Tampa, he discovered that it was too wide and deep to ford. His men would have to cross in a single dugout canoe, found at the site. In the midst of the time-consuming operation, when the troops were divided on opposite banks, Osceola and his followers attacked, killing four soldiers and injuring fifty-nine others, who were spared a worse fate by the poor quality of the Seminoles' gunpowder. The demoralized troops crossed back over the river that evening, and the entire column returned to Fort Drane. There, a medic treated the injured men, grinding through flesh and cutting and tugging with a knife to remove the lead balls.[19]

It is fitting that Osceola stood at the center of the war erupting between the United States and native peoples in the South. He had first encountered Andrew Jackson in 1813, when the general marched through the Creek Nation, razing villages and slaughtering the residents. Osceola, then known as Billy Powell, was about nine years old at the time. Soon after, Billy and his mother fled their devastated homelands for northern Florida, where they sought refuge with other Creeks and their Seminole relatives. In 1818, Jackson followed them, pursuing the "savage Enemies of the U. States" into the Florida Panhandle and Suwannee River region. With three thousand U.S. troops and two thousand Creek allies and mercenaries, the future president destroyed several towns and "confiscated" the residents' food supplies in the hope that they would starve. (By employing Creek gunmen, Jackson exploited the fact that Creeks had been bitterly divided since the U.S.-Creek War of 1813–14.) By one account, Jackson's troops briefly imprisoned Billy, after surprising an encampment and killing thirty-seven Creek men. One target eluded Jackson, however. Billy's great-uncle Peter McQueen, a renowned Creek prophet and one of the leaders of the resistance against the United States, remained beyond the general's reach.[20]

Osceola, whose entire life had been shaped by Jackson, proved to be the staunchest opponent of the president's efforts to deport the Seminoles. As a Creek, he had no particular claim to leadership among native peoples in Florida, but his eloquence and resolve earned him many followers. In October 1834, after the U.S. agent Wiley Thompson had described the "utter desolation and hopeless wretchedness" that awaited Seminoles who remained in Florida, it was Osceola who stood firm, even as older leaders wavered. Shortly afterward, Jackson ordered ten companies of U.S. troops into the Seminole homeland, setting the stage for Osceola's stunning triumph in the last week of 1835.[21]

The fateful four days between Dade's defeat and Clinch's ineffective campaign on the Withlacoochee mark a watershed in the history of the U.S. policy to deport native peoples. After this turning point midway through the 1830s, the United States could no longer sustain the fiction that Native Americans would play the acquiescent role predicted of them by experts. The War Department could no longer pretend that it was engaged in a humanitarian effort to save the continent's first peoples by moving them to the civilizing territory of Aboriginia. And the federal government could no longer hope that by some combination of compulsion, enticement, and duplicity it would complete the project to eliminate eighty thousand people without going to war. The admission was made on January 21, 1836, when Secretary of War Cass ordered General Winfield Scott to Florida to assume command of the operations against the Seminoles.[22] Instead of delivering food and supplies to dispossessed people on their journey west, the War Department would now conduct a military operation whose goal was the unconditional surrender of native villagers in Florida.

Across the South, as state militia headed off to war, towns feted their volunteer soldiers. When Alexander Beaufort Meek left Tuscaloosa, Alabama, for Florida with three companies of volunteers in February 1836, citizens lined the banks of the Black Warrior River, celebrating their local heroes with cannon salutes and cheers. It was "one of the most sublime, impressive and affecting scenes I ever saw," Meek wrote. Sixty miles downriver, the untested volunteers stopped for the evening and spent the night in "laughter and gayety." White residents in New Orleans, Darien, and Savannah also rallied around their troops, and in Augusta the "ladies" volunteered to make uniforms for their "gallant men." In Charleston, one South Carolina volunteer recalled the "last look of the beauteous maiden," with her lustrous eyes clouded by tears as his company embarked for Florida. "Go, brave and generous soldiers!" exclaimed the *Federal Union* of Milledgeville, Georgia. "March where glory, where patriotism, where humanity calls you!"[23]

General Scott, who had recently overseen the cholera-plagued war against Black Hawk, received unambiguous orders from the War Department: to "subdue" the Seminoles "unconditionally" until they agreed "to an immediate embarkation for the country west of the Mississippi." The fifty-year-old general, renowned for his mastery of European military strategy and tactics, planned a decisive blow against the partisans, but after a series of cumbersome and protracted maneuvers, U.S. troops became bogged down once again on the Withlacoochee. Its serpentine tributaries, islands, and swamps prompted the exasperated general to describe the river as "a Cretan labyrinth," as mysterious and impenetrable to white people, he said, "as the sacred groves of the Druids." For over a week, Seminoles laid siege to one thousand ill-provisioned troops, who survived by eating their horses and dogs. One angry officer charged that General Scott had devised the campaign on the rug "before his comfortable fire, allowing for no impassable country." "The Indians," he exclaimed, "were not so dull as to be swallowed up by an overwhelming force!"[24]

While the War Department evaluated the danger in Florida, native peoples assessed the extraordinary opportunity presented by the Seminole victories. Weeks before the signing of the Treaty of New Echota, Cherokees apparently caught wind of rumors that the British were planning to come to the Seminoles' aid, as the redcoats had twenty years earlier in the War of 1812. Cherokees reportedly anticipated an "insurrection in the south and west" and possibly even a war between the United States and Britain, events that they might profitably use to delay, or even end, plans for their deportation. They may have even possessed advance information about Osceola's plans, which by one account Seminoles had debated for a full year before launching the attacks in December 1835.[25]

Likewise, Creek villagers, who were in constant contact with their southern relatives, closely followed events in Florida. From their Alabama homelands, they were well-positioned to observe the mobilization of local militia. In Mobile, spectators crowded the wharves as companies of volunteers passed through the port, and "Creoles, mullattoes, Indians and Sailors"—all potential sources of intelligence for Creek people— regularly visited the city. Within a few weeks of Osceola's victories, it was rumored that Creeks were preparing to join the uprising. "Should such prove to be the case," warned the secretary of war, General Scott had orders "to reduce" both peoples to "unconditional submission."[26]

As the U.S. press circulated stories of Thompson's murder and Dade's annihilation, rumors quickly spread that the Cherokees intended to "massacre all the whites" and flee to Florida. "We need not be surprised if the difficulty with the Cherokees ends as with the Seminoles," a resident of north Georgia warned the governor, since there were "plenty" of men akin to Osceola in the Cherokee Nation. Or perhaps, as one U.S. Indian agent suggested, the Cherokees would join forces with the Creeks. In fact, the Creeks, inspired by Seminole victories or simply desperate to find sustenance for their starving families, had recently stepped up raids on the Georgia side of the Chattahoochee River.[27]

While the possibility that native peoples would combine forces alarmed white Americans, the prospect that they might make common cause with slave laborers terrified them. Georgia's citizens found it ominous that when Creeks attacked labor camps, they often spared the slaves, who were valuable to the looters as both allies and property, depending on the circumstance. The danger of an all-out race war appeared to be even more present in Seminole country, where numerous enslaved laborers from Florida and beyond had fled over the preceding decades. "You will allow no terms to the Indians," Secretary of War Cass ordered General Scott, "until every living slave in their possession belonging to a white man is given up." General Clinch himself owned hundreds of people and two expansive plantations in south Georgia and central Florida, and he shared the anxiety of many of his fellow planters that there was "a secret and improper communication carried on between the refractory Indians, Indian negroes, and some of the plantation negroes." He had seen the unnerving results once before, in 1816, when he led U.S. troops against the "Negro Fort," a redoubt on the Apalachicola River commanded by fugitive slaves and indigenous Americans. Navy boats obliterated it with a lucky shot to the powder magazine, but Clinch, who was long afterward celebrated for the fort's destruction, never forgot the threat. George Gibson assured him that this time the War Department would not permit an alliance to form between "lawless banditti" and "negroes," but Clinch nonetheless remained fearful that the "spirit" of murder and plunder would "extend to the plantation." It was hardly encouraging that scores of "Indian negroes" had participated in the attack on Dade.[28]

One South Carolina planter, who rushed an account of the war into print in 1836, avowed that the "mild character of slavery in the southern States, and the affection of the negro for his master" would preclude such a coalition from forming. The fugitives residing among the Seminoles, he insisted, had been forced "at the edge of the tomahawk" to leave their "happy and secure state of servitude." That was wishful thinking. Clinch's own slave, offered a "large reward" to carry an express letter for the general, instead fled to the Seminoles. Recaptured at a later date, he was "obstinate and surly" and refused to divulge any information. As Wiley Thompson had observed before his premature death, slave laborers preferred the "comparative liberty" in Seminole country to the "bondage and hard labour under overseers, on sugar and cotton plantations."[29]

After advocating unceasingly to expel Native Americans from the Deep South and then spending hundreds of thousands of dollars replacing the dispossessed with slaves, planter-politicians now faced the consequences. Over the course of the 1830s, the enslaved population in Alabama more than doubled to 253,000. By the end of the decade, nearly one out of every four slaves worked on land that only a few years earlier had belonged to the Creeks. Free people remained a slender majority in the state only because the northern mountain counties could not support profitable slave labor camps. In Mississippi, the demographic balance tipped in favor of African Americans with the forced migration of 100,000 enslaved people into the state in the six years after the passage of the expulsion act. By 1836, approximately 144,000 white Americans lived in Mississippi, while over 164,000 African Americans, imprisoned for life for no other reason than the accident of their birth, toiled in the cotton fields of the region's rapidly expanding plantations.[30]

The anxieties of white southerners about their tenuous control of hundreds of thousands of enslaved people were surpassed only by their interest in profiting from native dispossession.[31] One Mississippi planter who owned forty-eight people, reflecting the heightened fears of his class, suspected that slaves were poisoning their masters. He dreaded that, where they were "so numerous," the brutalized labor force would perpetrate a "great slaughter." The prospect weighed on him, even as he reveled in the productivity of the cotton land he had purchased in the Choctaw Nation. David Hubbard, Beers's southern associate, dismissed such concerns with unconvincing swagger: "We don't fear any other danger to our population than a little house burning here and there and now and then a few throats cut of the women and children and defenceless portion of our population." With so much profit so close at hand, he could endure an occasional sacrifice. Besides, white southerners would make examples "of all refractory slaves of every degree," he boasted, and inflict "the severest punishment upon the white incendiaries who encourage and incite them to crime."[32]

But no amount of posturing would calm the volatile world that planter-politicians had created. In Alabama and Mississippi alone, almost a half million people, held in perpetual bondage, had no loyalty to the South's expanding slave empire. In Florida, one thousand skilled Seminole marksmen were in arms and thwarting the U.S. Army at every turn. And in Alabama and the southern Appalachians, thirty-four thousand desperate and ill-treated Creeks and Cherokees appeared ready to join the uprising. The world created by the expulsion of native peoples seemed to be on the verge of exploding in an apocalypse of violence.

Far to the west, another threat loomed that would perhaps provide the spark to engulf the entire region in flames. In late 1835, slaveholding Anglo colonizers in Texas launched a rebellion against Mexico, which had threatened their supremacy by abolishing servitude six years earlier. General Antonio López de Santa Anna set out from Coahuila with six thousand Mexican troops to put down the proslavery secessionist movement. As the civil war continued into the new year, some planters in the neighboring slave states of the U.S. South feared that the conflagration would jump across the border.[33]

Congress debated the growing peril in the spring of 1836. Some representatives dismissed the danger that native peoples, Mexicans, and enslaved laborers posed to the South. It was greatly exaggerated, suggested Abijah Mann Jr. of New York. Or, as South Carolina's Waddy Thompson Jr. asserted, it could be met with an overpowering exhibition of manhood. Southern planters, according to this dubious line of thought, need only stand tall to subjugate any servile opposition. The ancient Scythians, he recounted, met a general revolt of their slaves with no other weapons than their whips, "at sight of which, the slaves all fled or surrendered." "The people of the slave States," he boasted, "need no other aid or weapons."[34]

Other congressmen, however, expressed deep concern. A representative from Louisiana worried that the war in Texas might spill into his own state, where it would be fueled by slaves who vastly outnumbered their masters. If General Santa Anna secured Texas and recruited "hordes of Indians," he said, Louisiana could collapse in an instant. One of Georgia's congressmen shared his own fears. In "the very heart of our Southern country," he observed, referring to the Seminole homeland, there existed "an Indian power" that the army had not been able to subdue. "The war belt," he warned, "is going the rounds, from Florida to the Upper Mississippi." President Jackson, in his final year in office and eager to secure his defining policy, believed that waging war indiscriminately, as he had done years earlier, would put an end to the uprising. By capturing or killing Seminole women and children, he said, the army in Florida could "more than amply destroy the Seminoles, then in three weeks destroy the Creeks and Cherokees."[35] He was badly mistaken.

As the debate unfolded in Washington City, a party of Creeks murdered several Georgia planters in the first week of May 1836, sparing the slaves. In one gruesome attack, they killed a family of seven and threw one of the dead children into the yard, where hogs nearly devoured the corpse. Pressured on all sides to act decisively, Secretary of War Cass directed General Thomas S. Jesup to secure the Creeks' "unconditional submission." General Winfield Scott, fresh off his ineffectual campaign against the Seminoles, soon arrived from Florida to assist. "The great object is to remove them immediately," Cass stressed in a letter to Jesup on May 19, "and to this other considerations must yield." That same day, he sent word that the federal government would no longer need the services of the commissary general's agents in the Creek Nation; expulsion would now be a military operation. A week later, the Senate barely ratified the controversial Treaty of New Echota, and soon after Secretary Cass deployed one thousand troops to the Cherokee Nation to guard against the possibility of a general uprising and to act decisively should Cherokees take up arms.[36]

Congress also took action. First, it authorized the president to engage the services of ten thousand volunteer soldiers to put down "Indian hostilities" and "repel invasions." The act doubled the number of ground troops available to the War Department. Second, Congress appropriated funds to initiate the construction of a "wall of defence to the far West." The twelve-hundred-mile military cordon would eventually run from present-day Minneapolis to the Gulf Coast, allowing troops to maintain "a continual *surveillance*" of the border.[37]

Since the formation of the Republic, politicians had fantasized about such a boundary line, and George Washington had even spoken of building a "Chinese wall" between the United States and the Cherokees. But until the 1830s, as Secretary of War Lewis Cass observed in February 1836, "No line could be drawn upon one side of which the Indians could be kept, and our citizens the other." Six years of deporting people "from the interior of the States beyond our western boundary" had now made such a line possible.[38]

The line was not only possible; it was desperately needed. The "inland frontier," as Congress called it, was lined with "savages," who were "creatures of passion and momentary impulse." Albert G. Harrison, a representative from Missouri, dramatized the danger. He warned that "vast hordes" bordered the western frontier. Holding up a map for his congressional colleagues from the East, he explained that before expulsion native peoples were "scattered over twenty-four States and three Territories." Living amid U.S. citizens, they had been merely "troublesome neighbors" rather than "dangerous enemies." "But now," he exclaimed, "this state of things is greatly changed." "Look at this map," he urged. "The map which I hold in my hand shows our exposed situation." According to one War Department estimate, as the military operation to expel native peoples continued to progress, the number of indigenous Americans on the outer edge of the U.S. Republic would soon approach

245,000 and would include angry and hostile populations, such as the Creeks and Seminoles.[39]

One of President Jackson's correspondents accurately summed up the situation in the spring of 1836: "It seems all the southern world is to be in a war."[40]

~~~

AS MILITIAMEN poured into Columbus, Georgia, on their way to fight Creek families in May 1836, the mood was celebratory. "We cannot speak in terms too high of the patriotism and high souled chivalry, which burns in the bosoms of these men," enthused the *Columbus Enquirer*. Distinctions between rich and poor had dissolved, the newspaper suggested. "We feel that we are yet *brethren*." Not all felt such solidarity, however; within a week the mood had soured and cracks appeared in the makeshift white alliance. Volunteers from neighboring counties accused the Columbus elite of hiding in their "store and counting-houses" and "attending to business," while rural farmers were mustered to protect "the lives and property of a few rich men." They called out Eli Shorter by name. A local universalist minister charged that the true "instigators" of the violence were the "few individuals" who had sought to "acquire overgrown fortunes." Militia would inevitably seek vengeance for the casualties they suffered against the Creeks. "That it may only fall where it is due," he said, "is my sincere desire and honest belief."[41]

The conflict that followed in the Creek Nation was vicious and chaotic. Creeks crossed into Georgia and seized nearby corncribs and smokehouses, stating "we were starving and were obliged to plunder." State militia retaliated but proved incompetent and undisciplined. Some militia dropped their arms and departed without leave; others were overeager and difficult to restrain. None seemed willing to remain behind to defend the baggage train, work that was monotonous and unheralded yet still dangerous. The one expedition that obtained "Major" Eli Shorter's services ended in disarray without a single encounter, and thereafter, Georgia militiamen were spared further ignominy when the governor forbade them from crossing into Alabama. Across the Chattahoochee, after an entire company from Montgomery County deserted, Alabama's governor offered a bounty of $10 per head to anyone who captured the runaway militia.[42]

Unnerved by endless accounts of the Seminoles' savagery—"Like wolves—they love the sight of blood, / And laugh to see life's wasting flood," wrote one would-be poet in the pages of the *Savannah Georgian*— white southerners stoked their own fears. Osceola would likely appear at any moment to lead the Creeks, speculated one newspaper, offering the dubious reassurance that if enemies killed or scalped members of the militia, their compatriots would avenge them. General William Irwin, recently returned from duty in Florida, panicked at the thought of Alabama slaves—he owned sixty-two of them—joining the uprising. They "have had uninterrupted intercourse with the Indians for a great length of time," he warned Georgia's governor, "and may have matured some plan of cooperation."[43]

Within Creek households, the uprising forced a difficult decision. On the one hand, resorting to violence might feed families in the short run and lead to a workable compromise with the United States in the future. On the other hand, a decision to lie low and be opportunistic, assisting the United States at some times, aiding the partisans at others, might forestall the worst possible outcome, the extermination of Creek peoples. Young men in the Creek Nation who did not remember the devastation wrought by Andrew Jackson's troops in the U.S.-Creek War of 1813–14 perhaps had an exaggerated sense of their capabilities. In late May 1836, one group of partisans boasted that they could "whip the white people" and that "our swamps are full of our young warriors." In the same conversation, however, they recognized the very real possibility that they could be "exterminated." This fear led the majority of people to attempt to sit out the conflict, a decision that hastened its end. In early

July, after Generals Scott and Jesup launched a series of poorly coordinated attacks, Scott declared that the war was "virtually over."[44]

For U.S. citizens, the war swept away the improbable but comforting narrative that native peoples would quietly march off to a western sanctuary. It exposed the dark impulse that underlay federal policy—a mounting desire to eliminate native families. "Removal or death," one gathering of Georgians toasted on July 4, 1836. General Jesup sought to eliminate native peoples by deporting them at the point of a bayonet. In early July, the U.S. Army rounded up 1,600 children, women, and men in eastern Alabama and marched them under guard toward Montgomery. The men walked in chains in double file, and each night of the six-day march, they slept within log fences, watched and defended by sentinels. Only the presence of U.S. troops prevented vigilantes from massacring the prisoners. On reaching Montgomery, the families were placed in a holding camp, where they spent the days waiting and the nights sleeping on the ground, forced to arrange themselves in rows, the men separated from their families. None of the refugees left accounts of the experience, but their despair was documented in other ways. One man slit his throat while being pulled through a Montgomery street in a cart. Another hanged himself. A third tried to cut his throat with a dull knife, and when that failed, plunged the blade into his chest. Alabama militia, charged with guarding the camp, kept order by bayonetting and shooting two Creeks, a father and son, who were attempting to escape.[45]

After a week, John W.A. Sanford and Company, the outfit that had contracted with the federal government to deport Creeks, assumed control of the deportation. Alabama militia herded the refugees, now numbering 2,300, onto two steamboats, including the *Lewis Cass*. Two platoons of forty men each accompanied the prisoners downriver. At Mobile, the troops debarked, and the steamboats, carrying the prisoners, continued along the Gulf Coast to New Orleans and then up to Rock Roe, on the Arkansas River. There, the chains were unloaded in barrels, and at night, the dispossessed rolled them into the water, where the rusting iron remains, a crumbling testament to the vicious and foundational policy embraced by the United States in the 1830s. Over 4 percent of the refugees died during this journey. Deportation by private contractors turned out to be neither less expensive for the federal government nor less deadly for the refugees.[46]

Six more detachments followed, totaling nearly fourteen thousand people. The Alabama Emigrating Company, as Sanford and Company had been renamed, oversaw the operations. To save time and money, the company made sure that the march west would be brisk and relentless. Since its profits depended on the difference between the per capita payment it received from the federal government and the actual cost of operations, the outfit had every interest in supplying the refugees with inferior and meager provisions. One group arrived by steamboat at Rock Roe to find that the company had failed to make any preparations at all. A federal officer, Edward Deas, scrambled to purchase corn from nearby farmers. Another group, after crossing the Mississippi at Memphis, discovered that the company had not set aside adequate provisions or fodder for the ninety-five-mile overland journey to Rock Roe. The "whole of the land operations," observed Deas, "have been badly conducted." The road was soon littered with dead horses and ponies. Tired, sick, and hungry, hundreds of refugees abandoned their detachments to search for food. "The feet of our old people bled," stated Opothle Yoholo. "Our young children cried."[47] The debacle was entirely predictable.

Most U.S. citizens in the South were overjoyed to see the region's oldest residents disappear on steamboats or overland for the distant West, and they asked few questions about the methods used. But thousands of other Creek people remained behind, and these people too became refugees. Many sought to escape across southeast Georgia to Seminole villages, where they hoped to find peace in the impenetrable swamps in Florida. Offended by this refusal to head west, Georgia and Alabama citizens set out to exterminate them. The refugees, said one Tennessee volunteer, would need to be "hunted up in the woods like wild beasts" and killed in small gangs. South of Columbus, a volunteer from Gwinnett County (now a suburb of Atlanta) dragged a Creek man into a small stockade and scalped him. A Colonel Wadsworth, who strutted around Columbus, Georgia, with a pair of large pistols in his waistband and a large bowie knife and two smaller pistols tucked into his breaches, shot a native man outside of town and then executed him with a shot to the head. He was notorious for such acts. A company of citizens from Russell County, Alabama, stormed a camp of friendly Creek families, whose men were serving with the United States in Florida. They cornered a ninety-year-old man in his cabin, shot him in the head, and stove in his skull with the butt of a musket. They raped several of the women and chased after a fifteen-year-old girl and shot her in the leg as she escaped into the bushes. The camp was under federal protection, but local militia rounded up several of the Creek boys and men. Under what authority? they were asked. "The people," they answered.[48]

The "people," organized as state militia, waded through mud and water in southwest Georgia in pursuit of the fugitives, "hunting up the Indians who yet infest the swamps," as one volunteer put it, and scattering the survivors. "The savage," proclaimed one army officer, "should be no longer permitted to polute our soil with his foot." The country was "infected." Week by week, militia tracked down the desperate refugees. They killed twelve on July 2, twenty-two on July 15, twenty-two on July 24, eighteen on July 26, and eighteen to twenty-three on August 13. They followed trails of blood and corpses, seizing the possessions dropped by the survivors—quilts, cloth, powder, and lead. Weak with hunger or simply too young, some Creek children could not keep up with the pace of flight. Their mothers smothered them to death. On occasion, women suffocated their crying babies to prevent them from revealing their locations. Nearing capture, they sometimes killed their children and committed suicide.[49]

Infrequently, the fugitives descended on farmsteads and murdered the occupants, acts that newspapers described in outrage.[50] White southerners had dispossessed the region's oldest residents and pursued the starving survivors through trackless swamps. Yet, even as they were exterminating Creek families, the perpetrators of the violence imagined themselves as the victims.

~~~

IT IS not clear if J.D. Beers ever met William Apess, who for a time was living in lower Manhattan not far from the financier's Wall Street office, or if Beers noticed the hearse in early April 1839, parked two blocks from his daughter's house, that carted Apess's body away to be buried in an anonymous grave. The Pequot minister had died at age forty after a sudden illness. Beers's forebears had arrived in New England with the great migration of Puritans in the 1630s, and one of his ancestors fought in both the Pequot War of 1637 and King Philip's War of 1675–76, two vicious conflicts that Anglo histories of the colonies celebrated as momentous victories. Apess's roots in the region of course extended far deeper, and his historical perspective reflected that fact. His final publication, *Eulogy on King Philip*, appeared in the pivotal year of 1836 and delved into New England's troubled relationship with the region's native residents, a subject that he lectured about extensively in the last few years of his life. In February 1837 at the New York Mercantile Library Association's Clinton Hall, he delivered a series of talks on Native American history that culminated in an examination of the "injuries" that native peoples had received under "proposed measures for their benefit." It is entirely possible that Beers was in the audience when Apess described the "inhuman" acts of New England's first colonists. The Pilgrims "possessed themselves of a portion of the country, and built themselves houses, and then made a treaty, and commanded them [native residents] to accede to it," he wrote in *Eulogy on King Philip*. Turning Puritan myths on their head, he asserted that

Miles Standish, the colony's military advisor, was "a vile and malicious fellow," that Puritans were "lewd," and that the famed minister Increase Mather was no more "pious" than the Christian who invited Apess to dine with him and then placed his dinner behind a door. The "walls of prejudice" that had been constructed by colonists, Apess predicted, would inevitably "fall upon their children."[51]

If Beers did not hear Apess or read his works, perhaps he had attended the lectures of the Cherokees Elias Boudinot and John Ridge, when they visited New York in 1832. The city's "most respectable citizens" held several meetings with the activists, contributed to a fundraising campaign, and adopted a resolution that condemned U.S. policy and demanded that the rights of the Cherokees be "fairly investigated and fully sustained." Morris Ketchum, a friend of Beers's and his associate as a founding partner of the New York and Mississippi Land Company, met with Boudinot and Ridge and even joined a standing committee to "diffuse information on the subject of the conditions and rights of the Cherokee Nation."[52]

The hypocrisy of raising funds for the Cherokees while financing the dispossession of indigenous families would not have surprised Apess. He repeatedly noted that despite all the declarations of piety and paternalism, avarice formed the basis of the relationship between colonizers and Native Americans. "I do not hesitate to say that through the prayers, preaching, and examples of those pretended pious," he charged, "has been the foundation of all the slavery and degradation in the American colonies toward colored people."[53]

Turning to current policy, Apess lampooned Andrew Jackson's paternalism, which the president continued to avow, despite sending U.S. troops against the Creeks and Seminoles. "We want your land for our use to speculate upon," he imagined the president saying; "it aids us in paying off our national debt and supporting us in Congress to drive you off." He continued, still in Jackson's voice:

You see, my red children, that our fathers carried on this
scheme of getting your lands for our use, and we have now
become rich and powerful; and we have a right to do with you
just as we please; we claim to be your fathers. And we think
we shall do you a great favor, my dear sons and daughters, to
drive you out, to get you away out of the reach of our civilized
people, who are cheating you, for we have no law to reach
them, we cannot protect you although you be our children.
So it is no use, you need not cry, you must go, even if the lions
devour you, for we promised the land you have to somebody
else long ago, perhaps twenty or thirty years; and we did it
without your consent, it is true. But this has been the way our
fathers first brought us up, and it is hard to depart from it;
therefore, you shall have no protection from us.[54]

With some mixture of cynicism and self-delusion, financiers under-
wrote philanthropic enterprises even as they speculated in indigenous
lands, as was the case with the stockholders of the American Land
Company. (The ever-enterprising J.D. Beers and his firm J.D. Beers and
Co. owned 850 shares of the company, with a total face value of $85,000.)
After spending $500,000 to speculate in indigenous lands in the South,
the "pious" part of the company, one newspaper mocked, felt "a little
conscience-stricken." At their first annual meeting in 1836, they therefore appropriated $1,000 of the company's $1,000,000—one tenth of one
percent of its capital—to purchase Bibles "to be distributed among the
benighted Indians of Alabama and Mississippi."[55] The exchange of a few
boxes of Bibles for immense tracts of valuable land neatly encapsulated
two centuries of clever maneuvering by self-righteous decision makers
in the Northeast.

As Wall Street financing and, in far smaller quantities, Wall Street–
financed Bibles flowed into indigenous lands, few people on either end
of the stream could fully grasp the connection between the South's dis-

integrating indigenous communities and the North's prospering investment banks. But the relationship was exposed briefly in early August 1836 on Ichawaynochaway Creek, in southwest Georgia, when state militia tracked down and attacked three hundred refugees who were fleeing southeast toward Seminole country. After the Creeks escaped a hard-fought battle, the militia discovered two crying infants hidden in a canebrake and a six-year-old girl. Their fates are unknown; we learn only that the children were reportedly "taken away by gentlemen who seemed pleased to have them." The militia found something else too, a note that one of the refugees, in the rush to escape, had dropped or perhaps thrown down in disgust. It said, "On demand I promise to pay Ectiarchi One hundred and forty dollars. This is not negotiable." The note was signed by J.D. Beers's associate, Eli Shorter.[56]

CHAPTER 10

AT THE POINT OF A BAYONET

~~~

THROUGH THE summer and fall of 1836, Cherokees struggled merely to survive. Early frosts in the previous year had killed off the corn crop, leaving farmers without a store of grain. Then a drought destroyed the spring planting. Hundreds of men, women, and children—white and Native American—wandered about Habersham County, in the foothills of northeast Georgia, begging for food. Indigenous farmers had long withstood the occasional poor harvest by relying on hunting to make up the difference. But U.S. citizens, fearing that the unrest among Creek and Seminole peoples would spread north, refused to sell ammunition to Cherokees. And General John E. Wool, commanding U.S. troops in the Cherokee Nation, required militant Cherokees in western North Carolina to give up their guns. At the same time, with the wars raging in Alabama and Florida, white Georgians felt newly entitled to run the Cherokees off their land, flogging them with cowhide whips, hickory withes, and wooden clubs. "We are not safe in our houses," Major Ridge and his son John Ridge wrote to Andrew Jackson; "our people are assailed by day & night by the rabble."[1]

Surveying this bleak landscape, John Ross and seven other Cherokee leaders recalled that during the congressional debate over the expulsion bill in 1830, its opponents had argued that its "secret design" was to make the situation of native peoples "so wretched and intolerable" that they would abandon their homelands. Others, and none more than the delegation from Georgia, had insisted that the measure was "founded in humanity." Now, with U.S. troops positioned throughout the South, the Cherokee leaders took satisfaction in declaring, "Who was right, let subsequent facts decide."[2]

Nonetheless, Cherokees refused to move. Federal agents, sent out to assess the value of native farms in the fall of 1836, as required by the Treaty of New Echota, recorded the quiet determination of the persecuted but resilient farmers. Tuelookee would not give his name or even speak to the valuators. Chudwelk and John Tatterhair told them bluntly that they were not willing to move. John Cahoossee's widow "could not be made to under stand our business"—or perhaps she did not want to understand. Canowsawksy gladly showed off his farm—it was "first rate creek bottom land"—but insisted he would not go west on any terms, "unless Ross says he shall." His resolve must have been fortified by the presence of Hogshooter and his family of eight, who had been living with him since U.S. citizens had torn the roof off their house and driven them away in 1833. Despite that traumatic experience, Hogshooter's family steadfastly refused to register for deportation. Others, such as Sicktowa and Whiteman Killer, also reported that white intruders had driven them off their farms.[3]

Moving through valleys and crossing ridges, the roving valuators enumerated houses, fields, fruit trees, corncribs, smokehouses, and horse lots, unintentionally documenting the diversity and abundance of the Cherokee Nation. Jackson Duck, dwelling with his family of six in northeastern Alabama, owned a small field and a cabin with a split-log puncheon floor and a wood and rock chimney. Possum, living nearby on Wills Creek, had a single cabin and a camp. Robert Brown was settled along the same creek and owned a cabin that was 30 feet by 14 feet, along with a stable, smokehouse, storehouse, horse lot, corncrib, and exterior kitchen. Summers must have been bountiful on Brown's farm, which had sixty-four peach trees, twenty-one apple trees, a cherry tree, and a Chickasaw plum tree. Nearby, Susannah, on North Wills Creek, owned several cabins, a cow pen, a cook camp, eight cherry trees, ten Chickasaw plum trees, thirty-eight peach trees, and forty-eight apple trees. She had twenty-five acres under cultivation, surrounded by a high nine-rail fence.[4]

Generally, the work of assessing Cherokee homes must have been tedious for the valuators and threatening and invasive for the families being dispossessed. The inventories are matter-of-fact, but in one instance a valuator paused long enough to appreciate the landscape, if not the plight of the residents. Crossing over a ridge in north Georgia, he was overcome by "perhaps the most splendidly striking mountain scenery upon the face of the Globe." "An amphitheatre of probably 50 miles in circuit is formed by the Brasstown Mountains," he marveled, "encircling a beautiful and fertile valley about 4 miles across interspersed with limpid streams and making upon the whole a picture unsurpassed and rare if ever to be equalled for the wildness and grandeur of its scenery."[5]

Brasstown is a mistranslation of the Cherokee word for "New green place," and Cherokees found the area as captivating as did the federal official sent to hasten their deportation. Drowning Bear, who lived at the head of Brasstown Creek, refused to show his property and said "he did not understand" the valuation process. John Walker said he would not enroll, did not want any money, and would remain on Brasstown Creek, where he farmed ten acres and tended eighteen peach and eight apple trees. Salagatahee refused to permit the valuator to visit his farm, stating that he would not go west. Two Dollar, though he had already been dispossessed of five acres of his farmland, also said he would not leave. Likewise, Sutt had lost six acres to an intruder but insisted he would not move west.[6]

The view of the Hiwassee River from Brasstown Bald, elevation 4,783 feet. The river was dammed to create Chatuge Lake in the 1940s.

The total value of Cherokee houses, fruit trees, crops, and the like, as determined by the valuators employed by the federal government, stood at $1.68 million. To this sum, the commissioners appointed by President Jackson added $416,000, their estimate of how much Cherokee property intruders had destroyed. On the other side of the ledger, they subtracted money that the federal government had advanced to the Cherokees or that private merchants and traders had purportedly loaned to them, a figure that totaled $1.35 million. That left $746,000, or about $125 per family. This paltry sum was all that Cherokee families who had cultivated farms in the region for generations would receive for their improvements. In practice, many received nothing, since their purported debts offset the assessed value of their homes and fields.[7]

The five leather-bound volumes that contain this reckoning are a monument to exacting procedure and moral obtuseness, as if the appearance of rigorous financial accounting would answer ethical questions about deporting thousands of families. Wilson Lumpkin, who in his fourth role after congressman, governor, and senator was now serving as one of Andrew Jackson's two special commissioners overseeing the process, declared that nothing "but a sense of duty, and a desire to promote the interest of the perishing Cherokees" had induced him to accept the assignment. He and his co-commissioner attended to the task "with great labour" by establishing an elaborate system of record keeping, with various payment registers, valuing books, receipts, duplicate receipts, vouchers, balance sheets, and the like, all in the service of preventing "embarrassment and error." No "business of similar magnitude, and complication, when all the circumstances are taken into view," Lumpkin bragged, "was ever in so short a period, systematized, partly settled, and brought into a form." If a few million dollars would buy the elimination of native families, Lumpkin was happy to adjudicate claims in a spirit of justice. Property should be valued "in a spirit of liberality and justice," he directed, avoiding "parsimony" on the one hand and "extravagance" on the other.[8]

He was less liberal with Cherokees who refused to cooperate. Lumpkin urged General Wool to put down any opposition by force, if necessary. In closing, he proclaimed bombastically that the Treaty of New Echota "will be executed, or it will be recorded 'that Georgia was.'" When Wool reported that starving Cherokees refused to accept federal aid, Lumpkin was gratified. Only those willing to abandon their homelands should be fed, he insisted. "We would invite all who are ready to perish, to come and partake of this benevolent provision," he and his fellow commissioner wrote. "Then if any suffer," they continued, "it would be justly chargeable to their own obstinacy." According to the moral calculation that satisfied Lumpkin, it seemed commendable to dispossess native families, feed the starving survivors who decided to move west, and blame those who did not for their own demise. (When planters punished enslaved people, they relied on a similar logic, blaming the victims when the planters themselves committed the original crime.)

But even then, Lumpkin resented feeding the starving refugees. The goal of the commissioners, as Lumpkin saw their task, was "to carry off emigrants" as fast as they could be collected, but rather than hurrying off to the West, hungry Cherokees were "fattening on the bounty of the Government." He consoled himself that, after the accounts were settled, Cherokees would be subject to "the imperative command" of the federal government: "To the West, march, march."⁹

~~~

WHILE THE War Department tightened its grip on the Cherokee Nation, John Ross continued to wage a tireless campaign to undermine the Treaty of New Echota. Deportation had proven to be so explosive that it became one of the rallying points for northern politicians who were unhappy with the Jackson administration, and even some southern politicians began cautiously opposing the president's Indian policy, if only to bolster their national ambitions. Ross hoped to outlast his long-time antagonist, who would leave office at the expiration of his second term on March 4, 1837. Jackson had been consistently hostile to native peoples from the start of his lengthy public career, even while professing a paternalistic devotion to them, the same fatherly concern, as the iron-fisted patriarch saw it, that defined his relationship with his slaves. He met some disobedient children with a whip in hand; others he confronted with armed militia.¹⁰

In public settings, native peoples occasionally professed to admire President Jackson. Like white Americans, they celebrated military prowess, and if they had not personally experienced his unsparing power, they knew of it by reputation. But it would be naive to take their expressions of respect at face value. The Chickasaws had questioned Jackson's paternalism in 1830 when negotiating with him in Franklin, Tennessee, as had at different times the Senecas, Choctaws, and Creeks. The public rebukes, cautious as they were, reveal native skepticism about Jackson's self-proclaimed benevolence. In private, what indigenous Americans said to each other is largely unknown, but a few extant letters hint at the depth of their hatred. John Ross noted that Jackson boasted "of never having told a red brother a lie, nor spoke to them with a forked tongue." The Cherokee leader continued, "We have a right, however, to judge of this bravado for ourselves from his own acts." No one was as forthright as the Cherokee John Ridge, who in a letter to a compatriot called President Jackson a "Chicken Snake" who hid in "the luxuriant grass of his nefarious hypocracy." It was necessary to "cut down this Snake's head," he exhorted, "and throw it down in the dust."[11]

While many of Jackson's admirers and detractors alike commented on his strong-willed personality, one Cherokee delegation came away with a different impression of the president. Meeting with him in 1834, they asked whether he had decided to disregard the "binding obligations" of U.S.-Cherokee treaties. "He did not desire to answer," one of the delegates reported. Rather than standing strong, Old Hickory "manifested a desire to equivocate" and "seemed to be afraid" to give a frank response. None of this surprised the Cherokees, who were "not ignorant of the true character of the white peoples chief."[12]

For a time, Cherokees had hoped that Martin Van Buren, Jackson's vice president and chosen successor, would lose the election of 1836, perhaps to Hugh Lawson White, a Tennessee senator who possessed a mawkish affection for native peoples. As the chairman of the Senate Committee on Indian Affairs, White had introduced the expulsion bill in the Senate in 1830, but he later broke with the president, as did a number of other Tennessee politicians. In 1834, he had supported a resolution recommending that the federal government purchase land from Georgia on behalf of the Cherokee Nation, a proposal that embarrassed Jackson and encouraged Ross and his allies.[13] Van Buren won the election, however, and in any case White would prove to be an unreliable ally.

Nonetheless, there were other avenues to pursue. Abolitionists, who were playing an increasingly vocal role in national politics, spoke loudly about the connection between plantation slavery and the deportation of native peoples. The Massachusetts Anti-Slavery Society stated in its annual report of 1838 that the "primary object of the South, through the instrumentality of the national government, is doubly atrocious." First, planter-politicians wished to take "forceful possession" of native lands. Then they intended to establish slavery, "with all its woes and horrors," on the stolen territory. The targets of this allegation saw no reason to debate the point, since they were proud of the empire of slave labor camps that they were building across the continent. The movement against expulsion, charged a slave-owning Tennessee congressman, was "nothing more nor less than a branch of Abolitionism in disguise." Seeking converts in the South, one northern activist sent copies of the abolitionist newspaper *Human Rights* to the Cherokee Nation.[14] Though John Ross and many other slaveholding Cherokees were themselves opposed to emancipation, any political division that split northern and southern politicians served their cause.

As late as November 1837, eighteen months after the Senate had ratified the Treaty of New Echota, Ross was still negotiating with the U.S. government for a permanent homeland in the South. He even rejected a preliminary offer from the United States that would have allowed Cherokees to remain in North Carolina and Tennessee in exchange for their Georgia and Alabama lands. The region was too small and mountainous, he said, holding out for a better agreement. If negotiations failed, he assured, Congress would still consider the matter "under circumstances more favorable, than at any other period heretofore."[15]

Ross correctly anticipated a groundswell of opposition to the Treaty of New Echota in the northern states. Sherlock Gregory, an incessant advocate from upstate New York, asked Congress to annul his citizenship until the United States atoned for its treatment of Native Americans and abolished slavery. On a single day in December 1837, the implacable Gregory fired off five petitions demanding congressional investigations of the treatment of Native Americans. When he was not calling for the liberation of native and enslaved peoples, he was railing against women's rights and Catholicism. Obviously, few people were as eclectic and vociferous as the impassioned Gregory. Still, thousands of Americans petitioned for the annulment of the treaty. Seventy women and men from Candor, New York, a rural area ten miles south of Ithaca, asserted that the treaty was "obtained by fraud." The citizens of Portland, Maine, demanded that, in justice to the Cherokees and "in belief of a God who is the Avenger of the oppressed," the United States should use "no means to compel the departure of said tribe." Seventy-two women from Holliston, Massachusetts, thirty miles west of Boston, asked Congress to defend Cherokees "from the cupidity and from the illegal and cruel aggressions of our own countrymen." Likewise, the citizens of Bristol, Connecticut, argued that enforcement of the treaty would be a "violation of principles of justice and of existing treaties" and "derogatory to the character of this confederated Republic," exposing the United States to "the judgments of the God of nations."[16]

In Union, New York, women and men observed that both Andrew Jackson and John Calhoun had made treaties with native nations. "Did they at that time, doubt the constitutionality of such engagements," they asked, "or that the treaty was binding on the several states, or the general govt?" "If our national faith is abandoned," they continued, "nothing of our vaunted republicanism worth contending for is left, and the days of our republic are numbered." "We are aware that the policy of removing Indians is asserted to be out of friendship to them," they wrote. "But is it friendship," they asked, "to expel a people from their beloved country by the sword?" From all present appearances, they concluded, the plans being put in place were not "in pursuit of the welfare of the Indian." Instead, federal policy obviously existed "to satisfy the craving of their white neighbours."[17]

Petitions arrived from Warren, Connecticut; Brooklyn, New York; and Orange, New Jersey. The residents of Concord, Massachusetts, including Ralph Waldo Emerson, told Congress that the Treaty of

New Echota was "an atrocious fraud" and "an outrage upon justice and humanity." In the Senate, a weary clerk counted signatures and recorded the results on the back of each petition: 45, 106, 114, 164, 88, 146, 197, 55, 21, 108, 213, 245, 404, and so on.[18] Nevertheless, the pushback from southern senators was considerable, so the protests were "laid upon the table," precluding debate on the matter. Clearly, Ross had miscalculated.

The longest petition came from the Cherokee Nation itself and surpassed all others in urgency. The "cup of hope is dashed from our lips; our prospects are dark with horror; and our hearts are filled with bitterness," it read. "Are we to be hunted through the mountains, like wild beasts, and our women, our children, our aged, our sick, to be dragged from their homes like culprits, and packed on board loathsome boats, for transportation to a sickly clime?" With 15,665 subscribers, the memorial, like a previous one from the Cherokees in 1836 that contained 14,910 names, was greeted with incredulity. Elias Boudinot, now residing with forces that viewed emigration as a necessity, had called the older petition a "fraud upon the world." After all, he maintained, there were now only about fifteen thousand Cherokees still remaining in the East. Ross "over shot the mark," charged John Schermerhorn, objecting that by his estimate there were only four thousand Cherokee men left in the region. To the Treaty Party that favored moving west, the petitions embodied Ross's faults, for the principal chief was humoring a "delusion" by failing to be candid with his fellow Cherokees. Ross asked his constituents, "Do you love your land?" and "Do you wish the white people driven out of the country?" Of course, the answers were uniformly positive. Posed differently—"Will you choose to live in this miserable condition among whites?"—the responses might have been very different. Ross belonged to a group of "rich half breeds" who did not share the interests of the common people, charged two Cherokees, who ironically were themselves wealthy and of mixed ancestry.[19]

The picture of a tyrannical Ross appealed to planter-politicians, who saw the Cherokee leader as the mirror image of themselves. As Wilson Lumpkin wrote to the like-minded Jackson, the vast majority of Cherokees were akin to slaves, "too ignorant and depraved" to think for themselves and "incapable of self government." They "should be treated as children." Ross ruled over them "just as much as the slave is governed by the opinion of his master," but while Lumpkin and his peers were benevolent fathers to their enslaved children, Ross, by comparison, was a tyrant to his. If only the Cherokees understood that Lumpkin, not Ross, had their best interests at heart, they would abandon their homes for the West. Of course, the logical conclusion to this exercise in arrogance and self-delusion was that U.S. planters should enslave native peoples for their own good, a determination reached by more than one southern apologist.[20]

Another white southerner saw Ross as the "slave, rather than the leader, of his nation," borne along by the overwhelming sentiment in the Cherokee Nation against expulsion. Perhaps this contrasting assessment better reflected the nature of leadership in many indigenous societies, including Ross's own. Though Ross had been elected as part of the Cherokee Nation's transition to a constitutional government, his authority rested on traditional sources, including the matrilineal clan, and his power depended on his ability to persuade. One missionary, a longtime resident in the nation, described a man who, soon after setting out for the West, stopped, loaded a rifle, and shot himself. "How vain then the reports that Mr. Ross has been keeping the people back from the west," the missionary wrote, "since it is so entirely beyond his power to make them willing to go."[21]

~~~

BY EARLY 1838, of the South's native residents, only the Cherokees and Seminoles remained in significant numbers. The United States had deported the Choctaws during the cholera times. A few years later, it had fought, defeated, and deported the Creeks. Then in late 1837, the

Chickasaws moved west. From their Mississippi homelands, they traveled a relatively short distance compared with other native southerners, enjoyed decent health, and avoided government contractors by funding their own journey. For these reasons, they suffered far less than others.[22]

With Ross and the vast majority of Cherokees remaining firmly opposed to deportation, the United States began preparing to conduct the expulsion by force of arms. By early 1838, the Engineering Corps had staked out roads through the Cherokee Nation in anticipation of an invasion. The War Department was particularly concerned about the region lying within present-day western North Carolina. If the Cherokees fought back, this area would surely become their stronghold, for it was filled with precipitous mountains and narrow valleys and ideal for concealment. In places, the creeks were "choked with thickets," wrote the topographical engineer William G. Williams, and mountain trails sometimes ascended too steeply for troop movements. The twenty-five-mile trail between Fort Lindsay and Fort Delany, in the present-day Nantahala National Forest, was "exceedingly rough," climbing along "dangerous rocky precipices of tremendous height and overhung by steep rocks and mountains." Other trails clung to mountainsides with no easy way down. "No descent could be obtained," wrote Williams, "that would not be very long and very expensive." Still others were hemmed in by high riverbanks and "might be easily annoyed at such points by ambuscades." To allow for the disposition of troops and munitions in this treacherous mountainous region, it was essential, wrote Williams, to survey the lands. The data "in case of emergency" would "contribute greatly to a prompt suppression of the Evil."[23]

The people who had cultivated Appalachia's green valleys "from time immemorial," the War Department learned from its topographical engineer, shared the common characteristics of "the Indian." The Cherokee was "Grave in his intercourse with whites, good tempered or sullen according to the treatment he receives from them." (Someone, perhaps from the War Department, later underlined this bit of useless information.) He was "Cunning and reserved" and "Poor, ignorant of economy, of time or money." Indians preferred "the chase of deer or sheer idleness to more useful employment." And they unsurprisingly favored their own language. In terms of appearance, the men were "athletic" and "supple," with an upright carriage and "elastic step." Though Cherokee men of fighting age perhaps numbered only four or five thousand, they were supported by an equal number of women, who were "inured to hardship" and "would yield great assistance in time of war." After completing this brief anthropological excursion, Williams concluded, "Little more need be said of these People."[24]

Despite the Cherokees' determination to keep their homes in the "mountain fastnesses" of southern Appalachia, the United States did have one essential advantage. With the federal government's quiet acquiescence, squatters, prospectors, and marauders had already reduced Cherokees to a "state of extreme poverty and privation." The first object of any military strategy against them would therefore be to occupy the fertile valleys that remained under Cherokee control and to seize the grain and cattle—in short, to starve them out. Reduced to extreme want, Cherokees would flee into the mountains, predicted Williams. Hogs and cattle had already destroyed many of the roots and plants that might otherwise contribute to the Cherokees' sustenance, and the refugees would therefore be forced to survive off the inner bark of the white oak. But, with this inadequate diet, they would be "shortly attended with disease." In their "precarious" situation, they would be easily brought to terms.[25] John Ross had been right. The government's "secret design"—begun with the passage of the expulsion act and culminating with the planned invasion of the Cherokee Nation—was to make their lives "so wretched and intolerable" that they would abandon their homelands.

On April 6, the War Department ordered Winfield Scott to report to the Cherokee Nation to oversee military operations, authorizing him to call up as many as three thousand volunteer soldiers from surrounding

states. An additional 1,500 soldiers would be transferred from the Florida
war to bolster Scott's command. (Most of the regulars, however, arrived
too late to be of use.) In preparation for the operation, the army had
already established twenty-three military posts in the Cherokee Nation,
and the quartermaster had shipped ordnance from Mobile. Scott traveled immediately to Athens, Tennessee, where he began studying the
local topography and making preparations for "an early vigorous system
of operations" to deport Cherokees. Though local native people showed
"the most inoffensive deportment," according to army intelligence, they
appeared unified in their determined stance. "The universal expression
amongst them is 'that they will make no resistance, but they must be
forced away.'"[26]

~~~

WHY DID U.S. politicians persist? By 1838, white southerners had
already seized the most valuable indigenous lands, situated in the rich
Black Prairie of Alabama and Mississippi. They could hardly have coveted the remote and mountainous Cherokee homeland in southern
Appalachia for extensive cotton cultivation. The chance discovery of
gold in Cherokee country in August 1829, it is true, attracted the interest of some of the most powerful men in the United States. The ubiqui-
tous J.D. Beers bought a share in a mine just inside the southern border
of the Cherokee Nation, and he acquired the output of surrounding
mining operations as well. In the same neighborhood, John C. Calhoun
also purchased an interest in a mine, using slave laborers to carry out the
backbreaking work, as he did on his South Carolina cotton plantation
one hundred miles to the east. George William Featherstonhaugh, the
British-born geographer, toured north Georgia's gold-laden mountains
with Calhoun in the fall of 1835 and noted that the valleys were "all dug
up." In the mad rush to strike it rich, miners had uprooted centuries-
old trees, rerouted mountain streams, and deposited tailings in large

unsightly mounds. The once-verdant valleys of the Appalachian foot-hills, he said, were "a picture of perfect desolation."[27]

And yet, by most accounts, gold mining peaked in the early 1830s, several years before the United States forced Cherokees to embark on the Trail of Tears. One scholar of the subject suggests that southern gold production, which was concentrated in Georgia and North Caro-lina, fell by 31 percent between 1834 and 1837. Those somewhat conjec-tural numbers err on the side of caution, and the decline may have been even greater. In 1838, one Georgia newspaper, hoping for a revival of the industry, admitted that the "high price of cotton, and consequently of labor, caused the Southern gold mines to be comparatively neglected for a few years."[28]

Regardless of the exact numbers, the peak years of mining in the early 1830s had proven that Georgia's citizens could exploit the gold deposits even while Cherokees remained on their homelands. In fact, most gold-bearing areas in the South did not lie within the Cherokee Nation, and most of the Cherokee Nation did not bear gold. As a result, large parts of the region did not interest colonizers. While thousands of fortunate drawers in the Georgia land lotteries had moved into the Cherokee Nation to seize their winnings, many others declined to claim their land, leading the legislature to extend the deadline to file paper-work every year until 1842. John Bell of Tennessee, the chairman of the House Committee on Indian Affairs, even suggested in May 1838 that his constituents would have acquiesced to the "permanent residence" of Cherokees on their "ancient possessions"—though he later underscored that events had since ruled out that possibility.[29]

Planter-politicians of course had other reasons besides cotton and gold to clear the South of native peoples, as Representative William Dawson of Georgia outlined in a fiery speech on the floor of the House in May 1838. President Van Buren's secretary of war, Joel Poinsett, had recently proposed delaying Cherokee expulsion by two years, and congressmen who opposed U.S. Indian policy had temporarily stalled a bill to fund

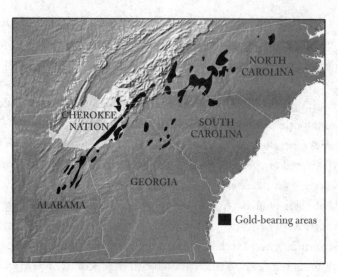

Gold-bearing areas in the South.

---

the Seminole war and Cherokee expulsion. As John Ross and a Cherokee delegation listened from the gallery, an outraged Dawson attacked his colleagues. The defenders of the Indians, he charged, were either ignorant or moved by "a prurient disposition to be esteemed the bold assailants of the supposed oppressors, and the vindicators of the oppressed." The Georgia congressman accused northerners of hypocrisy. "Go and read the tale of your own Indian wars," he goaded his northern colleagues.[30]

Dawson enumerated the reasons that the region's longtime residents must be expelled. Cherokees were lawless. White mothers in Georgia could not visit their daughters in Tennessee without crossing through the Cherokee Nation and putting themselves at risk of being raped. Entrepreneurs could not build roads and bridges through the region. Drivers of horses, mules, and hogs were compelled to travel great distances to pass around the Cherokee Nation. And the state could not proceed with the "great work of uniting by railroad the western waters with the Atlantic." All these inconveniences and injustices arose, he said, "because the

Cherokees claimed the unrestricted right to the country." If Georgia did not get its way, he threatened, it would secede. And if federal troops crossed into the state to "castigate" it, its citizens would meet them at the border with arms.[31]

As indignant as Dawson sounded, his reasons do not adequately account for the unshakable determination of Georgia's planter-politicians to expel Cherokees from southern Appalachia or the unbounded fury they directed at everyone who challenged them. While they postured by standing on states' rights, white supremacy in fact made up the bed-rock of their politics. As the citizens of Walker County, Georgia, in the northwestern corner of the state, put it, the Cherokees "invite to action our *internal* as well as *external* enemies." These stalwart defenders of white supremacy resolved that each citizen procure a firearm and fifty rounds of ammunition to meet the internal threat of a slave uprising and the external threat of a foreign invasion—and, when the time was right, to drive off the region's oldest residents "at the point of a bayonet."[32]

Perhaps some element of reason stoked the fears of Walker County's citizens. Practically speaking, the Cherokee Nation was a competing sovereign entity in the heart of the South, governed by people who were manifestly opposed to the guiding ideology of the region's white ruling class. In addition, its status as a "domestic dependent nation" created a special relationship with Washington City that invited federal power into the region. But Walker County was hardly a prime location for a slave rebellion. It had perhaps a thousand enslaved laborers who were outnumbered by a factor of ten to one.[33] The likelihood of Cherokees teaming up with a foreign power was even more remote.

Something more powerful than reason motivated Walker County's citizens. Thomas Jefferson, despite or because of his troubled relation-ship with enslaved African Americans, had put his finger on the source. Slavery, he said, turned planters into despots who were habituated to ruling but not being ruled. The habit extended to the South's non-slaveholding whites as well, who were empowered by law to lord over "colored people." The very existence of the Cherokee Nation insulted them. Representative George Washington Bonaparte Towns of Georgia, bearing the name of both a planter and a despot, warned Congress in May 1838 that his state would never be "castigated into submission" by being forced to recognize Cherokee rights. That was a punishment properly meted out "to the slave or the serf," the congressman declared, not to a proud slaveholding state that jealously guarded "her honor and her liberty."[34] By asserting their "rights," planter-politicians such as Dawson and Towns would bring to fruition the project they had launched in 1830. They would leave not a single indigenous person in the region, thereby making white men the masters of every square foot of the South. The expulsion of the Cherokees would realize the vision outlined in 1825 by Georgia's "Socrates." "We the people of Georgia" would become "we the white people of Georgia." Untroubled by sovereign Native Americans, planters would reign unchallenged over their African American slaves.

As he listened from the House gallery, it is not known what John Ross made of Dawson's ill-tempered speech, or whether he was on hand the next day to witness the fistfight that broke out between John Bell and a Tennessee colleague during the continuing debate over the Indian funding bill. On June 5, still in Washington City, a resigned Ross wrote, "The removal of the Cherokees from their native land, right or wrong, appears to be the fixed and unalterable determination of this government; it remains now only for the United States to promulgate the decree."[35] Ross was unaware that ten days earlier Winfield Scott had already launched the operation to deport the Cherokees from their eastern homelands.

~~~

THE CHEROKEE expulsion began on Saturday morning, May 26, 1838, eight years to the day after the House of Representatives had passed the "Act to provide for an exchange of lands with the Indians" by a five-vote margin and turned the deportation of eighty thousand people into federal policy. General Scott's orders to his troops were clear. He commanded his men to surround and arrest "as many Indians" as possible, leave them under guard in the nearest fort, and return for more. "These operations will be again and again repeated," he directed, until every indigenous person was imprisoned.[36]

The massive buildup of troops was large enough "to broil, pepper and eat the Cherokees," bragged the commander of the Georgia militia. With 3,500 soldiers, General Scott could field one soldier for every four deportees, a force "so large and so overwhelming," wrote one general, that resistance would be "hopeless." Sheer numbers seemed to ensure that the dispossession would unfold at lightning speed. Though state militia were undisciplined and often drunk, they swept over mountains and scoured river valleys, "taking Indians" through the day and leaving no time for the dispossessed to collect their belongings or even to gather their children. At night, they roused families from their homes, placed them under guard, and then slept in their still-warm beds. The next day, they continued the search from house to house, eventually marching the prisoners at bayonet-point to regional forts, where hundreds of people awaited transfer to one of the three central internment camps, Fort Payne in Alabama and the two larger military outposts in Tennessee, Ross's Landing and Fort Cass. It was fatiguing work, complained one volunteer, and not "what it was cracked up to be."[37]

Most Cherokees complied with the soldiers' orders, determined not to provoke armed men who, in the words of one general, thought it "no crime to kill an Indian." However, scores of people, especially from North Carolina's Cheoah Valley, in the extreme southwestern corner of the state, fled into the mountains when the troops arrived. "A more religious people than inhabits this valley cannot be found any where," wrote an admiring soldier. "Their preachers speak of the prospect of their speedy removal," he continued, "and the subject never fails to throw the congregation into Tears." Despite the War Department's careful preparations to move munitions and soldiers through North Carolina's alpine terrain, its officers could not capture the Cherokees. The fugitives formed the nucleus of what would become the Eastern Band of Cherokee Indians, recognized by the federal government as a distinct Indian nation in 1868.[38]

The terror that the soldiers spread as they moved through the nation can only be glimpsed through fragmentary records. They seized individuals who were engaged in the routine tasks of daily life, visiting friends, tending to livestock, and farming. They shot dead a deaf and dumb man, who tried to flee at the sight of the armed intruders. They drove two hundred children, women, and men through torrential rain, with scarcely a blanket to protect them. One soldier leveled a gun at a father and ordered him to board a barge, though the man had asked to wait for his young son. Infants and the aged especially suffered, since they were more susceptible to dysentery and to the effects of exposure. Soldiers forced one elderly woman, said to be nearly one hundred years old, to

Military forts and internment camps May–December, 1838.
The number of deportees, where given, is approximate.

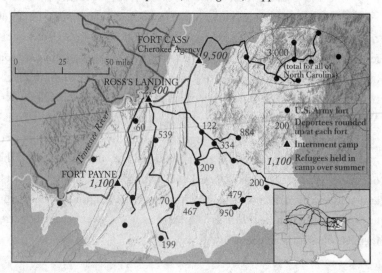

march all day and night to the point of exhaustion. They were suspected of killing another, who was unable to continue walking, and of hiding the body off the road.[39]

In mid-June, only a few weeks after the launch of the operation, the commander of the Georgia militia reported that the operation was complete. Scouts had recently searched north Georgia "in every direction, without seeing any Indians, or late Indian signs," but to be certain, mounted volunteers swept the country once more. The land was deserted. "Georgia has been entirely cleared of red population," announced General Scott a week later. The residents, numbering nearly fifteen thousand, had been herded into camps across the border in Tennessee and Alabama, where they awaited deportation. Many were "ragged and miserable," prompting the federal government to purchase clothing for them for the march west. The refugees rejected the false charity, stating that they had clothes of their own, which they had not been allowed to bring.[40]

Throughout the region, houses stood empty of residents and the objects of everyday life rested in place: a fiddle, chairs, a bed, a spinning wheel, a cooking pot, a bag of dried fruit, a playing horn. But this eerie absence of people was only temporary. Troops stole much of the Cherokees' property, and "work hands" followed soon after to collect what remained for auction by the federal government. John Dawson bought four axes that belonged to Teliska, tools that the planter probably turned over to his nine slaves. Mr. Sloan purchased Chewey's fiddle, Mr. McSpadden bought Crabgrass's canoe, John Oxford purchased Amateeska's pot, and Miss Godard bought Sopes's bed.[41] U.S. citizens moved into Cherokee houses, slept in their beds, and ate out of their pots. The occupiers used sheep shears, hoes, and fishing spears, augers, baskets, and fiddles that still bore the handprints of the original owners. The arrogation of Cherokee things, as bizarre as it was, went without comment in the southern press.

That June, the U.S. Army deported nearly three thousand people by steamboat. Taking the same route as Joseph Harris's detachment a year earlier, the transports followed the Tennessee River to the Ohio and Mississippi. Traveling down the Mississippi, they reached the Arkansas and ascended that river nearly to Fort Gibson. Mortality on the crowded and disease-ridden steamboats surpassed 10 percent during these summer deportations. As the water fell in western rivers and made steamboat travel unreliable, Cherokees arranged with the army to remain in internment camps in the East until the fall. When the cool weather arrived, Cherokees promised to transport themselves rather than depend on erratic and dishonest government contractors. At least 353 people died in the crowded and unsanitary camps during the hot southern summer.[42]

The majority of Cherokees, weakened after spending four months in camp under armed guard, set out for the West in October and November 1838. Nearly eleven thousand people in eleven separate detachments traveled northwest through Nashville, Tennessee, passing ten miles west of the Hermitage, Andrew Jackson's thousand-acre plantation, where the retired president commanded more than one hundred slave laborers. Continuing northwest, they crossed the frozen Ohio and then bore west through the southern end of Illinois. They crossed the Mississippi at Cape Girardeau and followed two slightly different routes through Missouri. One hundred miles from their destination, they turned nearly due south, before bearing west and crossing into present-day Oklahoma. The arduous seven-hundred-mile trek through mud, rain, and ice took four months to complete entirely on foot. Extrapolating from incomplete data, it appears that approximately 6 percent, or more than six hundred, of the nearly eleven thousand refugees who followed this northern route died during the journey.[43] Smaller numbers went by water or followed slightly more direct overland routes. But even the 660 deportees who took the shortest overland route, walking nearly due west through Tennessee and Arkansas, still covered 650 miles by foot.

Including the military's June deportations by steamboat and the Cherokee-led overland treks in the fall, approximately 1,000 people died directly during the months-long operation, representing nearly 7 percent of the population. A different accounting, which incorporates deaths in the holding camps as well as miscarriages, infertility, and other causes of reduced birth rate, produces a toll more than three times as large, at 3,500. The numbers do not capture the suffering. Three fatalities, horrendous but no different from hundreds of others, include an infant who succumbed from dysentery, a woman who was crushed by an overturned cart, and an elderly man, chilled to the bone, who dozed off too close to a campfire and burned to death.[44]

George Hicks, a friend of John Ross's, led one of the last detachments of Cherokees to leave their homeland. "It is with sorrow that we are

The "Trail of Tears," showing the routes that Cherokees traveled from their eastern homeland in the summer and fall of 1838. In some instances, I have extrapolated the number of deaths from the mortality rates of detachments that traveled the same route.

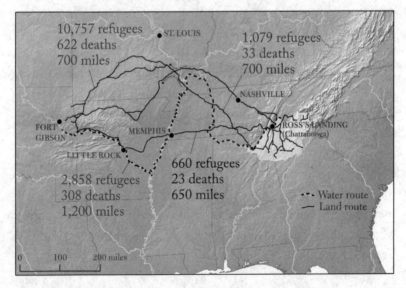

10,757 refugees
622 deaths
700 miles

ST. LOUIS

1,079 refugees
33 deaths
700 miles

NASHVILLE

FORT GIBSON

MEMPHIS

ROSS'S LANDING
(Chattanooga)

LITTLE ROCK

2,858 refugees
308 deaths
1,200 miles

660 refugees
23 deaths
650 miles

- - - Water route
——— Land route

0   100   200 miles

forced by the authority of the white man to quit the scenes of our child-hood," he wrote, describing how U.S. citizens robbed them in plain day-light as the massive caravan of 1,031 refugees, sixty wagons, six hundred horses, and forty pairs of oxen departed the Cherokee Nation. The long winter trek on the northern route took over four months, and seventy-nine people died along the way. When the survivors finally arrived in the West, the federal agent received them with rations of corn and beef that were unfit for human consumption. From "the promises made to us in the Nation East," Hicks jeered, "we did not Expect such Treatment."[45]

CHAPTER 11

'TIS NO SIN

~~~

Two weeks before Hicks and his party of Cherokee refugees arrived in Indian Territory, Captain Samuel Russell and seven men of the Second Infantry were descending the Miami River, heading to Fort Dallas in what is now downtown Miami. Seminole marksmen waited for the open boats to come within range and then fired a volley, hitting Russell in the chest. Russell ordered the boats to the opposite bank, climbed ashore, and was struck in the temple, dying instantly. Lieutenant Woodruff took command. The overmatched troops engaged in an hour-long firefight and suffered another fatal casualty, before retrieving Russell's body and continuing on to Fort Dallas. As usual, wrote one officer, the Seminoles' "*perfect* knowledge of the country enabled them to escape."[1]

Since the heady days of early 1836, when the South's citizens sent off their militia with great fanfare to fight in the swamps of Florida, the grind of war had shattered their expectations of easily won glory. Lewis Cass's confident assertion that a "display of a respectable force" would disabuse the "deluded" Seminoles of their illusions had turned out to be an illusion of its own.[2] Seminoles were far more tenacious than the secretary of war had anticipated and far more formidable than many volunteer soldiers imagined.

Florida's native families inherited a long tradition of defying colonial forces, stretching back to the mid-eighteenth century, when their great-grandparents had first carved out villages on the peninsula, safely distant from the expanding British colonies to the north but close enough to the Spanish to sustain a mutually profitable trade. The emigration of Creek dissidents periodically refreshed and strengthened Seminole militancy, most recently during the U.S.-Creek War of 1813–14 and the U.S.-Creek War of 1836. In the 1830s, the new arrivals were often young men, without families, who were driven to avenge the losses that their communities had suffered in Alabama. Though the men received a great deal of attention from the U.S. press—they were the iconic bloodthirsty warriors who thrilled readers in the Northeast and frightened those in the South—women played an equally essential role in the resistance. When not pouring lead bullets, they labored to wring subsistence from Florida's swamps and hammocks—the elevated patches of land that rose above surrounding waters—by cultivating and gathering food supplies and then hiding them effectively. They thwarted the primary strategy of the U.S. Army "to famish the savage out."[3]

Of course, not all thought it wise to challenge the U.S. Army. Charley Emathla, a Creek leader who had relocated to Seminole country, encouraged his people to move west, even while recognizing that he would "lose many on the path." Osceola executed him before he could depart, but his brother Holata Emathla and 407 others nonetheless gathered in Tampa to undertake the voyage. Their ordeal became an object lesson not to trust the federal government. Within three weeks of their departure in April 1836, an outbreak of measles aboard the steamboats carrying them across the Gulf reduced the party to 382. In western Arkansas, falling water forced them off the boats, and they continued the journey on foot. The number of sick continued to mount, reaching 150, and, in steady rain, they were reluctant to break camp. "We have had every difficulty to contend with," wrote the escorting U.S. officer, Jefferson Van Horne. "These people seem to have been pampered and indulged to such a degree," he complained to George Gibson, "that nothing can satisfy them or equal their extravagant expectations." Wagons foundered in the mud, and it was finally impossible to proceed. In camp, people died daily, and when the journey resumed again, after Van Horne and his assistants threatened the migrants and teamsters at gunpoint, the sick and dying had to be lifted into wagons, where they "lay in their own filth." The "effluvia and pestilential atmosphere" in the wagons and the "tainted air" in the camps was "almost insupportable," objected the unsympathetic Van Horne. "It would have had a wholesome effect had they been left to their fate," he wrote, "or driven at the point of a bayonet."[4]

Nearing their destination in what would become eastern Oklahoma, Holata Emathla fell ill. Expecting to die within a few hours, he asked that the party halt until he was dead and his body enshrined, but Van Horne denied the request, complaining that the refugees had "all along thrown every difficulty in the way." The party refused to move. Two days later, an eyewitness recorded, their "father, guardian, friend," and the "anchor of all their future hopes" died, leaving the migrants "disconsolate and broken hearted." Holata Emathla's family and followers cleared an area on a rise overlooking a creek, placed his body and possessions inside a five-foot-high wooden tomb, and kindled a fire nearby.[5]

A few days after this sorrowful event, the party arrived at their destination, numbering only 320. Nearly one out of every five had perished within the space of two months, and there was no sign that the deaths were abating. "Even while I count them," Van Horne reported, "I erase from the roll the name of those that die." The grieving survivors, destitute and in ill-health, struggled to sustain themselves in the strange, new land. Van Horne, consistent to the end, condemned the demoralized refugees as "dissipated, idle, and reckless."[6]

With little factual information at hand, the Seminoles who remained in Florida had to assume that their relatives had disappeared over the horizon, never to be heard from again. Or perhaps, beset by difficulties, they had died by the score during the journey and were continuing to despair in their new home. Neither scenario encouraged the Floridians to surrender to the United States. They were willing to do anything, confessed one Seminole leader, except board steamboats bound for the West.[7]

When their resolve flagged, they found encouragement from family and friends. Archaeological evidence reveals that European American ceramics are absent from Seminole settlements during the war, suggesting that residents were rejecting U.S. influence as part of a religious movement to revitalize and purify their communities. (Even in the midst of the conflict, there were opportunities to obtain foreign goods from traders.) Over the previous half century, similar movements had galvanized uprisings across the East. For the Seminoles, the multiyear conflict and the religious inspiration undergirding it united villagers in a common cause and catalyzed the formation of a distinct national identity.[8] To abandon the fight was to lose faith and to betray one's community.

~~~

WHILE SECRETARY Cass underestimated the commitment of Seminoles to remain in their homeland, his generals failed to recognize that Florida's native residents possessed a tremendous military advantage, sufficient to wear down the army and send it home in defeat. Before the start of renewed hostilities in 1836, Seminoles reportedly had watched U.S. soldiers taking target practice and had come away with a sense of their own superiority. Even the soldiers, aware that they were not well-trained in irregular warfare, could see that their ranks looked "ridiculous" when drilling in the woods in "Indian fighting." U.S. troops often moved with too much baggage, too many horses, and too much noise. The numbers did not favor them. According to quartermaster calculations, one thousand troops on the road for twelve days required 24,000 pounds of rations, hauled by sixty-four horses pulling sixteen wagons, four of which carried forage solely for the draft animals. This ponderous train of wagons, horses, livestock, and people does not even account for military supplies and food for the teamsters. If the commotion made by such a convoy did not alert Seminoles to U.S. troop movements, the army's practice of sounding bugles at daybreak and night foolishly announced their locations.[9]

Seminole land was unknown to the army, whose officers relied on faulty bookstore maps that Winfield Scott dismissed as "outlines filled up with unlucky guesses." A year into the conflict, Thomas Jesup, the commanding general, still had no topographical information and no reliable guides. "We have perhaps as little knowledge of the interior of Florida, as of the interior of China," he protested. Astoundingly, officers were voicing similar complaints in 1840, more than four years after the Seminoles had surprised and destroyed Dade's column. "Wholly ignorant of the country in which I am expected to operate," admitted one scout. Existing maps, he stated, were "erroneous in many important respects."[10]

Even as firsthand knowledge of the land slowly replaced guesswork, the terrain remained challenging. The region was "one vast forest castle, surrounded by moats, and guarded by difficult approaches," wrote a South Carolinian. Hammocks, morasses, scrublands, and dense forests made travel difficult, and if "celerity of movement" was "indispensable" to U.S. troops, as one soldier claimed, it was also impossible. The soldiers' spirits foundered in the region's inundated byways. Passing through knobby cypress swamps, U.S. troops unhitched their horses and pulled the wagons through the water themselves. Saw palmetto, an aptly named shrub with sharp-edged stalks, shredded their shoes and clothes and lacerated their skin. One naval officer, who spent weeks dragging canoes through the Everglades in pursuit of Seminole families, nearly lost both of his legs from infected wounds. Meanwhile, indigenous marksmen shot at the troops and retreated unseen. It was terrifying, confessed one soldier.[11]

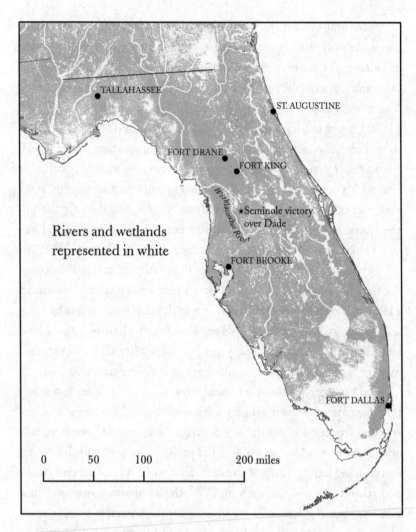

Large areas of the Seminole homeland were seasonally or permanently flooded, presenting challenges to U.S. troops. Seminole families took refuge along the Withlacoochee, whose low and marshy banks were covered with dense vegetation. One soldier wrote that it was as if nature had designed the river "as a covert and wall of defense for the savages."

By burning bridges and ambushing troops at every difficult pass, Seminole partisans were especially adept at using the region's rivers to their advantage. The army relied on hastily constructed rafts that sometimes sank and on makeshift bridges that were inadequate to the task. One "slight and crazy bridge" erected over the Ocklawaha River, in central Florida, could not support both a wagon and its team at the same time, so soldiers had to lead the draft animals over first and then return to pull the wagons by hand. With seventy wagons, crossing the sixty-foot-wide river took a day and a half. An experiment to build floating wagons, lined with rubber cloth, was a failure. Pontoon bridges, first demonstrated in the Creek Nation, were more effective but not yet in wide use. Even small mobile forces could not navigate the waters effectively. G.W. Allen led forty men down the Gulf Coast in light sailboats and proceeded up the Crystal River north of Tampa Bay. The troops debarked, discovered a large village, and pursued several people through hammocks and estuaries before running into deep water. They found a narrow strip of land and advanced directly into heavy gunfire before retreating. All they had to show for the expedition was the death of their sergeant.[12]

And yet, despite all of these handicaps, the United States ostensibly possessed a decisive technological advantage. Surely "the progress of liberty and law, service and the arts of civilization," as one Tennessee volunteer put it, would triumph over the primitive savage, with his "torch and scalping knife." This self-satisfied depiction did not hold true, however. Thanks to importations from Cuba, the Seminoles possessed better firearms than the army's standard-issue flintlock muzzle-loading musket, and the army's advanced weapons proved ineffective. "Destructive canisters," tin cases loaded with iron balls, were launched into the hammocks, where the shrapnel struck child and adult alike. In one instance, a soldier found an elderly man who had been killed by the indiscriminate bombardment, his skull "quartered and carried away." But the disadvantage of hauling heavy artillery through cypress swamps and across rivers outweighed their terrifying and deadly effect. Steamboats, the iconic

Sketch of a fictional hot-air balloon's "night ascension." In the U.S. encampment pictured on the left, uniformed, upright, and musket-bearing troops watch their marvelous wartime technology in operation. From the balloon's gondola, a soldier peers through a telescope at a desultory "Indian Encampment," where Seminoles are lying down, squatting, and milling about with tomahawks.

---

symbol of technological progress at the time, supplied coastal depots but proved useless in navigating Florida's shallow rivers. The War Department had great hope for the *Izard*, a lightweight vessel that drew only 2.5 feet of water. But it ran aground on one of the bars at the mouth of the Withlacoochee and within hours was a complete wreck. When the crew of twenty-eight finally made it back to safety, all but four had been "enfeebled and worn down by disease." Even the legendary arms manufacturer Samuel Colt could not help. He visited Florida with his new repeating rifle, but five of the thirty guns burst within ten days, seriously injuring those within range of the shrapnel.[13]

Perhaps the most aspiring of the wartime technologies arose in the form of the hot-air balloon, already familiar to armies in Europe but never before deployed in the United States. As proposed in 1840, a balloonist would ascend nightly above the peninsula's swamps and hammocks to scout out campfires, returning to earth in the morning, with a map in hand of enemy locations. One general imagined that the aerial contraption would also serve in conflicts on the "large undulating prairies of the far west," where "thousands of Indians" were often nearby but unknown to U.S. troops. After some initial encouragement, the plan was rejected as "entirely impracticable."[14]

The chimerical project was nonetheless conceived in the spirit of the war, which from the perspective of many U.S. citizens pitted civilization against nature. Where the "savages" had been "expelled," boasted a Florida congressional delegate, the forest was "falling before the axe of industry" and fields of cotton were "blooming." "I will shew you a city, in the place of a wigwam," he waxed, "and the press inculcating the mild precepts of Republicanism, where the war whoop was lately heard."[15] In a recurring theme of the American military, the arts of civilization would win the war for civilization.

With its presumed technological advantages proving inconsequential, the War Department cycled rapidly through seven commanding generals in the space of seven years in desperate search of victory. Winfield Scott, the first, devised a plan to win a European-style war, reflecting his expertise in French infantry tactics, the subject of the U.S. training manual he had authored. His successors plotted out other strategies, all of which failed in different ways. Certainly, it was not advisable to launch a summer campaign in the malarial climate of Florida, as General Richard Call did. General Thomas Jesup's strategy of employing small mobile forces proved somewhat effective, but he could not attain final victory against a people who were more mobile and more committed to the cause. Out of frustration, Jesup arrested and imprisoned Osceola under a flag of truce, a violation of the rules of war that he was still defending twenty years after the fact. Jesup finally gave up any hope for "the emigration of the Seminoles," declaring the proposition "impracticable under any circumstances." "The country can be rid of them," he said, "only by exterminating them." Was the government prepared to take such an extreme measure? he asked. It was. Jesup's friend and fellow officer Truman Cross reported that the secretary of war, the wealthy South Carolinian Joel Poinsett, "goes for 'extermination.'"[16]

In the spirit of Poinsett's ruthlessness, several officers and even one commanding general told their troops to take no prisoners. The "hackneyed phraseology of the day," wrote the disgusted Nathaniel Wyche Hunter, a free-thinking graduate of West Point, is thoroughly "unsatisfying." The native Georgian had grown to resent suspect platitudes: "that I have no right to discuss the propriety of any order; that it is the duty of a soldier to obey; that government is but enforcing a treaty; that our enemies are barbarious murderers of women and children; and last, that I am paid for acting not thinking." The government had ordered him to commit a crime, he charged, to defend a fraudulent treaty with "the vilest machinations man or demon could invent." Another soldier wrestled with his sympathy for the Seminoles, whom he said were "hunted like wolves" on their own lands. But when the time came to shoot a family after a daylong chase, he followed orders. "Its 'our vocation Hal' besides duty—fame—glory—necessity and all that," he sneered, quoting Shakespeare's Falstaff. In *Henry IV*, Falstaff, a dedicated highway robber, continues, "'tis no sin for a man to labour in his vocation."[17]

Even with the latitude to exterminate native families, Jesup's successors found no success in bringing the war to an end. General Zachary Taylor decided to divide the peninsula into twenty-mile squares, each patrolled by a centrally located garrison. "How absurd!" exclaimed one officer, after being ordered to scout squares no. 20 and no. 17. "It sounds well & looks well on paper," he scoffed. In practice, however, the "war of posts," as it was known, foundered on logistics. The garrisons were generally large enough to defend themselves behind breastworks but not to patrol their assigned squares without being "cut to pieces." In sum, Taylor's supremely rational plan was simply not feasible, as the U.S. Army finally conceded after laboring to construct 53 new posts, 848 miles of wagon roads, and 3,643 feet of causeways and bridges.[18]

In early 1838, Taylor presided over one of war's more controversial operations, when the War Department purchased thirty-three bloodhounds from Cuba to track Seminole families through Florida's morasses. The dogs proved ineffective in the swampy terrain, however, and their presence became a clear liability in public debates about the war. Nathaniel Wyche Hunter hoped that the Seminoles would take revenge for the "grand blood hound expedition." The dogs were "of no value whatever." "We must bear the odium," he fumed, "without reaping any benefits from the 'experiment.'" One Florida newspaper shamelessly suggested that the animals should be rebranded as "Peace-Hounds," but their association with slave catching could not be broken.[19] Northerners would not abide by the practice of tracking families with dogs, and top brass quietly withdrew the animals.

Succeeding Taylor, Walker Keith Armistead sketched a plan to drive Seminole families south of an east-west line, drawn across the peninsula through Fort King, in present-day Ocala. But even with 6,500 men, this plan proved to be impractical. The sharp-tongued Ethan Allen Hitchcock said that Armistead preferred to spend his time picking up seashells on the beach in Sarasota. He is "useless," wrote Hitchcock, and "a most dangerous man." Armistead, according to another officer, was an "imbecile dotard." Under his command, a peace initiative involved U.S. troops placing white flags on the smoldering ruins of houses and alongside the bodies of murdered Seminoles, with predictable results.[20]

~~~

AS DREAMS of easy victory evaporated under the Florida sun, soldiers lost whatever zeal they had once possessed for the cause. Approximately

30,000 militia served in the war. They were a much-needed source of manpower for the U.S. Army, which could only deploy a few thousand of its 11,000 troops to Florida at any one time. Though some militia eagerly departed for the front, their enthusiasm rarely lasted. Others arrived already disillusioned. When South Carolina initiated a draft, poor upcountry farmers reportedly regarded the conscription and "all the specious talk about the glorious necessity of volunteering, to save their own credit, and that of the State, as sheer nonsense." Those who could afford it simply paid for an able-bodied substitute. Meanwhile, planters from the low country, the site of some of the nation's largest and most brutal slave labor camps, excused themselves from service. "A great consideration in the matter," observed one white South Carolinian, "was the very dense <u>Black</u> population in the low country." Slave laborers out-numbered white people in the region by a margin of four to one. "Too many whites," he explained, "cannot be removed from this section of country with safety."[21]

U.S. regulars, though better trained, were no more committed to the cause. They received $6 to $7 per month for their services, equivalent to $20,400 a year in today's money, a welcome sum during the nationwide economic depression of the late 1830s and early 1840s but not enough to turn day laborers, farmers, and recent immigrants into dedicated sol-diers. Rather than serve in the deadly Florida campaign, officers could simply resign, as they did in droves, but privates had no recourse other than to fulfill their terms of duty, even if halfheartedly.[22]

The daily violence in the Second U.S.-Seminole War was both hor-rifying and numbing. Marching inland from Fort Brooke in Tampa to establish a weapons depot, Alexander Beaufort Meek described the terrifying and demoralizing experience of volunteers who just weeks earlier had left home as heroes. Seminole marksmen shot one in the back of the head, ambushed and scalped another, shot a third in the head, and hit a fourth in the torso. The threat seemed to be everywhere, and yet the "Indians could not be seen." William Bowen Campbell of

Tennessee had enlisted out of "excitement" and "patriotism," his only regret being that "we have no prospect of a <u>fight</u>." Since the volunteers would be "in no danger from the Indians," he lamented, wartime honors would be difficult to earn. Four months later, however, his company was "broken down, starved, worn out and unfit for service." Exchanging fire with Seminole sharpshooters on the Withlacoochee, he was feet away when his friend died within minutes of being struck by a bullet. Though Campbell had set out believing that native peoples would surrender immediately upon learning of the arrival of the vaunted Tennessee volunteers, a part of his company deserted soon after the firefight on the Withlacoochee.[23]

Perhaps worse than the constant fear of being shot was the "eternal dripping of death" brought on by Florida's "villainous climate." "The Dr. cannot, as yet, control the movements of my bowels," lamented Joseph Smith, an enlisted soldier who supposed he was writing his last letter to his wife. One seventeen-year-old German immigrant, who had run away from his parents, died in a delirium, hemorrhaging and calling for his mother. Another soldier, standing sentinel, went mad, shrieking "Indians, Indians!" He never recovered. Soldiers complained of a "general sinking of the system, a 'regular cave in' of the constitution," the effects of malaria that eventually left them "completely prostrated . . . in body and mind."[24]

William Pew, a lawyer practicing in Pittsburgh, volunteered for service in Florida and did two tours. Sent with the First Infantry to establish a fort about twenty miles east of Tallahassee, he watched dozens of people fall ill, eventually amounting to two-thirds of the entire company. His journal ends abruptly on June 2, 1839, after he noted that his commanding officer was sick. The officer would soon die, followed by Pew himself. A quotation from the Gospels stands alone on the last page of the volume: "like the voice of one crying in the wilderness."[25]

Seminoles and their African American allies enjoyed acquired immunity to malaria, a result of early and frequent exposure to the parasite, and they rarely suffered from the disease. But the vast majority of white Americans had no protection other than quinine. Extracted from the bark of the cinchona tree, quinine was the "whole stock in trade," admitted one doctor's assistant, and soldiers consumed the medication as if it were food. Nonetheless, the order to "lay him out," or prepare someone for burial, became so common that the command was given without a thought.[26]

In addition to malaria, soldiers suffered from a host of other infections and battle-inflicted injuries. "Medicines," including olive oil, turpentine, and silver nitrate, provided little to no relief, but at least opium dulled the pain from the amputating instruments, cupping glasses, dissecting tools, thumb lancets (for drawing blood), hernia trusses, splints, and trepanning instruments (for cutting holes in patients' skulls) that the U.S. Army requisitioned. Despite or because of such interventions, corpses multiplied. At Fort Drane in central Florida, when the wooden houses that passed for a hospital filled up with the dead and dying, troops hastily erected a lean-to outside the pickets to store more bodies. Sometimes they were forced to keep the deceased in tents with the living, a practice deemed safer than placing them in storehouses, where the flies swarming over the putrid bodies might contaminate provisions.[27]

Statistics from September 1841, an average month in terms of morbidity, capture the tremendous loss. Of about 4,100 U.S. forces stationed in Florida, over 1,800 were ill. By one estimate, approximately 30 percent never recovered. Those who were permanently "enfeebled and destroyed" were discharged to a life of "poverty, wretchedness, and woe." Others simply died. In fact, for every soldier who was killed on the battlefield, four others succumbed from disease.[28]

The thousands of day laborers, farmers, and glory seekers who fought against Florida's indigenous families salved their wounds and treated their misery with alcohol. One deputy quartermaster was said to be drunk from sunup to sundown. At Fort Heileman, not far from present-day Jacksonville, troops regularly drank to excess, and at Fort Cummings, in central Florida, soldiers raided the medical kit in search of alcohol. One company of militia received orders to muster after church, but by then the volunteers were too drunk to make an appearance. Self-medication extended up the chain of command. Richard Call, at one point the commanding general of the entire war, was reportedly a "drunkard, perfectly besotted," who continued to tipple even while campaigning. And General Robert Armstrong of the Tennessee volunteers was sometimes drunk for days on end; his staff often had to take him on the road to distance him from liquor.[29]

When alcohol proved ineffective, soldiers turned to stronger drugs. Nathaniel Wyche Hunter, who served in Florida for five years, described his spiraling descent into a life of disillusionment, sickness, and depression. Stationed temporarily in Georgia in March 1842, he could not forget the "harrowing spectacle" of discovering a half-burned corpse, purportedly the work of native people, though he suspected that whites had been involved. "What an awful scent," he wrote, "and how horrible to hear the frying of the old woman upon the live coals!" "My gorge rises at the bare remembrance." In constant pain, he resorted to large doses of "soporifics" in order to sleep through even part of the night. He tried drinking and womanizing but those diversions afforded no relief. Finally, in ruined health and broken spirit, he turned to opium.[30] He would die in 1849 in Athens, Georgia, at age thirty-eight.

John F. Lane also fell victim to the dripping of death during his service in Florida. Since deporting Ohio Shawnees in 1832 as a young, arrogant disbursing officer, he had risen to the rank of colonel. In October 1836, he led nine hundred troops to the Withlacoochee, where they engaged in a small skirmish with Seminoles before falling back to Fort Drane for supplies. Beset by fevers and fatigue, the twenty-six-year-old Lane retired to his tent and "ended his career by self-extermination," running his sword through his right eye and into his brain.[31]

~~~

FOR ALL of the suffering endured by U.S. troops, the violence struck native peoples even harder. A fundamental asymmetry distinguished the two sides. No native peoples were invading U.S. homelands and dispossessing the residents, and no U.S. citizens were starving because of it. "We have set them the example of violence," protested one officer, "by burning their homes and laying waste their very slender means of subsistence."[32]

Refugee families fled from camp to camp, scrambling to stay ahead of soldiers, who pursued them through miles of waist-high water and across densely forested hammocks. If captured, their fate was uncertain. A company of militia from South Carolina took several casualties before finally killing someone. The victim, wrote one witness, was "scalped, his body stretched naked on a pole, and brought into camp for the curious to look at." One hundred miles north of where Disney's Magic Kingdom now sits, a company of Tennessee militia surprised three people, chased them into a deep pond, and killed them. On a different occasion, the same volunteers shot three people through the head and chest, leaving them "all weltering in their blood." One evening they discovered an encampment of refugees and shot and killed eight, capturing four women and eight children. The prisoners cried "in a most pitiful and lamentable strain," wrote Henry Hollingsworth, one of the soldiers. He was unsympathetic, expressing more compassion for his famished horses. "Who," he asked, "can suppress a tear at the sight?"[33]

Surrounding and capturing Seminole families became commonplace, and soldiers referred to the practice as the "grab game" or "bagging the game." In one such instance, troops seized a five-year-old girl and her ten-year-old brother, the father and mother escaping by swimming across a river, almost certainly never to see their children again. Women captives were often "examined separately" for intelligence, by means that none of the interrogators or victims recorded. In another instance, troops waded through ten miles of swamps to strike a family as the father was mending his moccasins. His wife ran some ten or twenty yards before being tackled, and their two children were soon found hiding in the weeds. In celebration or despair, the troops drained a bottle of alcohol during their return.[34]

Seminole women, said one army surgeon, were "miserable, blackened, haggard, shriveled devils" and the children "ugly little nudities." The scornful characterization captured a truth. Seminole families were constantly on the run, forced to survive on wild plants. A more sympathetic observer, Richard Fields, a Cherokee who was part of a delegation that tried unsuccessfully to negotiate an end to the conflict, was appalled by what he saw. "I never so deeply felt before the miseries produced by war," he wrote. "Yes," he continued, "my heart sickened and sank within me at the many pictures of infant want and wretchedness." At one conference with U.S. officers, fifteen miles north of present-day West Palm Beach, Seminole women, clothed in discarded grain bags, begged the troops for food and snatched kernels of corn dropped from the mouths of army horses.[35]

The chickee, a thatched-roof shelter standing on six to eight posts, is today celebrated as the iconic Seminole house, yet it is a product of this period of violence and deprivation, when displaced families were forced to construct temporary lodgings. In the space of eighteen months, beginning in December 1836, the U.S. Army killed or captured 2,400 people, razed dozens of villages, slaughtered several thousand head of cattle and up to eight hundred horses and ponies, and destroyed nearly all of the Seminoles' cooking utensils, furniture, and other property, including their irreplaceable seed stock. The survivors had nothing left but their rifles.[36]

The violence spiraled out of control. Wandering through the comfortable lodgings and bountiful gardens of an abandoned Seminole village, one officer wrote that his sympathy for the dispossessed residents vanished after he discovered a desiccated scalp, and he silently rejoiced that "fate has swept the monsters from our land." A broken truce led a usually reflective observer to conclude that the "treacherous savages deserve little mercy." "Mercy to them is cruelty to the whites," he declared. One particularly horrific episode began when Waxehadjo reportedly killed and decapitated an express rider heading to Tampa Bay. After eating breakfast, Waxehadjo left the head upright on the coals. Soldiers later tracked him down, drove him into a pond, and shot him dead. Afterward, they fished his body out of the water and strung it up on a tree.[37]

~~~

THE SECOND U.S.-Seminole War stripped the "Act to provide for an exchange of lands with the Indians" of all humanitarian pretense. Avaricious U.S. citizens showed little interest in sending native residents off to an aboriginal paradise in the West. Instead, some coveted the fugitive slaves living in Seminole communities and wished to make the region safe for the business of running slave plantations. A South Carolina veteran even castigated the federal government for failing to make an effort "to discover the location of the negroes carried off from plantations." That goal, he suggested, ought to be foremost in the war effort. Speculators arrived from Georgia with "pockets full of powers of attorney" to claim the "negro property of the Indians," wrote an observer. One soldier was repulsed by the scene on New Year's Day, 1838, on Chickasawhatchee Creek north of Tallahassee, where he watched a second lieutenant consign two black Seminoles, a father and daughter, to a life of slavery. The father cried as the girl was "knocked off to the highest bidder."[38]

Other army officers speculated in land rather than people, even planning campaigns for the purpose of scouting desirable acreage. "I speak strictly the truth when I tell you that most of our reconnaissances have been made with an eye this way, rather than to the position of the enemy," wrote one soldier. The Core of Topographical Engineers, a branch of the army, surveyed and drafted maps "to further their infernal speculations," and it was even proposed to use the First Infantry to dig a canal to raise property values. None other than J.D. Beers bought an interest in eight million acres of Seminole land, an area more than twice the size of Connecticut. The "spirit of gain," not the "vindication of any principle," drove the war, concluded John T. Sprague, a disillusioned officer who wrote a jaundiced account of the conflict.[39]

And yet the mercenary reasons for fighting the war seem insuffi-cient. Thomas Jesup advised that Seminoles should be given a small dis-trict in Florida, since the more he saw of the peninsula, "a country of swamps and barren sand hills," the less he liked it. "If it were the will of Heaven to swallow the whole Peninsula in the ocean," agreed his friend, "geography would certainly gain far more than agriculture would lose." J.R. Poinsett, the secretary of war, promptly rejected Jesup's rec-ommendation. Compromise would invite resistance from other indig-enous Americans east of the Mississippi, he asserted, and "betray great weakness" and "tarnish" the honor of the army. Jesup, breaking with military protocol to weigh in again on government policy, continued to insist that the object was not worth the cost. Rebuffing Jesup a second time, Poinsett instructed that fugitive families "ought to be captured or destroyed." He replaced the pessimistic general with Zachary Taylor soon afterward. By the end of 1840, Ethan Allen Hitchcock wrote, the United States was fighting solely "to avoid the mortification of defeat."[40]

By the time the Second U.S.-Seminole War drew to a close in May 1842, the United States had deported 3,824 people at a cost of between thirty and forty million dollars, leaving several hundred Seminoles remaining in the Everglades. (Today, their descendants constitute the Seminole Tribe of Florida and the Miccosukee Tribe of Indians of Florida.) Of the ten thousand regular soldiers deployed, 1,466 lost their lives. The thirty thou-sand militia who served in the conflict suffered fewer battlefield casualties than their regular counterparts, but if they succumbed to disease at even half the rate, then the sum total of U.S. deaths is approximately 3,200.[41]

Unfortunately, incomplete population data make it impossible to determine with any accuracy how many Seminole people lost their lives; the number may be as high as 1,000, or 20 percent of the population. In absolute terms, fatalities in other nineteenth-century wars, epidemics, and natural disasters far surpassed the loss of lives in the Second U.S.-Seminole War. The Seminoles were never numerous to begin with, however, and the modest size of their villages only underscores the colossal waste of lives and resources occasioned by the United States's relentless pursuit of them. The numbers do not reflect well on the effort. For every four people that it deported, the United States killed one person, lost three soldiers, and spent $32,000. In today's dollars, that is equivalent to $8.5 million for every single Seminole person shipped west.[42]

As the U.S. Army deported indigenous families west, it shifted troops and officers across the Mississippi, including William S. Harney, a veteran of the U.S. war with Black Hawk, the Second U.S.-Seminole War, and the U.S.-Mexican War. In the 1850s, Harney would lead the campaign against Sioux people, clearing the way for U.S. expansion in the Dakotas, but in 1840, he was pulling boats through mud and grass in the Everglades, chasing Seminole families to the very edge of the continent. The operations in southern Florida marked the grim culmination of the U.S. policy to expel native peoples, enacted with so much manufactured fanfare ten years earlier. Spotting two canoes, Harney's troops gave chase through water and over land. With Harney looking on and cheering, they "disabled" two men, "accidentally wounded" a woman who was fleeing with a child on her back, and "overhauled" another woman, with a young girl and two small children. Afterward, Harney, a "creature of impulses" and "unresisting victim of his passions," according to one contemptuous soldier, hanged the men from a tall tree and left the bodies to rot. The injured woman died the next day; there is no record of the fate of her child.[43]

The soldiers were not done. Nearby, they discovered Chakaika, a noted Seminole leader, and chased, shot, and scalped him. By the end of the night, they had killed or captured twenty-five people. Harney hanged two more prisoners on a tall tree and strung up Chakaika's scalped body by their side. "The night was beautiful," wrote one soldier. The exhausted troops went to sleep beneath the corpses, silhouetted by the bright rising moon.[44]

THE PRICE OF EXPULSION

~~~

ISAAC MCCOY died in June 1846, twenty-three years after he was seized with the idea of creating an "Indian Canaan." He had successfully realized the first part of his vision, the deportation of eighty thousand people across the Mississippi. But the second part, the creation of an aboriginal western paradise, remained as distant as ever. McCoy was naive to the end. "He must be blind," McCoy insisted in 1840, "who can perceive no difference in the tenure by which Indians hold lands now." For the first time since the arrival of Europeans in North America, McCoy declared, native peoples resided securely on territory of their own.[1] But forty-one years after his death, the United States would again drive indigenous Americans from their homes with the passage of the Dawes Act of 1887. The Dawes Act broke up tribal domains and distributed the land to individual native citizens, leaving the owners subject to predatory speculators.

Lewis Cass, after stepping down as Andrew Jackson's secretary of war, remained a prominent Democratic politician, dedicated to placating southern slaveholders at every turn. In 1850, he played a key role in drafting the notorious Fugitive Slave Act, which created a federal network of slave catchers in the northern states. Two years later, he proposed that the United States "swallow Cuba" so that southern planters could reap profits from the island's more than three hundred thousand enslaved laborers. In 1857, he welcomed the Supreme Court's *Dred Scott* ruling that African Americans could never become U.S. citizens and that Congress could not prohibit slavery in the territories. It required "greater moral courage" to "hold back, to survey the whole subject coolly and impartially, and to restore harmony to a distracted country" by defending perpetual and hereditary slavery, he rationalized, than it did "to minister to the popular feeling where we live" by fighting against the institution. Political moderation, as Cass practiced it in the 1850s, meant keeping four million people in bondage, just as in the 1830s it had meant deporting eighty thousand indigenous Americans. Though he remained loyal to the Union in the Civil War, he excoriated the North for raising "that abominable Negro question."[2] He died in 1866.

Wilson Lumpkin, the Georgia congressman, governor, and senator, was so delighted with his role in deporting native peoples that he gave a blow-by-blow account of the victory in a two-volume manuscript of approximately 270,000 words, nearly three times the length of this book. It was his "particular mission, instrumentally," he recalled, "to do something to relieve Georgia from the incumbrance of her Indian population, and at the same time benefit the Indians." He lived to witness the emancipation of his fifteen slaves in Athens, Georgia, and died in 1870. A part of the University of Georgia now sits on his former plantation. Lumpkin's fellow Georgian, Eli Shorter, the avaricious Columbus land speculator, died in 1836. His premature death, after a life of striving so hard to accumulate so much, brings to mind the timeless observation of Cusseta Micco. In 1771, the Creek leader advised the grasping British that, no matter how much land any one person acquired, at death, he or she "could only rot on one spot of it."[3]

George Gibson directed the Office of the Commissary General of Subsistence until his death in 1861. In later years, he was often seen sitting in front of McClery & Clements, a drugstore on the corner of Pennsylvania Avenue and 14th Street, leaning with both hands on his gold-headed cane or whittling a piece of wood. "He was a simple-hearted old-fashioned soldier," recalled an acquaintance, "and everybody loved him." Neighbors stopped by to speak with the ancient commissary general, now in his eighties. They included the Mississippi senator Jefferson Davis, the one-time Georgia representative Alexander Stephens, and the Georgia senator Robert Toombs.[4] A few months before Gibson's death in September 1861, these three men would assume the offices of president, vice president, and secretary of state of the Confederate States of America. Gibson, by overseeing the deportations that extended white supremacy across the South, had advanced the cause that culminated in the creation of the would-be transcontinental Confederate slave empire.

The victims of these U.S. statesmen and business leaders had less to celebrate. After Black Hawk's defeat in the U.S.-Sauk War of 1832, the army sent the Sauk leader down the Mississippi to Jefferson Barracks, south of St. Louis. As the steamboat passed by "fine houses" and "rich harvests," Black Hawk "reflected upon the ingratitude of the whites." The Sauks had "never received a dollar," he stated, and "the whites were not satisfied until they took our village and our grave-yards from us, and removed us across the Mississippi."[5]

At Jefferson Barracks, guards shackled Black Hawk to an iron ball, and he and ten other emaciated Sauks passed the long winter of 1832 in confinement. In the spring, the War Department sent the prisoners to Washington City to meet President Jackson, followed by a voyage up the East Coast to Baltimore, Philadelphia, and New York. "You will see the strength of the white people," the slave-owning president told the prisoners. If Sauks killed "a few women and children," Jackson threatened, whites as numerous "as the leaves in the woods" would "destroy" their "whole tribe."[6] The War Department released Black Hawk after the journey, and he retired to the Iowa River, west of the Mississippi.

Enlightened by his visit to the populous East Coast, the aging leader decided to embrace John Ross's strategy of "intellectual warfare" against the United States. Rather than taking up arms, he would narrate and publish his life story. In a dedication to his old adversary General Atkinson, Black Hawk remembered being "in his native forests . . . once as proud and bold as yourself." He hoped that the general would "never experience the humility that the power of the American government has reduced me to." After Black Hawk died in 1838, at age seventy-two, a local doctor disinterred the corpse and transported it to St. Louis. The Iowa governor eventually seized the body and deposited it in the Burlington Geological and Historical Society, where it was consumed by flames when the building burned down in 1855.[7]

Opothle Yoholo, the Creek leader who compared speculators to demons, steered his nation through the U.S.-Creek War of 1836 by trying to mollify U.S. commanders. Though "there was a difference in our colour and complexions," he reminded General Jesup, and "although the skin of the one was white and that of the other red we were nevertheless brothers." Despite their differences, he said, "they were all of the family of human nature." After moving west, Opothle Yoholo remained the foremost leader in the Creek Nation and managed to accumulate a large number of slaves. Unlike the unfree laborers in the Deep South, however, Opothle Yoholo's slaves had farms of their own, owing a portion of their harvests to their master. When the Civil War erupted and the Confederacy invaded Indian Territory, the Creek Nation splintered. The United States had promised to protect them, the seventy-something Opothle Yoholo wrote to President Abraham Lincoln, but "no body has come." Men "who are strangers tread our soil," he reported; "our children are frightened and the mothers cannot sleep for fear." Opothle Yoholo freed his slaves and led them along with three thousand followers north into Kansas through extreme cold and sleet. Clothed in rags, over one hundred of the starving refugees lost their "frosted limbs" to amputation during the bitter winter of 1861–62.[8] Opothle Yoholo died in March 1863 in a refugee camp in Kansas.

John Ross continued to work tirelessly on behalf of his nation, despite believing that "the only chance of justice" for native peoples was "in History." The deportation was not only a political failure for him; his wife Quatie died in Little Rock during the journey to Indian Territory. In the West, he set to work mending the political factions that had fractured Cherokees in the 1830s, and he rebuilt the constitutional government that the United States had worked so hard to undermine. In the 1840s, as the principal chief, he presided over the creation of a public school system in the Cherokee Nation, the first to be chartered west of the Mississippi. During the Civil War, he displayed the same political savvy that had frustrated President Jackson three decades earlier. This time, he protected Cherokee sovereignty by establishing nominal alliances, first with the Confederacy, then with the Union, as wartime circumstances dictated.[9] Ross died 1866.

Osceola, captured by General Jesup under a white flag in October 1837, was marched with 237 other captives to St. Augustine and confined in Fort Marion. Within months, fifteen of the destitute prisoners died from measles in their cramped quarters. After sixteen others escaped, General Jesup sent Osceola and the remaining captives on the *Poinsett*—named for the secretary of war who had resolved to exterminate them—to Sullivan's Island, one of the debarkation points for the 160,000 Africans who were funneled through Charleston into the South's slave labor camps. Imprisoned in Fort Moultrie, Osceola became a curiosity, and local residents flocked to see the ailing Seminole leader, who was suffering from both long-term and acute illnesses. Nearing death, the thirty-four-year-old asked the attending doctor, Frederick Weedon, to return his body to Florida "to remain in peace." He "regretted his country had been taken from him," Osceola told Weedon, and that the Seminoles' "natural Birth right had been wrested from them by the strong & oppressive hand of the white people."[10] Osceola died the next day, on January 30, 1838.

Weedon severed and embalmed Osceola's head, leaving the decapitated body to be interred on Sullivan's Island. Carrying his gruesome trophy to St. Augustine, the doctor displayed it in his drugstore. In 1843, a renowned New York surgeon, Valentine Mott, accepted the specimen for his "cabinet of heads." It remained in Mott's lower Manhattan home, on the southwest corner of Bleecker and Thompson streets, until the surgeon's death in 1865. From there, Osceola's head disappeared.[11]

Behind these political leaders—the men who represented indigenous communities to the outside world—eighty thousand other people endured the "Act to provide for an exchange of lands." Elzira, a Choctaw girl, suffered an accident during the journey west and had to have her arm amputated. (There is no record whether she survived.) Unnamed Shawnee women groped their way through the dark in frigid weather in western Missouri to set up tents in the snow and build campfires. A Creek woman gave birth to a child on January 7, 1836, on the *Alpha*, as the steamboat ascended the Arkansas River. Tetolahih's three children died during deportation from the North Carolina mountains, as did Lucy's husband, Nancy Long Bullet's child, and three of Cheesquah's children. These and thousands of similar stories make up the "experiment" that the United States launched in the 1830s.[12]

~~~

THE FEDERAL government expended about $75 million to expel native peoples from their homelands, equivalent today to a trillion dollars, or about $12.5 million for each deportee. Vast sums passed through the War Department to fund the dispossession. In the pivotal year of 1836, more than 40 percent of every federal dollar went to enforce the "Act to provide for an exchange of lands," a peak reached again in 1838, in the midst of the Cherokee deportation. The War Department did not use the appropriations to compensate the dispossessed fairly, transport the refugees safely to the West, or build McCoy's trans-Mississippi "Indian Canaan."

Instead, it contracted with provisioners, steamboat captains, and other opportunistic Americans in a futile effort to carry out the deportation cheaply and quickly. When the time came, it purchased munitions and supplies and mobilized U.S. troops and state militia to fight the seven-year war against Seminole families. The enormous expenditures during the decade of deportation must be compared with the nearly $80 million that the federal government received over the same period by selling expropriated native lands.[13] Not coincidentally, the sales of native lands—called "public lands" by the federal government—kept pace with the costs of dispossession, even though the General Land Office disposed of native lands at bargain prices.

Expulsion generated additional profits for the Republic and its citizens. The lands that the federal government expropriated in the decade of deportation furnished nearly 160 million pounds of ginned cotton in 1850, equal to 16 percent of the entire crop in the United States. Native

Profits from the sale of indigenous lands kept pace with the costs of deportation.

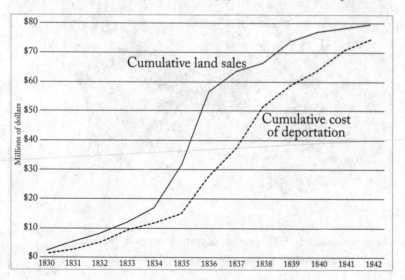

lands produced 40 percent of the total value of the agricultural output in Mississippi and Alabama. In the nation as a whole, they produced 6 percent of the total value of agricultural output.[14] Clearly, as a profit-seeking enterprise, the mass deportations of the 1830s made sense.

But the costs to Americans cannot be captured solely by a balance sheet. White colonizers enforced a racial hierarchy that was markedly more oppressive than anything that had existed before on native lands. Jim Tom witnessed the transformation. Said by federal commissioners to be "half negro and half Indian" and "black as negro," he and his Choctaw wife Shim-mah-ho-ya and their four children lived on the eastern edge of the Choctaw Nation on the Tombigbee River, about forty miles southwest of Tuscaloosa, Alabama, in the early 1830s. They cultivated a

Cotton produced on the lands of the dispossessed in 1850.

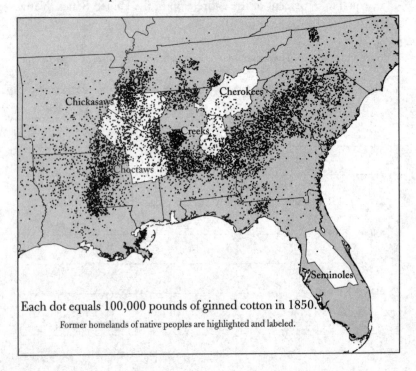

Each dot equals 100,000 pounds of ginned cotton in 1850.
Former homelands of native peoples are highlighted and labeled.

common field with Shim-mah-ho-ya's mother, Salla Ho Yo, who lived adjacent to them in the opposite side of a double house. Jim Tom's father, a free black man, resided nearby. The extended family of Choctaws and African Americans "boiled the same pot, and divided the food." Sometime after Alabama created Sumter County and extended its jurisdiction over his lands in 1832, Jim Tom smartly sold his farm before he was dispossessed. His wife, children, and mother-in-law, by contrast, applied to the federal agent William Ward to receive title to land under the Treaty of Dancing Rabbit Creek. As in so many other instances, however, the drunken officer failed to register their names.[15]

Dispossessed of their inheritance, the family survived for a time on land belonging to Jim Tom's father, but the community of mixed Choctaws and African Americans dwindled under Alabama's body of oppressive laws targeting "colored people." By 1840, some 13,900 white people commanded 15,900 slave laborers in Sumter County, all recent arrivals since the dispossession of the Choctaws. They vastly outnumbered the small number of 116 free "colored people." The inequality continued to worsen. As wealthy landowners added to their holdings and expanded their slave labor camps, the number of white residents declined, and the enslaved population rose. By 1860, approximately 5,900 white people ruled over 18,100 imprisoned laborers in Sumter County. The free black population had shrunk to 25, and the U.S. Census listed not a single native person. (Toms Creek, Alabama, just south of the small town of Gainesville, still marks the former location of Jim Tom's family.)[16]

James Nance, a young enterprising North Carolinian, was one of the white newcomers. After purchasing 320 acres about thirty miles north of Jim Tom's farm, he wrote home urging his father to sell his land near Raleigh, North Carolina, for "Young negroes" under the age of twenty-five. Nance set his slaves to work transforming the rich Black Prairie land. The laborers cut down twenty-foot-high river cane and chased or killed off the wild game. Four years later, in 1836, Nance boasted that his plantation "grew some of the best cotton you ever seen." He complained only that "Negroes" were too expensive, an enslaved man costing as much as $1,500. Nonetheless, by 1850 Nance commanded twenty-four unfree laborers, a number that would continue to grow until their emancipation fifteen years later.[17]

Nance's were among the 236,000 slaves in Mississippi and Alabama in 1850—fully 36 percent of the unfree population in those states—who toiled on lands that only two decades earlier had belonged to indigenous peoples. The "Act to provide for an exchange of lands with the Indians" had transformed the region and the Republic. To meet the demand of labor camp owners, slave traders had separated enslaved workers from their families in the Chesapeake and Carolinas and marched them west to the newly acquired lands.[18] The cost of expulsion to these Americans was immeasurable.

The wealth extracted by speculators, colonizers, and cotton barons has lasted for generations, as has the damage done to the victims. Joseph D. Beers founded the North American Trust and Banking Company in 1838, using capital earned from native lands, including $52,500 in New York and Mississippi Land Company stock. The bank was a house of cards, built with fictitious certificates of deposit to benefit Beers and his partners. When it collapsed in 1841, the receiver found among other items a mahogany office clock, a green-covered table, a circular desk, and a map of Auburn, New York, the location of a massive penitentiary. One wag asked, "did some of the managers contemplate its ample state prison?"[19] But despite this setback, Beers continued to sit atop Wall Street as one of New York's most prominent financiers.

When Beers died in 1863, the family sold off $31,000 in furniture—tables, vases, rosewood chairs, crimson damask armchairs, satin damask curtains, a Gobelin carpet, a rosewood piano, an Aubusson carpet, candelabras, and more—amounting to the equivalent of $5.4 million today. Beers also owned various railroad stocks, shares in what became the New York City subway, and dozens of lots in Manhattan. His $15,000 in

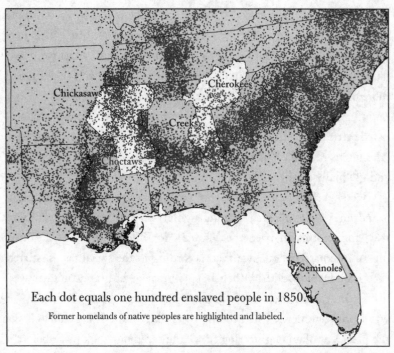

Chickasaws

Cherokees

Creeks

Choctaws

Seminoles

Each dot equals one hundred enslaved people in 1850.
Former homelands of native peoples are highlighted and labeled.

The spread of slavery onto the lands of the dispossessed, 1850.

stock in the New York and Mississippi Land Company had depreciated by the end of the Civil War to a value of only $1,000. It represented the last of his holdings in the Chickasaw Nation.[20]

This wealth—accumulated in part by dispossessing indigenous families—enriched his heirs. J.D. Beers's dissolute grandson, it is true, did not fare well. His $3,000 annuity (the equivalent today of over $500,000) proved insufficient to support his expensive habits in Paris. He had inherited a share in Beers's lands in the Florida Panhandle and, in one feverish letter written from Freiburg in the Black Forest in 1865, sketched out a project to ship German emigrants to the area to grow cotton, corn, hemp, and tobacco. "You will be looked up to by these people as a King," he wrote to his skeptical brother, assuring him, "This may look like a crazy idea, but I do not see why it is not true." A year and half later, he was committed to an insane asylum. His brother Benjamin had more of his grandfather in him. Just as J.D. had expected slaves to labor on indigenous lands in the 1830s, Benjamin insisted that newly emancipated African Americans must be put to work. If they refused, he stated, "the negro race like the Indian race before them will begin to decline and gradually disappear."[21]

Beers's other descendants were more successful than his ailing grandson. One of his great-granddaughters married an Italian prince in 1885, and another married the Marquis de Talleyrand-Perigord, forming an international alliance that, according to the social pages, stirred the "fashionable world." When Beers's great-great-granddaughter wed in 1923 in "one of the most brilliant social marriages of the season," it was front-page news. The groom, a Harvard and MIT graduate, was the president of an engineering firm. The ceremony took place before a console table and a large wall mirror, heirlooms that had once stood in J.D. Beers's Manhattan house.[22]

In more ways than one, the wall mirror was "an Indian's looking glass for the white man," to borrow the title of one of William Apess's most unsparing essays. The Pequot minister held up his metaphorical mirror to show white Americans their crimes. They had robbed native peoples "almost of their whole continent," murdered "their women and children," and deprived the survivors of "their lawful rights." Then they had forced Africans to till the land "and welter out their days under the lash." J.D. Beers's wall mirror, purchased at least partially with the proceeds of speculating in native lands, served a different purpose. In the flickering candlelight of the bride's palatial estate, it reflected the concentrated and compounded family wealth generated by the sordid saga of dispossession nearly a century earlier. When J.D. Beers's great-great-granddaughter died in 1990, sixty-seven years after her marriage, the *New York Times* reported that the "93-year-old banking heiress" left an $18 million estate.[23]

The mirror image of this wealth was the poverty of the dispossessed. By a conservative estimate, Chickasaw families lost $4,000,000 in the sales of their allotments, money pocketed by speculators rather than by the original landowners. Since some families were paid in depreciated paper money and received advances rather than the stipulated contractual price, the losses could reasonably approach $7,000,000 or more. By the same conservative estimate, the Chickasaw Nation lost $3,000,000 in the auctions conducted by the General Land Office, bringing total losses from individual allotments and national lands to between $7,000,000 and $10,000,000. That sum, if invested instead of transferred to speculators, could have capitalized one of the three largest corporations in the United States at the time. It amounts to $4,200 for every deported family. In today's dollars, the loss per household ranges from $117,000 to well over $1,000,000, depending on the method of currency conversion—equivalent to the net worth of all but the wealthiest families in the United States. Likewise, a conservative estimate suggests that Choctaws lost about $10 million and that Creeks lost between $4 million and $8 million.[24] These staggering figures do not capture the psychological and emotional impact of being stripped of one's multigenerational inheritance in the space of a few years. Nor do they account for the premature deaths of so many of the dispossessed.

A full accounting must also include the loss of cultural knowledge specific to eastern homelands. In some instances, as with the mixed community of Senecas, Mohawks, Cayugas, and Oneidas in Ohio, the impact was minimal, since the targets of deportation had migrated into the region only recently. But in other cases, as with indigenous peoples in the Southeast, the dispossessed lost the accumulated place-based knowledge of a thousand years.

~~~

EXPULSION REMADE the geographic relationship between native peoples and the United States. In the first eight years of the policy, the indigenous population east of the Mississippi plummeted from nearly one hundred thousand to barely fifteen thousand. Midway through the decade of deportation, the Senate Committee on Indian Affairs reviewed the status of native peoples in the Republic and happily concluded, "They are on an *outside* of us, and in a place which will ever remain an *outside*."[25]

Admittedly, dozens of small indigenous settlements remained in the East. A few thousand Cherokees still lived in the mountains of North Carolina; hundreds of Creeks, Choctaws, and Seminoles survived on marginal lands in Alabama, Mississippi, and Florida; dozens of Odawa, Ojibwa, Stockbridge, and Menominee families continued to reside in

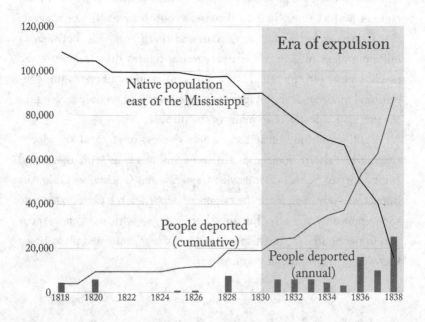

Expulsion eliminated most native peoples who
lived within the United States.

Michigan and Wisconsin; and over four thousand Iroquois remained in New York. From a national perspective, however, native peoples and U.S. citizens were now segregated by a line down the middle of the continent. In 1834, before the Cherokees' expulsion, John Ross had compared his nation to "a solitary tree in an open space." All the "forest trees around," he said, had been "prostrated by a furious tornado—save one."[26] Four years later, not a single tree remained standing in the South.

The geographical segregation created by the "Act to provide for an exchange of lands" had profound implications, for it inscribed the Republic's racial fixation on the land itself, creating a militarized front that the U.S. Army patrolled and then advanced toward the Pacific Ocean. For a time, the military cordon that the War Department had begun building in 1836 marked the dividing line between native peoples and U.S. settlements. Like so many other ambitious but underfunded state projects, however, the cordon fell far short of the goal set for it by administrators. Construction continued piecemeal for a decade, and by the time one portion was complete, others were already in disrepair.[27] By the 1850s, the "inland frontier" had jumped over the ill-considered "wall of defence," and the U.S. Army was conducting military operations four hundred miles to the west of the onetime boundary.

Frederick Douglass, the fugitive slave turned public intellectual and one of the most incisive critics of race in the United States, recognized how geography shaped the lives of black and native Americans. "The only reason why the negro has not been killed off, as the Indians have been, is, that he is so close under your arm, that you cannot get at him," he told the American Anti-Slavery Society in 1869, in the wake of a series of massacres of indigenous communities in the West. "If we had set up a separate nationality, gone off on the outer borders of your civilization, right before your bayonets and swords," he continued, "we should have been pushed off, precisely as the Indians have been pushed off."[28]

The consequences of being "on an outside" of the expanding Republic were deadly. William Harney was one of many insiders who enforced the geographical segregation. In September 1855, he led six hundred troops against 250 Brulé and Oglala families in western Nebraska, descending on the camp at daybreak. Armed with long-range rifles, the soldiers shot and killed eighty-six people who were scrambling to escape through a narrow ravine. As he had in the Florida Everglades fifteen years earlier, Harney watched from on high as the assault unfolded.[29]

~~~

WHITE AMERICANS liked to think that the mass deportation of the 1830s and the westward-moving line that it created were inevitable. The federal government, they insisted, was too weak to protect indigenous residents, white people too vigorous to leave native lands untouched, and native peoples too backward to help themselves. Even from our perspective today, given what unfolded in the nineteenth century, expulsion can appear to have been inexorable, albeit for slightly different reasons: U.S. citizens were too rapacious, the forces of capital too relentless and too powerful, and the federal government too feeble to check belligerent southern states. And yet the same was said about slavery, and in that case, after generations of colluding, enough white Americans joined forces with enslaved people to compel the federal government to intervene.

The deeply intertwined causes of slavery and dispossession were more alike than not. Both generated enormous profits; both earned the support of northerners who were sympathetic to the cause of white supremacy and often personally invested in the oppressive policies; and both generated a vocal opposition in Congress that remained a minority, in part because the three-fifths compromise skewed representation in favor of the slave South. Southern slaveholders mocked and condemned anti-expulsion activists and abolitionists with equal contempt, and they met resistance to their transcontinental aspirations by threatening to break up the Union. Just as the federal government protected slavery at every

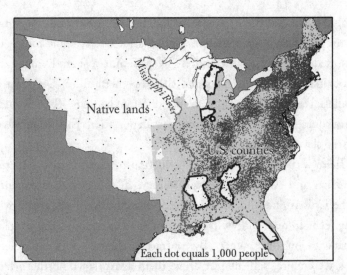

The United States and its territories in 1830, when many indigenous nations still stood amid U.S. settlements. I have highlighted some of the larger territories belonging to native peoples. Small indigenous communities in the Midwest and in New York are not visible at this scale.

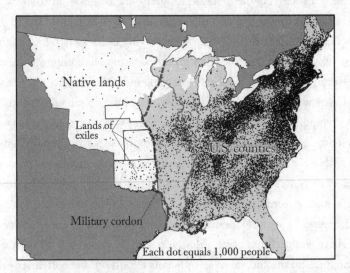

The United States and its territories in 1842, after the "furious tornado" spawned by the "Act to provide for an exchange of lands" had toppled almost every indigenous nation in the East. The War Department began constructing the military cordon to separate U.S. citizens and native peoples in 1836.

turn, it facilitated the expulsion of indigenous Americans by overseeing the logistics of the operation, setting aside western land for the dispossessed, and turning the entire enterprise into a sham humanitarian victory for planter-politicians and their northern allies. Despite these parallels, the two causes came to very different endings. There would be no reckoning over state-sponsored mass deportation. Expulsion was the war the slaveholders won.

There was one fundamental distinction between Native American expulsion and African American slavery. In the westward expansion of the United States, common interest in acquiring land united white Americans to put Andrew Jackson in the White House and expel the continent's longtime owners. By contrast, in the westward expansion of the slave empire, self-interest drove them apart, since northern farmers and wage laborers feared being displaced in fields and factories by unpaid laborers. Yet the politics surrounding dispossession were not so simple. U.S. citizens never faced a binary choice between total expulsion of native peoples and full recognition of indigenous land rights. Few Native Americans insisted on preserving every square foot of their remaining territory. Instead, they proposed numerous compromises, ceding some regions but not others, accepting individual land titles, practicing Christianity (at least superficially), adopting U.S. farming practices, and even agreeing to U.S. citizenship. These were pragmatic and workable concessions, formulated to meet the unjust political challenges of the 1830s. Rejecting the deterministic narrative peddled by the advocates of dispossession, John Ross insisted that expulsion was a matter of policy, not, as some would have it, a chapter in the inevitable conquest of the world by white Americans. Deportation was a political choice.[30]

There was an alternative. Though native peoples drew on their own distinct traditions and values in opposing expulsion, they often appealed to the values of the American Revolution, a rhetorical appropriation that was strategic rather than cynical, and prescriptive rather than naive.

Paraphrasing the Declaration of Independence while at the same time invoking their own supreme being, Creek leaders had observed in 1830 that "the great master of Breath . . . created mankind in equal, in possession of an unmolested enjoyment of life, and the blessings of Self Government." A "great and enlightened Republic," they asserted, stood by those values. Likewise, Seneca leaders reminded President Jackson of the example of imperial Rome, whose story in the era of the Revolution was often recounted as a frightening and edifying lesson in the dangers of tyranny. Chickasaws appealed to the "liberty" bequeathed to Americans by George Washington. And as early as 1824, Cherokee leaders demanded their rights "under that *memorable* declaration, 'that all men are created equal; that they are endowed by their Creator with certain unalienable rights; that among these are, life, liberty, and the pursuit of happiness.'"[31]

U.S. citizens made similar appeals when calling on their government to honor its treaties with indigenous nations. In Luzerne County, Pennsylvania, residents wrote, "the Liberty that we Enjoy was originally attained by constant Sacrifices of Life and property on the Altar of Eternal Justice and the Original and indefeasible Rights of man." In Chesterfield, Maine, residents warned that if the federal government expelled native peoples, "we fear those rights of Man, for which our Fathers fought and bled in the Revolutionary conflict will be trampled under foot; and the publick faith of our Nation, the glory of our Republick, sinks into disgrace." In Lafayette, New York, they quoted the Declaration of Independence and concluded that efforts to "wrest" the land from native peoples was "tyrannical and oppressive." In Lincoln County, Maine, they warned that, with the deportation of native peoples, "the only free govt on earth" would be "converted into a Despotism of the most frightful character."[32] U.S. citizens were wishfully reimagining the Republic's early history—which was hardly favorable to indigenous Americans—but they were also drawing on a very real radical tradition rooted in the American Revolution, a once-powerful current in U.S. politics that had ebbed by the 1830s, overwhelmed by the massive profits flowing into the pockets of the South's planter-politicians and the North's textile mill owners and investment bankers.

Though it may be difficult to envision the decade of deportation unfolding differently, even the most determined and imperious administrators can be undermined by the objects of their policy. Had the Republic's revolutionary values swayed five votes in the House of Representatives, native peoples would have remained in the East, where they would have resisted and adapted in ways that were imaginative and unpredictable, deflecting U.S. politics in ways that we cannot know.

Beyond the cordon, indigenous Americans rebuilt their communities, though the loss of generations of wealth and thousands of human lives continues to resonate. "The Indian question now is oer / The Indian question now is oer," wrote the Choctaw composer of "The New Jawbone" on his way west, satirizing the dangerous language of state administrators. Rejecting the myriad rationalizations for deportation— the predictions of doom in the East, the assurances of salvation in the West, professions of good faith, accusations of indolence and dissipation, and declarations of inevitability—the dispossessed was unwavering in his conviction:

> *When we have gone to the West*
> *You will say tis for the best*
> *We shall never think it so*
> *We shall never think it so.*[33]

ACKNOWLEDGMENTS

~~~

I AM GRATEFUL to many people who on my behalf made strategic forays into archives and libraries around the country: Felecia Caples (Ripley, Mississippi), Brian Carnaby (Topeka, Kansas), Ross Corsair (Garrison, New York), Ahmed Deidán de la Torre (Austin, Texas), Courtney DeFelice and Menika Dirkson (Philadelphia, Pennsylvania), Marisela Emperatriz Esparza (Oakland, California), Andrew Epstein (New Haven, Connecticut), Meggan Farish (Durham, North Carolina), Nicole Gallucci (Athens, Georgia), Nina Halty (Cambridge, Massachusetts), Jeff Hobbs (Madison, Wisconsin), Elana Krischer (Albany, New York), Lana Newhart-Kellen (Fishers, Indiana), James Owen (Athens, Georgia), Sarah Pickman (New Haven and New York City), Alex Post (Oakland, California), Sherri Sheu (Washington, D.C.), Adam Tate (Clayton, Georgia), Kurt Windisch (Montgomery, Alabama), and Laurie Woodson (Phenix City, Alabama).

I'd also like to thank a number of other individuals who contributed to this project in various ways. Patrick Del Percio of the D'Arcy McNickle Center for American Indian and Indigenous Studies at the

Newberry Library took on several challenging Cherokee translations. Jack Baker, the president of the Oklahoma Historical Society and one of the world's experts on Cherokee history, generously shared with me his knowledge of mortality statistics on the Trail of Tears. Andrew Zawacki helped pull me along on more than one occasion and also took the author photo.

Throughout this multiyear project, my editor at W. W. Norton, Tom Mayer, remained enthusiastic and optimistic. He is both exacting and accommodating, a difficult balance to strike. Likewise, my agent Lisa Adams at the Garamond Agency was supportive from beginning to end and always willing to weigh in when I needed her experienced advice. Thanks too to Nneoma Amadi-obi for reading the manuscript and steering it through the production process.

Several of my colleagues at the University of Georgia shared their expertise with me when I went to them with questions, including Sergio Bernardes, Steve Berry, Oscar Chamosa, Jamie Kreiner, Stephen Mihm, Scott Nelson, Dan Rood, Steve Soper, and Jace Weaver. In addition, a number of friends and colleagues elsewhere helped me clarify my thoughts, especially on the financing of dispossession. They include the participants in the Johns Hopkins Seminar and the 2017 Harvard capitalism conference, as well as Sven Beckert, Ann Daly, Christine A. Desan, and Robert Wright. Michael Kwass provided essential computer assistance. Peter Wood deserves special mention for generously agreeing to chair a critical "Unconference" in Athens, Georgia, on very short notice in late March 2019.

Above all, I'd like to thank Rachel for her unconditional support and loving companionship and Leo and Milo for their good humor, magic shows, updates on the Giro, pappardelle and pizza, and all the other wonderful and unpredictable diversions that they bring to my life.

ABBREVIATIONS

ASPIA	*American State Papers: Indian Affairs* (Washington, D.C., 1832 and 1834), 2 vols.
CGLR	Records Relating to Indian Removal, Records of the Commissary General of Subsistence, Letters Received, 1830–36, RG 75, entry 201
CGLS	Records Relating to Indian Removal, Records of the Commissary General of Subsistence, Letters Sent, 1830–36, RG 75, entry 202
COIA	Committee on Indian Affairs
CSE	*Correspondence on the Subject of the Emigration of Indians* (Washington, D.C., 1834–35), 5 vols.
DMR	David M. Rubenstein Rare Book and Manuscript Library, Duke University
EAH	Ethan Allen Hitchcock Collection on Indian Removal, Western Americana Collection, Beinecke Rare Book and Manuscript Library, Yale University
HCP	Hitchcock-Coit Papers, Special Collections and Archive, F.W. Olin Library, Mills College, Oakland, California
IRW	Indian Removal to the West, 1832–1840, Files of the Office of the Commissary General of Subsistence (LexisNexis microfilm)
LC	Library of Congress, Manuscript Division, Washington, D.C.

LPC	Lewis Perry Curtis Family Papers (MS 587), Manuscripts and Archives, Yale University Library
LR	Letters received
LS	Letters sent
MP	Isaac McCoy Papers, Kansas State Historical Society
NA	National Archives, Washington, D.C.
NACP	National Archives, College Park, Maryland
NYMS	New York and Mississippi Land Company Records, Letter book, State Historical Society of Wisconsin, Archives Division, Madison
OIA	Office of Indian Affairs
PAJ	*The Papers of Andrew Jackson Digital Edition*, ed. Daniel Feller (Charlottesville: University of Virginia Press, 2015–)
PCJR	*The Papers of Chief John Ross*, ed. Gary E. Moulton (Norman: University of Oklahoma Press, 1985), 2 vols.
PM	Petitions and memorials
PPP	Peter Pitchlynn Papers, Helmerich Center for American Research, Gilcrease Museum, Tulsa, Oklahoma
RG	Record group
RDC	*Register of Debates in Congress* (Washington, D.C., 1825–37), 14 vols.
SHC	Southern Historical Collection, Wilson Library, University of North Carolina at Chapel Hill

NOTES

1. James A. Folsom to Peter Pitchlynn, Oct. 31, 1831, 4026.3212, PPP.

INTRODUCTION: "WORDS ARE DELUSIVE"

1. *Southern Banner* (Athens, Ga.), July 16, 1836, 2–3.
2. *Southern Banner*, July 16, 1836, 2–3; John Page to George Gibson, July 2, 1836, CGLR, box 9, Creek, NA; Benjamin Young to Thomas Jesup, July 6, 1836, box 12, The Office of the Adjutant General, Generals' Papers and Books, General Jesup, entry 159, RG 94, NA; Major Ridge and John Ridge to Andrew Jackson, June 30, 1836, LR, OIA, reel 80, M-234, NA; Josiah Shaw to Lewis Cass, June 28, 1836, LR, OIA, reel 80, M-234, NA; Joseph W. Harris to Lewis Cass, July 25, 1836, LR, OIA, reel 290, frame 91, M-234, NA.
3. The first usage I have found of "Indian Removal" is in the *Evening Post* (New York, N.Y.), Jan. 26, 1830. There are surely earlier occurrences, but regardless it is clear that the policy's proponents favored the term. *RDC*, 6:2, p. 1070 ("words are delusive").
4. Several scholars have fruitfully explored the genocide of Native Americans, including Jeffrey Ostler, *Surviving Genocide: Native Nations and the United States from the American Revolution to Bleeding Kansas* (New Haven: Yale University Press, 2019); Benjamin Madley, *An American Genocide: The United States and the California Indian Catastrophe, 1846–1873* (New Haven: Yale University Press, 2016); and Andrew Woolford, Jeff Benvenuto, and Alexander Laban Hinton, eds., *Colonial Genocide in Indigenous North America* (Durham: Duke University Press, 2014). Raphael Lemkin, the Polish Jew who coined the term in the wake of World War II, kept extensive notes on "Indian Removal" and recorded instances of "physical" and "cultural genocide" that were committed at the time by "white genocidists." Raphael Lemkin Collection, P-154, box 9, folder 14, American Jewish Historical Society, New York, N.Y. On terminology, see also Alf Lüdtke, "Explaining Forced Migration," in *Removing Peoples: Forced Removal in the Modern World*, ed. Bessel and Haake (Oxford: Oxford University Press, 2009), 17–18; Pavel Polian, *Against Their Will: The History of Geography and Forced Migrations in the USSR* (Budapest: Central European University Press, 2004), 1–2; Norman M. Naimark, *Fires of Hatred: Ethnic Cleansing in Twentieth-Century Europe* (Cambridge: Harvard University Press, 2001), 2–3.
5. Examples of the use of "expulsion" include Memorial of Creeks, Feb. 3, 1830, PM, Protection of Indians, SEN21A-H3, NA; Memorial of Inhabitants of Augusta, Maine, Feb. 2, 1832, PM, COIA, SEN22A-G7, NA. For "extermination," see [W.W. Smith], *Sketch of the Seminole War and Sketches During a Campaign, by a*

Lieutenant (Charleston, 1836), 68, 115; James D. Elderkin, *Biographical Sketches and Anecdotes of a Soldier of Three Wars* (Detroit, 1899), 19; Jacob Rhett Motte, *Journey into Wilderness: An Army Surgeon's Account of Life in Camp and Field during the Creek and Seminole Wars, 1836–1838,* ed. James F. Sunderman (Gainesville: University of Florida Press, 1953), 208; *Southern Banner,* Mar. 11, 1838, 2.

6. Naimark, *Fires of Hatred,* 97 (march of "civilization" against the Chechens and Ingush); Hans-Lukas Kieser, "Removal of American Indians, Destruction of Ottoman Armenians: American Missionaries and Demographic Engineering," *European Journal of Turkish Studies* 7 (2008): 3 ("necessity" of deporting Armenians from Turkey); Tara Zahra, *The Great Departure: Mass Migration from Eastern Europe and the Making of the Free World* (New York: W. W. Norton, 2016), 150 ("only with difficulty assimilate," referring to Jews in Poland in 1938); Nicolas Werth, *Cannibal Island: Death in a Siberian Gulag* (Princeton: Princeton University Press, 2007), 24 ("grandiose plan" to deport people to Siberia).

7. "The Indian question" entered the U.S. lexicon during the gubernatorial election of 1825 in Georgia and became widespread in the 1830s. "The Jewish question" began circulating widely in English in the 1840s, though Russian administrators invented the problem in the late eighteenth century. John Klier, *Russia Gathers Her Jews: The Origins of the "Jewish Question" in Russia, 1772–1825* (Dekalb, Ill.: Northern Illinois University Press, 1986); *Georgia Journal* (Milledgeville, Ga.), Aug. 30, 1825, 1–3 ("Indians"); "Memorial," *Cherokee Phoenix,* Apr. 29, 1829, 1–4 ("exterminating").

8. Alexis de Tocqueville, *Democracy in America* (New York, 1838), 321; Jennifer Pitts, "Introduction," in Alexis de Tocqueville, *Alexis de Tocqueville: Writings on Empire and Slavery* (Baltimore: Johns Hopkins University Press, 2000), xv–xxviii; Benjamin C. Brower, *A Desert Named Peace: The Violence of France's Empire in the Algerian Sahara, 1844–1902* (New York: Columbia University Press, 2009), 19–20 ("indigènes"); *Procès-verbaux et rapports de la comission d'Afrique instituée par ordonnance du Roi du 12 Décembre 1833* (Paris, 1834), 67 ("talked about incessantly").

9. Stephen D. Shenfield, "The Circassians: A Forgotten Genocide?" in *The Massacre in History,* ed. Mark Levene and Penny Roberts (New York: Berghahn Books, 1999), 156 ("These Circassians"); Jens-Uwe Guettel, "From the Frontier to German South-West Africa: German Colonialism, Indians, and American Westward Expansion," *Modern Intellectual History* 7, no. 3 (Nov. 2010): 523–52; Jens-Uwe Guettel, *German Expansionism, Imperial Liberalism, and the United States, 1776–1945* (New York: Cambridge University Press, 2012), 13 ("indigenous inhabitants"); Edward B. Westermann, *Hitler's Ostkrieg and the Indian Wars* (Norman: University of Oklahoma Press, 2016); Sven Beckert, "American Danger: United States Empire, Eurafrica, and the Territorialization of Industrial Capitalism, 1870–1950," *American Historical Review* 122, no. 4 (Oct. 2017): 1137–70.

10. On the long history of population engineering in the United States, see Paul Frymer, *Building an American Empire: The Era of Territorial and Political Expansion* (Princeton: Princeton University Press, 2017).

11. The 1830s marked the emergence of the United States as "a modern nation-state," writes Leonard Sadosky. Sadosky, *Revolutionary Negotiations: Indians, Empires, and Diplomats in the Founding of America* (Charlottesville: University of Virginia Press, 2009), 215. On "removal" as a turning point, see Christina Snyder, *Great Crossings: Indians, Settlers, and Slaves in the Age of Jackson* (New York: Oxford University Press, 2017). Ostler's *Surviving Genocide* arrived just as my own book was going to press,

and I was unable to incorporate its findings. Nehah Micco et al. to John H. Eaton, Apr. 8, 1831, *CSE*, 2:424–25 ("the worst evil"); John Ross et al. to Lewis Cass, Feb. 14, 1833, *CSE*, 4:98 ("scheme"); George Colbert et al. to John Eaton and John Coffee, Aug. 25, 1830, LR, OIA, reel 136, M-234, NA ("act of usurpation"); Petition of residents of Mendon, Monroe County, New York, Feb. 14, 1831, COIA, Petitions, Feb. 14, 1831, HR21A-G8.2, NA ("indelible"); Petition of inhabitants of Brumfield, Portage County, Ohio, Jan. 17, 1831, COIA, Petitions, Feb. 14, 1831, HR21A-G8.2, NA ("whether the future Historian").

12. Jeremiah Evarts, "Draft of a Protest against the Principles and Policy of the Indian Bill of May, 1830," in Evarts, *Cherokee Removal: The "William Penn" Essays and Other Writings*, ed. Francis Paul Prucha (Knoxville: University of Tennessee Press, 1981), 250–51 ("the banishment"); William Howitt, *Colonization and Christianity* (London, 1838), 410.

13. A recent, provocative exploration of the frontier in American history is Greg Grandin, *The End of the Myth: From the Frontier to the Border Wall in the Mind of America* (New York: Henry Holt, 2019).

14. Historians draw a crude if sometimes useful distinction between settler and extractive colonies. The now-voluminous literature on this subject began with Patrick Wolfe, "Settler Colonialism and the Elimination of the Native," *Journal of Genocidal Research* 8, no. 4 (Dec. 2006): 387–409.

15. Abraham Lincoln, "Second Inaugural Address," Mar. 4, 1865, https://avalon.law .yale.edu/19th_century/lincoln2.asp (accessed June 8, 2019); John Quincy Adams, *Memoirs of John Quincy Adams* (Philadelphia, 1876), 10:492.

16. I do not draw a categorical distinction between modern and premodern mass expulsions, as some scholars have. The literature on the subject is voluminous, but I have found the following books to be most useful: Michael Mann, *The Dark Side of Democracy: Explaining Ethnic Cleansing* (Cambridge: Cambridge University Press, 2005); Naimark, *Fires of Hatred*; Daniel Kanstroom, *Deportation Nation: Outsiders in American History* (Cambridge: Harvard University Press, 2007); Donald Bloxham, *Genocide, the World Wars and the Unweaving of Europe* (London: Vallentine Mitchell, 2008); Bessel and Haake, eds., *Removing Peoples*; and Zahra, *The Great Departure*.

CHAPTER 1: ABORIGINIA

1. Isaac McCoy, Journal (typescript), Mar. 17, 1831, p. 138, MP; Randolph Orville Yaeger, "Indian Enterprises of Isaac McCoy—1817–1846" (Ph.D. diss., University of Oklahoma, 1954), 414–15, 451–52, 556, 585.

2. Yaeger, "Indian Enterprises of Isaac McCoy," 13–15; Kurt William Windisch, "A Thousand Slain: St. Clair's Defeat and the Evolution of the Constitutional Republic" (Ph.D. diss., University of Georgia, 2018), 181–85; J. Stoddard Johnston, ed., *Memorial of Louisville* (Chicago: American Biographical Publishing, n.d.), 1:58; Sami Lakomäki, *Gathering Together: The Shawnee People through Diaspora and Nationhood, 1600–1870* (New Haven: Yale University Press, 2014), 102–26.

3. McCoy, Autobiography (typescript), 7, MP.

4. McCoy, Autobiography, 23 ("strange and wicked"), 28 (green flies), 35 ("not so difficult"); George A. Schultz, *An Indian Canaan: Isaac McCoy and the Vision of an Indian State* (Norman: University of Oklahoma Press, 1972), 8, 13–14.

5. McCoy, Journal (typescript), Mar. 8, 1829, p. 56, MP.

6. McCoy, Journal, Nov. 12, 1831, p. 198 ("pious"), May 29, 1822, p. 302 ("How grossly"); May 29, 1822, p. 302 ("How depraved"); Isaac McCoy, *Remarks on the*

Practicability of Indian Reform, Embracing their Colonization (Boston, 1827), 14 ("the very filth").

7. Isaac McCoy to Luther Rice, July 10, 1823, reel 3, frame 51, MP ("civilized" and "barbarous countryment"); Isaac McCoy to John S. Mechan, Dec. 10, 1824, reel 3, frame 991, MP ("hunted"); Isaac McCoy to John S. Mechan, Dec. 29, 1824, reel 3, frame 1042, MP ("The great mass"); McCoy, *Remarks on the Practicability of Indian Reform*, 17–18 ("total extermination").

8. Isaac McCoy to Luther Rice, July 10, 1823, reel 3, frame 51, MP ("scheme"); McCoy, *Remarks on the Practicability of Indian Reform*, 25 ("the perishing tribes"), 30 ("morality").

9. Isaac McCoy to Lewis Cass, Mar. 6, 1832, *CSE*, 3:240 ("one body politic" and "I am not enthusiastic"); Isaac McCoy to the Commissioners West, Oct. 15, 1832, *CSE*, 3:492 ("uniting the radii").

10. The exact number of Cherokee individuals who moved to Arkansas Territory in the early nineteenth century is unknown. "I. Draft Amendment, on or before 9 July 1803," *Founders Online*, National Archives, http://founders.archives.gov/documents/Jefferson/01-40-02-0523-0002. Christian B. Keller attempts to bring some logic to Jefferson's thinking on expulsion in Keller, "Philanthropy Betrayed: Thomas Jefferson, the Louisiana Purchase, and the Origins of Federal Indian Removal Policy," *Proceedings of the American Philosophical Society* 144, no. 1 (2000): 39–66. See also Anthony F.C. Wallace, *Jefferson and the Indians: The Tragic Fate of the First Americans* (Cambridge: Harvard University Press, 1999), 224–26, 256–56; Treaty with the Cherokees, 1817, and Treaty with the Delawares, 1818, Charles J. Kappler, *Indian Affairs: Laws and Treaties* (Washington, D.C., 1904), 140–44, 170–71, 269–70; S. Charles Bolton, "Jeffersonian Indian Removal and the Emergence of Arkansas Territory," *Arkansas Historical Quarterly* 62, no. 3 (Autumn 2003): 253–71.

11. Isaac McCoy to Lewis Cass, June 23, 1823, reel 2, frame 1071, MP.

12. Most native peoples in the Northwest were eventually expelled, a story recounted in John P. Bowes, *Land Too Good for Indians: Northern Indian Removal* (Norman: University of Oklahoma Press, 2016), Meehchikilita quotation on 68; Schultz, *Indian Canaan*, 181 ("other colour"); Potawattomies to A.C. Pepper, July 14, 1835, CGLR, box 13, NA ("We are poor").

13. John Metoxen to Isaac McCoy, July 20, 1821, reel 2, frame 39, MP ("farmers and macanics"); John McElvain to Thomas L. McKenney, May 27, 1830, *CSE*, 2:57 ("I . . . can truly say"); Shannon Bontrager, "'From a Nation of Drunkards, We Have Become a Sober People': The Wyandot Experience in the Ohio Valley during the Early Republic," *Journal of the Early Republic* 32, no. 4 (Winter 2012): 628 ("*a cruelty*"); Elizabeth Neumeyer, "Michigan Indians Battle Against Removal," *Michigan History* 55, no. 4 (1971): 279 ("far better").

14. Henry C. Brish to S.S. Hamilton, Nov. 28, 1831, *CSE*, 2:691–92; Ben Secunda, "The Road to Ruin? 'Civilization' and the Origins of a 'Michigan Road Band' of Potawatomi," *Michigan Historical Review* 34, no. 1 (2008): 118–49; *White Pigeon Republican* (St. Joseph, Mich.), Aug. 28, 1839, reprinted in *Collections and Researches made by the Pioneer Society of the State of Michigan* (Lansing, 1908), 10:170–72 ("they hunt with us").

15. Bowes, *Land Too Good for Indians*, 141–42 ("terms of intimacy"); Susan E. Gray, "Limits and Possibilities: White-Indian Relations in Western Michigan in the Era of Removal," *Michigan Historical Review* 20, no. 2 (Fall 1994): 79, 82–85, 88 ("We could not have done"); James M. McClurken, "Ottawa Adaptive Strategies to Indian Removal," *Michigan Historical Review* 12, no. 1 (Spring 1986): 38–39, 47–48, 51.

16. Peter C. Mancall, "Men, Women, and Alcohol in Indian Villages in the Great Lakes Region in the Early Republic," *Journal of the Early Republic* 15, no. 3 (Autumn 1995): 425–48; Bontrager, "'From a Nation of Drunkards, We Have Become a Sober People,'" 627 ("maintain them").

17. William Hicks and John Ross, annual message, Oct. 13, 1828, *PCJR*, 1:144 ("burlesque"); John Ross to William Wirt, Nov. 11, 1831, *PCJR*, 1:231 ("ere long"); George Colbert et al. to John Eaton and John Coffee, Aug. 25, 1830, LR, OIA, reel 136, M-234, NA ("as long as the grass grows"); Peter Pitchlynn[?] to David Folsom, May 19, 1830, 4026.3186, PPP ("If we go").

18. Mark F. Boyd, "Horatio S. Dexter and Events Leading to the Treaty of Moultrie Creek with the Seminole Indians," *Florida Anthropologist* 11, no. 3 (Sept. 1958): 89 ("I am satisfied"); Alan K. Craig and Christopher Peebles, "Ethnoecologic Change among the Seminoles, 1740–1840," *Geoscience and Man* 5 (1974): 83–96.

19. James Stuart, *Three Years in North America* (Edinburgh, 1833), 2:132 ("Europeans"); Tiya Miles, *The House on Diamond Hill: A Cherokee Plantation Story* (Chapel Hill: University of North Carolina Press, 2010), 29 ("aristocratic"), 143; Michael F. Doran, "Negro Slaves of the Five Civilized Tribes," *Annals of the Association of American Geographers* 68, no. 3 (Sept. 1978): table 2, p. 346.

20. Cherokee Account Book, 1823–1835, Box 5, William Holland Thomas Papers, DMR; Theda Perdue, *Cherokee Women: Gender and Culture Change* (Lincoln: University of Nebraska Press, 1998), 115–58.

21. John Clark to the Governor of Alabama, Sept. 29, 1821, John Clark Letter, Western Americana Collection, Beinecke Rare Book and Manuscript Library, Yale University ("suffered to intermix"); George Strother Gaines, *Reminiscences of George Strother Gaines: Pioneer and Statesman of Early Alabama and Mississippi*, ed. James P. Pate (Tuscaloosa: University of Alabama Press, 1998), 78 ("pretty good").

22. Thomas Jefferson to Caspar Wistar, Oct. 22, 1815, *Founders Online*, National Archives, last modified November 26, 2017, http://founders.archives.gov /documents/Jefferson/03-09-02-0091 ("a great pity"); *RDC* (1825), 1:639–40 ("dispirited and degraded"); *RDC* (1828), vol. 4, 2:1564 (melting snow); *RDC* (1825–26), vol. 2, appendix, 40 ("in despair"); Ruth Miller Elson, *Guardians of Tradition: American Schoolbooks of the Nineteenth Century* (Lincoln: University of Nebraska Press, 1964), 69, 79; Jill Lepore, *The Name of War: King Philip's War and the Origins of American Identity* (New York: Knopf, 1998), 191–226.

23. Thomas Jefferson, *Notes on the State of Virginia* (Philadelphia, 1788), 64–65; Alison Bashford and Joyce E. Chaplin, *The New Worlds of Thomas Robert Malthus: Rereading the* Principle of Population (Princeton: Princeton University Press, 2016), 116–45; Benjamin Rush, *Medical Inquiries and Observations* (Philadelphia, 1805), 1:48; Elbert Herring to Lewis Cass, Nov. 19, 1831, p. 475, LS, OIA, reel 7, M-21, NA.

24. I am using Douglas H. Ubelaker's conservative numbers. Ubelaker, "North American Indian Population Size: Changing Perspectives," in *Disease and Demography in the Americas*, ed. John W. Verano and Douglas H. Ubelaker (Washington, D.C.: Smithsonian Institution Press, 1992), 173; Memorial of the Cherokees, Dec. 1829, Committee of the Whole House, Petitions, "Various Subjects," HR21A-H1.1, NA. Translation from the original Cherokee by Patrick Del Percio.

25. I am relying on the numbers compiled by Jon Muller, "Historic Southeastern Native American Population," available from the author. Perhaps the most detailed examination of health and reproduction in the early modern indigenous world is Seth Archer, *Sharks upon the Land: Colonialism, Indigenous Health, and Culture in Hawai'i,*

1778–1855 (New York: Cambridge University Press, 2018); Judge Harper, "Memoir on Slavery, Part I," *Southern Literary Messenger* 4, no. 10 (Oct. 1838): 609–18; W. Williams to J.J. Abert, Feb. 8, 1838, Records of the Office of the Chief of Engineers, Map File, RG 77, U.S. 125–6, NACP.

26. John Ross, annual message, Oct. 24, 1831, *PCJR*, 1:229 ("our population"); *Cherokee Phoenix*, July 21, 1828, 2 ("We repeat again"); Memorial of Creeks, Feb. 3, 1830, PM, Protection of Indians, SEN21A-H3, NA.

27. Isaac McCoy to the Commissioners West, Oct. 15, 1832, *CSE*, 3:493; Nicholas Guyatt, *Bind Us Apart: How Enlightened Americans Invented Racial Segregation* (New York: Basic Books, 2016), 281–305.

28. Douglas R. Egerton, "'Its Origin Is Not a Little Curious': A New Look at the American Colonization Society," *Journal of the Early Republic* 5, no. 4 (1985): 463–80.

29. William Miles, "'Enamoured with Colonization': Isaac McCoy's Plan of Indian Reform," *Kansas Historical Quarterly* 38, no. 3 (1972): 269, 278–79; Thomas Jefferson, Autobiography, Jan. 6–July 29, 1821, *Founders Online*, National Archives, http://founders.archives.gov/documents/Jefferson/98-01-02-1756; U.S. Congress, *Journal of the House of Representatives of the United States*, 18th Cong., 2nd sess. (1825), 190, 215, 295, 309; H.N. Sherwood, "Early Negro Deportation Projects," *Mississippi Valley Historical Review* 2, no. 4 (Mar. 1916): 484–508.

30. Michael P. Johnson, "Denmark Vesey and His Co-Conspirators," *William and Mary Quarterly* 58, no. 4 (Oct. 2001): 915–76; Lacy Ford, "Reconfiguring the Old South: 'Solving' the Problem of Slavery, 1787–1838," *Journal of American History* 95, no. 1 (June 2008): 116; *Acts of the General Assembly of the State of Georgia* (Milledgeville, 1827), 199–201 ("wild, fanatical and destructive").

31. *RDC* (1825), 1:640. The expansionist ambitions of Southern planters extended well beyond the indigenous lands in Mississippi, Alabama, and Georgia, as Matthew Karp describes in *This Vast Southern Empire: Slaveholders at the Helm of American Foreign Policy* (Cambridge: Harvard University Press, 2016).

32. The office of Superintendent of Indian Trade, existing between 1806 and 1822, predated the office of Superintendent of Indian Affairs, which was created in 1824. Thomas L. McKenney to Isaac Thomas, Dec. 14, 1816, Library of Congress Collection, RG 233, entry 756, box 57, NA; John Ross et al. to Lewis Cass, Feb. 14, 1833, *CSE*, 4:98.

33. James Barbour to William McLean, Apr. 29, 1828, LS, OIA, Miscellaneous Immigration, RG 75, entry 84, M21, book D, 485, NA; *RDC* (1830), vol. 6, 2:1017 ("admirably adapted"); Lewis Cass to the Chiefs of the Creek Tribe, Jan. 16, 1832, *CSE*, 2:743; Removal of the Indians, Feb. 24, 1830, COIA, HR21A-D11.2, NA ("wrongs").

34. Thomas L. McKenney to John Cocke, Jan. 23, 1827, LS, OIA, Miscellaneous Immigration, RG 75, entry 84, M21, book C, 326, NA; Map no. 157, RG 75, Central Map File, Indian Territory, NACP.

35. *RDC* (1828), vol. 4, 2:1549.

36. Herman J. Viola, *Exploring the West* (Washington, D.C.: Smithsonian Books, 1987), 29–30 ("American Sahara"); *Account of an Expedition from Pittsburgh to the Rocky Mountains Performed in the Years 1819 and '20 under the Command of Stephen H. Long* (Philadelphia, 1823), 2:361; G. Malcolm Lewis, "William Gilpin and the Concept of the Great Plains Region," *Annals of the Association of American Geographers* 56, no. 1 (Mar. 1966): 35–36; Isaac McCoy to P.B. Porter, Jan. 29, 1829, Report of Committee on Indian Affairs, 20th Cong., 2nd sess., H.Rep. 87, p. 17; J.B. Clark to George Gibson, Apr. 13, 1831, *CSE* 1:548 ("greatly exaggerated").

37. "Great system" is the phrase of the Superintendent of Indian Affairs, Thomas

L. McKenney. McKenney to Isaac McCoy, Oct. 13, 1826, LS, OIA, Miscellaneous Immigration, RG 75, entry 84, M21, book C, 188, NA.

38. Inventory of Articles, Oct. 8, 1824, reel 3, frame 901, MP; Isaac McCoy to Lucious Bolles, Sept. 27, 1826, reel 5, frame 234, MP ("We have none" and "They could not compete").

39. Thomas Jefferson to William Henry Harrison, Feb. 27, 1803, *Founders Online*, National Archives, http://founders.archives.gov/documents/Jefferson/01-39-02 -0500; Thomas C. McKenney to Wyandott Chiefs, Mar. 24, 1825, LS, OIA, Miscellaneous Immigration, RG 75, entry 84, M21, book A, 424, NA ("He is your friend"). Though the literature on the "plan of civilization" is immense, a good starting place is Anthony F.C. Wallace, *Jefferson and the Indians: The Tragic Fate of the First Americans* (Cambridge: Belknap Press, 1999). Bernard Sheehan argues that Jefferson's policy to civilize native peoples was tightly linked to the desire to make them disappear. Bernard Sheehan, *Seeds of Extinction: Jeffersonian Philanthropy and the American Indian* (Chapel Hill: University of North Carolina Press, 1973).

40. Thomas L. McKenney to Isaac Thomas, Dec. 14, 1816, Library of Congress Collection, RG 233, entry 756, box 57 of LC box 183, NA.

41. John C. Calhoun to James Monroe, Mar. 29, 1824, LS, OIA, Miscellaneous Immigration, RG 75, entry 84, M21, book A, 9, NA ("humane & benevolent"); John C. Calhoun to John Crowell, Aug. 12, 1824, LS, OIA, Miscellaneous Immigration, RG 75, entry 84, M21, book A, 177, NA ("in a short time"); "Civilization of the Indians," *ASPIA*, 2:458 ("It requires"); Thomas L. McKenney to James B. Finley, Feb. 22, 1825, LS, OIA, Miscellaneous Immigration, RG 75, entry 84, M21, book A, 366, NA.

42. *RDC* (1825–26), vol. 2, appendix, 40–43 ("approaching catastrophe"); John Joseph Wallis, "Federal government employees, by government branch and location relative to the capital: 1816–1992," table Ea894-903 in *Historical Statistics of the United States, Earliest Times to the Present: Millennial Edition*, ed. Susan B. Carter, Scott Sigmund Gartner, Michael R. Haines, Alan L. Olmstead, Richard Sutch, Gavin Wright (New York: Cambridge University Press, 2006); Department of Defense, *Selected Manpower Statistics, Fiscal Year 1997* (Washington, D.C.: U.S. Government Printing Office, 1997), 46–47, table 2.

43. D.A. Reese to Lewis Cass, Mar. 10, 1832, *CSE* 3:255; Bustenay Oded, *Mass Deportations and Deportees in the Neo-Assyrian Empire* (Wiesbaden: Reichert, 1979); Mark Edward Lewis, *China Between Empires: The Northern and Southern Dynasties* (Cambridge: Harvard University Press, 2009), 78–79; David Abulafia, "The Last Muslims in Italy," *Dante Studies* 125 (2007): 271–87; John R. Perry, "Forced Migration in Iran during the Seventeenth and Eighteenth Centuries," *Iranian Studies: Bulletin of the Society for Iranian Cultural and Social Studies* 8, no. 4 (1975): 199–215.

44. Robert Walsh, *An Appeal from the Judgments of Great Britain Respecting the United States of America* (London, 1819), 92; David Ramsay, *The History of South-Carolina* (Charleston, 1809), 1:15.

45. "Indian Affairs," *Niles' Weekly Register*, Aug. 30, 1828, 13 ("in modern times"); "Examination of the Controversy between Georgia and the Creeks," *Vermont Gazette* (Bennington, Vt.), Aug. 23, 1825, 1–2 ("the partitioners").

46. *RDC* (1825–26), vol. 2, appendix, 40–43.

47. Duke of Saxe-Weimar Eisenach Bernhard, *Travels through North America during the Years 1825 and 1826* (Philadelphia, 1828), 1:170; William Faux, *Memorable Days in America: Being a Journal of a Tour to the United States* (London, 1823), 438.

CHAPTER 2: THE WHITE PEOPLE OF GEORGIA

1. *Georgia Journal* (Milledgeville, Ga.), Aug. 30, 1825, 1–3.

2. *RDC* (1825), 1:643 ("must be very valuable"); *Southern Recorder* (Milledgeville, Ga.), May 15, 1830, 3 ("savages"); *Southern Recorder*, June 19, 1830, 3 ("tributaries"); *The Athenian* (Athens, Ga.), Nov. 10, 1829, 2 (small tax); Sven Beckert, *Empire of Cotton: A Global History* (New York: Knopf, 2015), 117–20.

3. *Georgia Journal*, Jan. 16, 1830, 2 ("negrophiles"), Feb. 10, 1831, 3 ("Indianites"), May 25, 1819, 3 ("waste public lands"), July 10, 1830, 2 ("Georgia may forgive"), Oct. 3, 1829, 2 ("to some distant point"), Aug. 30, 1825, 1–3 ("submit").

4. Daniel Immerwahr, *How to Hide an Empire: A History of the Greater United States* (New York: Farrar, Straus and Giroux, 2019), chaps. 1–2; Malcolm Rohrbough, *The Land Office Business: The Settlement and Administration of American Public Lands, 1789–1837* (New York: Oxford University Press, 1968), 174–75; and Paul Frymer, *Building an American Empire: The Era of Territorial and Political Expansion* (Princeton: Princeton University Press, 2017), 1–127.

5. Memorial of the Head Men and Warriors of the Creek Nation of Indians, Feb. 6, 1832, *The New American State Papers* (Wilmington, Del.: Scholarly Resources, 1972), 9:192–96.

6. Population figures compiled from the *Handbook of North American Indians* (Washington, D.C.: Smithsonian Institution, 1978–2008), 20 vols.; Martin Van Buren, *Autobiography of Martin Van Buren* (Washington, D.C., 1920), 2:293.

7. Conference of John Ross, Edward Gunter, and John Mason, Jr., Nov. 6, 1837, *PCJR*, 1:537–40.

8. The causes of the South's shifting cultivation, which gave rise to the barren landscape described by the *Augusta Chronicle*, are still hotly debated. *Augusta Chronicle* (Augusta, Ga.), Nov. 24, 1830; John Majewski and Viken Tchakerian, "The Environmental Origins of Shifting Cultivation: Climate, Soils, and Disease in the Nineteenth-Century U.S. South," *Agricultural History* 81, no. 4 (Fall 2007): 522–49.

9. *Federal Union* (Milledgeville, Ga.), Dec. 11, 1835, 2 ("by force"); *Southern Recorder*, Dec. 29, 1831, 2–3 ("mere *mockery*"). The sectional politics within Georgia were more complicated than Nesbit implied. Watson W. Jennison, *Cultivating Race: The Expansion of Slavery in Georgia, 1750–1860* (Lexington: University Press of Kentucky, 2012), 194–217.

10. *RDC* (1825), 1:639–40.

11. Trip Henningson, "Princetonians in Georgia," *Princeton and Slavery*, https://slavery .princeton.edu/stories/princetonians-in-georgia (accessed Feb. 1, 2018); Joseph Yannielli, "Student Origins," *Princeton and Slavery*, https://slavery.princeton.edu /stories/origins (accessed Feb. 1, 2018); *Chronicles of Erasmus Hall* (Brooklyn, N.Y., 1906), 47, 55.

12. Edward J. Harden, *The Life of George M. Troup* (Savannah, Ga., 1859), 194 ("great moral and political truths"), 197 ("positive obligations"), 204 ("simply *occupants*"), 205 ("breach of faith"), 217 ("birthright"), 230 ("indisputable"), 351 ("the Governor of this State"), Edmund P. Gaines as quoted on 390 ("little European despot"), 401 ("Chief Magistrate"), 531 ("Where principal"); Articles of Agreement and Cession, Apr. 25, 1802, Governor's Subject Files, Executive Dept., Governor, RG 1-1-5, Georgia Archives.

13. Harden, *Life of George M. Troup*, 207 ("Of all the old States"), 405 ("civilizing plan"); John Ross et al. to the Senate and House of Representatives, Mar. 12, 1825, *PCJR*, 1:104–5.

14. Michael D. Green, *The Politics of Indian Removal: Creek Government and Society in Crisis* (Lincoln: University of Nebraska Press, 1982), 69–97; Report of special agent, June 28, 1825, enclosed in T.P. Andrews to James Barbour, July 4, 1825, LR, OIA, reel 219, frames 363–71, M-234, NA.

15. Harden, *Life of George M. Troup*, 232 ("fomenting"), 289 ("the servant").

16. *The Constitutionalist* (Augusta, Ga.), Sept. 2, 1825, 3; Jennison, *Cultivating Race*, 194–95.

17. "To Socrates," *Georgia Journal*, Aug. 9, 1825, 2 ("Troup and the Treaty"); *RDC* (1830), vol. 6, 2:1102 ("at the first prattle"); "To the People of the State of Georgia," *Savannah Republican*, as reprinted in the *Southern Recorder*, Sept. 27, 1825, 1–2 ("A Native Georgian").

18. *RDC* (1826), 2:775; Harden, *Life of George M. Troup*, 467.

19. Green, *Politics of Indian Removal*, 123; General Humming Bird et al. to Generals William Clark, Thomas Hinds, and John Coffee, Nov. 14, 1826, *ASPIA*, 2:713 ("with great unanimity"); Levi Colbert et al. to Thomas Hinds and John Coffee, Oct. 24, 1826, *ASPIA*, 2:720 ("We have no lands"); 20th Cong., 2nd sess., H.Doc. 6, pp. 2–7 (Cherokees); Harden, *Life of George M. Troup*, 175. "Southern empire" became a common phrase in the 1830s. See Matthew Karp, *This Vast Southern Empire: Slaveholders at the Helm of American Foreign Policy* (Cambridge: Harvard University Press, 2016).

20. John Martin, "John McKinley: Jacksonian Phase," *Alabama Historical Quarterly* 28, nos. 1–2 (1966): 7–31; *RDC* (1827), 71–76 (Reed); *RDC* (1825), 1:648–60 (Cobb).

21. *Southern Recorder*, Apr. 9, 1827, 2–3.

22. William H. Crawford to John Gaillard, Mar. 13, 1816, *ASPIA*, 2:28 ("It is believed"); "Crawfordism," *Macon Telegraph* (Macon, Ga.), Apr. 30, 1827, 1; John Demos, *The Heathen School: A Story of Hope and Betrayal in the Age of the Early Republic* (New York: Knopf, 2014); *RDC* (1828), vol. 4, 2:1566 ("a mixture"); Harden, *Life of George M. Troup*, 206.

23. U.S. Constitution, Article 4, Section 4; Garry Wills, *"Negro President": Jefferson and the Slave Power* (Boston: Houghton Mifflin, 2003), 11.

24. *Southern Recorder*, Apr. 9, 1827, 2–3.

25. *Southern Recorder*, Apr. 9, 1827, 2–3. On southern domination of the federal government, see Leonard L. Richards, *The Slave Power: The Free North and Southern Domination, 1780–1860* (Baton Rouge: Louisiana State University Press, 2000).

26. William G. McLoughlin, *Cherokee Renascence in the New Republic* (Princeton: Princeton University Press, 1986), 396–424.

27. *Southern Recorder*, Apr. 9, 1827, 2–3.

28. *Georgia Journal*, May 25, 1819, 3.

29. David Eltis, "Estimates of the Slave Trade," *Voyages: The Trans-Atlantic Slave Trade Database*, http://www.slavevoyages.org/estimates/ygVmZkq4 (accessed Feb. 8, 2018).

30. Existing records show that 130 different ships, many owned by different investors, delivered over 38,000 of the enslaved people who arrived in the United States in the final two years of the trade. David Eltis, "Slave Trade Database," *Voyages: The Trans-Atlantic Slave Trade Database*, http://www.slavevoyages.org/voyages/qWuTxkC5 (accessed Feb. 8, 2018), and http://www.slavevoyages.org/voyages/CakpCwJY (accessed Feb. 8, 2018); James McMillin, *The Final Victims: Foreign Slave Trade to North America, 1783–1810* (Columbia: University of South Carolina Press, 2004). The number of permissible deaths is a common calculation in twenty-first-century humanitarian operations. Eyal Weizman, *The Least of All Possible Evils: Humanitarian Violence from Arendt to Gaza* (New York: Verso, 2012).

31. Steven Deyle, *Carry Me Back: The Domestic Slave Trade in American Life* (New York: Oxford University Press, 2006), table 4.1, p. 140; Calvin Schermerhorn, *The Business of Slavery and the Rise of American Capitalism, 1815–1860* (New Haven: Yale University Press, 2015), 142–43, 150–51; Robert H. Gudmestad, *A Troublesome Commerce: The Transformation of the Interstate Slave Trade* (Baton Rouge: Louisiana State University Press, 2003), 93; James Fenimore Cooper, *The Last of the Mohicans* (New York, 1859), 443.

32. Deyle, *Carry Me Back*, 99, 102–4, 107, 113–19.

33. Gudmestad, *A Troublesome Commerce*, 53; David L. Lightner, *Slavery and the Commerce Power: How the Struggle against the Interstate Slave Trade Led to the Civil War* (New Haven: Yale University Press, 2006), 16–36, 46.

34. Harden, *Life of George M. Troup*, 458; *Southern Recorder*, Apr. 9, 1827, 2–3.

35. *New Hampshire Observer* (Concord), June 20, 1825, 2 ("seditious"); *Essex Register* (Salem, Mass.), July 4, 1825, 1 ("imbecile menaces"); *Franklin Post and Christian Freeman* (Greenfield, Mass.), Aug. 16, 1825, 2 ("madness and folly"); *Rhode Island Republican* (Newport, R.I.), Feb. 15, 2017, 3 ("bold and decisive stand"); *Commercial Advertiser* (New York, N.Y.), Aug. 13, 1825, 2 ("righteous retribution"); Laurence M. Hauptman and George Hamell, "George Catlin: The Iroquois Origins of His Indian Portrait Gallery," *New York History* 84, no. 2 (Spring 2003): 130.

36. "Georgia and the Creeks," *The New-York Review, and Atheneum* 1 (1825–26): 174, 187, 188, 189, 190.

37. *Georgia Journal*, Aug. 9, 1825, 2 ("doggerel verse"); "To the People of Georgia," *Southern Recorder*, Aug. 9, 1825, 1 ("tender hearted"); Richard R. John, "Taking Sabbatarianism Seriously: The Postal System, the Sabbath, and the Transformation of American Political Culture," *Journal of the Early Republic* 10, no. 4 (1990): 517–67.

38. Atticus, "To the People of Georgia," *Southern Recorder*, Aug. 9, 1825, 1; "The Late Treaty," *Georgia Journal*, Nov. 8, 1825, 2 ("were got rid of" and "sentimental trash"); *Georgia Journal*, May 31, 1824, 3 ("cant of the day"); *Charleston Courier* (Charleston, S.C.), Nov. 16, 1825, 2.

39. John Ross et al. to the U.S. Senate, Apr. 16, 1824, *ASPIA*, 2:502; "Address of the Creeks to the citizens of Alabama and Georgia," *Niles' Weekly Register* 37 (Aug. 29, 1829), 12.

40. John P. Bowes, *Land Too Good for Indians: Northern Indian Removal* (Norman: University of Oklahoma Press, 2016), 67–68; Reply of the Head Chief Hicks to the talk delivered by the Commissioner Col. White, May 5, 1827, LR, OIA, reel 806, frame 5, M-234, NA.

41. Isaac McCoy, *Remarks on the Practicability of Indian Reform, Embracing their Colonization* (Boston, 1827), 12.

42. Robert V. Remini, *Andrew Jackson and His Indian Wars* (New York: Viking, 2001), 62–79 (quotation on 63–64).

43. Robert V. Remini, *Andrew Jackson: The Course of American Freedom, 1822–1832* (Baltimore: Johns Hopkins University Press, 1998), 147–48.

44. Remini, *Andrew Jackson: The Course of American Freedom*, 172–77 (quotation on 175); Jeremiah Evarts to Joseph Nourse, Mar. 9, 1829, no. 18, ABC 11.1, vol. 2, Letters from Officers of the Board, American Board of Commissioners for Foreign Missions, Houghton Library, Harvard College Library; "First Inaugural Address of Andrew Jackson," Mar. 4, 1829, http://avalon.law.yale.edu/19th_century/jackson1 .asp, (accessed May 2, 2019). Two drafts of the address include a second sentence regarding native peoples: "A just and liberal policy is due to their dependent situation, and to our national character." "Inaugural Address," 1829, *PAJ*.

45. Martin Van Buren, *Autobiography of Martin Van Buren* (Washington, D.C., 1920), 2:295; Isaac McCoy, Journal (typescript), Feb. 27, 1829, p. 61, MP.

CHAPTER 3: THE DEBATE

1. *Salem Gazette* (Salem, Mass.), Dec. 15, 1829, 2; *Delaware Gazette and State Journal* (Wilmington, Del.), Dec. 18, 1829, 2; *Savannah Georgian* (Savannah, Ga.), Jan. 11, 1830, 2; Anthony R. Fellow, *American Media History*, 3rd. ed. (Boston: Wadsworth, 2013), 83.

2. Ellen Cushman, *The Cherokee Syllabary: Writing the People's Perseverance* (Norman: University of Oklahoma Press, 2011), 39–70, 89–129; John Ross to George Gist, Jan. 12, 1832, *PCJR*, 1:234.

3. Memorial of the Cherokees, Dec. 1829, Committee of the Whole House, Petitions, "Various Subjects," HR21A-H1.1, NA.

4. Translations by Patrick Del Percio of the D'Arcy McNickle Center for American Indian and Indigenous Studies, Newberry Library.

5. "Memorial of the Cherokees," *Cherokee Phoenix* (New Echota, Cherokee Nation), Dec. 30, 1829, 3; Tiya Miles, "'Circular Reasoning': Recentering Cherokee Women in the Antiremoval Campaigns," *American Quarterly* 61, no. 2 (2009): 221–43; Theda Perdue, *Cherokee Women: Gender and Culture Change, 1700–1835* (Lincoln: University of Nebraska Press, 1998), 91–108.

6. John Huss to [?], June 19, 1828, in *Cherokee Phoenix*, July 2, 1828, 2–3 ("the land they love").

7. Memorial of Creeks, Feb. 3, 1830, PM, Protection of Indians, SEN21A-H3, NA.

8. *Journal of the House of Representatives of the United States* (Washington, D.C., 1829), 262, 265; Charles Caldwell, *Thoughts on the Original Unity of the Human Race* (New York, 1830), 136.

9. *Commercial Advertiser* (New York, N.Y.), Mar. 18, 1828, 2; *Augusta Chronicle* (Augusta, Ga.), Mar. 7, 1828, 1; *Cherokee Phoenix*, Feb. 11, 1829, 3; Thomas L. McKenney to Elias Boudinot, May 17, 1828, LS, OIA, Miscellaneous Immigration, RG 75, entry 84, M21, book D, 454, NA.

10. George M. Troup to John Forsyth, Apr. 6, 1825, *ASPIA*, 2:780; E. Merton Coulter, *Joseph Vallence Bevan: Georgia's First Official Historian* (Athens: University of Georgia Press, 1964), 53–72; Hasan Crockett, "The Incendiary Pamphlet: David Walker's Appeal in Georgia," *Journal of Negro History* 86, no. 3 (Summer 2001): 309–10; Arthur Foster, *A Digest of the Laws of the State of Georgia* (Philadelphia, 1831), 314–17, 319; John MacPherson Berrien to Andrew Jackson, June 25, 1830, LR, OIA, reel 76, M-234, NA.

11. John Demos, *The Heathen School: A Story of Hope and Betrayal in the Age of the Early Republic* (New York: Knopf, 2014), 165–71; "Address of Dewi [*sic*] Brown," *Proceedings of the Massachusetts Historical Society* 12 (1871–73): 32–33 ("had the natives"); Joel W. Martin, "Crisscrossing Projects of Sovereignty and Conversion: Cherokee Christians and New England Missionaries during the 1820s," in *Native Americans, Christianity, and the Reshaping of the American Religious Landscape*, ed. Joel W. Martin, Mark A. Nichols, and Michelene E. Pesantubbee (Chapel Hill: University of North Carolina Press, 2010), 67–92; "Letter from David Brown," *Essex Register* (Salem, Mass.), June 27, 1825, 3 ("How would the Georgians").

12. Maureen Konkle, *Writing Indian Nations: Native Intellectuals and the Politics of Historiography, 1827–1863* (Chapel Hill: University of North Carolina Press, 2004); William Apess, *A Son of the Forest: The Experience of William Apes, A Native of the Forest* (New York, 1829), 14–15, 66 ("good people"), 140 ("exaggerated account"); Drew

Lopenzina, *Through an Indian's Looking-Glass: A Cultural Biography of William Apess, Pequot* (Amherst: University of Massachusetts Press, 2017), 227–42.

13. *Missionary Herald* 15, no. 4 (Apr. 1819): 75; Perdue, *Cherokee Women*, 156–58; Miles, "'Circular Reasoning'"; M. Amanda Moulder, "Cherokee Practice, Missionary Intentions: Literacy Learning among Early Nineteenth-Century Cherokee Women," *College Composition and Communication* 63, no. 1 (Sept. 2011): 75–97.

14. Ronald N. Satz, *American Indian Policy in the Jacksonian Era* (1974; reprint, Norman: University of Oklahoma Press, 1975), 14–15 ("This sort of machinery"); Francis Paul Prucha, "Thomas L. McKenney and the New York Indian Board," *Mississippi Valley Historical Review* 48, no. 4 (Mar. 1962): 635–55.

15. Isaac McCoy to Rice McCoy, Dec. 21, 1829, reel 7, frame 270, MP; Satz, *American Indian Policy,* 14–15; [Lewis Cass,] "Removal of the Indians," *North American Review* 30, no. 66 (Jan. 1830): 67, 71, 73, 74, 83.

16. [Lewis Cass,] "Manners and Customs of Several Indian Tribes, *North American Review* 22, no. 50 (Jan. 1826): 116, 119.

17. *Bangor Register* (Maine), Apr. 13, 1830, 3; Joseph Griffin, ed., *History of the Press of Maine* (Brunswick, Maine, 1872), 129; Jason M. Dorr, "Changing Their Guardians: The Penobscot Indians and Maine Statehood, 1820–1849" (University of Maine: M.A. thesis, 1998).

18. Manisha Sinha, *The Slave's Cause: A History of Abolition* (New Haven: Yale University Press, 2016), 214–17; John Stauffer, *The Black Hearts of Men: Radical Abolitionists and the Transformation of Race* (Cambridge: Harvard University Press, 2002), 97–105; John A. Andrew III, *From Revivals to Removal: Jeremiah Evarts, the Cherokee Nation, and the Search for the Soul of America* (Athens: University of Georgia Press, 1992), 148–49; Mary Hershberger, "Mobilizing Women, Anticipating Abolition: The Struggle against Indian Removal in the 1830s," *Journal of American History* 86, no. 1 (June 1999): 15–40; J. Orin Oliphant, *Through the South and the West with Jeremiah Evarts in 1826* (Lewisburg, Pa.: Bucknell University Press, 1956), 1–62; Jeremiah Evarts, *Cherokee Removal: The "William Penn" Essays and Other Writings,* ed. Francis Paul Prucha (Knoxville: University of Tennessee Press, 1981), 11, 74, 109, 177–78.

19. Memorial of Inhabitants of Topsfield, Massachusetts, Apr. 17, 1830, PM, Protection of Indians, SEN21A-H3, NA; Petition of inhabitants of Windham County, Connecticut, Feb. 8, 1830, COIA, Petitions, Feb. 1, 1830 to Jan. 18, 1831, folder 1, HR21A-G8.2, NA; Memorial from citizens of the City of New York, Apr. 3, 1830, Petitions, SEN21A-H3; Memorial of Citizens of Massachusetts, Feb. 8, 1830, PM, Protection of Indians, SEN 21A-H3, NA; Memorial of Inhabitants of Philipsburg, New Hampshire, Apr. 7, 1830, PM, Protection of Indians, SEN21A-H3, NA; Report of Senate Committee on Indian Affairs, Mar. 29, 1830, PM, Indian Affairs, SEN21A-D7, NA (burdensome duty); *RDC* (1830), vol. 6, 2:1019 ("contented majorities"), 1080 ("were nothing").

20. Petition of citizens of New York, Dec. 28, 1829, PM, Indian Affairs, SEN21A-G8, NA; Memorial of inhabitants of Pennsylvania, Jan. 7, 1830, PM, Indian Affairs, SEN21A-G8, NA; Petition of the Inhabitants of Brunswick, Maine, Mar. 6, 1830, PM, Protection of Indians, SEN21A-H3, NA; Memorial of Inhabitants of North Yarmouth, Maine, Mar. 29, 1830, PM, Protection of Indians, SEN21A-H3, NA. On colonialism and Protestant evangelism in the early modern era, see Edward E. Andrews, *Native Apostles: Black and Indian Missionaries in the British Atlantic World* (Cambridge: Harvard University Press, 2013).

21. Petition of citizens of New York, Dec. 28, 1829, PM, Indian Affairs, SEN21A-G8, NA (dark stain); Petition of Inhabitants of Lexington, New York, Feb. 8, 1830,

COIA, Petitions, Feb. 1, 1830 to Jan. 18, 1831, folder 1, HR21A-G8.2, NA; Petition of citizens of Pennsylvania, Feb. 15, 1830, COIA, Petitions, Feb. 1, 1830 to Jan. 18, 1831, folder 2, HR21A-G8.2, NA; Memorial of the Officers of Dartmouth College, May 3, 1830, COIA, Petitions, Feb. 1, 1830 to Jan. 18, 1831, folder 1, HR21A-G8.2, NA; Memorial of the Inhabitants of Lafayette, New York, Jan. 7, 1830, PM, Protection of Indians, SEN21A-H3, NA ("tyrannical and oppressive"); Memorial of Inhabitants of North Yarmouth, Maine, Mar. 29, 1830, PM, Protection of Indians, SEN21A-H3, NA ("unparalleled perfidy"); Memorial of Inhabitants of Farmington, Connecticut, Feb. 27, 1830, PM, Indian Affairs, SEN21A-G8, NA ("atrocious outrage"); Memorial of the Ladies, Inhabitants of Pennsylvania, Mar. 3, 1830, PM, Protection of Indians, SEN21A-H3, NA ("lasting dishonor").

22. Petition of Inhabitants of Farmington, Jan. 6, 1830, COIA, Petitions, Feb. 1, 1830 to Jan. 18, 1831, folder 1, HR21A-G8.2, NA; Hershberger, "Mobilizing Women"; Miles, "'Circular Reasoning'"; Alisse Portnoy, *Their Right to Speak: Women's Activism in the Indian and Slave Debates* (Cambridge: Harvard University Press, 2005).

23. Memorial of Sundry Ladies of Hallowell, Maine, Jan. 8, 1830, PM, Indian Affairs, SEN21A-G8, NA ("domestic altar" and "endearments"); Petition of inhabitants of Lewis, New York, Jan. 24, 1831, COIA, Petitions, Jan. 24 to Feb. 8, 1831, folder 2, HR21A-G8.2, NA; Memorial of the Ladies of Burlington, New Jersey, Jan. 7, 1830, PM, Protection of Indians, SEN21A-H3, NA ("feebler sex"); Portnoy, *Their Right to Speak,* 67–71.

24. "To the People of Georgia," *Southern Recorder* (Milledgeville, Ga.), Aug. 9, 1825, 1 ("meek"); *The Athenian* (Athens, Ga.), Aug. 17, 1830, 2 ("sickly"); *The Athenian*, Feb. 16, 1830, 3 ("morbid"); *Georgia Journal* (Milledgeville, Ga.), Mar. 24, 1831, 1–3 ("fearless, manly exercise"); "The Southern Indians—Again," *Southern Recorder*, Feb. 13, 1830, 3 ("FEMALE petitions," quoting the *Pittsburgh Mercury*); "Georgia Indians," *Southern Recorder*, Feb. 6, 1830, 3 ("The ladies," quoting the *New England Review*).

25. *RDC* (1830), vol. 6, 1:108–9 ("no reliance"); Harriet Martineau, *Retrospect of Western Travel* (London, 1838), 1:300; *RDC* (1836), vol. 12, 4:4041 ("Anglo-Saxon").

26. Neha Micco et al. to the President, Jan. 21, 1830, LR, OIA, reel 222, frame 274, M-234, NA; Tuskee-Neha-Haw et al. to John H. Eaton, Oct. 20, 1829, 21st Cong., 2nd sess., H.Rep. 109, p. 3.

27. George Lowrey, Lewis Ross, William Hicks, R. Taylor, Joseph Vann, and W.S. Coodey to John Eaton, Feb. 11, 1830, LR, OIA, reel 74, M-234, NA ("emboldened"); George Lowrey, Lewis Ross, William Hicks, R. Taylor, Joseph Vann, and W.S. Coodey to Andrew Jackson, Mar. 26, 1830, LR, OIA, reel 74, M-234, NA.

28. Phill Grierson vs. Sockahpautia, box 10, 1st series, no. 22, Creek Removal Records, entry 300, RG 75, NA; Phill Grierson vs. the Creek Nation, box 10, 1st series, no. 28, Creek Removal Records, entry 300, RG 75, NA; Cowemaltha et al. to John H. Eaton, Apr. 12, 1829, HR21A-D11.2, NA; George Lowrey, Lewis Ross, William Hicks, R. Taylor, Joseph Vann, and W.S. Coodey to Andrew Jackson, Feb. 25, 1830, LR, OIA, reel 74, M-234, NA ("It cannot be supposed"); James Williams to Hugh Montgomery, Mar. 4, 1830, LR, OIA, reel 74, M-234, NA.

29. "Indian Depredations," *Southern Recorder*, Mar. 6, 1830, 2–3 ("the first fruits"); "Removal of the Indians," *Georgia Journal*, Mar. 13, 1830, 3 ("rude and impudent," "Fanatics," "white savages"); *Georgia Journal*, Jan. 16, 1830, 2 ("local concerns").

30. Isaac McCoy to Rice McCoy, Dec. 21, 1829, reel 7, frame 270, MP ("I hope"); List of recipients of "Indian Report," [Feb. 24, 1829?], reel 7, frame 67, MP; Isaac McCoy to Rice McCoy, Dec. 21, 1829, reel 7, frame 270, MP ("of the spirit").

31. Talbot W. Chambers, *Memoir of the Life and Character of the Late Hon. Theo. Frelinghuysen* (New York, 1863).

32. Frelinghuysen, in some instances, appears to have borrowed language from two Creek and Cherokee petitions that had arrived in Congress a few months before his speech. *RDC* (1830), vol. 6, 1:311, 318; Memorial of Creeks, Feb. 3, 1830, PM, Protection of Indians, SEN21A-H3, NA; Memorial of the Cherokees, Dec. 1829, Committee of the Whole House, Petitions, "Various Subjects," HR21A-H1.1, NA.

33. I am inferring the number of hours of Forsyth's speech by word count. *RDC* (1830), vol. 6, 1:326, 328, 329, 336.

34. Ambrose Spencer to William Buell Sprague, Mar. 9, 1830, William Buell Sprague Papers, DMR; *RDC* (1830), vol. 6, 2:1014.

35. Remarks submitted to the Hon. Mr. Bell, Jan. 19, 1830, reel 7, frame 358, MP; Jeremiah Evarts to David Greene, Mar. 20, 1829, no. 24, ABC 11.1, vol. 2, Letters from Officers of the Board, American Board of Commissioners for Foreign Missions, Houghton Library, Harvard College Library ("Our treatment"); William S. Coodey to John Ross, May 17, 1838, *PCJR*, 1:639–40.

36. *RDC* (1830), vol. 6, 2:1016, 1018, 1020, 1021, 1022.

37. Bell's speech was not transcribed, but other congressmen quoted his phrase "mere device" several times. *RDC* (1830), vol. 6, 2:998 ("It requires no skill"), 1050 ("its hired patrole"), 1108 ("a mere device").

38. *RDC* (1830), vol. 6, 2:1015 ("vindicate"), 1030 ("the eyes of the world"), 1103 ("indulge," "The Indians melt," and "bound in conscience").

39. Memorial of the Cherokees, Dec. 1829, Committee of the Whole House, Petitions, "Various Subjects," HR21A-H1.1, NA; Memorial of Creeks, Feb. 3, 1830, PM, Protection of Indians, SEN21A-H3, NA.

40. *RDC* (1830), vol. 6, 2:1061 ("are the very means"), 1110 ("with the horrors").

41. B. Brown to Charles Fisher, May 30, 1830, box 1, folder 3, in the Fisher Family Papers #258, SHC ("I have never witnessed"); John E. Owens, "The Proto-Partisan Speakership: Andrew Stevenson, Jacksonian Agent in the US House?" working paper, Annual Meeting of the Southern Political Science Association, New Orleans, 2014, 32–33 ("Slaves of the Executive"). Available online at https://www.researchgate.net/profile /John_Owens7/publication/282150870_The_Proto-Partisan_Speakership_Andrew _Stevenson_Jacksonian_Agent_in_the_US_House/links/5605234e08ae8e08c08ae357 /The-Proto-Partisan-Speakership-Andrew-Stevenson-Jacksonian-Agent-in-the-US -House.pdf?origin=publication_detail (accessed Aug. 24, 2018).

42. Martin Van Buren, *Autobiography of Martin Van Buren* (Washington, D.C., 1920), 2:289.

43. *New-York Observer* (New York, N.Y.), Aug. 28, 1830, 2 ("threats and terrors"); *Pennsylvania Intelligencer* (Harrisburg, Pa.), June 8, 1830, 1 ("the *highest authority*"); David J. Russo, "The Major Political Issues of the Jacksonian Period and the Development of Party Loyalty in Congress, 1830–1840," *Transactions of the American Philosophical Society* 62, no. 5 (1972): 3–51.

44. The *Journal of the House of Representatives* mistakenly lists James Ford as James Finch. *Journal of the House of Representatives of the United States*, 21st Cong., 1st sess. (Washington, D.C., 1829), 730; *RDC* (1830), vol. 6, 2:1135; John Ross, "Message to the General Council," July 1830, *PCJR*, 1:191.

45. *Pennsylvania Intelligencer*, June 8, 1830, 1 ("an *ignoramus*"); *Daily National Journal* (Washington, D.C.), Aug. 25, 1830, 3.

46. *Pennsylvania Intelligencer*, June 1, 1830, 3; *Pennsylvania Intelligencer*, June 15, 1830, 3.

47. There is more than one way to calculate the effect of the three-fifths clause. Leonard

L. Richards, *The Slave Power: The Free North and Southern Domination, 1780–1860* (Baton Rouge: Louisiana State University Press, 2000), 45, 89, 103n40, 125, 126–27 ("southern measure"), 164.

48. *RDC* (1830), vol. 6, 2:1080 ("The Indians"), 1127 ("zealously"); *Georgia Journal,* July 10, 1830, 2; Deborah A. Rosen, "Colonization through Law: The Judicial Defense of State Indian Legislation, 1790–1880," *American Journal of Legal History* 46, no. 1 (Jan. 2004): 26–54.

49. *College for colored youth: an account of the New-Haven city meeting and resolutions, with recommendations of the college, and strictures upon the doings of New-Haven* (New York, 1831), 22.

50. William Apess, *Indian Nullification of the Unconstitutional Laws of Massachusetts Relative to the Marshpee Tribe* (Boston, 1835), 69; William Apess, "An Indian's Looking-Glass for the White Man," in Apess, *The Experiences of Five Christian Indians of the Pequod Tribe* (Boston, 1833), 60.

51. The amendment was proposed by William Ramsey, one of the key swing votes in Pennsylvania. *U.S. Statutes at Large* 4 (1846): 411–12; *Journal of the House of Representatives,* 21st Cong., 1st sess., 23:705; *New-York Morning Herald* (N.Y.), May 28, 1830, 2.

52. *RDC* (1830), vol. 6, 2:1076.

CHAPTER 4: "FORKED TONGUE AND SHALLOW HART"

1. "A poem composed by a Choctaw of P.P. Pitchlynn's party while emigrating last winter to the West," [1832], 4026.8176, PPP.

2. Isaac McCoy, "To Philanthropists in the United States, Generally, and to Christians in Particular, on the Condition and Prospects of the Indians," [Dec. 1, 1831?], reel 7, frame 861, MP; John Henry Eaton to Andrew Jackson, Sept. 1, 1830, *PAJ*; Gabriel L. Lowe, Jr., "The Early Public Career of John Henry Eaton" (M.A. thesis, Vanderbilt University, 1951), 31 ("It is hard to say").

3. Herman J. Viola, *Thomas L. McKenney: Architect of America's Early Indian Policy: 1816–1830* (Chicago: Swallow Press, 1974), 112 ("not well-informed"), 223–36 ("It was my misfortune" on 235); Poem regarding the Treaty of Dancing Rabbit, [1843], 4026.3162, PPP ("good talker").

4. 21st Cong., 1st sess., H.Rep. 319, pp. 196 and 200; Deborah A. Rosen, "Colonization through Law: The Judicial Defense of State Indian Legislation, 1790–1880," *American Journal of Legal History* 46, no. 1 (2004): 26–54; Mary Stockwell, *The Other Trail of Tears: The Removal of the Ohio Indians* (Yardley, Pa: Westholme Publishing, 2014), 186.

5. Andrew Jackson to William Berkeley Lewis, Aug. 25, 1830, and John Coffee to Andrew Jackson, July 10, 1830, *PAJ*.

6. Margaret Kinard, "Frontier Development of Williamson County," *Tennessee Historical Quarterly* 8, no. 2 (June 1949): 127–53.

7. Andrew Jackson to the Chickasaw Indians, Aug. 23, 1830, *PAJ*.

8. Andrew Jackson to the Chickasaw Indians, Aug. 23, 1830, *PAJ*; *Baltimore Patriot* (Baltimore, Md.), Aug. 27, 1830, 2; Andrew Jackson to the Chickasaws, Aug. 23, 1830, and Levi Colbert et al. to John Eaton and John Coffee, Aug. 25, 1830, *CSE*, 2:240–44 ("unparalleled").

9. John Eaton and John Coffee to the Chickasaws, Aug. 26, 1830, *CSE*, 2:246 ("Misery"); *Evening Post* (New York, N.Y.), Sept. 15, 1830, 1 ("earnest hope"); Andrew Jackson to James Knox Polk, Aug. 31, 1830, *PAJ*.

10. John Eaton and John Coffee to the Choctaws, Sept. 18, 1830, *CSE*, 2:256–57; Andrew Jackson to the Choctaw Indians, Aug. 26, 1830, *PAJ*.

11. *The Athenian* (Athens, Ga.), Aug. 17, 1830, 2–3 ("Again and again"); George W. Harkins, "The Choctaw's Farewell," *New-York Observer* (New York, N.Y.), Dec. 31, 1831, 3.

12. John Eaton and John Coffee to the Choctaws, Sept. 18, 1830, *CSE*, 2:256.

13. "A poem composed by a Choctaw of P.P. Pitchlynn's party while emigrating last winter to the West," [1832], 4026.8176, PPP.

14. "Basis of a Treaty to be submitted to the Commissioners of the United States," Sept. 25, 1830, 4826.29a and b, PPP; Choctaw leaders [anon.] to John Eaton and John Coffee," Sept. 25, 1830, 4026.3191 ("truly distressing"), PPP.

15. Isaac McCoy to the Honorable Senate and House of Representatives, Dec. 15, 1829, reel 7, frame 255, MP; Comstick et al. to Andrew Jackson, Sept. 22, 1830, *PAJ*; John P. Bowes, *Land Too Good for Indians: Northern Indian Removal* (Norman: University of Oklahoma Press, 2016), 115–37 ("the deposit" on 119).

16. Petition of citizens of county of Seneca, Ohio, Dec. 1829, COIA, Petitions, "Various Subjects," HR21A-G8.2, NA ("useless"); Memorial of the representatives of the Religious Society of Friends in the states of Indiana, Illinois, and the western parts of Ohio, Apr. 8, 1830, PM, Protection of Indians, SEN21A-H3, NA ("insatiable avarice"); Memorial of Inhabitants of New Petersburg, Ohio, Apr. 12, 1830, PM, Protection of Indians, SEN21A-H3, NA; Petition of residents from Claridon, Geauga County, Ohio, Jan. 1831, COIA, Petitions, Feb. 14, 1831, HR21A-G8.2, NA ("it would be manifest"); Stockwell, *The Other Trail of Tears*, 199.

17. Laurence H. Hauptman, *Conspiracy of Interests: Iroquois Dispossession and the Rise of New York State* (Syracuse: Syracuse University Press, 1999), 101–90; Mary H. Conable, "A Steady Enemy: The Ogden Land Company and the Seneca Indians" (Ph.D. diss., University of Rochester, 1994), 1–138; William G. Mayer, "The History of Transportation in the Mohawk Valley," *Proceedings of the New York State Historical Association* 14 (1915): 227; Big Kettle, Seneca White, and Thomson Harris to Andrew Jackson, Jan. 11, 1831, *PAJ*.

18. Big Kettle, Seneca White, and Thomson Harris to Andrew Jackson, Jan. 11, 1831, *PAJ*; James Kent, *Commentaries on American Law* (New York, 1826), 1:6.

19. 21st Cong., 1st sess., H.Rep. 319, p. 199; C.C. Clay, *A Digest of the Laws of the State of Alabama* (Tuskaloosa, Ala., 1843), 272, pp. 600–601; *RDC* (1830), 6:338–39; *Georgia Journal* (Milledgeville, Ga.), June 19, 1830, 3 ("the dearest rights"); *Federal Union* (Milledgeville, Ga.), Sept. 22, 1831, 1 ("Indian testimony").

20. *Laws of the State of Mississippi Embracing All Acts of a Public Nature from January Session, 1824, to January Session 1838, Inclusive* (Jackson, Miss., 1838), 349; John G. Aikin, *A Digest of the Laws of the State of Alabama: Containing All the Statutes of a Public and General Nature, in Force at the Close of the Session of the General Assembly, in January 1833* (Tuskaloosa, Ala., 1833), 396; Oliver H. Prince, *A Digest of the Laws of the State of Georgia* (Athens, Ga., 1837), 800, 810; 21st Cong., 1st sess., H.Rep. 319, p. 197 ("strolling").

21. *Southern Recorder* (Milledgeville, Ga.), Apr. 9, 1827, 3 (*"Abstractly"*); 21st Cong., 1st sess., H.Rep. 319, p. 242 ("said persons"); Prince, *A Digest of the Laws of the State of Georgia*, 808, 811; D. A. Reese to Lewis Cass, Mar. 10, 1832, *CSE* 3:253–56 ("real Indians"); Charles Caldwell, *Thoughts on the Original Unity of the Human Race*, (New York, 1830), 82 ("hybrid offspring"); *The Athenian*, Sept. 28, 1830, 2 ("aristocratical half breeds"); John Ridge and Stand Watie to John F. Schermerhorn, Feb. 28, 1836, enclosed in Schermerhorn to Lewis Cass, Feb. 27, 1836, LR, OIA, reel 80, M-234, NA ("nearly a white man"); Lewis Ross to John Ross, Feb. 23, 1834, LR, OIA, reel 76, M-234, NA ("motley crew").

22. John L. Allen to John H. Eaton, Feb. 7, 1830, LR, OIA, reel 136, M-234, NA ("native freedom"); Tuskee-Neha-Haw et al. to John H. Eaton, Oct. 20, 1829, 21st Cong., 2nd sess., H.Rep. 109, p. 3 ("tied"); Opothle Yoholo et al. to the House and Senate, Jan. 24, 1832, COIA, HR22A-G8.2, NA ("We have never been").

23. *Commercial Advertiser* (New York, N.Y.), Jan. 12, 1831, 2.

24. John Ross, annual message, Oct. 11, 1830, *PCJR*, 1:201–3 ("a stamp"); John Ross to Elias Boudinot, Feb. 4, 1831, *PCJR*, 1:212–14 ("piercing cold").

25. Nehah Micco et al. to John H. Eaton, Apr. 8, 1831, *CSE*, 2:424–25; "Oto Cho" (Ishtehotopa) et al. to Andrew Jackson, May 28, 1831, *PAJ*; Opothle Yoholo et al. to the House and Senate, Jan. 24, 1832, COIA, HR22A-G8.2, NA.

26. John H. Eaton to the Red Men of the Muscogee nation, May 16, 1831, *CSE*, 2:290; Return J. Meigs, extract from journal, Aug. 9, 1834, "Documents Relating to Frauds, &c., in the sale of Indian Reservations of Land," 24th Cong., 1st sess., S.Doc. 425, serial 445, p. 168 ("degraded"); Andrew Jackson to John Pitchlynn, Aug. 5, 1830 ("I feel conscious"), and Andrew Jackson to William Berkeley Lewis, Aug. 25, 1830 ("I have used"), *PAJ*.

27. *Commercial Advertiser*, Jan. 12, 1831, 2.

28. Clayton would later express regret for his role in the trial, an apology that came too late for the Cherokees. *Southern Recorder*, Nov. 13, 1830, 2; *Augusta Chronicle* (Augusta, Ga.), Nov. 17, 1830, 2; *The Constitutionalist* (Augusta, Ga.), Apr. 2, 1830, 2 ("wandering savages"); *Cherokee Phoenix* (New Echota, Cherokee Nation), Oct. 1, 1830, 1 ("intermeddling"); Tim Alan Garrison, *The Legal Ideology of Removal: The Southern Judiciary and the Sovereignty of Native American Nations* (Athens: University of Georgia Press, 2002), 111–24; "An Act to authorize the survey and disposition of lands," Dec. 21, 1830, Prince, *A Digest of the Laws of the State of Georgia*, 561.

29. John Ross to Hugh Montgomery, July 20, 1830, *PCJR*, 1:194; *Commercial Advertiser*, Jan. 12, 1831, 2; *Vermont Gazette* (Bennington, Vt.), Jan. 25, 1831, 1; Robert S. Davis, "State v. George Tassel: States' Rights and the Cherokee Court Cases, 1827–1830," *Journal of Southern Legal History* 12 (2004): 41–72; Garrison, *Legal Ideology of Removal*, 122 ("a vast multitude").

30. Jill Norgren, *The Cherokee Cases: The Confrontation of Law and Politics* (New York: McGraw-Hill, 1996), 167.

31. John Berrien, "To the Public," *Savannah Georgian* (Savannah, Ga.), Aug. 2, 1831, 1–2; Royce Coggins McCrary, Jr., "John MacPherson Berrien of Georgia (1781–1856)" (Ph.D. diss.: University of Georgia, 1971), 144n174.

32. William Wirt also referred to a guardianship relationship in one of his opinions as attorney general in 1828, but he insisted that indigenous nations were nonetheless "independent" and "governed solely by their own laws." William Wirt to the President of the United States, July 28, 1828, and John MacPherson Berrien to the Secretary of War, Dec. 21, 1830, *Official Opinions of the Attorneys General of the United States* (Washington, D.C., 1852), 2:133, 402–4; *Cherokee Nation v. Georgia*, 30 U.S. (5 Pet.), 22, 44 (1831).

33. John Ross to the Cherokees, April 14, 1830, *PCJR*, 1:217; D.A. Reese to George Gilmer, June 8, 1831, LR, OIA, reel 74, M-234, NA.

34. Jonathan Elliot, *Historical Sketches of the Ten Miles Square forming the District of Columbia* (Washington, D.C., 1830), 166–67; Ronald N. Satz, *American Indian Policy in the Jacksonian Era* (Norman: University of Oklahoma Press, 1975), 165–66; Viola, *Thomas L. McKenney*, 95.

35. Elliot, *Historical Sketches*, 165–67 ("impressed"); Isaac McCoy to General Noble, [Feb. 2, 1828?], reel 6, frame 268, MP; *RDC* (1828), vol. 4, 2:1568–69; "Speech of the Hon R.B. Rhett" *Charleston Mercury* (Charleston, S.C.), July 13, 1860, 4.

36. John A. Andrew III, *From Revivals to Removal: Jeremiah Evarts, the Cherokee Nation, and the Search for the Soul of America* (Athens: University of Georgia Press, 1992), 182; John H. Eaton to John Coffee, Oct. 12, 1830, John Coffee Papers, Beinecke Rare Book and Manuscript Library, Yale University ("Economy in expenditure"); John H. Eaton to Superintendents and Agents of Indian Affairs, Jan. 14, 1831, p. 126, LS, OIA, reel 7, M-21, NA ("The Indian business"); John H. Eaton to Isaac McCoy, Apr. 13, 1830, *CSE*, 2:276.

37. Grant Foreman, "An Unpublished report by Captain Bonneville with Introduction and Footnotes," *Chronicles of Oklahoma* 10, no. 3 (Sept. 1932): 329–30; Isaac McCoy to John H. Eaton, Apr. 1831, *CSE*, 2:432, 435.

38. M. Stokes to Lewis Cass, Aug. 5, 1833, *CSE*, 4:495 ("general and correct"); John H. Eaton to John Bell, Jan. 17, 1831, LS, OIA, reel 7, p. 126, M-21, NA ("each tribe"); John H. Eaton to Isaac McCoy, Apr. 13, 1831, p. 179, LS, OIA, reel 7, M-21, NA ("We have no satisfactory"); Lewis Cass to Andrew Jackson, Feb. 16, 1832, *CSE*, 2:768 ("imperfect"); Lewis Cass to M. Stokes, H.L. Ellsworth, and J.F. Schermerhorn, Mar. 18, 1833, *CSE*, 3:617 ("vague and unsatisfactory").

39. John H. Eaton to John Coffee, May 16, 1831, *CSE*, 2:291–92.

40. John H. Eaton to John Bell, Jan. 17, 1831, LS, OIA, reel 7, p. 126, M-21, NA; John H. Eaton to Isaac McCoy, Apr. 13, 1831, LS, OIA, reel 7, p. 179, M-21, NA; Isaac McCoy to the Secretary of War, Aug. 18, 1831, *CSE*, 2:563; M. Stokes to Lewis Cass, Aug. 5, 1833, *CSE*, 4:495 ("greatly embarrassed").

41. Isaac McCoy to the Secretary of War, Aug. 18, 1831, *CSE*, 2:561–66; Roley McIntosh et al. to Andrew Jackson, Oct. 21, 1831, *PAJ* ("ultimate ruin"); RG 77, Civil Works Map File, I.R. 50, NACP; RG 75, Central Map File, Indian Territory, no. 105, NACP.

42. M. Stokes to Lewis Cass, Aug. 5, 1833, *CSE*, 4:496 ("I am much mistaken" and "incorrect"); D. Kurtz to William Clark, Aug. 13, 1833, *CSE*, 3:748 ("Upon examining"); Elbert Herring to William Clark, Nov. 29, 1833, *CSE*, 4:736; Matthew Arbuckle to John H. Eaton, Dec. 11, 1830, LR, OIA, reel 136, M-234, NA.

43. Lewis Cass to Andrew Jackson, Feb. 16, 1832, *CSE*, 2:781.

44. J. Montgomery to John H. Eaton, Mar. 27, 1831, *CSE*, 2:421–22 ("perseverance"); "Letter from David Brown," *Essex Register* (Salem, Mass.), June 27, 1825, 2; "Journal of Isaac McCoy for the Exploring Expedition of 1828," *Kansas Historical Quarterly* 5, no. 3 (1936): 250; Opothle Yoholo et al. to the House and Senate, Jan. 24, 1832, COIA, HR22A-G8.2, NA.

45. Lewis Cass to the Chiefs of the Creek Tribe, Jan. 16, 1832, *CSE*, 2:742–43 ("fine country"); John H. Eaton to the Red Men of the Muscogee nation, May 16, 1831, *CSE*, 2:290 ("altogether favorable"); Copy of a petition by the Principal Men of the Pottawatamis, Ottawas, and Chippewas to Andrew Jackson, Sept. 30, 1835, CGLR, box 2, Chicago, NA ("deceived"); Reply of the Head Chief Hicks to the talk delivered by the Commissioner Col. White, May 5, 1827, LR, OIA, reel 806, frame 5, M-234, NA ("it is bad"); Christina Snyder, *Great Crossings: Indians, Settlers, and Slaves in the Age of Jackson* (New York: Oxford University Press, 2017), 131 ("good for nothing"); James Gould et al. to the Chiefs of the Wyandot Nation, Dec. 15, 1831, *CSE*, 3:165–68 ("the most abandoned").

46. Reply of the Head Chief Hicks to the talk delivered by the Commissioner Col. White, May 5, 1827, LR, OIA, reel 806, frame 5, M-234, NA ("Bad Indians"); Levi Colbert to Andrew Jackson, Feb. 23, 1832, LR, OIA, reel 136, M-234, NA; Charles Dickens, *American Notes* (London, 1842), 2:95–100; Snyder, *Great Crossings*, 131 ("long separated"); John Ross to James C. Martin, Nov. 5, 1837, *PCJR*, 1:536; David La Vere,

Contrary Neighbors: Southern Plains and Removed Indians in Indian Territory (Norman: University of Oklahoma Press, 2000).

47. Nehah Micco et al. to John H. Eaton, Apr. 8, 1831, *CSE*, 2:424–25; Western Creeks to Andrew Jackson, June 12, 1830, *PAJ* ("sorrows"); Richard M. Hannum to John Pope, Dec. 13, 1832, *CSE*, 3:551–52 ("Young women"); John Dougherty to William Clark, Oct. 29, 1831, *CSE*, 2:718–19 ("monstrous").

48. "Oto Cho" (Ishtehotopa) et al. to Andrew Jackson, May 28, 1831, *PAJ* ("Some of our people"); Levi Colbert to Andrew Jackson, Feb. 23, 1832, LR, OIA, reel 136, M-234, NA; Guy B. Braden, "The Colberts and the Chickasaw Nation," *Tennessee Historical Quarterly* 17, no. 3 (Sept. 1958): 232–33.

49. Memorial of the Chickasaw Chiefs to the President of the United States, Nov. 22, 1832, LR, OIA, reel 136, M-234, NA.

50. U.S. officials claimed that white men were behind the Chickasaw petition, a charge that some historians have accepted, though there is no real evidence. A delegation of Chickasaw representatives and their allies hand-carried the letter to Washington, but the Jackson administration refused to negotiate with them. Memorial of the Chickasaw Chiefs to the President of the United States, Nov. 22, 1832, LR, OIA, reel 136, M-234, NA; James R. Atkinson, *Splendid Land, Splendid People: The Chickasaw Indians to Removal* (Tuscaloosa: University of Alabama Press, 2003), 228–30; Amanda L. Paige, Fuller L. Bumpers, and Daniel F. Littlefield, Jr., *Chickasaw Removal* (Ada, Okla.: Chickasaw Press, 2010), 44–46.

51. B. Brown to Charles Fisher, May 30, 1830, box 1, folder 3, in the Fisher Family Papers #258, SHC; John Henry Eaton to Andrew Jackson, Sept. 1, 1830, *PAJ*; Henry Leavenworth to Samuel Preston, Feb. 21, 1830, Henry Leavenworth, Letters to Samuel Preston, Western Americana Collection, Beinecke Rare Book and Manuscript Library, Yale University ("There is a set").

52. Grant Foreman, *Indian Removal: The Emigration of the Five Civilized Tribes of Indians* (Norman: University of Oklahoma Press, 1932), 42; John W. Barriger, *Legislative History of the Subsistence Department of the United States Army* (Washington, D.C., 1877), 73 ("He will make"); Thomas P. Roberts, *Memoirs of John Bannister Gibson* (Pittsburgh, 1890), 229 ("was always in order").

53. Records of the Commissary General of Subsistence, General Correspondence, LR, Entry 10, RG 192, NA; Department of Defense, *Selected Manpower Statistics, Fiscal Year 1997* (Washington, D.C.: U.S. Government Printing Office, 1997), 47, table 2-11.

54. *RDC* (1830), vol. 6, 2:1070 ("Whoever"); John Eaton to Greenwood LeFlore, May 7, 1831, reel 2, IRW ("We are preparing"); J.H. Hook to Greenwood LeFlore, June 23, 1831, *CSE*, 1:17 ("promptitude"); James R. Stephenson to George Gibson, Apr. 1, 1831, *CSE*, 1:852–53.

CHAPTER 5: THE PLAN OF OPERATIONS

1. "A poem composed by a Choctaw of P.P. Pitchlynn's party while emigrating last winter to the West," [1832], 4026.8176, PPP.

2. Robert Mills, *Guide to the National Executive Offices and the Capitol of the United States* (Washington, D.C., 1841), 20; *A Full Directory for Washington City, Georgetown, and Alexandria* (Washington, D.C., 1834); Harriet Martineau, *Retrospect of Western Travel* (London, 1838), 1:266 ("Its seven").

3. Stephanie L. Gamble, "Capital Negotiations: Native Diplomats in the American Capital" (Ph.D. diss., Johns Hopkins University, 2014), 1–2, 104–7; "Letters

from Washington," *New-York Observer* (New York, N.Y.), Feb. 12, 1831, 4 ("public tables").

4. Lewis Cass, Regulations Concerning the Removal of the Indians, May 15, 1832, *CSE*, 1:343–49 ("systematic"); George Gibson to Lewis Cass, Nov. 12, 1835, CGLS, vol. 3, pp. 338–50, NA ("complete accountability"); Return J. Meigs, extract from journal, Aug. 9, 1834, "Documents Relating to Frauds, &c., in the sale of Indian Reservations of Land," 24th Cong., 1st sess., S.Doc. 425, serial 445, p. 169 ("made all nature"); George Gibson to Lewis Cass, Jan. 30, 1835, CGLS, vol. 2, pp. 427–28, NA ("of a multifarious").

5. Thomas L. McKenney to John H. Eaton, Mar. 18, 1829, LS, OIA, Miscellaneous Immigration, RG 75, entry 84, M21, book E, 353, NA ("unremitting"); John Bell to Lewis Cass, July 17, 1835, LR, OIA, reel 136, M-234, NA ("in the best" and "A bungler"); John Kennedy and Thomas W. Wilson to C.A. Harris, Dec. 6, 1837, LR, OIA, reel 114, M-234, NA ("competent"); John C. Mullay to C.A. Harris, Apr. 19, 1837, LR, OIA, reel 82, M-234, NA ("great number" and "to an immense"); John C. Mullay to C.A. Harris, Nov. 6, 1837, LR, OIA, reel 114, M-234, NA; Extract of a letter from M. Stokes, Apr. 3, 1838, LR, OIA, reel 82, frame 683, M-234, NA.

6. Michael Zakim, "Paperwork," *Raritan* 33, no. 4 (Spring 2014): 52–53; Shelf list of Records Relating to Indian Removal, Records of the Commissary General of Subsistence, NA; George Gibson to J. Van Horne, Oct. 31, 1836, CGLS, vol. 4, p. 217, NA ("Finis").

7. I am estimating the linear length of records relating to the 1830s, since they are not filed chronologically. Records of the Accounting Officers of the Department of the Treasury, Settled Indian Accounts, RG 217, entry 525, NA. The early history of the bureaucracy of the Bureau of Indians Affairs is explored in Stephen J. Rockwell, *Indian Affairs and the Administrative State in the Nineteenth Century* (Cambridge: Cambridge University Press, 2010).

8. J.H. Hook to William Armstrong, Oct. 1, 1832, *CSE*, 1:171 ("Where medical"); George Gibson to John Page, July 15, 1834, CGLS, vol. 2, pp. 229–38, NA ("when actually required" and "must be"); J.T. Sprague, Dec. 3, 1836, Records of the Accounting Officers of the Department of the Treasury, Settled Indian Accounts, RG 217, entry 525, box 257, account 547, NA.

9. Papers Relating to Claims for Commutation Pay by Heirs of George Gibson, box 1, Gibson-Getty-McClure Papers, LC; Kurt Windisch, "A Thousand Slain: St. Clair's Defeat and the Evolution of the Constitutional Republic" (Ph.D. diss., University of Georgia, 2018), 16; Biography of George Gibson, 1818–1854 and undated, box 1, Gibson-Getty-McClure Papers, LC; Thomas P. Roberts, *Memoirs of John Bannister Gibson* (Pittsburgh, 1890), 228; Erna Risch, *Quartermaster Support of the Army: A History of the Corps, 1775–1939* (1962; reprint, Washington, D.C.: Center of Military History, U.S. Army, 1989), 178–79; George Gibson to Jacob Brown, Jan. 16, 1835, CGLS, vol. 2, p. 417, NA ("It will not do"); Ethan Davis, "An Administrative Trail of Tears: Indian Removal," *American Journal of Legal History* 50, no. 1 (Jan. 1, 2008): 49–100.

10. George Gibson to J.P. Simonton, July 11, 1832, *CSE*, 1:117 ("of the size"); George Gibson to Jacob Brown, Jan. 14, 1835, CGLS, vol. 2, pp. 413–15, NA ("numbers"); George Gibson to William Clark, Oct. 13, 1834, CGLS, vol. 2, pp. 334–37, NA ("muster roll"); George Gibson to William Clark, May 6, 1834, CGLS, vol. 2, pp. 190–92, NA ("with a view"); George Gibson to John Page, July 15, 1834, CGLS, vol. 2, pp. 229–38, NA ("detachment"); George Gibson to William Armstrong, July 19, 1834, CGLS, vol. 2, pp. 257–61, NA; J.H. Hook to William Armstrong, Oct. 1, 1832, *CSE*,

1:171 ("It is not warranted"); Lewis Cass, Regulations Concerning the Removal of the Indians, May 15, 1832, *CSE*, 1:344; J.B. Clark to George Gibson, May 5, 1831, reel 2, IRW ("It placed me").

11. Mark Walson, *Birthplace of Bureaus: The United States Treasury Department* (Washington, D.C.: Treasury Historical Society, 2013), 14–16; John T. Sprague, *The Origin, Progress, and Conclusion of the Florida War* (New York, 1848), 103 ("rigid economy").

12. George Gibson to W.S. Colquhuon, Sept. 21, 1831, *CSE*, 1:44; George Gibson to J.P. Taylor, July 13, 1831, *CSE*, 1:24; George Gibson to S.V.R. Ryan, Nov. 9, 1831, *CSE*, 1:50; George Gibson to George S. Gaines, Mar. 31, 1832, *CSE*, 1:75–77; George Gibson to Jacob Brown, Aug. 12, 1833, *CSE*, 1:287 ("The word *inclusive*"); George Gibson to John Page, July 15, 1834, CGLS, vol. 2, pp. 229–38, NA ("from" and "to"); J. Brown to George Gibson, May 30, 1832, *CSE*, 3:450–51 ("waste and extravagance"); George Gibson to Jacob Brown, July 11, 1834, CGLS, vol. 2, pp. 222–24, NA ("It gives me").

13. George Gibson to J.R. Stephenson, Dec. 27, 1830, *CSE*, 1:5–6 ("Too much"); George Gibson to Jacob Brown, Apr. 12, 1832, *CSE*, 1:77–78 ("strictly economical" and "and lop it off"); George Gibson to John Page, July 15, 1834, CGLS, vol. 2, pp. 229–38, NA ("I would impress"); J.H. Hook to A.C. Pepper, Aug. 12, 1834, CGLS, vol. 2, pp. 282–84, NA ("You are urged"); George Gibson to Wiley Thompson, Feb. 28, 1835, CGLS, vol. 2, pp. 477–83, NA ("Let nothing"); George Gibson to J.P. Simonton, May 5, 1835, CGLS, vol. 3, pp. 96–97, NA ("Wherever money").

14. William Armstrong to George Gibson, Oct. 13, 1832, *CSE*, 1:386–87 ("every exertion"); John Page to George Gibson, Jan. 6, 1835, CGLR, box 8, Creek, 1834, NA ("incur"); John Page to George Gibson, Apr. 25, 1835, CGLR, box 8, Creek, 1834, NA ("enormous"); John Page to George Gibson, May 1, 1835, CGLR, box 8, Creek, NA ("I never did"); A.M.M. Upshaw to C.A. Harris, Aug. 1, 1838, LR, OIA, reel 143, frame 689, M-234, NA ("We are moved").

15. Upshaw, despite his occasional sympathy for Chickasaws, was not above cheating them of their funds. Amanda L. Paige, Fuller L. Bumpers, and Daniel F. Littlefield, Jr., *Chickasaw Removal* (Ada, Okla.: Chickasaw Press, 2010), 253; George Gibson to Templin W. Ross, Oct. 1, 1834, CGLS, vol. 2, pp. 314–18, NA ("with every regard"); George Gibson to Joseph Kerr, July 21, 1832, *CSE*, 1:126 ("consistent"); George Gibson to Lewis Cass, Nov. 12, 1835, CGLS, vol. 3, pp. 338–50, NA ("With respect"); Davis, "An Administrative Trail of Tears," 92.

16. Davis, "An Administrative Trail of Tears," 99; George Gibson to William Clark, Oct. 13, 1834, CGLS, vol. 2, pp. 334–37, NA.

17. Thomas L. McKenney to James Barbour, Jan. 4, 1828, LS, OIA, Miscellaneous Immigration, RG 75, entry 84, M21, book D, 229, NA; J.T. Sprague, Oct. 23, 1836, Records of the Accounting Officers of the Department of the Treasury, Settled Indian Accounts, RG 217, entry 525, box 257, account 547, NA.

18. Ronald N. Satz, *American Indian Policy in the Jacksonian Era* (1974; reprint, Norman: University of Oklahoma Press, 1975), 73; "On Claims to Reservations under the Fourteenth Article of the Treaty of Dancing Rabbit Creek, with the Choctaw Indians," 24th Cong., 1st sess., H.Doc. 1523, *American State Papers: Public Lands* (Washington, D.C., 1861), 8:691–93 ("negro servant"); Records Relating to Indian Removal, Records of the Commissary General of Subsistence, Choctaw Removal Records, Journal of Pray, Murray, and Vroom, RG 75, entry 268, box 1, p. 167 ("soured") and p. 168 ("confused and impaired"), NA; James Murray and Peter D. Broom to the President of the United States, Records Relating to Indian Removal, Records of

the Commissary General of Subsistence, Choctaw Removal Records, Pray, Murray, and Vroom, Evidence, 1837–38, RG 75, entry 270, box 3, NA ("arbitrary").

19. Mary E. Young, "Indian Removal and Land Allotment: The Civilized Tribes and Jacksonian Justice," *American Historical Review* 64, no. 1 (Oct. 1958): 38.

20. By one estimate, five thousand Choctaw people remained in Mississippi as late as 1838, fully seven years after deportation began, suggesting that between a third and half of the entire nation had intended to stay in the region and become citizens of the state. That figure is in line with the one given by the Choctaw Nation in the 1850s. James Murray and Peter D. Broom to the President of the United States, Records Relating to Indian Removal, Records of the Commissary General of Subsistence, Choctaw Removal Records, Pray, Murray, and Vroom, Evidence, 1837–38, RG 75, entry 270, box 3, NA; "Claims of the Choctaw Nation," 44th Cong., 1st sess., H.Misc.Doc. 40, p. 23, Records Relating to Indian Removal, Records of the Commissary General of Subsistence, Choctaw Removal Records, Journal of Pray, Murray, and Vroom, RG 75, entry 268, box 1, NA ("to suffer"); William Ward to Samuel Hamilton, June 21, 1831, 4026.3194, PPP; "On Claims to Reservations under the Fourteenth Article of the Treaty of Dancing Rabbit Creek, with the Choctaw Indians," 24th Cong., 1st sess., H.Doc. 1523, *American State Papers: Public Lands*, 8:691 ("emigrating agents"); Deposition of Adam Jones, Jan. 31, 1838, Records Relating to Indian Removal, Records of the Commissary General of Subsistence, Choctaw Removal Records, Journal of Pray, Murray, and Vroom, RG 75, entry 268, box 1, NA ("there were too many"); Deposition of Captain Bob, alias Mingohomah, July 12, 1844, Records Relating to Indian Removal, Records of the Commissary General of Subsistence, Choctaw Removal Records, Pray, Murray, and Vroom, Evidence, 1837–38, RG 75, entry 270, box 3, NA.

21. Records Relating to Indian Removal, Records of the Commissary General of Subsistence, Choctaw Removal Records, Journal of Pray, Murray, and Vroom, RG 75, entry 268, box 1, NA; Mahlon Dickerson to George W. Martin, Sept. 5, 1833, U.S. Congress, Senate, *Report from the Secretary of the Treasury*, 24th Cong., 1st sess., S.Doc. 69, pp. 13–14; J.H. Eaton to Lewis Cass, Sept. 20, 1833, *CSE*, 4:565 ("so torn").

22. [?] to Peter Pitchlynn, Aug. 8, 1834, 4026.3351, PPP.

23. Patrick B. McGuigan, "Bulwark of the American Frontier: A History of Fort Towson," in *Early Military Forts and Posts in Oklahoma*, ed. Odie B. Faulk, Kenny A. Franks, and Paul F. Lambert (Oklahoma City: Oklahoma Historical Society, 1978), 9–25; Robert Gudmestad, "Steamboats and the Removal of the Red River Raft," *Louisiana History* 52, no. 4 (Fall 2011): 389–416; Benjamin Reynolds and George S. Gaines to John H. Eaton, Feb. 7, 1831, *CSE*, 1:674–75.

24. J.H. Hook to P.G. Randolph, July 2, 1831, *CSE*, 1:21–22; George Gibson to J.R. Stephenson, Aug. 27, 1831, *CSE*, 1:36–37; George Gibson to John B. Clark, Apr. 5, 1831, *CSE*, 1:8–9 ("proper intervals"); J.H. Hook to Greenwood LeFlore, June 23, 1831, *CSE*, 1:15–17; J.H. Hook to Wm. S. Colquhoun, July 5, 1831, *CSE*, 1:27–28; George Gibson to T.S. Jesup, Sept. 21, 1831, *CSE*, 1: 43; George Gibson to Jacob Brown, Nov. 4, 1831, *CSE*, 1:49–50; J.B. Clark to George Gibson, Oct. 19, 1831, *CSE*, 1:586; J.B. Clark to George Gibson, July 30, 1831, *CSE*, 1:561–62 ("No one").

25. I am excluding for the moment those who tried to stay in Mississippi. Approximately 2,400 Choctaw families were expelled, and, assuming 6 people per family on average, only 100 families were compensated under Article 19 of the Treaty of Dancing Rabbit Creek. *Liabilities of Choctaw Indians to Individuals*, 43rd Cong., 2nd sess., H.Exec.Doc. 47, pp. 12–13; John Coffee to Andrew Jackson, Sept. 23, 1831, *CSE*, 2:600 ("almost nothing").

26. George Wilson Pierson, *Tocqueville in America* (Baltimore: Johns Hopkins University Press, 1938), 595–98.

27. Walter Johnson, *River of Dark Dreams: Slavery and Empire in the Cotton Kingdom* (Cambridge: Harvard University Press, 2013), 73–96; Michael Chevalier, *Society, Manners, and Politics in the United States* (Boston, 1839), 223–24 ("So much"); Robert H. Gudmestad, *Steamboats and the Rise of the Cotton Kingdom* (Baton Rouge: Louisiana State University Press, 2011), 80–82.

28. Steamboat explosions were not unusual. Gudmestad, *Steamboats and the Rise of the Cotton Kingdom*, 105–11. William S. Colquhoun to George Gibson, Dec. 10, 1831, *CSE*, 1:593 ("disgusting sight"); James B. Gardiner to George Gibson, June 20, 1832, *CSE*, 1:690 ("their native modesty"); [?] to Lewis Cass, May 2, 1832, 4026.3220, PPP ("well agree"); James B. Gardiner to George Gibson, June 2, 1832, *CSE*, 1:687–88 ("scalded").

29. William S. Colquhoun to George Gibson, Dec. 10, 1831, *CSE*, 1:427; J. Brown to George Gibson, Dec. 15, 1831, *CSE*, 1:593; Thomas Nuttall, *Journal of Travels into the Arkansas Territory During the Year 1819* (Philadelphia, 1821), 75–78.

30. J. Brown to George Gibson, Dec. 22, 1831, *CSE*, 1:428; J. Brown to George Gibson, Dec. 29, 1831, *CSE*, 1:431–32 ("horrid"); J. Brown to George Gibson, Jan. 4, 1832, *CSE*, 1:432; J. Brown to George Gibson, May 4, 1832, *CSE*, 1:447–48 ("indifferently made").

31. "A poem composed by a Choctaw of P.P. Pitchlynn's party while emigrating last winter to the West," [1832], 4026.8176, PPP.

32. F.W. Armstrong to Lewis Cass, Feb. 8, 1832, *CSE*, 3:191–92; Grant Foreman, *Indian Removal: The Emigration of the Five Civilized Tribes of Indians* (Norman: University of Oklahoma Press, 1932), 58.

33. Foreman, *Indian Removal*, 58–59, 59n16.

34. The per capita cost of $25 does not include the year of rations to be paid after deportation. *RDC* (1830), vol. 6, 2:1076 ("five times five millions"); "Estimate of the expense of removing seven thousand Chaktaw from their old to their new homes by waggons," reel 2, frame 456, IRW; George Gibson to Lewis Cass, Apr. 18, 1836, CGLS, vol. 3, p. 511, NA.

35. Records Relating to Indian Removal, Records of the Commissary General of Subsistence, Estimates, 1832–36, RG 75, entry 205, NA; Elbert Herring to Col. William Ward, Mar. 19, 1832, *CSE*, 2:800 ("What amount"); William S. Colquhoun to George Gibson, Apr. 15, 1832, *CSE*, 1:604 ("quite insufficient").

36. Greenwood LeFlore to the Secretary of War, June 7, 1831, reel 2, William S. Colquhoun to George Gibson, Jan. 3, 1832, reel 2, and F.W. Armstrong to Elbert Herring, Mar. 8, 1833, reel 3, IRW; Peter Pitchlynn[?] to David Folsom, May 19, 1830, 4026.3186, PPP ("in a precipitate manner"); "A poem composed by a Choctaw of P.P. Pitchlynn's party while emigrating last winter to the West," [1832], 4026.8176, PPP ("tyrant"); Mushulatubbe at al. to John Henry Eaton, June 2, 1830, *PAJ*; Greenwood LeFlore to Lewis Cass, Mar. 6, 1834, LR, OIA, reel 170, M-234, NA ("compensate"); Records Relating to Indian Removal, Records of the Commissary General of Subsistence, Choctaw Removal Records, Journal of Pray, Murray, and Vroom, RG 75, entry 268, box 1, pp. 212–13, NA ("We dreaded"); R. Halliburton, Jr., "Chief Greenwood LeFlore and His Malmaison Plantation," in *After Removal: The Choctaw in Mississippi*, ed. Samuel J. Wells and Rosseana Tubby (Jackson: University of Mississippi Press, 1986), 56–63.

37. Some 300 people entered the swamp, but the captain of the *Talma* reported rescu-

ing only 265. Joseph Kerr to Lewis Cass, June 14, 1832, *CSE*, 1:1719–20; William A. Taylor, "Senator Joseph Kerr," *The "Old Northwest" Genealogical Quarterly* 6 (Jan. 1903): 69; Foreman, *Indian Removal*, 62n24; George Gibson to Joseph Kerr, July 21, 1832, *CSE*, 1:126.

38. Petition of citizens of county of Seneca, Ohio, December 1829, COIA, Petitions, "Various Subjects," HR21A-G8.2, NA ("useless"); To the Honorable the Senate and House of Representatives, Jan. 31, 1831, *CSE*, 2:403–4; *History of Seneca County, Ohio* (Chicago, 1886), 310.

39. List of Sales, Mar. 20, 1832, *CSE*, 3:328, 331, 332, 333, 335, 338, 339, 343, 345, 348, 353; "Indian Sale," Sept. 8, 1831, *CSE*, 2:597; Henry C. Brish to S.S. Hamilton, Nov. 28, 1831, *CSE*, 2:691–92; John McElvain to Elbert Herring, Feb. 7, 1832, *CSE*, 3:190.

40. List of Sales, Mar. 20, 1832, *CSE*, 3:332, 335, 338; Henry C. Brish to William Clark, July 16, 1832, *CSE*, 5:118–20 ("immense quantity").

41. The precise numbers of deportees vary slightly in different accounts. William Clark to William B. Lewis, Nov. 18, 1833, *CSE*, 5:113; Henry C. Brish to S.S. Hamilton, Nov. 28, 1831, *CSE*, 2:691–92; Mary Stockwell, *The Other Trail of Tears: The Removal of the Ohio Indians* (Yardley, Pa.: Westholme, 2014), 207–12; Henry C. Brish to S.S. Hamilton, Nov. 16, 1831, *CSE*, 2:725; Henry C. Brish to William Clark, Nov. 26, 1831, *CSE*, 2:723–24 ("extremely dissipated" and "blood-thirsty").

42. Steve Ehlmann, *Crossroads: A History of St. Charles County, Missouri* (Marceline, Mo.: Walsworth Publishing Company, 2004), 45–61; Henry C. Brish to William Clark, Dec. 13, 1831, *CSE*, 2:725–26; William Clark to Elbert Herring, Dec. 20, 1831, *CSE*, 2:722–23.

43. John McElvain to Lewis Cass, Nov. 15, 1831, *CSE*, 2:684–85 ("live well"); Small Cloud Spicer et al. to William Clark, Dec. 10, 1831, *CSE*, 3:9–10; Henry C. Brish to Samuel S. Hamilton, Jan. 20, 1832, *CSE*, 3:24–25; Henry C. Brish to Samuel S. Hamilton, Jan. 20, 1832, *CSE*, 3:24–25; Postscript to Small Cloud Spicer et al. to William Clark, Dec. 10, 1831, *CSE*, 3:9 ("what then remains").

44. Henry C. Brish to William Clark, May 8, 1832, Henry C. Brish to William Clark, May 16, 1832, and Henry C. Brish to William Clark, July 16, 1832, *CSE*, 5:116–20 (quotations).

45. Of the 398 deportees who left Ohio, only 352 reached their destination, but some families turned back along the way. Henry C. Brish to William Clark, July 16, 1832, *CSE*, 5:118–20; Stockwell, *The Other Trail of Tears*, 211.

46. J. Brown to George Gibson, Sept. 13, 1832, *CSE*, 1:476–77.

47. John McElvain to S.S. Hamilton, Feb. 21, 1832, *CSE*, 3:213–14; F.W. Armstrong to Lewis Cass, Apr. 20, 1832, *CSE*, 3:302–3.

48. Lewis Cass, Regulations Concerning the Removal of the Indians, May 15, 1832, *CSE*, 1:343–49.

49. Steve R. Waddell, *United States Army Logistics: From the American Revolution to 9/11* (Santa Barbara: ABC-CLIO, 2010), 30–45; Risch, *Quartermaster Support of the Army*, 143–44, 181–83, 202; 13th Cong., 3rd sess., H.Doc., 53, p. 9 ("palm"); "A poem composed by a Choctaw of P.P. Pitchlynn's party while emigrating last winter to the West," [1832], 4026.8176, PPP.

50. Lewis Cass, Regulations Concerning the Removal of the Indians, May 15, 1832, *CSE*, 1:343–49.

51. George Gibson to George S. Gaines, Aug. 13, 1831, *CSE*, 1:32; J. Brown to George Gibson, Dec. 15, 1831, *CSE*, 1:427.

CHAPTER 6: THE CHOLERA TIMES

1. Kerry A. Trask, *Black Hawk: The Battle for the Heart of America* (New York: Henry Holt, 2007), 32.

2. John A. Walthall, *Galena and Aboriginal Trade in Eastern North America*, Illinois State Museum Scientific Papers, vol. 17 (Springfield: Illinois State Museum, 1981), 12; Lucy Eldersveld Murphy, *Gathering of Rivers: Indians, Métis, and Mining in the Western Great Lakes, 1737–1832* (Lincoln: University of Nebraska Press, 2000), 97, 102, 105, 117.

3. Alexander Macomb to Henry Atkinson, May 5, 1832, *The Black Hawk War, 1831–32* (Springfield: Illinois State Historical Library), vol. 2, 1:351; Alfred A. Cave, *Sharp Knife: Andrew Jackson and the American Indians* (Santa Barbara: Praeger, 2017), 133–34; Patrick J. Jung, *The Black Hawk War of 1832* (Norman: University of Oklahoma Press, 2007), 70–72; George Rollie Adams, *General William S. Harney: Prince of Dragoons* (Lincoln: University of Nebraska Press, 2001), 37–42.

4. The editor of the *Galenian* practiced what he preached, volunteering in the militia and taking several scalps, which he later put on display in his home. Murphy, *Gathering of Rivers*, 162–65; Jung, *The Black Hawk War of 1832*, 89, 149–51; Lewis Cass to William Clark, May 22, 1832, *Black Hawk War, 1831–32*, vol. 2, 1:405; Trask, *Black Hawk*, 262.

5. Jung, *Black Hawk War of 1832*, 79, 98–100, 115, 127; Jackson's endorsement of John Robb to Andrew Jackson, June 12, 1832, *PAJ* ("must be chastised").

6. "Asiatic Cholera Pandemic of 1826–37," George Childs Kohn, ed., *Encyclopedia of Plague and Pestilence, from Ancient Times to the Present* (New York: Facts on File, 2008), 15; G.F. Pyle, "The Diffusion of Cholera in the United States in the Nineteenth Century," *Geographical Analysis* 1 (1969): 59–75; J.S. Chambers, *The Conquest of Cholera: America's Greatest Scourge* (New York: MacMillan, 1938), 86–88.

7. Chambers, *Conquest of Cholera*, 95; David A. Sack et al., "Cholera," *Lancet* 363 (Jan. 17, 2004): 223–33.

8. "The Cholera Epidemic of 1873 in the United States," 43rd Cong., 2nd sess., H. Ex. Doc. 95, pp. 572–76 ("paper barrier" and "brought disease"); Chambers, *Conquest of Cholera*, 90, 94, 97, 577; Charles E. Rosenberg, *The Cholera Years: The United States in 1832, 1849, and 1866* (1962; Chicago: University of Chicago Press, 1987), 74–79; Trask, *Black Hawk*, 275.

9. Some Ho-Chunks (Winnebagos), Potawatomis, and Menominees aided the U.S. war effort for their own strategic reasons, as described in John W. Hall, *Uncommon Defense: Indian Allies in the Black Hawk War* (Cambridge: Harvard University Press, 2009); Trask, *Black Hawk*, 270–71, 277 ("extracted"), 282–89 ("work of death" on 284); Jung, *The Black Hawk War of 1832*, 172; Hall, *Uncommon Defense*, 195–205.

10. "Indian War," *Baltimore Gazette and Daily Advertiser* (Baltimore, Md.), June 18, 1832, 2 ("dispassionate"); *Commercial Advertiser* (New York, N.Y.), Aug. 17, 1832, 2 ("in the injustice").

11. "The Cholera Epidemic of 1873 in the United States," 43rd Cong., 2nd sess., H. Ex. Doc. 95, p. 577. Ramon Powers and James N. Leiker, "Cholera among the Plains Indians: Perceptions, Causes, and Consequences," *Western Historical Quarterly* 29, no. 3 (Autumn 1998): 320–21, 331–33; Chambers, *Conquest of Cholera*, 102–3.

12. J. Brown to George Gibson, Apr. 20, 1832, *CSE*, 1:443–44.

13. "An Act, to amend an act entitled, 'an act further to define and carry into effect the act to extend the laws of this state over the persons, and property of the persons

called Indians, in this state,'" Dec. 9, 1831, *Laws of the State of Mississippi Embracing All Acts of a Public Nature from January Session, 1824, to January Session 1838, Inclusive* (Baltimore, 1838), 358; William Armstrong to George Gibson, Sept. 1, 1832, *CSE*, 1:376–78; Journal of William S. Colquhoun, Sept. 13, 1832 to Dec. 20, 1832, CGLR, box 6, Choctaw, 1833, NA; William Armstrong to George Gibson, Sept. 10, 1832, *CSE*, 1:378–79; F.W. Armstrong to George Gibson, Oct. 28, 1832, *CSE*, 1:391; F.W. Armstrong to George Gibson, Oct. 21, 1832, *CSE*, 1:388–89 (quotations).

14. Journal of William S. Colquhoun, Sept. 13, 1832 to Dec. 20, 1832, CGLR, box 6, Choctaw, 1833, NA.

15. A.S. Langham to George Gibson, Nov. 8, 1832, *CSE*, 1:737–38; William Armstrong to George Gibson, Nov. 10, 1832, *CSE*, 1:398–99; F.W. Armstrong to George Gibson, Nov. 21, 1832, *CSE*, 1:400 ("Scarce a boat"); Roads 51 (1833), Civil Works Map File, RG 77, NACP; Roads 1 (Dec. 10, 1827), Civil Works Map File, RG 77, NACP; William Howard to J.J. Abert, May 3, 1834, 23rd Cong., 2nd sess., H.Doc. 83, serial 445, pp. 1–14.

16. William Armstrong to George Gibson, Nov. 10, 1832, *CSE*, 1:398 ("*cholera times*"); Journal of J.P. Simonton, Nov. 16, 1832 to Dec. 19, 1832, CGLR, box 6, Choctaw, 1833, NA ("sheer want" and "Having received"); Journal of J. Van Horne, Nov. 2, 1832 to Dec. 18, 1832, CGLR, box 6, Choctaw, 1833, NA ("old, lame").

17. Journal of J. Van Horne, Nov. 2, 1832 to Dec. 18, 1832, CGLR, box 6, Choctaw, 1833, NA.

18. George Strother Gaines to Anthony Winston Willard, Aug. 8, 1857, in Gaines, *Reminiscences of George Strother Gaines: Pioneer and Statesman of Early Alabama and Mississippi*, ed. James P. Pate (Tuscaloosa: University of Alabama Press, 1998), 123 ("pet"), 124 ("useless agencies"); Carolyn Thomas Foreman, "The Armstrongs of Indian Territory," *Chronicles of Oklahoma* 30, no. 4 (1952): 294 ("talked loudly"); Lieut. Montgomery to F.W. Armstrong, Mar. 22, 1833, reel 3, IRW ("spoiled" and "largely economised"); F.W. Armstrong to George Gibson, Mar. 31, 1833, reel 3, IRW; Journal of William S. Colquhoun, Sept. 13, 1832 to Dec. 20, 1832, CGLR, box 6, Choctaw, 1833, NA ("naked"); F.W. Armstrong to Lewis Cass, Nov. 21, 1832, reel 2, IRW ("tyrant and cruel" and "outrageous").

19. Copy of Lieut. J.A. Phillips' Journal, Nov. 14, 1832 to Dec. 9, 1832, CGLR, box 6, Choctaw, 1833, NA.

20. A.S. Langham to George Gibson, Nov. 8, 1832, *CSE*, 1:737–38; Journal of J.P. Simonton, Nov. 16, 1832 to Dec. 19, 1832, CGLR, box 6, Choctaw, 1833, NA ("suffered dreadfully"); F.W. Armstrong to George Gibson, Dec. 2, 1832, *CSE*, 1:401–2 ("We have been"); Journal of J. Van Horne, Nov. 2, 1832 to Dec. 18, 1832, CGLR, box 6, Choctaw, 1833, NA.

21. Isaac McCoy to the Commissioners West, Oct. 15, 1832, *CSE*, 3:497 ("the path"); G.J. Rains to George Gibson, Apr. 5, 1833, *CSE*, 1:841–42 ("except by age"); G.J. Rains to George Gibson, June 10, 1833, *CSE*, 1:831; J.H. Hook to G.J. Rains, May 6, 1833, *CSE*, 1:255 ("much to be lamented").

22. G.J. Rains to George Gibson, June 19, 1833, *CSE*, 1:845; F.W. Armstrong to Elbert Herring, Sept. 20, 1833, LR, OIA, reel 170, M-234, NA ("Will the Government"); F.W. Armstrong to Elbert Herring, Nov. 8, 1833, LR, OIA, reel 170, M-234, NA; George Gibson to G.J. Rains, Jan. 21, 1834, CGLS, vol. 2, p. 141, NA ("This is a disagreeable"); G.J. Rains to George Gibson, Apr. 18, 1834 to Dec. 18, 1832, CGLR, box 7, Choctaw, 1834, NA ("let to starve").

23. G.J. Rains to George Gibson, Nov. 4, 1833, *CSE*, 1:851; John Campbell to Elbert Herring, Nov. 20, 1833, *CSE*, 4:722.

24. George Gibson to J.B. Gardiner, June 28, 1832, *CSE*, 1:102 ("the plan of removal"); Daniel Dunihue, "Journal of Occurrences," Aug. 21, 1832, Conner Prairie Museum Archives, Fishers, Indiana ("It will [be] but a short time"); George Gibson to J.B. Gardiner, Sept. 1, 1832, *CSE*, 1:153; James B. Gardiner to Lewis Cass, Feb. 25, 1833, *CSE*, 4:113.

25. J.F. Lane to George Gibson, Sept. 25, 1832, *CSE*, 1:730; J.J. Abert to George Gibson, Oct. 2, 1832, *CSE*, 1:384 ("swelled"); Carl Wittke, ed., *History of the State of Ohio* (Columbus: Ohio State Archaeological and Historical Society, 1941), 3:36; James B. Gardiner to George Gibson, Oct. 8, 1832, *CSE*, 1:706 ("settled plan"); Daniel R. Dunihue to Alexander R. Dunihue, Sept. 11, 1832, "Removal of Indians from Ohio: Dunihue Correspondence of 1832," *Indiana Magazine of History* 35, no. 4 (Dec. 1939): 419; J.B. Gardiner to Daniel R. Dunihue, July 28, 1832, "Removal of Indians from Ohio," 414 ("flowery"); Henry Harvey, *History of the Shawnee Indians, From the Year 1681 to 1854, Inclusive* (Cincinnati, 1855), 227–28 ("they would get to see" and "My friend").

26. Daniel Dunihue, Diary, Sept. 2, 5, and 13, 1832, Conner Prairie Museum Archives, Fishers, Indiana; Stephen Warren, *The Worlds the Shawnees Made: Migration and Violence in Early America* (Chapel Hill: University of North Carolina Press, 2014), 200–201; "Journal of John Shelby," *A Sorrowful Journey*, ed. Randall L. Buchman (Defiance, Ohio: Defiance College Press, 2007), 15–16 ("offending").

27. Daniel R. Dunihue to Alexander R. Dunihue, Sept. 29, 1832, "Removal of Indians from Ohio," 420 ("tawney"); James B. Gardiner to Lewis Cass, Oct. 1, 1832, *CSE*, 3:478–79 ("miserable"); Dunihue, Diary, Oct. 3, 1832.

28. James B. Gardiner to Lewis Cass, Feb. 25, 1833, *CSE*, 4:115; Daniel R. Dunihue to Alexander R. Dunihue, Oct. 23, 1832, "Removal of Indians from Ohio," 423.

29. "The Cholera," *Arkansas Gazette* (Little Rock, Ark.), Oct. 31, 1832, 2 ("Keep cool" and "trust," quoting the *Republican*); "The Cholera," *Alexandria Gazette* (Alexandria, Va.), Nov. 5, 1832, 4; "The Cholera," *Rochester Union and Advertiser* (Rochester, N.Y.), Nov. 17, 1832, 2; Dunihue, "Journal of Occurrences," Oct. 25, 1832.

30. James B. Gardiner to William Clark, Oct. 25, 1832, *CSE*, 4:118; "Journal of John Shelby," 42, 44; J.J. Abert to George Gibson, Nov. 9, 1832, *CSE*, 1:396–97; J.J. Abert to George Gibson, Nov. 17, 1832, *CSE*, 1:399; "Journal of John Shelby," 47–50 ("wept bitterly").

31. Dunihue, Diary, Sept. 28, Nov. 9, Nov. 15, 1832 ("laughing"), Dec. 9, 1832.

32. "Journal of John Shelby," 62–65; James B. Gardiner to William Clark, Oct. 25, 1832, *CSE*, 4:117; Sami Lakomäki, "From Ohio to Oklahoma and Beyond: The Long Removal of the Lewistown Shawnees," *The Eastern Shawnee Tribe of Oklahoma: Resilience through Adversity*, ed. Stephen Warren (Norman: University of Oklahoma Press, 2017), 48; "Journal of John Shelby," 57–59, 62 ("various changes").

33. Reuben Holmes to B. McCary, *Black Hawk War, 1831–32*, vol. 2, 1:414–16.

34. Black Hawk, *Black Hawk's Autobiography*, ed. Roger L. Nicholas (1833; Ames: Iowa State University Press, 1999), 13, 82–84 ("war chiefs"); "From the Seat of War," *American* (New York, N.Y.), June 12, 1832, 2 ("of undoubted bravery"); John Ridge to Stand Watie, Apr. 6, 1832, *Cherokee Cavaliers: Forty Years of Cherokee History as Told in the Correspondence of the Ridge-Watie-Boudinot Family*, ed. Edward Everett Dale and Gaston Litton (1939; Norman: University of Oklahoma Press, 1995), 8 ("intellectual warfare").

35. The commander of the Georgia Guard threatened Boudinot with "a sound whipping" if he were "too free" in his remarks about the armed force. The Supreme Court had jurisdiction by writ of error under the twenty-fifth section of the Judi-

ciary Act of 1789. *Cherokee Phoenix* (New Echota, Cherokee Nation), Mar. 12, 1831, 3, and Sept. 3, 1831, 2–3; *Samuel A. Worcester v. the State of Georgia*, 31 U.S. Reports 515, 516 (1832).

36. John Sergeant's notes, box 5, file 18, pp. 16–19, John Sergeant Papers, Historical Society of Pennsylvania, Philadelphia ("a State"); *Cherokee Phoenix*, Oct. 21, 1829, 2, and Apr. 14, 1830, 1; Memorial of the Cherokees, Dec. 1829, Committee of the Whole House, Petitions, "Various Subjects," HR21A-H1.1, NA; Jill Norgren, *The Cherokee Cases: The Confrontation of Law and Politics* (New York: McGraw-Hill, 1996), 117.

37. *Samuel A. Worcester v. the State of Georgia*, 31 U.S. Reports 515, 559, 561 (1832).

38. William M. Davis to Lewis Cass, June 24, 1832, *CSE*, 3:381 ("It was trumpted"); Elias Boudinot to Stand Watie, Mar. 7, 1832, *Cherokee Cavaliers*, 4–6; John Ridge to Stand Watie, Apr. 6, 1832, *Cherokee Cavaliers*, 10.

39. John Ridge to Stand Watie, Apr. 6, 1832, *Cherokee Cavaliers*, 8; *RDC* (1833), vol. 8, 2:2013–14.

40. *RDC* (1833), vol. 8, 2:2027–28.

41. *The Constitutionalist* (Augusta, Ga.), Apr. 2, 1830, 2; John Brown, *Slave Life in Georgia: A Narrative of the Life, Sufferings, and Escape of John Brown, A Fugitive Slave* (London, 1855), 21, 27–30, 45–48 (quotations); F.N. Boney, "Thomas Stevens, Antebellum Georgian," *South Atlantic Quarterly* 72 (1973): 226–42.

42. *Georgia Journal* (Milledgeville, Ga.), Apr. 12, 1832, 3 ("the perpetuity"); *Southern Recorder* (Milledgeville, Ga.), Apr. 19, 1832, 3 ("A palpable"); *The Constitutionalist*, May 4, 1832, 2 ("rights and interests"); *Georgia Journal*, May 24, 1832, 2 ("*local concerns*").

43. William M. Davis to Lewis Cass, June 24, 1832, *CSE*, 3:381–82 ("perilous"); Copy of letter from John McLean to Chief John Ross, May 23, 1832, 4026.107-a.1, John Ross Papers, Helmerich Center for American Research, Gilcrease Museum, Tulsa, Oklahoma; U.S. Statutes at Large 2 (1802): 141; Gerard N. Magliocca, "The Cherokee Removal and the Fourteenth Amendment," *Duke Law Journal* 53 (2003): 897 and n135.

44. Elisha W. Chester to John Ross, July 20, 1832, *CSE*, 3:424; Elisha W. Chester to Lewis Cass, Aug. 11, 1832, LR, OIA, reel 75, M-234, NA ("pressing evils").

45. H. David Williams, "Gambling Away the Inheritance: The Cherokee Nation and Georgia's Gold and Land Lotteries of 1832–33," *Georgia Historical Quarterly* 73, no. 3 (Fall 1989): 519–39; David A. Nichols, "Land, Republicanism, and Indians: Power and Policy in Early National Georgia, 1780–1825," *Georgia Historical Quarterly* 85, no. 2 (Summer 2001): 199–226; John Ridge to John Ross, Feb. 2, 1833, *PCJR*, 1:259.

46. William W. Freehling, *Prelude to Civil War: The Nullification Controversy in South Carolina, 1816–1836* (New York: Harper & Brothers, 1965), 250–51, 254–59 (quotation on 257); Richard Sutch, "Slave prices, value of the slave stock, and annual estimates of the slave population: 1800–1862," table Bb209–214 in *Historical Statistics of the United States, Earliest Times to the Present: Millennial Edition*, ed. Susan B. Carter, Scott Sigmund Gartner, Michael R. Haines, Alan L. Olmstead, Richard Sutch, and Gavin Wright (New York: Cambridge University Press, 2006).

47. William Wirt to John Sergeant, Dec. 22, 1832, reel 23, William Wirt Papers, Maryland Historical Society; Norgren, *The Cherokee Cases*, 126–30; Tim Alan Garrison, *The Legal Ideology of Removal: The Southern Judiciary and the Sovereignty of Native American Nations* (Athens: University of Georgia Press, 2002), 191–97.

48. John Ross, Annual Message, Oct. 10, 1832, *PCJR*, 1:255.

49. *Columbus Enquirer* (Columbus, Ga.), Mar. 31, 1832, 3; John H. Martin, *Columbus,*

Geo., from its Selection as a "Trading Town" in 1827, to its Partial Destruction by Wilson's Raid, in 1865 (Columbus, Ga., 1874), 7, 8, 10, 35.

50. Stephen F. Miller, *The Bench and Bar of Georgia* (Philadelphia, 1858), 2:202, 248–54.

51. *Columbus Enquirer,* Apr. 14, 1832, 3 ("the dearest interest"); Memorial of Creeks, Feb. 3, 1830, PM, Protection of Indians, SEN21A-H3, NA.

52. *Columbus Enquirer,* Aug. 25, 1832, 2 ("system"); Eli S. Shorter et al. to Lewis Cass, Oct. 16, 1835, "Documents Relating to Frauds, &c., in the sale of Indian Reservations of Land," 24th Cong., 1st sess., S.Doc. 425, serial 445; Shorter, Tarver, & Co. et al. to Lewis Cass, Nov. 18, 1835, "Documents Relating to Frauds," 363 ("bare-naked"); Opothle Yoholo et al. to the House and Senate, Jan. 24, 1832, COIA, HR22A-G8.2, NA; Eli S. Shorter to John B. Hogan, Feb. 24, 1836, LR, OIA, reel 243, frame 768, M-234, NA ("scrupulously regardful").

CHAPTER 7: THE FINANCIERS

1. Stephen F. Miller, *The Bench and Bar of Georgia* (Philadelphia, 1858), 2:256 ("I have been"), 260 ("itched"); Oliver H. Prince, *A Digest of the Laws of the State of Georgia* (Athens, Ga., 1837), 90; *Savannah Georgian* (Savannah, Ga.), Dec. 9, 1831, 2 ("more real capital," quoting the *Columbus Enquirer*).

2. John H. Martin, *Columbus, Geo., from its Selection as a "Trading Town" in 1827, to its Partial Destruction by Wilson's Raid, in 1865* (Columbus, Ga., 1874), 8 ("strip"); *Savannah Georgian,* June 15, 1831, 4; *Federal Union* (Milledgeville, Ga.), May 2, 1833, 3; *Columbus Enquirer* (Columbus, Ga.), Nov. 23, 1833. 1; *Georgia Journal* (Milledgeville, Ga.), Nov. 10, 1831, 3.

3. On one occasion, a "general panic pervaded the Indians" when the Montgomery County sheriff entered the Creek Nation with a party of volunteer militia. As the troops advanced, "every hut and shelter was abandoned, and not an Indian was to be seen." *Georgia Journal,* Feb. 27, 1830, 3; *Southern Recorder* (Milledgeville, Ga.), Mar. 27, 1830, 3; William Moor to Nehah Micco, Dec. 6, 1831, and Neha Micco, Tuskemhow, and Nehah Locko Opoy to John Crowell, Dec. 13, 1831, CSE, 2:708–9; Neha Micco et al. to the President, Jan. 21, 1830, frame 274, John Crowell to Lewis Cass, Dec. 15, 1831, frame 545, John Crowell to John H. Eaton, June 30, 1830, frames 315–316, and John Crowell to John H. Eaton, Aug. 8, 1830, frames 319–324, LR, OIA, reel 222, M-234, NA; Sandy Grierson vs. the Creek Nation, box 10, 1st series, no. 31, Creek Removal Records, entry 300, RG 75, NA; Abraham Smith vs. Sandy Grayson, 1831, box 10, 1st series, no. 19, Creek Removal Records, entry 300, RG 75, NA.

4. Nehah Micco et al. to John H. Eaton, Apr. 8, 1831, CSE, 2:424–25; John H. Eaton to the Red Men of the Muscogee nation, May 16, 1831, CSE, 2:290; Opothle Yoholo et al. to the House and Senate, Jan. 24, 1832, COIA, HR22A-G8.2, NA ("We admit").

5. Tuskeneah to Andrew Jackson, May 21, 1831, *PAJ.*

6. Garland B. Terry et al. to Andrew Jackson, May 31, 1831 *PAJ* ("intense suffering"); *Southern Recorder,* June 23, 1831, 3 ("beyond description").

7. For a modern-day analogue in which states privatized indigenous lands, see Joe Bryan and Denis Wood, *Weaponizing Maps: Indigenous Peoples and Counterinsurgency in the Americas* (New York: Guilford Press, 2015), 96–126. John H. Eaton to George R. Gilmer, June 17, 1831, CSE, 2:307–8; Samuel S. Hamilton to John Crowell, July 25, 1831, p. 306, LS, OIA, reel 7, M-21, NA ("regrets"); Lewis Cass to the Chiefs of the Creek Tribe, Jan. 16, 1832, CSE, 2:742–43; Michael D. Green, *The Poli-*

tics of Indian Removal: Creek Government and Society in Crisis (Lincoln: University of Nebraska Press, 1982), 169–73.

8. *Columbus Enquirer*, Feb. 25, 1832, 3.

9. Allan Greer, *Property and Dispossession: Natives, Empires and Land in Early Modern North America* (New York: Cambridge University Press, 2018), 27–64, 311–54; Andro Linklater, *Measuring America: How the United States Was Shaped by the Greatest Land Sale in History* (New York: Penguin, 2002), 160–75; C. Albert White, *A History of the Rectangular Survey System* (Washington, D.C.: Bureau of Land Management, 1983), 18–96.

10. Elijah Hayward to F.W. Armstrong, Apr. 28, 1832, *Report from the Secretary of the Treasury*, 24th Cong., 1st sess., S.Doc. 69, p. 6.

11. John Robb to Enoch Parsons, Oct. 14, 1833, *CSE*, 3:787; Peter S. Onuf, "Liberty, Development, and Union: Visions of the West in the 1780s," *William and Mary Quarterly* 43, no. 2 (Apr. 1986): 186–88.

12. George W. Martin to Lewis Cass, Aug. 9, 1833, LR, OIA, reel 188, M-234, NA; "TO THOSE WHO CLAIM RESERVATIONS," 1831, 3026.337, PPP.

13. B.F. Butler to Lewis Cass, Dec. 28, 1833, LR, OIA, reel 188, M-234, NA; Records Relating to Indian Removal, Records of the Commissary General of Subsistence, Choctaw Removal Records, Journal of Pray, Murray, and Vroom, RG 75, entry 268, box 1, NA.

14. B.S. Parsons and Thomas Abbot to Lewis Cass, Sept. 7, 1832, LR, OIA, frames 307–9, reel 223, M-234, NA; Ne-Hah Micco et al. to the Secretary of War, Nov. 15, 1832, *CSE*, 3:527–28.

15. Ishtehotopa King to Andrew Jackson, July 17, 1835, LR, OIA, reel 136, frame 608, M-234, NA; Claudio Saunt, *Black, White, and Indian: Race and the Unmaking of an American Family* (New York: Oxford University Press, 2005); Thomas J. Abbott to Lewis Cass, Sept. 29, 1832, *CSE*, 3:471; B.S. Parsons to Lewis Cass, Oct. 16, 1832, LR, OIA, frames 281–282, reel 223, M-234, NA ("in Every way"); B.S. Parsons to Lewis Cass, Oct. 21, 1832, LR, OIA, frames 283–285, reel 223, M-234, NA ("negro woman").

16. Thomas J. Abbott to Lewis Cass, May 1833, *CSE*, 4:236; Tuckabatchee Hadjo and Octeahchee Emathla to Andrew Jackson, Feb. 18, 1831, *PAJ*.

17. Creek Census, 1832, *CSE*, 4:334, 394; Choctaw Census, *CSE*, 3:149; Arrell Gibson, *The Chickasaws* (Norman: University of Oklahoma Press, 1971), 179.

18. In the ranking of corporations, I have excluded firms whose maximum authorized capital is unknown. I have calculated the slave population using the 1840 U.S. Census. Where counties lay only partially within the boundaries of the Creek, Choctaw, and Chickasaw nations in the 1830s, I took a proportional fraction. For the value of slaves, I used the average price in 1836 of $547. Robert E. Wright, "US Corporate Development 1790–1860," *The Magazine of Early American Datasets (MEAD)*, https://repository.upenn.edu/mead/7/ (accessed Sept. 25, 2018); Richard Sutch, "Slave prices, value of the slave stock, and annual estimates of the slave population: 1800–1862," table Bb209–214 in *Historical Statistics of the United States, Earliest Times to the Present: Millennial Edition*, ed. Susan B. Carter, Scott Sigmund Gartner, Michael R. Haines, Alan L. Olmstead, Richard Sutch, and Gavin Wright (New York: Cambridge University Press, 2006).

19. Walter Barrett, *The Old Merchants of New York City* (New York, 1870), vol. 2, 2:107–10 ("a clever man," "quick," "as affable," and of "great wealth"); Andrew Beers to Joseph D. Beers, Oct. 1801, box 26, folder 787, LPC ("all manner"); Joseph D. Beers to Starr, Feb. 24, 1812, box 26, folder 787, LPC; Alice Curtis Desmond, *Yankees and Yorkers*

(Portland, Me: Anthoensen Press, 1985), 14–23, 69 ("became the best customer"); J.D. Beers to Benjamin Curtis, Jan. 2, 1857, box 27, folder 818, LPC; J.D. Beers to Joseph Curtis, July 1, 1861, box 27, folder 819, LPC.

20. Henry Reed Stiles, *Genealogies of the Stranahan, Josselyn, Fitch and Dow Families in North America* (Brooklyn, 1868), 77–78; E. Mils to J.D. Beers, Jan. 30, 1825, box 26, folder 790, LPC; Sven Beckert, *Empire of Cotton: A Global History* (New York: Knopf, 2015), 117–20; Walter Johnson, *River of Dark Dreams: Slavery and Empire in the Cotton Kingdom* (Cambridge: Harvard University Press, 2013), 259–62; J.D. and Mary Beers to Eliza and Lewis Curtis, Jan. 25, 1835, box 26, folder 795, LPC; J.D. and Mary Beers to Eliza and Lewis Curtis, Jan. 10, 1835, box 26, folder 795, LPC ("The poor Negroes"); William Wilberforce, *An Appeal to the Religion, Justice, and Humanity of the Inhabitants of the British Empire in behalf of the Negro Slaves in the West Indies* (London, 1823), 1.

21. "Slave labor camp" is Peter H. Wood's term. J.D. and Mary Beers to Eliza and Lewis Curtis, Mar. 27, 1835, box 26, folder 796, LPC ("don't think"); J.D. and Mary Beers to Eliza and Lewis Curtis, Feb. 6, 1835, box 26, folder 795, LPC ("Oh you don't know"); J.D. and Mary Beers to Eliza and Lewis Curtis, Feb. 28, 1835, box 26, folder 795, LPC ("is all done"); J.D. and Mary Beers to Eliza and Lewis Curtis, Jan. 25, 1835, box 26, folder 795, LPC ("makes it another"); Desmond, *Yankees and Yorkers*, 37; Peter H. Wood, "Slave Labor Camps in Early America: Overcoming Denial and Discovering the Gulag," in *Inequality in Early America*, ed. Carla Gardina Pestana and Sharon V. Salinger (Hanover, N.H.: University Press of New England, 1999), 222–39.

22. Eric Kimball, "'What have we to do with slavery?' New Englanders and the Slave Economies of the West Indies," and Calvin Schermerhorn, "The Coastwise Slave Trade and a Mercantile Community of Interest," in *Slavery's Capitalism: A New History of American Economic Development*, ed. Sven Beckert and Seth Rockman (Philadelphia: University of Pennsylvania Press, 2016), 181–94, 209–24; *Niles' Register*, Sept. 5, 1835, 9.

23. Poem regarding the Treaty of Dancing Rabbit, [1843], 4026.3162, PPP.

24. In the Antebellum era, it was common for southern states to purchase large stakes in state-chartered banks. *Laws of the State of Mississippi Embracing All Acts of a Public Nature from January Session, 1824, to January Session 1838, Inclusive* (Jackson, Miss., 1838), 237 ("give impulse"), 298–99, 436; Charles Hillman Brough, "The History of Banking in Mississippi," *Publications of the Mississippi Historical Society* (1900), 3:317–40; Howard Bodenhorn, *State Banking in Early America: A New Economic History* (New York: Oxford University Press, 2003), 123–54, 219–48; Fritz Redlich, *Molding of American Banking: Men and Ideas* (New York: Hafner, 1951), 2:333–35; "State Bonds Sold," *Alexandria Gazette* (Alexandria, Va.), Sept. 11, 1833, 2; Account Sales, 1833–34, box 40, folder 1077, LPC.

25. George R. Gilmer, *Sketches of some of the First Settlers of Upper Georgia, of the Cherokees, and the Author* (New York, 1840), 468 ("cotton"); *An Act to Establish a Branch of the Bank of the State of Alabama in the Tennessee Valley* (New York, 1833), 27 ("Indian titles"), 31–32.

26. Nathan Mitchell and J.B. Toulmin to Baring Bros, Nov. 3, 1832, p. 2636, reel C-1372, Baring Papers, LR, General, Public Archives, Canada ("Like all new states"); William H. Brantley, *Banking in Alabama, 1816–1860* (privately printed, 1961), 1:267–73; Daniel Bell and Son to Frederick Huths and Co., May 22, 1833, Daniel Bell and Son Letter, Alabama Department of Archives and History, Montgomery; *Dublin Morning Register*, May 29, 1833, 2; Thomas Wilson and Co. to J.D. Beers and Co., Sept. 14, 1832 [1833?], box 35, folder 969, LPC.

27. David Hubbard to J.D. Beers, Nov. 17, 1834, box 39, folder 1058, LPC ("Our sections"); David Hubbard to J.D. Beers, Jan. 10, 1835, box 39, folder 1058, LPC ("pouring in"); Articles of Association, Mar. 2, 1835, box 39, folder 1058, LPC.

28. For a history of land companies during Indian Removal, see Mary Elizabeth Young, *Redskins, Ruffleshirts, and Rednecks: Indian Allotments in Alabama and Mississippi, 1830–1860* (Norman: University of Oklahoma Press, 1961); Boston and Mississippi Cotton Land Company Papers, DMR.

29. Report of John Bolton, Sept. 18, 1835, p. 48 and 60, Letter book, NYMS; John D. Haeger, *The Investment Frontier: New York Businessmen and the Economic Development of the Old Northwest* (Albany: State University of New York Press, 1981), 110, 156–57; Memorandum of Agreement, Oct. 15, 1835, box 36, folder 989, LPC; Thomas M. Barker to Lewis Cass, July 17, 1834, LR, OIA, reel 136, M-234, NA ("at the Cost"). In the ranking of corporations, I have excluded firms whose maximum authorized capital is unknown. Robert E. Wright, "US Corporate Development 1790–1860," *The Magazine of Early American Datasets (MEAD)*, https://repository.upenn.edu/mead/7/ (accessed Sept. 25, 2018).

30. Callie B. Young, ed., *From These Hills: A History of Pontotoc County* (Fulton, Miss.: Pontotoc Woman's Club, 1976), 69–76; John Bolton to the Trustees of the New York and Mississippi Land Company, Apr. 25, 1835, p. 16, NYMS ("rather bitter"); John Bolton to the Trustees of the New York and Mississippi Land Company, June 16, 1835, p. 39, NYMS ("really Hot").

31. John Bolton to the Trustees of the New York and Mississippi Land Company, Mar. 25, 1835, p. 3, NYMS ("immense profits"); John Bolton to the Trustees of the New York and Mississippi Land Company, Apr. 20, 1835, p. 15, NYMS ("the rich planter"); John Bolton to the Trustees of the New York and Mississippi Land Company, Apr. 25, 1835, p. 16, NYMS ("deep rich"); John Bolton to the Trustees of the New York and Mississippi Land Company, May 25, 1835, p. 33, NYMS.

32. Wendy Cegielski, "A GIS-Based Analysis of Chickasaw Settlement in Northeast Mississippi: 1650–1840" (M.A. thesis, University of Mississippi, 2010), 64; John Howard Blitz, *An Archaeological Study of the Mississippi Choctaw Indians*, vol. 16, Archaeological Report (Jackson: Mississippi Department of Archives and History, 1985), 34–35; Robbie Ethridge, *Creek Country: The Creek Indians and Their World* (Chapel Hill: University of North Carolina Press, 2003), 120–21; William G. Siesser, "Paleogene Sea Levels and Climates: U.S.A. Eastern Gulf Coastal Plain," *Palaeogeography, Palaeoclimatology, Palaeoecology* 47 (1984): 261–75.

33. *Public Dinner Given in Honor of the Chickasaw and Choctaw Treaties* (Mississippi, 1830), 3 ("exchange"); David Hubbard to J.D. Beers, Jan. 10, 1835, box 39, folder 1058, LPC ("sought for"); *Columbus Enquirer*, Apr. 24, 1835, 3 ("It is confidently").

34. Ethridge, *Creek Country*, 96, 132–33, 155, 170–71, 280n24; Mary Theresa Bonhage-Freund, "Botanical Remains," *Archaeology of the Lower Muskogee Creek Indians, 1715–1836*, ed. Mary Theresa Bonhage-Freund, Lisa D. O'Steen, and Howard Thomas Foster (Tuscaloosa: University of Alabama Press, 2007), 190–92; Blitz, *Archaeological Study of the Mississippi Choctaw Indians*, 17 (names of months); Cegielski, "A GIS-Based Analysis of Chickasaw Settlement," 27; John Bolton to the Trustees of the New York and Mississippi Land Company, June 1835, p. 35, NYMS.

35. *Public Dinner Given in Honor of the Chickasaw and Choctaw Treaties*, 2, 4; L. Atkison to Farish Carter, June 5, 1833, folder 9, in the Farish Carter Papers #2230, SHC ("the best"); John Bolton to the Trustees of the New York and Mississippi Land Company, May 6, 1835, p. 22, NYMS.

36. Poem regarding the Treaty of Dancing Rabbit, [1843], 4026.3162, PPP; Nehah

Micco et al. to John H. Eaton, Apr. 8, 1831, *CSE*, 2:424–25; Opothle Yoholo et al. to Lewis Cass, Sept. 4, 1835, "Documents Relating to Frauds, &c., in the sale of Indian Reservations of Land," 24th Cong., 1st sess., S.Doc. 425, serial 445, p. 318; "The Late Treaty," *Georgia Journal*, Nov. 8, 1825, 2.

37. Bonhage-Freund, "Botanical Remains," 150–56.

38. R. Alfred Vick, "Cherokee Adaptation to the Landscape of the West and Overcoming the Loss of Culturally Significant Plants," *American Indian Quarterly* 53, no. 3 (Summer 2011): 394–417; Steven G. Platt, Christopher G. Brantley, and Thomas R. Rainwater, "Native American Ethnobotany of Cane (Arundinaria spp.) in the Southeastern United States: A Review," *Castanea* 74, no. 3 (Sept. 2009): 271–85.

39. Peter Pitchlynn[?] to David Folsom, May 19, 1830, 4026.3186, PPP; Opothle Yoholo et al. to the House and Senate, Jan. 24, 1832, COIA, HR22A-G8.2, NA ("white brethren"); John Ross, Annual Message, Oct. 10, 1832, *PCJR*, 1:255.

40. *Cherokee Phoenix* (New Echota, Cherokee Nation), Nov. 18, 1829, 2–3; Thomas L. McKenney to John Cocke, Jan. 23, 1827, Library of Congress Collection, RG 233, entry 756, NA box 57 of LC box 184, NA; Opothle Yoholo et al. to the House and Senate, Jan. 24, 1832, COIA, HR22A-G8.2, NA ("slowly and reluctantly").

41. Isaac McCoy, Journal (typescript), Apr. 15, 1838, p. 483, MP; William Armstrong to George Gibson, Sept. 14, 1833, *CSE*, 1:414.

42. G.J. Rains to George Gibson, July 29, 1834, CGLR, box 7, Choctaw, 1834, NA; Abraham Redfield to David Greene, Aug. 25, 1834, frames 846–847, reel 779, Unit 6, ABC 18.4.4, Letters from Officers of the Board, American Board of Commissioners for Foreign Missions, Houghton Library, Harvard College Library; David Carter to Hugh Montgomery, Aug. 30, 1834, LR, OIA, reel 76, M-234, NA ("government and government agents"); Benjamin F. Currey to Lewis Cass, Sept. 15, 1834, LR, OIA, reel 76, M-234, NA ("Let me").

43. Joseph Glover Baldwin, *The Flush Times of Alabama and Mississippi: A Series of Sketches* (New York, 1853), 81–83, 238.

44. Isham Harrison to James T. Harrison, Feb. 10, 1836, folder 4, James T. Harrison Papers #02441, SHC ("Virgin lands"); Baldwin, *Flush Times*, 83 ("rose"); Neah Micco et al. to Lewis Cass, Sept. 27, 1832, *CSE*, 3:464.

CHAPTER 8: "A COMBINATION OF DESIGNING SPECULATORS"

1. Walter Barrett, *The Old Merchants of New York City* (New York, 1866), 110 ("high-toned"); Map of real estate, box 38, folder 1031, LPC; Inventory of real estate, box 30, folder 867, LPC; Joseph Curtis to Lewis Curtis, July 6, 1863, box 27, folder 821, LPC ("a consistent"); *Columbus Enquirer* (Columbus, Ga.), Dec. 13, 1836, 2 ("distinguished"); Stephen F. Miller, *The Bench and Bar of Georgia* (Philadelphia, 1858), 2:248 ("a man").

2. Opothle Yoholo's exact words: "The homes which have been rendered valuable by the labor of our hands, are torn from us by a combination of designing speculators, who haunt your office, and who, like the man among the tombs, are so fierce that no one can pass that way." Opothle Yoholo et al. to Robert W. McHenry, Mar. 23, 1835, Records Relating to Indian Removal, Records of the Commissary General of Subsistence, Creek Removal Records, Reports, 1836–38, RG 75, entry 293, box 3, NA; Joseph Glover Baldwin, *The Flush Times of Alabama and Mississippi: A Series of Sketches* (New York, 1853), 82 ("mesmeric"); Samuel Gwin to the Commissioner of the General Land Office, Nov. 24, 1835, *Report from the Secretary of the Treasury*, 24th Cong., 1st sess., S.Doc. 69, pp. 18–19 ("ravenous"); Elizabeth Arnold and James McConnell, "Hijacked Humanity: A Postcolonial Reading of Luke 8:26–39,"

Review & Expositor 112, no. 4 (Nov. 1, 2015): 591–606; Christopher Burdon, "'To the Other Side': Construction of Evil and Fear of Liberation in Mark 5.1–20," *Journal for the Study of the New Testament* 27, no. 2 (2004): 149–67; Joshua Garroway, "The Invasion of a Mustard Seed: A Reading of Mark 5.1–20," *Journal for the Study of the New Testament* 32, no. 1 (Sept. 1, 2009): 57–75. Thanks to Jamie Kreiner for references regarding the story of the Gerasene demoniac.

3.   Opothle Yoholo et al. to Lewis Cass, Sept. 4, 1835, "Documents Relating to Frauds, &c., in the sale of Indian Reservations of Land," 24th Cong., 1st sess., S.Doc. 425, serial 445, p. 318; Opothle Yoholo et al. to the House and Senate, Jan. 24, 1832, COIA, HR22A-G8.2, NA; Samuel George Morton, *Catalogue of Skulls of Man and the Inferior Animals*, 3rd. ed. (Philadelphia, 1849); Cameron B. Strang, *Frontiers of Science: Imperialism and Natural Knowledge in the Gulf South Borderlands, 1500–1850* (Chapel Hill: University of North Carolina Press, 2018), 225–26, 308–14; Robert E. Bieder, *Science Encounters the Indian, 1820–1880: The Early Years of American Ethnology* (Norman: University of Oklahoma Press, 1986), 55–103; James Colbert to Lewis Cass, June 29, 1835, LR, OIA, reel 136, frame 614, M-234, NA.

4.   Treaty of Dancing Rabbit Creek and supplement, 1830, Charles J. Kappler, ed., *Indian Affairs: Laws and Treaties* (Washington, D.C., 1903–), 2:310–19; 44th Cong., 1st sess., H.Misc.Doc. 40, p. 73; *Choctaw Nation v. United States*, Nov. 15, 1886, 119 U.S. 1 (7 S.Ct. 75, 30 L.Ed. 306), https://www.law.cornell.edu/supremecourt/text/119/1 (accessed Oct. 23, 2018).

5.   Choctaws should have received two to three million acres, depending on how one estimates family size. "Claims of the Choctaw Nation," 44th Cong., 1st sess., H.Misc.Doc. 40, p. 23; 43rd Cong., 2nd sess., H.Exec.Doc. 47, p. 17; 44th Cong., 1st sess., H.Misc.Doc. 40, p. 23.

6.   The speculators' schemes are summarized in Mary Elizabeth Young, *Redskins, Ruffleshirts, and Rednecks: Indian Allotments in Alabama and Mississippi, 1830–1860* (Norman: University of Oklahoma Press, 1961), 47–72. John Coffee to Andrew Jackson, Sept. 23, 1831, *CSE*, 2:600 ("almost nothing"); William S. Colquhoun to Samuel S. Hamilton, Nov. 19, 1831, *CSE*, 2:687; John W. Byrn to the Secretary of War, Dec. 18, 1831, *CSE*, 2: 717; John W. Byrne to the Indian Office, Apr. 18, 1832, LR, OIA, reel 170, M-234, NA ("His sun"); John W. Byrne to the Secretary of War, Dec. 18, 1831, *CSE*, 2:717; Records Relating to Indian Removal, Records of the Commissary General of Subsistence, Choctaw Removal Records, Journal of Pray, Murray, and Vroom, pp. 215–34, RG 75, entry 268, box 1, NA ("collected"); William S. Colquhoun to Lewis Cass, Sept. 20, 1833, *CSE*, 4:566.

7.   23rd Cong., 2nd sess., S.Doc. 22, serial 267, vol. 2, pp. 33, 49–50, 95, 105, 128; "Message from the President of the United States, with Documents relating to the Character and Conduct of Samuel Gwin," 24th Cong., 2nd sess., S.Doc. 213, serial 298, vol. 2, pp. 1–4, 17; Malcolm Rohrbough, *The Land Office Business: The Settlement and Administration of American Public Lands, 1789–1837* (New York: Oxford University Press, 1968).

8.   23rd Cong., 2nd sess., S.Doc. 22, serial 267, vol. 2, pp. 151–53; "Message from the President of the United States, with Documents relating to the Character and Conduct of Samuel Gwin," 24th Cong., 2nd sess., S.Doc. 213, serial 298, vol. 2, pp. 1–2 ("Fraudulent" and "confined"), 4.

9.   23rd Cong., 2nd sess., S.Doc. 22, serial 267, vol. 2, pp. 11–12, 99, 117; "Message from the President of the United States, with Documents relating to the Character and Conduct of Samuel Gwin," 24th Cong., 2nd sess., S.Doc. 213, serial 298, vol. 2, pp. 73 and 76 (quotations); James P. Shenton, *Robert John Walker: A Politician from Jackson to Lincoln* (New York: Columbia University Press, 1961), 11–13, 25–26, 33, 121,

127–30, 148, 158, 160; *Vicksburg Register* (Vicksburg, Miss.), Oct. 8, 1835, 1. The purchases of the Chocchuma Land Company were compiled using the U.S. Bureau of Land Management patent database and include all Mississippi patents belonging to four partners, Robert J. Walker, Thomas G. Ellis, Malcolm Gilchrist, and Robert Jemison.

10. Deposition of Captain Bob, alias Mingohomah, July 12, 1844, Records Relating to Indian Removal, Records of the Commissary General of Subsistence, Choctaw Removal Records, Pray, Murray, and Vroom, Evidence, 1837–38, RG 75, entry 270, box 3, NA.

11. Choctaw Claims, n.d., box 10, folder 79, in the Fisher Family Papers #258, SHC.

12. Claims 160 (Immaka), 187 (Oakalarcheehubbee), 196 (Illenowah), and 199 (Okshowenah), Records Relating to Indian Removal, Records of the Commissary General of Subsistence, Choctaw Removal Records, Pray, Murray, and Vroom, Evidence, 1837–38, RG 75, entry 270, box 1, NA.

13. Claims 242 (Elitubbee), 251 (Abotaya), 205 (Shokaio), 245 (Chepaka), 250 (Hiyocachee), Records Relating to Indian Removal, Records of the Commissary General of Subsistence, Choctaw Removal Records, Pray, Murray, and Vroom, Evidence, 1837–38, RG 75, entry 270, box 1, NA; Case 20 (Ahlahubbee), J.F.H. Claiborne, Minutes, 1842–43, folder 40, J.F.H. Claiborne Papers #00151, SHC.

14. [?] to Peter Pitchlynn, Aug. 8, 1834, 4026.3351, PPP ("deep reflection"); Reuben H. Grant to Peter Pitchlynn, Nov. 12, 1836, 4026.3436, PPP ("There is a great").

15. U.S.-Chickasaw treaties of 1832 and 1834, Kappler, ed., *Indian Affairs*, 2:356–62, 418–23.

16. James Colbert to Lewis Cass, June 29, 1835, LR, OIA, reel 136, frame 614, M-234, NA; William S. Colquhoun to Lewis Cass, Sept. 20, 1833, *CSE*, 4:566; Statement of Gordon D. Boyd, Mar. 7, 1837, LR, OIA, reel 146, frame 548, M-234, NA ("cholera cases"); Statement of Samuel Ragsdale, May 17, 1838, LR, OIA, reel 146, frame 581, M-234, NA ("very <u>poor</u>"); U.S. Censuses of 1830 and 1840.

17. Records Relating to Indian Removal, Records of the Commissary General of Subsistence, Chickasaw Removal Records, Reports of Land Sales and Deeds, 1836–39, RG 75, entry 255, box 1, NA; William S. Colquhoun to Lewis Cass, Sept. 20, 1833, *CSE*, 4:566; David Hubbard to Lewis Curtis, June 2, 1837, box 1, NYMS; Benjamin Reynolds to C.A. Harris, June 2, 1837, LR, OIA, reel 146, M-234, NA.

18. The General Land Office sold approximately 4,400 square miles of Chickasaw land between 1836 and 1840. It auctioned most of the remaining land by 1850. 31st Cong., 2nd sess., S.Exec.Doc. 2, p. 14; "Chickasaw Fund," 29th Cong., 1st sess., H.Doc. 8, p. 75 ("residue"); Richard Bolton to Lewis Curtis, Sept. 8, 1835, p. 67, letter book, NYMS; Isham Harrison to James T. Harrison, July 27, 1835, folder 4, James T. Harrison Papers #02441, SHC ("speculation"); Article 7, U.S.-Chickasaw treaty of 1832, Kappler, ed., *Indian Affairs*, 2:358–59; Richard Bolton to Lewis Curtis, July 27, 1835, p. 55, NYMS; John Bolton to Lewis Curtis, July 16, 1835, NYMS; Statement of Gordon D. Boyd, March 7, 1837, LR, OIA, reel 146, M-234, NA ("capitalists").

19. "Chickasaw Fund," 29th Cong., 1st sess., H.Doc. 8.

20. "Chickasaw Fund," 29th Cong., 1st sess., H.Doc. 8.

21. "Chickasaw Fund," 29th Cong., 1st sess., H.Doc. 8, pp. 75–86.

22. I am converting the dollar amount by using the labor cost of an unskilled worker. Samuel H. Williamson, "Seven Ways to Compute the Relative Value of a U.S. Dollar Amount, 1774 to Present," MeasuringWorth, 2019, www.measuringworth.com /uscompare/; *Exceptions to the Account stated, under the direction of the Secretary of the*

Interior, exhibiting in detail all the moneys which from time to time had been placed, in the Treasury to the credit of the Chickasaw Nation (Washington, D.C., 1869), 1, 2, 3, 7.

23. Memorial of the Chickasaw Chiefs to the President of the United States, Nov. 22, 1832, LR, OIA, reel 136, M-234, NA.

24. B.M. Lowe to Levi Woodbury, May 3, 1836, Correspondence of the Secretary of Treasury Relating to the Administration of Trust Funds for the Chickasaw and Other Indian Tribes, S Series, 1834–72, RG 56, M-749, NA; J.D. Beers to Elbert Herring, Mar. 4, 1836, LR, OIA, Stocks, reel 853, RG 75, M-234, NA ("Under the circumstances"); J.D. Beers to Levi Woodbury, Mar. 21, 1836, no. 29, Correspondence of the Secretary of Treasury Relating to the Administration of Trust Funds for the Chickasaw and Other Indian Tribes, S Series, 1834–72, RG 56, M-749, NA ("this pressing time"); "Chickasaw Fund," 29th Cong., 1st sess., H.Doc. 8, p. 67; Richard E. Sylla, Jack Wilson, and Robert E. Wright, "Price Quotations in Early United States Securities Markets, 1790–1860," Inter-university Consortium for Political and Social Research (New York: New York University, Stern School of Business, 2002), table DS5; Robert J. Ward to F.P. Blair, Oct. 27, 1836, p. 130, Correspondence of the Secretary of Treasury Relating to the Administration of Trust Funds for the Chickasaw and Other Indian Tribes, S Series, 1834–72, RG 56, M-749, NA.

25. The total Chickasaw investment in the Decatur bank was $750,000, but only $500,000 was loaned out in the form of specie certificates. 35th Cong., 2nd sess., S.Misc.Doc. 8, pp. 8–9; Levi Woodbury to Charles Macalester and J.D. Beers, Jan. 28, 1836, no. 13, J.W. Garth to Levi Woodbury, March 25, 1836, no. 39, and Levi Woodbury to Andrew Jackson, June 30, 1836, Correspondence of the Secretary of Treasury Relating to the Administration of Trust Funds for the Chickasaw and Other Indian Tribes, S Series, 1834–72, RG 56, M-749, NA; James Durno to Levi Woodbury, July 28, 1836, 24th Cong., 2nd sess., H.Rpt. 194, pp. 79–80; "State Bonds created for the Branch Bank at Montgomery," Bank of the State of Alabama, Branch Bank at Montgomery, General Financial Statements, 1839–1848, Alabama Department of Archives and History, Montgomery; Charles C. Mills to Farish Carter, Sept. 11, 1836, folder 12, Farish Carter Papers #2230, SHC ("decided advantage" and "There has never been").

26. Opinion of Alfred Balch on the contract of Aug. 28, 1836, LR, OIA, reel 243, frame 320, M-234, NA ("On one side"); Creek chiefs to the President, May 21, 1831, LR, OIA, reel 222, frames 441–43, M-234, NA; William Moor to Nehah Micco, Dec. 6, 1831, *CSE*, 2:710 ("an old helpless"); List of white intruders living in the Creek Nation, Dec. 13, 1831, LR, OIA, reel 222, frames 549–51, M-234, NA; Neah Micco and Tus-Ke-Neah-Haw to the Secretary of War, Dec. 20, 1832, *CSE*, 3:565–66.

27. John B. Hogan to Uriah Blue, Apr. 3, 1835, CGLR, box 8, Creek, NA; U. Blue to George Gibson, Dec. 21, 1835, CGLR, box 8, Creek, NA; Extract of a letter from Jeremiah Austill to the Secretary of War, July 26, 1833, *CSE*, 4:487; Jeremiah Austill to Lewis Cass, July 31, 1833, *CSE*, 4:493; Copy of bond and oath, 1836, LR, OIA, reel 243, frames 908–09, M-234, NA ("indenture" and "highly respectable"); Opothle Yoholo et al. to the President of the United States, Jan. 7, 1836, LR, OIA, reel 243, frame 505, M-234, NA.

28. Opothle Yoholo et al. to Dr. McHenry, Mar. 23, 1835, box 3, correspondence of certifying agents, entry 293, RG 75, NA; Eli S. Shorter to Lewis Cass, May 2, 1834, "Documents Relating to Frauds," 129; Deposition of John Taylor, Jan. 16, 1837, *The New American State Papers* (Wilmington, Del.: Scholarly Resources, 1972), 10:58–61 ("it made no difference"); John B. Hogan to Uriah Blue, Apr. 3, 1835, CGLR, box 8, Creek, NA ("white proof").

29. "Documents Relating to Frauds," 181 ("malefactors"), 182, 222, 228, 236.

30. Elijah Corley to Scott and Cravens, Mar. 25, 1835, *New American State Papers*, 9:513–514 ("rogued"); Eli Shorter to John S. Scott and M.M. and N.H. Craven, Jan. 28, 1835, *New American State Papers*, 9:510–11 ("Give up" and "Swear off"); Eli Shorter to John S. Scott and E. Corley, and M.M. and N.H. Craven, Mar. 1, 1835, *New American State Papers*, 9:511–13 ("*Stealing*"); Benjamin P. Tarver to M.A. Craven, Mar. 1, 1835, *New American State Papers*, 9:513 ("Hurrah").

31. J.W.A. Sanford to George Gibson, Sept. 30, 1835, CGLR, box 8, Creek, NA; Christopher D. Haveman, *Rivers of Sand: Creek Indian Emigration, Relocation, and Ethnic Cleansing in the American South* (Lincoln: University of Nebraska Press, 2016), 138–39.

32. William Hunter to John B. Hogan, Aug. 12, 1835, CGLR, box 8, Creek, NA ("would die"); Opothle Yoholo et al. to the President of the United States, Jan. 14, 1836, LR, OIA, reel 225, frames 38–41, M-234, NA; George Gibson to John B. Hogan, Jan. 25, 1836, CGLS, vol. 3, p. 426, NA; Cass quoted in Haveman, *Rivers of Sand*, 139.

33. See the accounts in Christopher D. Haveman, ed., *Bending Their Way Onward: Creek Indian Removal Documents* (Lincoln: University of Nebraska Press, 2018), 118–76.

34. George F. Salli to Lewis Cass, May 13, 1836, LR, OIA, reel 225, frames 151–52, M-234, NA ("There was no garbage"); David Hubbard to Lewis Cass, May 1, 1834, LR, OIA, reel 237, frames 425–28, M-234, NA ("clotted"); John Page to C.A. Harris, May 8, 1836, LR, OIA, reel 243, frame 1327, M-234, NA ("I talk to them").

35. *Columbus Enquirer*, May 1, 1835, 2; Copy of petition drafted by Eli Shorter, Feb. 14, 1836, LR, OIA, reel 243, frame 744, M-234, NA ("insolent"); John B. Hogan to George Gibson, Jan. 23, 1836, CGLR, box 9, Creek, NA ("contemptible").

36. George Gibson to Jacob Brown, Oct. 20, 1835, CGLS, vol. 3, pp. 307–11, NA ("perfectly"); George Gibson to Lewis Cass, Nov. 12, 1835, CGLS, vol. 3, pp. 338–50, NA ("uncertain").

37. This small contingent of Cherokees was about half of what Harris had expected. The rest remained in their cabins or took refuge in the mountains. Joseph W. Harris to George Gibson, Mar. 8, 1834, CGLR, box 1, Cherokee, NA; March 23 and 31, Journal of Occurrences of a Company of Cherokee Emigrants, for the months of February, March, April, May, 1834, CGLR, box 1, NA.

38. April 5, 6, 7, 9, and 10, Journal of Occurrences of a Company of Cherokee Emigrants, for the months of February, March, April, May, 1834, CGLR, box 1, NA.

39. Joseph W. Harris to Drs. Alders Sprague and Bushrod W. Lic, Records of the Accounting Officers of the Department of the Treasury, Settled Indian Accounts, RG 217, entry 525, box 274, account 1109–A(13), NA ("a proper police"); April 11 and 12, Journal of Occurrences of a Company of Cherokee Emigrants, for the months of February, March, April, May, 1834, Records of the Commissary General of Subsistence, Letters Received, 1831–36, RG 75, entry 201, box 1, NA.

40. April 14, 15, 16, and 30, May 5 and 6, Journal of Occurrences of a Company of Cherokee Emigrants, for the months of February, March, April, May, 1834, CGLR, box 1, NA.

41. Joseph W. Harris to Drs. Alders Sprague and Bushrod W. Lic, Records of the Accounting Officers of the Department of the Treasury, Settled Indian Accounts, RG 217, entry 525, box 274, account 1109-A(13), NA; Joseph W. Harris to George Gibson, May 9, 1834, CGLR, box 1, Cherokee, NA; Journal of Occurrences of a Company of Cherokee Emigrants, for the months of February, March, April, May 15, 1834, CGLR, box 1, NA ("easy journeys"); Joseph W. Harris to George Gibson, June 5, 1834, CGLR, box 1, Cherokee, NA.

42. J.W. Harris to Wiley Thompson, Aug. 23, 1835, CGLR, box 15, Creek, NA.

43. J.W. Harris to Wiley Thompson, Plan of Operations in Detail for the Removal of Florida Indians, Aug. 23, 1835, CGLR, box 15, Creek, NA.

44. J.W. Harris to Wiley Thompson, Aug. 23, 1835, CGLR, box 15, Creek, NA.

45. George Gibson to Lewis Cass, Nov. 12, 1835, CGLS, vol. 3, pp. 338–50, NA; J.P. Simonton to George Gibson, Sept. 2, 1834, CGLR, box 12, Creek, NA ("hard and flinty" and "sickly").

46. S. Grantland to Farish Carter, Apr. 3, 1836, folder 12, Farish Carter Papers; Samuel Gwin to the Commissioner of the General Land Office, May 7, 1835, *Report from the Secretary of the Treasury*, 24th Cong., 1st sess., S.Doc. 69; John B. Hogan to Andrew Jackson, Apr. 22, 1836, LR, OIA, reel 243, frame 892, M-234, NA; Samuel Given to Lewis Cass, May 22, 1832, LR, OIA, reel 188, M-234, NA.

CHAPTER 9: 1836: THE SOUTHERN WORLD AT WAR

1. Larry E. Rivers, "Leon County, Florida, 1824 to 1860," *Journal of Negro History* 66, no. 3 (Autumn 1981): 235–45; Heintzelman diary, Nov. 15, 1839, reel 3, Samuel Peter Heintzelman Papers, LC.

2. Jeffrey Ostler, "'To Extirpate the Indians': An Indigenous Consciousness of Genocide in the Ohio Valley and Lower Great Lakes 1750s–1810," *William and Mary Quarterly* 72, no. 4 (Oct. 2015): 587–622.

3. *RDC* (1828), vol. 4, 2:1584–85 ("distinguished individuals"); Wilson Lumpkin to Lewis Cass, May 31, 1833, LR, OIA, reel 75, M-234, NA ("speedy extermination"); *Southern Banner* (Athens, Ga.), Apr. 14, 1838, 2 ("evil").

4. [?] to Peter Pitchlynn, Aug. 8, 1834, 4026.3351, PPP.

5. Memorial of the Cherokee Nation, May 17, 1833, PM, COIA, SEN23A-G6, NA.

6. Kenneth L. Valliere, "Benjamin Currey, Tennessean Among the Cherokees: A Study of the Removal Policy of Andrew Jackson, Part I," *Tennessee Historical Quarterly* 41, no. 2 (Summer 1982): 140–58; Benjamin F. Currey to Elbert Herring, Nov. 13, 1831, *CSE*, 2:681; John Robb to Benjamin F. Currey, Nov. 24, 1831, p. 487, LS, OIA, reel 7, M-21, NA; Benjamin F. Currey to Elbert Herring, Apr. 20, 1833, LR, OIA, reel 75, M-234, NA; Benjamin F. Currey to Elbert Herring, Sept. 9, 1833, LR, OIA, reel 75, M-234, NA; Lewis Ross to John Ross, Feb. 23, 1834, LR, OIA, reel 76, M-234, NA; Extract of a letter from Lewis Ross to John Ross, Mar. 5, 1834, enclosed in Currey to Herring, Feb. 7, 1834, LR, OIA, reel 76, M-234, NA; Kenneth L. Valliere, "Benjamin Currey, Tennessean Among the Cherokees: A Study of the Removal Policy of Andrew Jackson, Part II," *Tennessee Historical Quarterly* 41, no. 3 (Fall 1982): 251–59; John Ross to a Gentleman of Philadelphia, May 6, 1837, *PCJR*, 1:490–503; John Ross to John Howard Payne, Mar. 5, 1836, *PCJR*, 1:390 ("demonical").

7. James William Van Hoeven, "Salvation and Indian Removal: The Career Biography of the Rev. John Freeman Schermerhorn, Indian Commissioner" (PhD diss., Vanderbilt University, 1972), 27–28 ("foreign missionary"), 35–36, 56, 69–70, 94 ("in the dark"), 97; John Freeman Schermerhorn to Andrew Jackson, May 14, 1824, *PAJ* ("your old friend").

8. John Freeman Schermerhorn to Andrew Jackson, June 23, 1831, *PAJ*.

9. Van Hoeven, "Salvation and Indian Removal," 21.

10. Van Hoeven, "Salvation and Indian Removal," 141 ("bigoted"), 166 ("more designing"), 204 ("prostituted"); Isaac McCoy, Journal (typescript), Dec. 14, 1834, p. 389, MP; George A. Schultz, *An Indian Canaan: Isaac McCoy and the Vision of an Indian State* (Norman: University of Oklahoma Press, 1972), 140.

11. Laurence M. Hauptman, *Conspiracy of Interests: Iroquois Dispossession and the Rise of New York State* (Syracuse: Syracuse University Press, 1999), 181 ("certain notorious"); Van Hoeven, "Salvation and Indian Removal," 204 ("Sginuhyona"); Patrick Del Percio to the author, Dec. 13, 2018; John Ross in answer to inquiries from a friend, July 2, 1836, *PCJR*, 1:427–44.

12. Van Hoeven, "Salvation and Indian Removal," 270; James Gadsden to Andrew Jackson, Nov. 14, 1829, LR, OIA, reel 806, frame 8, M-234, NA; Leonard L. Richards, *The California Gold Rush and the Coming of the Civil War* (New York: Vintage Books, 2007), 125 ("a social blessing"); W.S. Steele, "The Last Command: The Dade Massacre," *Tequesta* 46 (1986): 6 ("19/20"); James Gadsden to Lewis Cass, June 2, 1832, *CSE*, 3:368–69 ("half-starved"); Treaty with the Seminoles, 1832, Charles J. Kappler, ed., *Indian Affairs: Laws and Treaties* (Washington, D.C., 1903–), 2:344.

13. Woodburne Potter, *The War in Florida* (Baltimore: Lewis and Coleman, 1836), 38 ("hard and unconscionable"), 60 ("I never"); John Eaton to Lewis Cass, Mar. 8, 1835, LR, OIA, reel 806, frame 101, M-234, NA; Lewis Cass to John H. Eaton, Mar. 27, 1835, CGLS, vol. 3, pp. 42–44, NA; James Gadsden to Lewis Cass, Nov. 1, 1834, LR, OIA, reel 806, frame 81, M-234, NA ("White man's treaty"); Ethan Allen Hitchcock to Samuel Cooper, Oct. 22, 1840, box 2, folder 7, EAH; Diary of Nathaniel Wyche Hunter, Dec. 23, 1840, HCP ("out of his element"); C.S. Monaco, "'Wishing that Right May Prevail': Ethan Allen Hitchcock and the Florida War," *Florida Historical Quarterly* 93, no. 2 (Fall 2014): 167–94.

14. Treaty of Dancing Rabbit Creek and supplement, 1830, Kappler, ed., *Indian Affairs*, 2:395; Monaco, "'Wishing that Right May Prevail,'" 181–82 ("made"); Ethan Allen Hitchcock to Samuel Cooper, Oct. 22, 1840, box 2, folder 7, EAH.

15. Major Ridge et al. to the Senate and House, Nov. 28, 1834, COIA, HR23A-G7.2, NA; John Ridge et al. to Benjamin F. Currey, Nov. 1, 1834, enclosed in Currey to Herring, Nov. 10, 1834, LR, OIA, reel 76, M-234, NA; Memorial of the Cherokee Indians, Nov. 28, 1834, PM, COIA, SEN23A-G6, NA ("can now alone"); John Ross to John H. Eaton, May 29, 1834, *PCJR*, 1:294–95.

16. John Ross to John Ridge, Sept. 12, 1823," *PCJR*, 1:303; Valliere, "Benjamin Currey . . . Part II," 251 ("prostituted"); Memorial of the Cherokee Indians, Nov. 28, 1834, PM, COIA, SEN23A-G6, NA ("patriots"); John Ross to Lewis Cass, Feb. 9, 1836, *PCJR*; Thurman Wilkins, *Cherokee Tragedy: The Story of the Ridge Family and the Decimation of a People* (New York: MacMillan, 1970), 254–78.

17. J.W. Harris to George Gibson, Dec. 30, 1835, CGLR, box 15, Creek, NA; John T. Sprague, *The Origin, Progress, and Conclusion of the Florida War* (New York, 1848), 91 ("cruelly").

18. Frank Laumer, *Dade's Last Command* (Gainesville: University Press of Florida, 1995), 9, 16, 180, 192–96; [W.W. Smith], *Sketch of the Seminole War and Sketches During a Campaign, by a Lieutenant* (Charleston, 1836), 39.

19. J.W. Harris to George Gibson, Dec. 30, 1835, CGLR, box 15, Creek, NA; Frank Laumer, "Encounter by the River," *Florida Historical Quarterly* 46, no. 4 (Apr. 1968): 322–39; [Smith], *Sketch of the Seminole War*, 46; John Bemrose, *Reminiscences of the Second Seminole War*, ed. John K. Mahon (Gainesville: University of Florida Press, 1966), 58.

20. Andrew Jackson to José Masot, May 23, 1818, *PAJ* ("savage"); Robert V. Remini, *Andrew Jackson and His Indian Wars* (New York: Viking, 2001), 150–52, 154 ("confiscated"); Mark F. Boy, "Asi-Yaholo or Osceola," *Florida Historical Quarterly* 33, no. 3/4 (Jan.–Apr. 1955): 257–58.

21. Patricia R. Wickman, *Osceola's Legacy* (Tuscaloosa: University of Alabama Press, 1991), 1–22; Wiley Thompson to Elbert Herring, Oct. 28, 1834, LR, OIA, reel 806, frame 84, M-234, NA; John K. Mahon, *History of the Second Seminole War, 1835–1842* (Gainesville: University of Florida Press, 1967), 93–94.

22. Lewis Cass to Winfield Scott, Jan. 21, 1836, *American State Papers: Military Affairs* (Washington, D.C., 1861), 6:61–63.

23. Alexander Beaufort Meek, "Journal of the Florida Expedition, 1836," Alexander Beaufort Meek Papers, DMR; Potter, *War in Florida*, 60–62 ("ladies" and "gallant men"); Myer M. Cohen, *Notices of Florida and the Campaigns* (Charleston, S.C., 1836), 115 ("last look"); *Federal Union* (Milledgeville, Ga.), Feb. 12, 1836, 3.

24. Scott was the author of *Infantry-Tactics*, a three-volume manual for the "exercise and manoevres of the United States' infantry," published in 1835. Lewis Cass to Winfield Scott, Jan. 21, 1836, *American State Papers: Military Affairs*, 6:61–63; "Major General Scott's Address," *American State Papers: Military Affairs*, 7:197 ("a Cretan labyrinth"); Mahon, *History of the Second Seminole War*, 147–49; Bemrose, *Reminiscences of the Second Seminole War*, 77, 88–89; James Barr, *A Correct and Authentic Narrative of the Indian War in Florida* (New York, 1836), 17.

25. *Federal Union*, Dec. 11, 1835, 2; John B. Hogan to Thomas Jesup, June 24, 1836, Letters Received during the Creek War, 1836–38, from Camps and Forts, box 15, The Office of the Adjutant General, Generals' Papers and Books, General Jesup, entry 159, RG 94, NA; Mahon, *History of the Second Seminole War*, 103.

26. John K. Mahon, "The Journal of A.B. Meek and the Second Seminole War, 1836," *Florida Historical Quarterly* 38, no. 4 (Apr. 1960): 305 ("Creoles"); Lewis Cass to John B. Hogan, Jan. 21, 1836, CGLS, vol. 3, p. 417, NA.

27. A Cherokee to William Schley, Feb. 1, 1836, LR, OIA, reel 76, M-234, NA ("massacre"); Isaac Baker to William Schley, Feb. 1, 1836, LR, OIA, reel 76, M-234, NA; Sarah H. Hill, "'To Overawe the Indians and Give Confidence to the Whites': Preparations for the Removal of the Cherokee Nation from Georgia," *Georgia Historical Quarterly* 95, no. 4 (Winter 2011): 469; Isaac Baker to William Schley, Feb. 1, 1836, LR, OIA, reel 76, M-234, NA ("We need").

28. John Page to George Gibson, May 12, 1836, CGLR, box 9, Creek, NA; Lewis Cass to Winfield Scott, Jan. 21, 1836, *American State Papers: Military Affairs*, 6:61–63; Duncan Clinch to Roger Jones, Oct. 9, 1835, order book, 1834–35, Duncan Lamont Clinch Papers, LC; Claudio Saunt, *A New Order of Things: Property, Power, and the Transformation of the Creek Indians, 1733–1816* (New York: Cambridge University Press, 1999), 273–90; George Gibson to D.L. Clinch, Oct. 22, 1835, CGLS, vol. 3, pp. 312–13, NA; Duncan Clinch to Roger Jones, Dec. 9, 1835, order book, 1834–35, Duncan Lamont Clinch Papers, LC ("spirit"); John C. Casey to Thomas Basinger, Jan. 2, 1836, folder 1, in the William Starr Bassinger Papers #1266-Z, SHC ("Indian negroes"); Laumer, *Dade's Last Command*, 235–39.

29. [Smith], *Sketch of the Seminole War*, 20–22 ("mild character"); J.W. Phelps to Helen M. Phelps, Jan. 16, 1837, John Wolcott Phelps Papers, LC ("large reward"); Wiley Thompson to Lewis Cass, Apr. 27, 1835, LR, OIA, reel 806, frame 105, M-234, NA.

30. I determined the number of slaves working on Creek land by examining county-level data, using fractional figures when counties spanned the border between the Creek Nation and the United States. John Hebron Moore, *Agriculture in Ante-Bellum Mississippi* (New York: Bookman Associates, 1958), 69.

31. Joshua D. Rothman, *Flush Times and Fever Dreams: A Story of Capitalism and Slavery in the Age of Jackson* (Athens: University of Georgia Press, 2012).

32. Isham Harrison to James T. Harrison, July 27, 1835, folder 4, James T. Harrison

Papers #02441, SHC ("so numerous"); Isham Harrison to James T. Harrison, Oct. 14, 1834, folder 3, James T. Harrison Papers; David Hubbard to John Bolton, Aug. 23, 1835, p. 62, NYMS.

33. Brian DeLay, *War of a Thousand Deserts: Indian Raids and the US-Mexican War* (New Haven: Yale University Press, 2008), 71–75.

34. *RDC* (1836), vol. 12, 3:3335–36.

35. *RDC* (1836), vol. 12, 3:3342 ("hordes"); 3345–47 ("the very heart"). Jackson wrote one response on the back of a letter from Georgia governor William Schley, and Secretary of War Cass conveyed it to the Governor. William Schley to the President, Feb. 23, 1836, LR, OIA, reel 76, frame 936, M-234, NA; Lewis Cass to William Schley, Feb. 23, 1836, *American State Papers: Military Affairs,* 6:628; Extract of a private letter from General Andrew Jackson to the Secretary of War, Oct. 1, 1837, letter book 6, Thomas Sidney Jesup Papers, LC.

36. John Page to George Gibson, May 8, 1836, CGLR, box 9, Creek, NA; John Page to George Gibson, May 16, 1836, CGLR, box 9, Creek, NA; Lewis Cass to Thomas Jesup, May 19, 1836, LR, OIA, reel 225, frames 26–30, M-234, NA; Lewis Cass to George Gibson (memorandum), May 19, 1836, CGLR, box 9, Creek, NA; Laurence M. Hauptman, "John E. Wool in Cherokee Country, 1836–1837: A Reinterpretation," *Georgia Historical Quarterly* 85, no. 1 (Spring 2001): 1, 10–11.

37. "An Act Authorizing the President of the United States to accept the service of volunteers, and to raise an additional regiment of dragoons or mounted riflemen," Chapter 80, 24th Cong., 1st sess., *U.S. Statutes at Large* 5 (1836): 32–33; Department of Defense, *Selected Manpower Statistics, Fiscal Year 1997* (Washington, D.C.: U.S. Government Printing Office, 1997), 46–47, table 2; 24th Cong., 1st sess., S.Doc. 77, p. 3 ("a continual"); "An Act to provide for better protection of the western frontier," Chapter 258, 24 Cong., 1st sess., *U.S. Statutes at Large* 5 (1836): 67.

38. George Washington to Timothy Pickering, July 1, 1796, *Founders Online,* National Archives, https://founders.archives.gov/documents/Washington/99-01-02-00674 (accessed April 11, 2019); Paul Frymer, *Building an American Empire: The Era of Territorial and Political Expansion* (Princeton: Princeton University Press, 2017), 45; James P. Ronda, "'We Have a Country': Race, Geography, and the Invention of Indian Territory," *Journal of the Early Republic* 19, no. 4 (Dec. 1999): 739–55; Lewis Cass to Thomas H. Benton, Feb. 19, 1836, *American State Papers: Military Affairs,* 6:150–52; *American State Papers: Military Affairs,* 6:149 ("from the interior"), 154.

39. Residents of Jackson County, Missouri, to the Senate and House, May 10, 1836, COIA, HR25A-G7.2, NA; *RDC* (1836), vol. 12, 3:3337–39 (quotations); *American State Papers: Military Affairs,* 6:154.

40. A.R. Turk to Andrew Jackson, June 13, 1836, LR, OIA, reel 76, M-234, NA.

41. *Columbus Enquirer* (Columbus, Ga.), May 20, 1836, 3 ("We cannot"); *Columbus Enquirer,* May 27, 1836, 3 ("store and counting-houses"); *Columbus Enquirer,* June 9, 1836, 3; *Columbus Enquirer,* June 16, 1836, 2 ("instigators").

42. John Page to George Gibson, May 16, 1836, CGLR, box 9, Creek, NA; John Page to George Gibson, May 30, 1836, CGLR, box 9, Creek, NA ("we were starving"); Diary of Thomas Sidney Jesup, box 2, folder 6, EAH; John T. Ellisor, *The Second Creek War: Interethnic Conflict and Collusion on a Collapsing Frontier* (Lincoln: University of Nebraska Press, 2010), 205–10.

43. *Macon Weekly Telegraph* (Macon, Ga.), Mar. 17, 1836, 1 (quoting the *Savannah Georgian*); Ellisor, *Second Creek War,* 210–11, 260; John Hope Franklin and Loren Schweninger, *Runaway Slaves: Rebels on the Plantation* (New York: Oxford University Press, 1999), 88 ("have had uninterrupted").

44. John Page to George Gibson, May 30, 1836, CGLR, box 9, Creek, NA ("whip"); Ellisor, *Second Creek War*, 211–21, 245–47, 257–58, 263 ("virtually over").

45. *Columbus Enquirer*, July 14, 1836, 3 ("removal"); Sylvester Churchill Journals, July 3 to July 11, 1836, Sylvester Churchill Papers, LC; *Southern Banner*, July 16, 1836, 2; Christopher D. Haveman, *Rivers of Sand: Creek Indian Emigration, Relocation, and Ethnic Cleansing in the American South* (Lincoln: University of Nebraska Press, 2016), 186–87.

46. The second auditor determined that ninety-seven people died along the way. The final cost was $28.50 per person, which does not compare favorably with deportations conducted by the federal government. J. Waller Barry to George Gibson, Aug. 10, 1836, CGLR, box 9, Creek, NA; A. Iverson to C.A. Harris, June 17, 1837, enclosure, J.W.A. Sanford, Records of the Accounting Officers of the Department of the Treasury, Settled Indian Accounts, RG 217, entry 525, box 261, account 691, NA.

47. Contract with the Alabama Emigrating Company, Aug. 13, 1836, *Bending Their Way Onward: Creek Indian Removal in Documents*, ed. Christopher D. Haveman (Lincoln: University of Nebraska Press, 2018), 226–31; Edward Deas to George Gibson, Nov. 22, 1836, LR, OIA, frames 553–556, reel 237, M-234, NA; Opothle Yoholo et al. to Andrew Jackson, Dec. 25, 1836, box 3, folder 13, EAH.

48. William Bowen Campbell to David Campbell, Correspondence, June 20, 1836, Campbell Family Papers, DMR ("hunted"); *Southern Banner*, July 2, 1836, 2; Heintzelman diary, Aug. 18, 1836, reel 2, Samuel Peter Heintzelman Papers, LC; Jonathan G. Reynolds to Henry Wilson, Mar. 31, 1837, box 5, EAH ("The people").

49. William Bowen Campbell to Fanny Campbell, Correspondence, July 29, 1836, Campbell Family Papers, DMR ("hunting"); *Georgia Journal* (Milledgeville, Ga.), Aug. 2, 1836, 3 ("The savage"); *Georgia Journal*, Feb. 7, 1837, 3 ("infected"); Benjamin Young to Thomas Jesup, July 6, 1836, box 12, The Office of the Adjutant General, Generals' Papers and Books, General Jesup, entry 159, RG 94, NA; J.S. McIntosh to Thomas Jesup, Aug. 13, 1836, box 12, The Office of the Adjutant General, Generals' Papers and Books, General Jesup, entry 159, RG 94, NA; *Southern Recorder* (Milledgeville, Ga.), Aug. 23, 1836, 2; *Federal Union*, Aug. 23, 1836, 3; *Southern Banner*, Aug. 27, 1836, 3; Jacob Rhett Motte, *Journey into Wilderness: An Army Surgeon's Account of Life in Camp and Field during the Creek and Seminole Wars, 1836–1838*, ed. James F. Sunderman (Gainesville: University of Florida Press, 1953), 69–70; Ellisor, *Second Creek War*, 268, 271–72, 284, 288, 292, 293, 301.

50. Ellisor, *Second Creek War*, 267, 379.

51. Drew Lopenzina, *Through an Indian's Looking-Glass: A Cultural Biography of William Apess, Pequot* (Amherst: University of Massachusetts Press, 2017), 238–40, 243–45; Alice Curtis Desmond, *Yankees and Yorkers* (Portland, Maine: Anthoensen Press, 1985), 34; *Christian Intelligencer* (New York, N.Y.), Feb. 18, 1837, 4 ("injuries"); William Apess, *Eulogy on King Philip*, in Barry O'Connell, ed., *On Our Own Ground: The Complete Writings of William Apess, a Pequot* (Amherst: University of Massachusetts Press, 1992), 279, 280, 284, 288, 305.

52. *New-York Observer* (New York, N.Y.), Feb. 11, 1832, 2 ("most respectable"); "Meeting in Aid of the Cherokees," *New-York Observer*, Feb. 11, 1832, 2 ("diffuse").

53. Apess, *Eulogy on King Philip*, 304, 308.

54. Apess, *Eulogy on King Philip*, 307.

55. American Land Company, *First Annual Report of the Trustees of the American Land Company* (New York, 1836), 27; "Government Land Speculators," *Alexandria Gazette* (Alexandria, Va.), Nov. 23, 1839, 2 ("pious").

56. H.W. Jernigan to J.W.A. Sanford, Aug. 5, 1836, John W.A. Sanford Papers, Alabama Department of Archives and History, Montgomery.

CHAPTER 10: AT THE POINT OF A BAYONET

1. J.R. Mathews et al. to Lewis Cass, June 24, 1836, LR, OIA, reel 80, M-234, NA; George M. Lavender to John Ridge, May 3, 1836, LR, OIA, reel 80, M-234, NA; Josiah Shaw to Lewis Cass, June 28, 1836, LR, OIA, reel 80, M-234, NA; Spencer Jarnigan to C.A. Harris, Aug. 26, 1836, LR, OIA, reel 80, M-234, NA; Major Ridge and John Ridge to Andrew Jackson, June 30, 1836, LR, OIA, reel 80, M-234, NA.

2. Memorial of the Cherokee Nation, May 17, 1833, PM, COIA, SEN23A-G6, NA; John Ross et al. to the Senate and House of Representatives, June 21, 1836, PCJR, 1:437.

3. Tuelookee, Oct. 24, 1836, p. 84, John Cahoossee's widow, Oct. 19, 1836, p. 66, Canowsawsky, Oct. 24, 1836, p. 83, Tatterhair, Oct. 24, 1836, p. 85, Whiteman Killer, Oct. 24, 1836, p. 88, Records Relating to Indian Removal, Records of the Commissary General of Subsistence, Cherokee Removal Records, First Board, Property Valuations, 1835–39, RG 75, entry 224, box 3, Hutchins, Shaw, and Kellog, NA.

4. Nos. 8, 9, 10, and 11, Records Relating to Indian Removal, Records of the Commissary General of Subsistence, Cherokee Removal Records, First Board, Property Valuations, 1835–39, RG 75, entry 224, box 1, NA.

5. Yohnuguskee or Drowning Bear, Oct. 21, 1836, Records Relating to Indian Removal, Records of the Commissary General of Subsistence, Cherokee Removal Records, First Board, Property Valuations, 1835–39, RG 75, entry 224, box 3, Hutchins, Shaw, and Kellog, p. 74, NA.

6. James Mooney, Myths of the Cherokee (1900; reprint, New York: Dover, 1995), 523; Yohnuguskee or Drowning Bear, Oct. 21, 1836, p. 74, John Walker and Salagatahee, Oct. 21, 1836, p. 73, Two Dollar, Oct. 22, 1836, p. 75, Sutt, Oct. 22, 1836, p. 76, Records Relating to Indian Removal, Records of the Commissary General of Subsistence, Cherokee Removal Records, First Board, Property Valuations, 1835–39, RG 75, entry 224, box 3, Hutchins, Shaw, and Kellog, NA.

7. Book E, Records Relating to Indian Removal, Records of the Commissary General of Subsistence, Cherokee Removal Records, First Board, General Abstract of Valuations and Spoliations, RG 75, entry 238, box 1, NA.

8. Wilson Lumpkin to B.F. Butler, Oct. 26, 1836, Records Relating to Indian Removal, Records of the Commissary General of Subsistence, Cherokee Removal Records, First Board, LS, 1836–39, RG 75, entry 223, box 1, pp. 32–34, NA ("but a sense"); Wilson Lumpkin to Martin Van Buren, June 19, 1837, LR, OIA, reel 82, M-234, NA ("with great labour" and "business"); Wilson Lumpkin and John Kennedy to Lieutenant Van Horne, May 31, 1837, LR, OIA, reel 114, M-234, NA ("embarrassment and error"); John C. Mullay to C.A. Harris, Apr. 19, 1837, LR, OIA, reel 82, M-234, NA; Wilson Lumpkin and John Kennedy to Messrs. Welch and Jarrett, Nov. 22, 1837, LR, OIA, reel 114, M-234, NA ("in a spirit").

9. Wilson Lumpkin to J.E. Wool, Sept. 24, 1836, Records Relating to Indian Removal, Records of the Commissary General of Subsistence, Cherokee Removal Records, First Board, LS, 1836–39, RG 75, entry 223, box 1, pp. 18–19, NA ("will be executed"); Wilson Lumpkin to C.A. Harris, Oct. 26, 1836, Records Relating to Indian Removal, Records of the Commissary General of Subsistence, Cherokee Removal Records, First Board, LS, 1836–39, RG 75, entry 223, box 1, pp. 28–31, NA; Wilson Lumpkin and John Kennedy to John E. Wool, Jan. 23, 1837, Records Relating to Indian Removal, Records of the Commissary General of Subsistence, Cherokee Removal Records, First Board, LS, 1836–39, RG 75, entry 223, box 1, pp. 70–72, NA ("We would invite"); Wilson Lumpkin and John Kennedy to C.A. Harris, June 5,

1837, Records Relating to Indian Removal, Records of the Commissary General of Subsistence, Cherokee Removal Records, First Board, LS, 1836–39, RG 75, entry 223, box 1, pp. 23–26, NA ("to carry off"); Wilson Lumpkin and John Kennedy to Nathaniel Smith, Oct. 24, 1837, Records Relating to Indian Removal, Records of the Commissary General of Subsistence, Cherokee Removal Records, First Board, LS, 1836–39, RG 75, entry 223, box 1, pp. 77–78, NA ("the imperative command").

10. Fred S. Rolater, "The American Indian and the Origin of the Second American Party System," *Wisconsin Magazine of History* 76, no. 3 (Spring 1993): 180–203; Michael Paul Rogin, *Fathers and Children: Andrew Jackson and the Subjugation of the American Indian* (New York: Knopf, 1975), 56–57.

11. John Ross to Richard Taylor et al., Apr. 28, 1832, *PCJR*, 1:242–43; John Ridge to Stand Watie, Apr. 6, 1832, *Cherokee Cavaliers: Forty Years of Cherokee History as Told in the Correspondence of the Ridge-Watie-Boudinot Family*, ed. Edward Everett Dale and Gaston Litton (1939: reprint, Norman: University of Oklahoma Press, 1995), 8.

12. Richard Taylor to Elijah Hicks, Mar. 12, 1834, LR, OIA, reel 76, M-234, NA.

13. Steven D. Byas and Stephen D. Byas, "James Standifer, Sequatchie Valley Congressman," *Tennessee Historical Quarterly* 50, no. 2 (Summer 1991): 90–97; Nancy N. Scott, ed., *A Memoir of Hugh Lawson White* (Philadelphia, 1856), 154, 170; W.H. Underwood to Benjamin F. Currey, Mar. 7, 1836, enclosed in Currey to Herring, Apr. 6, 1836, LR, OIA, reel 80, M-234, NA; Benjamin F. Currey to Andrew Jackson, Nov. 24, 1834, LR, OIA, reel 76, M-234, NA; Hugh Lawson White to J.A. Whiteside, Sept. 17, 1835, *National Banner and Nashville Whig* (Nashville, Tenn.), Sept. 17, 1835, 3.

14. Linda K. Kerber, "The Abolitionist Perception of the Indian," *Journal of American History* 62, no. 2 (Sept. 1975): 271–95; Manisha Sinha, *The Slave's Cause: A History of Abolition* (New Haven: Yale University Press, 2016), 378; *Sixth Annual Report of the Board of Managers of the Massachusetts Anti-Slavery Society* (Boston, 1838), 4 ("primary object"); Hopkins Turney in the *Congressional Globe* (Washington, D.C., 1838), vol. 6, Appendix, 358 ("nothing more"); Joshua Holden to Benjamin F. Currey, Feb. 11, 1836, enclosed in Currey to Herring, Apr. 6, 1836, LR, OIA, reel 80, M-234, NA; Rezin Rawlings to Benjamin F. Currey, Feb. 18, 1836, enclosed in Currey to Herring, Apr. 6, 1836, LR, OIA, reel 80, M-234, NA.

15. Conference of John Ross, Edward Gunter, and John Mason, Jr., Nov. 6, 1837, *PCJR*, 1:537–40; John Ross to Lewis Ross, Nov. 6 – Nov. 11, 1837, *PCJR*, 1:542 ("under circumstances").

16. John Quincy Adams to Sherlock S. Gregory, Nov. 23, 1837, Adams Family Papers, Massachusetts Historical Society, reel 153; Sherlock Gregory to the Senate and House, Feb. 13, 1838, COIA, HR25A-G7.2, NA; Sherlock Gregory to the Senate and House, Dec. 3, 1837, COIA, HR25A-G7.2, NA; John L. Brooke, *Columbia Rising: Civil Life on the Upper Hudson from the Revolution to the Age of Jackson* (Chapel Hill: University of North Carolina Press, 2010), 594n76; Memorial of Citizens of Condor, New York, Apr. 30, 1838, PM, COIA, SEN25A-H6, NA; Memorial of Citizens of Portland, Maine, May 7, 1838, PM, COIA, SEN25A-H6, NA; Memorial of Citizens of Holliston, Massachusetts, May 7, 1838, PM, COIA, SEN25A-H6, NA; Memorial of Citizens of Bristol, Connecticut, May 11, 1838, PM, COIA, SEN25A-H6, NA.

17. Memorial of Citizens of Union, New York, May 11, 1838, PM, COIA, SEN25A-H6, NA.

18. Memorial of Citizens of Concord, Massachusetts, May 11, 1838, PM, COIA, SEN25A-H6, NA.

19. 25th Cong., 2nd sess., H.Doc. 316, pp. 2, 3 ("cup of bitterness"); 24th Cong., 1st sess., H.Doc. 286; 25th Cong., 2nd sess., S.Doc. 121, p. 36 ("fraud" and "delusion"); John F. Schermerhorn to Lewis Cass, Mar. 3, 1836, LR, OIA, reel 80, M-234, NA ("overshot"); John Ridge and Stand Watie to John F. Schermerhorn, Feb. 28, 1836, enclosed in Schermerhorn to Lewis Cass, Feb. 27, 1836, LR, OIA, reel 80, M-234, NA ("Do you love" and "rich").

20. Wilson Lumpkin to Andrew Jackson, Sept. 24, 1836, LR, OIA, reel 80, M-234, NA ("too ignorant"); Wilson Lumpkin, *The Removal of the Cherokee Indians from Georgia* (New York: Dodd, Mead, 1907), 1:167 ("treated as children"); Wilson Lumpkin to Andrew Jackson, Sept. 24, 1836, LR, OIA, reel 80, M-234, NA ("just as much"); *Southern Banner* (Athens, Ga.), Nov. 12, 1835, 2; William Drayton, *The South Vindicated from the Treason and Fanaticism of the Northern Abolitionists* (Philadelphia, 1836), 102; Chancellor Harper, *Memoir on Slavery* (Charleston, 1838), 11–12.

21. William Lindsay to C.A. Harris, July 20, 1837, LR, OIA, reel 114, M-234, NA ("slave"); Theda Perdue, "Clan and Court: Another Look at the Early Cherokee Republic," *American Indian Quarterly* 24, no. 4 (Autumn 2000): 562–69; Daniel S. Butrick, *Cherokee Removal: The Journal of Rev. Daniel S. Butrick* (Park Hill, Okla.: Trail of Tears Association, 1998), 36 ("How vain").

22. Amanda L. Paige, Fuller L. Bumpers, and Daniel F. Littlefield, Jr., *Chickasaw Removal* (Ada, Okla.: Chickasaw Press, 2010), 115–70.

23. W. Williams to J.J. Abert, Feb. 8, 1838, Records of the Office of the Chief of Engineers, Map File, RG 77, U.S. 125–6, NACP.

24. W. Williams to J.J. Abert, Feb. 8, 1838, Records of the Office of the Chief of Engineers, Map File, RG 77, U.S. 125–6, NACP.

25. W. Williams to J.J. Abert, Feb. 8, 1838, Records of the Office of the Chief of Engineers, Map File, RG 77, U.S. 125–6, NACP.

26. Alexander Macomb to Winfield Scott, Apr. 6, 1838, and Alexander Macomb to Winfield Scott, May 3, 1838, 25th Cong., 2d sess., H.Doc. 453, pp. 1–2; Winfield Scott to Joel Poinsett, May 18, 1838, 25th Cong., 2d sess., H.Exec.Doc. 219, pp. 7–8 ("an early"); W. Williams to J.J. Abert, Feb. 8, 1838, Records of the Office of the Chief of Engineers, Map File, RG 77, U.S. 125–6, NACP ("the most inoffensive").

27. John Niven, *John C. Calhoun and the Price of Union: A Biography* (Baton Rouge: Louisiana State University Press, 1988), 215; *Federal Union* (Milledgeville, Ga.), June 6, 1833, 3; *Washington News* (Washington, Ga.), April 6, 1830, p. 3; George Washington Featherstonhaugh, *A Canoe Voyage up the Minnay Sotor* (London, 1847), 2:255–56.

28. After placer mining was exhausted in the early 1830s, there was a second boom in the 1840s, set off by hard rock mining. Otis E. Young, "The Southern Gold Rush, 1828–1836," *Journal of Southern History* 48, no. 3 (1982): 391; *Georgia Constitutionalist* (Augusta, Ga.), Aug. 2, 1838, 2 ("high price"). None other than J.D. Beers dominated the gold mining industry in Georgia in the early 1830s, and he declined to reveal how much gold he was shipping abroad. I am indebted to Ann Daly for sharing her knowledge of gold mining in the 1830s.

29. *Southern Banner*, Nov. 25, 1842, p. 2; *Congressional Globe* (Washington, D.C., 1838), vol. 6, Appendix, 562 ("permanent residence").

30. *Congressional Globe*, vol. 6, Appendix, 480, 484–85.

31. *Congressional Globe*, vol. 6, Appendix, 480, 484–85.

32. Stephen Neal Dennis, *A Proud Little Town: LaFayette, Georgia: 1835–1885* (Walker County, Georgia Governing Authority, 2010), 209, 211.

33. The 1850 U.S. Census enumerates 1,664 enslaved people and 11,408 white people.
34. Thomas Jefferson, *Notes on the State of Virginia* (Philadelphia, 1788), 172–73; *Congressional Globe*, vol. 6, Appendix, 361.
35. *Congressional Globe*, 6:423; John Ross to Mrs. Bayard, June 5, 1838, *PCJR*, 1:644.
36. Orders, No. 34, May 24, 1838, 25th Cong., 2d sess., H.Doc. 453, pp. 14–15; *Federal Union*, Apr. 24, 1838, 2.
37. There were thirty-one companies of militia in the Cherokee Nation when Scott arrived, and eventually twenty-six companies of regulars joined them, though Scott then began dismissing the volunteers. Winfield Scott to Joel Poinsett, May 18, 1838, and Winfield Scott to Joel Poinsett, June 15, 1838, 25th Cong., 2d sess., H.Doc. 453, pp. 7–8, and 22–23; Sarah H. Hill, "'To Overawe the Indians and Give Confidence to the Whites': Preparations for the Removal of the Cherokee Nation from Georgia," *Georgia Historical Quarterly* 95, no. 4 (Winter 2011): 473 ("to broil"), 477–78, 483 ("so large"); N.W. Pittman and H.P. Strickland to Henchin Strickland, June 6, 1838, folder 1, in the John R. Peacock Collection #1895-Z, SHC ("taking Indians" and "what it was cracked up"); Butrick, *Cherokee Removal*, 1–2. Sarah H. Hill, "Cherokee Removal Scenes: Ellijay, Georgia, 1838," *Southern Spaces*, Aug. 23, 2012, http://southernspaces.org/2012/cherokee-removal-scenes-ellijay-georgia-1838 (accessed July 7, 2016).
38. Hill, "'To Overawe the Indians," 490 ("no crime"); John Gray Bynum to J.H. Simpson, June 5, 1838, folder 25, in the William Preston Bynum Papers #117, SHC ("A more religious"); John R. Finger, *The Eastern Band of Cherokees, 1819–1900* (Knoxville: University of Tennessee Press, 1984), 20–40, 105; Sharlotte Neely, *Snowbird Cherokees: People of Persistence* (Athens: University of Georgia Press, 2002), 11–35.
39. Butrick, *Cherokee Removal*, 1–3, 6, 8, 9.
40. Dennis, *A Proud Little Town*, 256–57 ("in every direction"); Winfield Scott to A.P. Bagby, June 26, 1838, LR, OIA, reel 82, M-234, NA; John Kennedy, Thomas W. Wilson, and James Liddell to C.A. Harris, May 4, 1838, LR, OIA, reel 82, M-234, NA ("ragged"); Butrick, *Cherokee Removal*, 4.
41. Return of Property left by Indians and sold by the Agents in Cass County, Georgia, and Return of Property for the Counties of Cherokee, AL, and Cobb, Gilmer, Floyd . . . in Georgia, Records Relating to Indian Removal, Records of the Commissary General of Subsistence, Cherokee Removal Records, First Board, Returns of Property, 1838, RG 75, entry 227, box 1, NA; Return of Property left by the Indians in Macon County, North Carolina ("work hands"), Records Relating to Indian Removal, Records of the Commissary General of Subsistence, Cherokee Removal Records, First Board, Returns of Property, 1838, RG 75, entry 227, box 2, NA.
42. Matthew T. Gregg and David M. Wishart, "The Price of Cherokee Removal," *Explorations in Economic History* 49, no. 4 (Oct. 1, 2012): table 4, p. 431.
43. Since data are incomplete for three of the detachments that followed the northern and Hildebrand routes, I am extrapolating from the mortality rates of other detachments that traveled along the same route. Gregg and Wishart, "The Price of Cherokee Removal," table 4, p. 431; Robert Remini, *Andrew Jackson and the Course of American Democracy* (New York: Harper & Row, 1984), 435–36.
44. Russell Thornton's estimate of a total loss of eight thousand is the most often-cited figure, but Jack D. Baker, the president of the Oklahoma Historical Society and a citizen of the Cherokee Nation, points out that Thornton erred in his calculation by assuming that the Drennon Roll of 1851 included all Cherokees living in the West,

when in fact it contained only those who had migrated after the Treaty of New Echota, plus their descendants. The Old Settler Roll of 1851 must be added to the Drennon Roll for a complete count of Cherokees. Baker also notes that, given the Old Settler Roll's enumeration of 3,273 individuals in 1851, Thornton's estimate of 5,000 in 1835 seems unlikely. After correcting for these errors, a reprojection yields a figure of about 3,500. The figure of 1,000 deaths comes from extrapolating from known data. On three deaths: Butrick, *Cherokee Removal*, 41, 43, 45, 46, 47.

45. Grant Foreman, *Indian Removal* (Norman: University of Oklahoma Press, 1932), 305, 311; George Hicks and Collins McDonald to John Ross, Mar. 15, 1839, *PCJR*, 1:701.

CHAPTER 11: 'TIS NO SIN

1. *Pensacola Gazette* (Pensacola, Fla.), Mar. 16, 1839, 2 (*"perfect* knowledge").

2. Lewis Cass to John H. Eaton, Mar. 27, 1835, CGLS, vol. 3, pp. 42–44, NA.

3. Claudio Saunt, *A New Order of Things: Property, Power, and the Transformation of the Creek Indians, 1733–1816* (New York: Cambridge University Press, 1999), 34–37; John T. Sprague, *The Origin, Progress, and Conclusion of the Florida War* (New York, 1848), 94, 272–73, 283; John Bemrose, *Reminiscences of the Second Seminole War*, ed. John K. Mahon (Gainesville: University of Florida Press, 1966), 88 ("famish").

4. Wiley Thompson to Elbert Herring, Oct. 28, 1834, LR, OIA, reel 806, frame 84, M-234, NA ("lose many"); J.W. Harris to George Gibson, May 11, 1836, CGLR, box 15, Creek, NA; J. Van Horne to George Gibson, May 23, 1836, CGLR, box 15, Creek, NA ("These people"); J. Van Horne to George Gibson, June 5, 1836 [mistakenly dated May 5], CGLR, box 15, Creek, NA ("It would have had a wholesome effect"); other Van Horne quotations: Journal of a party of Seminole Indians conducted by Lieut. J. Van Horne, May 23, 1836, CGLR, box 15, Creek, NA.

5. Joseph W. Harris to Lewis Cass, July 25, 1836, LR, OIA, reel 290, frame 91, M-234, NA (quotations); Journal of a party of Seminole Indians conducted by Lieut. J. Van Horne, May 23, 1836, CGLR, box 15, Creek, NA.

6. Journal of a party of Seminole Indians conducted by Lieut. J. Van Horne, May 23, 1836, CGLR, box 15, Creek, NA; J. Van Horne to George Gibson, June 5, 1836 [mistakenly dated May 5], CGLR, box 15, Creek, NA ("even while"); Joseph W. Harris to Lewis Cass, July 25, 1836, LR, OIA, reel 290, frame 91, M-234, NA; J. Van Horne to George Gibson, Aug. 23, 1836, CGLR, box 15, Creek, NA ("dissipated").

7. Jacob Rhett Motte, *Journey into Wilderness: An Army Surgeon's Account of Life in Camp and Field during the Creek and Seminole Wars, 1836–1838*, ed. James F. Sunderman (Gainesville: University of Florida Press, 1953), 205.

8. Brent R. Weisman, "Nativism, Resistance, and Ethnogenesis of the Florida Seminole Indian Identity," *Historical Archaeology* 41, no. 4 (2007): 198–212; Samuel Watson, "Seminole Strategy, 1812–1858: A Prospectus for Further Research," in *America's Hundred Years' War: U.S. Expansion to the Gulf Coast and the Fate of the Seminole, 1763–1858*, ed. William S. Belko (Gainesville: University Press of Florida, 2011), 155–80.

9. I have interpolated from the figures in Erna Risch, *Quartermaster Support of the Army: A History of the Corps, 1775–1939* (1962; reprint, Washington, D.C.: Center of Military History, U.S. Army, 1989), 228; Bemrose, *Reminiscences of the Second Seminole War*, 25 ("ridiculous"); Reynold M. Wik, "Captain Nathaniel Wyche Hunter and the Florida Indian Campaigns, 1837–41," *Florida Historical Quarterly* 39, no. 1 (July 1960): 68.

10. Sprague, *Origin, Progress, and Conclusion of the Florida War*, 143 ("outlines"); Thomas S. Jesup to J.R. Poinsett, Apr. 9, 1837, LR, OIA, reel 290, frame 138, M-234, NA; Diary of Nathaniel Wyche Hunter, Feb. 27, 1840, HCP ("Wholly ignorant").

11. [W.W. Smith], *Sketch of the Seminole War and Sketches During a Campaign, by a Lieutenant* (Charleston, S.C., 1836), 69 ("one vast"), 73 ("celerity"); Myer M. Cohen, *Notices of Florida and the Campaigns* (Charleston, S.C., 1836), 154; Motte, *Journey into Wilderness*, 189, 300; George Henry Preble, "A Canoe Expedition into the Everglades in 1842," *Tequesta* 5 (1945): 44, 49; William Bowen Campbell to David Campbell, Correspondence, Nov. 9, 1836, Campbell Family Papers, DMR.

12. Motte, *Journey into Wilderness*, 32, 124; Frank Laumer, *Dade's Last Command* (Gainesville: University Press of Florida, 1995), 2; Horn, "Tennessee Volunteers," 244; Motte, *Journey into Wilderness*, 68–69 ("slight"); Risch, *Quartermaster Support of the Army*, 229; Proceedings of the Board of Examination, Aug. 23, 1836, letter book 6, Thomas Sidney Jesup Papers, LC; G.W. Allen to William S. Foster, Feb. 10, 1837, box 3, folder 15, EAH.

13. John Campbell to David Campbell, Correspondence, July 10, 1836, Campbell Family Papers ("the progress"); [Smith], *Sketch of the Seminole War*, 28; Woodburne Potter, *The War in Florida* (Baltimore, 1836), 143, 147 ("quartered"); John K. Mahon, *History of the Second Seminole War, 1835–1842* (1967; revised ed., Gainesville: University of Florida Press, 1985), 120; Edward A. Mueller, "Steamboat Activity in Florida during the Second Seminole War," *Florida Historical Quarterly* 64, no. 4 (Apr. 1986): 407–31; *Army and Navy Chronicle*, July 1 to Dec. 31, 1836, vol. 3, 299 ("enfeebled"); Sprague, *Origin, Progress, and Conclusion of the Florida War*, 379.

14. Michael G. Schene, "Ballooning in the Second Seminole War," *Florida Historical Quarterly* 55, no. 4 (Apr. 1977): 480–82 ("entirely impracticable" on 481); F. Stansbury Haydon, "First Attempts at Military Aeronautics in the United States," *Journal of the American Military Foundation* 2, no. 3 (Autumn 1938): 131–38 (Gaines quotation on 135).

15. James M. White to James Barbour, June 4, 1831, LR, OIA, reel 290, frame 68, M-234, NA.

16. Thomas Jesup's account of the Capture of Osceola, 1858, box 5, EAH; Thomas S. Jesup to C.A. Harris, June 5, 1837, LR, OIA, reel 290, frame 149, M-234, NA (Jesup quotations); Thomas S. Jesup to J.R. Poinsett, June 7, 1837, LR, OIA, reel 290, frame 151, M-234, NA; Truman Cross to Thomas Jesup, July 27, 1837, box 5, EAH.

17. Diary of Nathaniel Wyche Hunter, Apr. 14, 1840, HCP; Diary of Nathaniel Wyche Hunter, Apr. 15, 1840, HCP ("hackneyed"); Robert M. McLane to Catherine Mary McLane, Nov. 24, 1837, Box 2, Louis McLane Papers, LC; *Henry IV*, part 1, 1.2.99–100.

18. Diary of Nathaniel Wyche Hunter, Mar. 17, 1842, pp. 169–70, HCP ("How absurd!"); J.R. Vinton to Thomas S. Jesup, May 10, 1844, Correspondence, Thomas Sidney Jesup Papers, DMR ("war of posts"); Mahon, *History of the Second Seminole War*, 119, 261, 282.

19. Diary of Nathaniel Wyche Hunter, Apr. 2 and 15, 1840, HCP; John Campbell, "The Seminoles, the 'Bloodhound War,' and Abolitionism, 1796–1865," *Journal of Southern History* 72, no. 2 (May 2006): 281 ("Peace-Hounds"); Mahon, *History of the Second Seminole War*, 265–67.

20. Mahon, *History of the Second Seminole War*, 119, 261, 282; Ethan Allen Hitchcock to Samuel Cooper, Dec. 16, 1840, box 2, folder 7, EAH; Diary of Nathaniel Wyche Hunter, May 18, 1840, HCP ("imbecile dotard").

21. Department of Defense, *Selected Manpower Statistics, Fiscal Year 1997* (Washington, D.C.: U.S. Government Printing Office, 1997), 46–47; Sprague, *Origin, Progress, and Conclusion of the Florida War,* 103–6; [Smith], *Sketch of the Seminole War,* 112–13 "all the specious talk"); James M. Denham and Canter Brown, Jr., "South Carolina Volunteers in the Second Seminole War: A Nullifier Debacle as Prelude to the Palmetto State Gubernatorial Election of 1836," in *America's Hundred Years' War,* 213–15; John Burbidge to Rosina Mix, Feb. 23, 1836, folder 1, Rosina Mix Papers #02201-z, SHC ("A great consideration").

22. W.S. Steele, "The Last Command: The Dade Massacre," *Tequesta* 46 (1986): 9; James M. Denham, "'Some Prefer the Seminoles': Violence and Disorder among Soldiers and Settlers in the Second Seminole War, 1835–1842," *Florida Historical Quarterly* 70, no. 1 (July 1991): 39. Dollar conversion is by relative labor earnings. Samuel H. Williamson, "Seven Ways to Compute the Relative Value of a U.S. Dollar Amount, 1774 to Present," MeasuringWorth, 2019.

23. Alexander Beaufort Meek, "Journal of the Florida Expedition, 1836," Alexander Beaufort Meek Papers, DMR ("Indians"); William Bowen Campbell to David Campbell, Correspondence, June 19, 1836, Campbell Family Papers ("excitement"); William Bowen Campbell to Fanny Campbell, Correspondence, Oct. 23, 1836, Campbell Family Papers ("broken down").

24. Diary of Nathaniel Wyche Hunter, July 1845, p. 151, HCP ("eternal dripping"); John K. Mahon, "Letters from the Second Seminole War," *Florida Historical Quarterly* 36, no. 4 (Apr. 1958): 339 ("The Dr."); "Recollections of a Campaign in Florida," *Yale Literary Magazine* 11, no. 11 (Dec. 1845): 77; Bemrose, *Reminiscences of the Second Seminole War,* 102 ("Indians, Indians!"); Sprague, *Origin, Progress, and Conclusion of the Florida War,* 379 ("general sinking"); Capt. P. Morrison to J.R. Poinsett, July 26, 1838, LR, OIA, reel 290, frame 436, M-234, NA ("completely prostrated").

25. "The Last Days of Fort Roger Jones," 1839, William W. Pew Papers, DMR, Duke University.

26. James D. Elderkin, *Biographical Sketches and Anecdotes of a Soldier of Three Wars* (Detroit, 1899), 35 ("whole stock"); Bemrose, *Reminiscences of the Second Seminole War,* 94, 99 ("lay"); Denise L. Doolan, Carlota Dobaño, and J. Kevin Baird, "Acquired Immunity to Malaria," *Clinical Microbiology Reviews* 22, no. 1 (Jan. 2009): 13–36.

27. C. Casey, Records of the Accounting Officers of the Department of the Treasury, Settled Indian Accounts, RG 217, entry 525, box 240, account 20458, NA; I. Clark, Records of the Accounting Officers of the Department of the Treasury, Settled Indian Accounts, RG 217, entry 525, box 260, account 629, NA; L.B. Webster, Records of the Accounting Officers of the Department of the Treasury, Settled Indian Accounts, RG 217, entry 525, box 260, account 638, NA; Bemrose, *Reminiscences of the Second Seminole War,* 94, 102.

28. Mahon, *History of the Second Seminole War,* 325; Sprague, *Origin, Progress, and Conclusion of the Florida War,* 401, 447.

29. Horn, "Tennessee Volunteers," 174; "Recollections of a Campaign in Florida," *Yale Literary Magazine* 11, no. 11 (Dec. 1845): 76; Diary of Nathaniel Wyche Hunter, Dec. 20, 1840, p. 102, HCP; Heintzelman diary, Dec. 22, 1840, reel 3, Samuel Peter Heintzelman Papers, LC; William Bowen Campbell to David Campbell, Correspondence, Nov. 2, 1836, Campbell Family Papers ("drunkard").

30. Diary of Nathaniel Wyche Hunter, Mar. 7, 1842, p. 166, ("harrowing"), Mar. 7, 1842, p. 168, ("soporifics"), and July [?], 1845, p. 152, HCP.

31. John W. Phelps, "Letters of Lieutenant John W. Phelps, U.S.A., 1837–1838," *Florida Historical Quarterly* 6, no. 2 (Oct. 1927): 70.

32. Potter, *War in Florida*, 40.

33. Cohen, *Notices of Florida and the Campaigns*, 189–90; [Smith], *Sketch of the Seminole War*, 247 ("scalped"); Horn, "Tennessee Volunteers," 356 ("weltering"), 358, 360 ("Who . . . can suppress"), 366 ("in a most").

34. Electus Backus, "Diary of a Campaign in Florida, in 1837–8," *The Historical Magazine* 10 (Sept. 1866): 282 ("grab game"); Diary of Nathaniel Wyche Hunter, Dec. 19, 1840, HCP ("bagging the game"); Phelps, "Letters of Lieutenant John W. Phelps," 67–84; Heintzelman diary, Oct. 29, 1836, reel 2, Samuel Peter Heintzelman Papers ("examined"); Diary of Nathaniel Wyche Hunter, Dec. 16, 1840, HCP.

35. Motte, *Journey into Wilderness*, 120 ("miserable"), 205, 218–19; Frank L. White, Jr., "The Journals of Lieutenant John Pickell, 1836–1837," *Florida Historical Quarterly* 38, no. 2 (Oct. 1959): 165; Richard Fields to John Ross, Dec. 6, 1837, *PCJR*, 1:564–66 ("I never").

36. Nathan R. Lawres, "Reconceptualizing the Landscape: Changing Patterns of Land Use in a Coalescent Culture," *Journal of Anthropological Research* 70, no. 4 (2014): 563–64; Thomas Jesup, June 6, 1838, letter book 7, Thomas Sidney Jesup Papers, LC; Mahon, "Letters from the Second Seminole War," 345.

37. "Recollections of a Campaign in Florida," *Yale Literary Magazine* 11, no. 111 (Jan. 1846): 130–37 ("fate"); Heintzelman diary, Aug. 7, 1839, reel 3, Samuel Peter Heintzelman Papers ("treacherous"); Sprague, *Origin, Progress, and Conclusion of the Florida War*, 254.

38. John Eaton to Lewis Cass, Mar. 8, 1835, LR, OIA, reel 806, frame 101, M-234, NA; Horn, "Tennessee Volunteers," 248; Denham and Brown, "South Carolina Volunteers," 226 ("to discover"); Samuel Forry, "Letters of Samuel Forry, Surgeon U.S. Army, 1837: Part I," *Florida Historical Quarterly* 6, no. 3 (Jan. 1928): 134 ("pockets"); Diary of Nathaniel Wyche Hunter, Nov. 1839, pp. 28–29, HCP ("knocked").

39. Robert M. McLane to Louis McLane, Jan. 6, 1838, Box 2, Louis McLane Papers, LC ("I speak"); *Articles of Agreement and Association of the Florida Peninsula Land Company* (New York, 1836); John Lee Williams, *The Territory of Florida* (New York, 1837), 301; Sprague, *Origin, Progress, and Conclusion of the Florida War*, 287 ("spirit").

40. Thomas S. Jesup to J.R. Poinsett, June 16, 1837, LR, OIA, reel 290, frame 158, M-234, NA; Truman Cross to Thomas Jesup, July 27, 1837, box 5, EAH; J.R. Poinsett to Thomas S. Jesup, July 25, 1837, *Court of Inquiry—Operations in Florida*, 25th Cong., 2nd sess., H.Doc. 78, serial 323, no. 3, p. 33; Thomas Jesup to J.R. Poinsett, Feb. 11, 1838, 25th Cong., 2d sess., H.Exec.Doc. 219, pp. 5–7; Sprague, *Origin, Progress, and Conclusion of the Florida War*, 202 ("ought to be"); Ethan Allen Hitchcock to Samuel Cooper, Oct. 22, 1840, box 2, folder 7, EAH ("to avoid").

41. 28th Cong., 1st sess., H.Doc. 82, p.2; Mahon, *History of the Second Seminole War*, 325; Williamson, "Seven Ways to Compute the Relative Value of a U.S. Dollar Amount."

42. Estimates of the size of the Seminole population varied widely. If there were five thousand people, then approximately 20 percent died during the war, but that estimate may be too high. The uncertainty reflects just how little the United States knew about the people it was fighting. In converting to 2018 dollars, I am using labor cost, which is measured as a multiple of the average wage of unskilled workers. Williamson, "Seven Ways to Compute the Relative Value of a U.S. Dollar Amount."

43. George Rollie Adams, *General William S. Harney* (Lincoln: University of Nebraska Press, 2001); "Notes on the Passage Across the Everglades," *Tequesta* 20 (1960): 57–65.

44. "Notes on the Passage Across the Everglades," 57–65.

AFTERWORD: THE PRICE OF EXPULSION

1. Isaac McCoy, *History of Baptist Indian Missions* (Washington, D.C., 1840), 581–82 ("He must be"); George A. Schultz, *An Indian Canaan: Isaac McCoy and the Vision of an Indian State* (Norman: University of Oklahoma Press, 1972), 182–203.

2. Leonard L. Richards, *The Slave Power: The Free North and Southern Domination, 1780–1860* (Baton Rouge: Louisiana State University Press, 2000), 162–64, 179–84; Leslie Friedman Goldstein, "A 'Triumph of Freedom' After All? Prigg v. Pennsylvania Re-examined," *Law and History Review* 29, no. 3 (Aug. 2011): 786n81; Rebecca J. Scott, *Slave Emancipation in Cuba: The Transition to Free Labor, 1860–1899* (Pittsburgh: University of Pittsburgh Press, 1985), p. 7, table 1; W.L.G. Smith, *The Life and Times of Lewis Cass* (New York, 1856), 702 ("greater moral"); Willard Carl Klunder, *Lewis Cass and the Politics of Moderation* (Kent, Ohio: Kent State University Press, 1996), 289 ("swallow Cuba"), 296–97, 310 ("the abominable").

3. Wilson Lumpkin, *The Removal of the Cherokee Indians from Georgia* (New York: Dodd, Mead, 1907), 1:40 ("particular mission"); Head men and warriors of Upper Creeks to James Wright, May 1, 1771, enclosed in Memorial of James Wright to the Lords of Trade, 1771, *Colonial Records of the State of Georgia* (Athens: University of Georgia Press, 1976), vol. 28, 2:806–15.

4. Virginia Miller, "Dr. Thomas Miller and His Times," *Records of the Columbia Historical Society* 3 (1900): 308–9.

5. Black Hawk, *Black Hawk's Autobiography*, ed. Roger L. Nicholas (1833; Ames: Iowa State University Press, 1999), 79.

6. "The President's Visit," *Niles' Register*, June 15, 1833, 256; Black Hawk, *Black Hawk's Autobiography*, 80–85.

7. Black Hawk, *Black Hawk's Autobiography*, 7, and introduction, xiv–xv; Roger L. Nichols, *Black Hawk and the Warrior's Path*, 2nd. ed. (Malden, Mass.: Wiley & Sons, 2017), 164.

8. Hopoethle-Yoholo to T.S. Jesup, June 12, 1836, Correspondence, Thomas Sidney Jesup Papers, DMR; Opoithleyahola to Abraham Lincoln, Aug. 15, 1861, LR, OIA, reel 230, frames 595–596, M-234, NA; A.B. Campbell to Joseph K. Barnes, Feb. 5, 1862, and George W. Collamore to William P. Dole, Apr. 21, 1862, *The War of the Rebellion: A Compilation of the Official Records of the Union and Confederate Armies* (Washington, D.C., 1899), series 2, 4:6–7, 11–12.

9. The Choctaws chartered a school system a year after the Cherokees but put it into operation in 1842, nearly a decade before their Cherokee neighbors. William G. McLoughlin, *After the Trail of Tears: The Cherokees' Struggle for Sovereignty, 1839–1880* (Chapel Hill: University of North Carolina Press, 1993), 86–120; Christina Snyder, *Great Crossings: Indians, Settlers, and Slaves in the Age of Jackson* (New York: Oxford University Press, 2017), 272–96; John Ross to John Howard Payne, Mar. 5, 1836, *PCJR*, 1:390 ("the only chance"); Clarissa W. Confer, *The Cherokee Nation in the Civil War* (Norman: University of Oklahoma Press, 2007).

10. "Trans-Atlantic Slave Trade Database," https://www.slavevoyages.org/voyages /SzPhOxXs (accessed May 8, 2019); Patricia R. Wickman, *Osceola's Legacy* (Tuscaloosa: University of Alabama Press, 1991), 89–103 (quotation on 100).

11. Wickman, *Osceola's Legacy*, 144–53 (quotation on 150).

12. John T. Fulton, Records of the Accounting Officers of the Department of the Treasury, Settled Indian Accounts, RG 217, entry 525, box 240, account 20610, NA; "Journal of John Shelby," *A Sorrowful Journey*, ed. Randall L. Buchman (Defiance, Ohio: Defiance College Press, 2007), 49; Journal of Edward Deas, Feb. 4, 1836,

CGLR, box 9, Creek, NA; Census of North Carolina Cherokees, 1840, William Holland Thomas Papers, DMR; "To Philanthropists in the United States, Generally, and to Christians in Particular, on the Condition and Prospects of the Indians," [Dec. 1, 1831?], reel 7, frame 861, MP ("experiment").

13. There is no precise way of calculating the cost of expulsion, given that some of the expenses were absorbed by the U.S. Army in fighting wars or conducting operations against native peoples. The difference between the sum total of the average annual expenses of the army and the Indian Department between 1820–29, before expulsion, and 1830–42, during expulsion, is approximately $75 million. To approximate federal expenditures on deportation in 1836 and 1838, I subtracted the average annual War Department and Indian Department expenditure between 1820 and 1829 from the expenditures in 1836 and 1838. Budget statistics are available in U.S. Bureau of the Census, *Historical Statistics of the United States, 1789–1945* (U.S. Department of Commerce, 1949). I am converting to 2018 dollars by measuring the cost of deportation as a percentage of the output of the entire economy. Samuel H. Williamson, "Seven Ways to Compute the Relative Value of a U.S. Dollar Amount, 1790 to Present," MeasuringWorth, 2019.

14. Figures calculated from data available in Steven Ruggles, Sarah Flood, Ronald Goeken, Josiah Grover, Erin Meyer, Jose Pacas, and Matthew Sobek, IPUMS USA: Version 8.0 [dataset] (Minneapolis, Minn.: IPUMS, 2018), https://doi.org/10.18128/D010.V8.0.

15. Records Relating to Indian Removal, Records of the Commissary General of Subsistence, Choctaw Removal Records, Claiborne, Graves, Tyler, Gaines, and Rush, Journal of Proceedings, 1842–45, RG 75, entry 274, box 2, NA.

16. U.S. Census of 1840 and 1860, Steven Manson, Jonathan Schroeder, David Van Riper, and Steven Ruggles, *IPUMS National Historical Geographic Information System: Version 13.0* [Database] (Minneapolis: University of Minnesota, 2018), http://doi.org/10.18128/D050.V13.0; Virginia O. Foscue, "The Place Names of Sumter County, Alabama," *Publication of the American Dialect Society* 65, no. 1 (1978): 62.

17. Nance's first two purchases were just outside the Choctaw Nation, but as the General Land Office patent database shows, he later purchased 200 acres within its former boundaries. James Nance to George Nance, Sept. 10, 1832, James Nance to his sister, Jan. 7, 1833, and James Nance to George Nance, Sept. 11, 1836, James Nance Letters, Alabama Department of Archives and History, Montgomery; U.S. Census of 1850 and 1860.

18. Michael Tadman, *Speculators and Slaves: Masters, Traders, and Slaves in the Old South* (Madison: University of Wisconsin Press, 1989), 133–78.

19. *David Leavitt Reciever &c. against Richard M. Blatchford, John L. Gramham, & Lewis Curtis . . . Million and First Half Million Trusts* (New York, 1852), 100, 403; Fritz Redlich, *Molding of American Banking: Men and Ideas* (New York: Hafner, 1951), 2:342–43; William L. MacKenzie, *The Lives and Opinions of Benj'n Franklin Butler* (Boston, 1845), 147 ("did some").

20. To convert dollar values in this instance I am using the multiple of the average wage that a worker would need to purchase the commodities. Statement of Sales of Furniture at No. 30 West 14th St, box 30, folder 867, LPC; Williamson, "Seven Ways to Compute the Relative Value of a U.S. Dollar Amount"; Assets belonging to the Estate of J.D. Beers, August 1865, box 30, folder 867, LPC; Inventory of real estate, box 30, folder 867, LPC.

21. I am using relative labor earnings to convert to 2018 dollars. Lewis Curtis to William Giles, n.d., box 29, folder 857, LPC; Joseph Curtis to Benjamin Curtis, Sept. 12,

1865, box 27, folder 823, LPC; Benjamin Curtis to Joseph Curtis, Feb. 3, 1866, box 27, folder 823, LPC.

22. "American Women Near European Thrones," *Evening Star* (Washington, D.C.), Sept. 12, 1908, 6 ("fashionable"); "Heirlooms and Flowers Mark Society Wedding," *Bridgeport Telegram* (Bridgeport, Conn.), Aug. 17, 1923, 1 ("one of the most brilliant").

23. William Apess, "An Indian's Looking Glass for the White Man," in *On Our Own Ground: The Complete Writings of William Apess, a Pequot*, ed. Barry O'Connell (Amherst: University of Massachusetts Press, 1992), 157; "Garrison Journal; At the Fish Library, a Chronicle of Death and Taxes," *New York Times*, Jan. 6, 1992, B4.

24. One speculator's accounting of 120 square miles of land showed an 80 percent profit, yet the trustees of the New York and Mississippi Land Company insisted on a minimum profit of 200 percent. I calculated Chickasaw losses by assuming that speculators resold property for twice what they paid for it on paper. That estimate is sufficiently conservative to allow for the cost of doing business. Individual reserves sold for a total of $3,827,236. For unreserved lands, I include only the three million acres that sold for $3,073,570 through 1841, when land companies were most active. On profits: David Hubbard to J.D. Beers, Jan. 10, 1835, box 39, folder 1058, LPC; Richard Bolton to Lewis Curtis, Dec. 9, 1836, box 1, NYMS; Richard Bolton to John Bolton, Sept. 25, 1835, box 1, NYMS. On reserve sales: Records Relating to Indian Removal, Records of the Commissary General of Subsistence, Chickasaw Removal Records, Reports of Land Sales and Deeds, 1836–39, RG 75, entry 255, box 1, NA. On the size of corporations in the 1830s: Robert E. Wright, "US Corporate Development 1790–1860," *The Magazine of Early American Datasets (MEAD)*, https://repository.upenn.edu/mead/7/ (accessed Sept. 25, 2018). Using the 1847 Chickasaw Census, I am assuming 3.6 people per family, excluding slaves, since they were considered a form of wealth. Regarding Choctaw losses, in 1860, the U.S. Senate estimated that the Choctaws were owed nearly $3 million, but that sum does not account for the collusion between speculators and the forced sale of millions of acres, which lowered market prices. Assuming that speculators averaged a 100 percent profit, it is easy to arrive at losses exceeding $10 million. Creek losses must be figured by subtracting the price paid to Creeks (3¢ per acre, if on average they received $10 for every allotment) from the price at which speculators sold Creek lands (anywhere from $2 to $4 per acre). 44th Cong., 1st sess., H.Misc. Doc. 40, pp. 31–32; Mary Elizabeth Young, *Redskins, Ruffleshirts, and Rednecks: Indian Allotments in Alabama and Mississippi, 1830–1860* (Norman: University of Oklahoma Press, 1961), 107–12.

25. 24th Cong., 1st sess., S.Doc. 246, p. 5.

26. John R. Finger, *The Eastern Band of Cherokees, 1819–1900* (Knoxville: University of Tennessee Press, 1984); J. Anthony Paredes, "Back from Disappearance: The Alabama Creek Indian Community," in *Southeastern Indians since the Removal Era*, ed. Walter L. Williams (Athens: University of Georgia Press, 1979), 123–41; John P. Bowes, *Land Too Good for Indians: Northern Indian Removal* (Norman: University of Oklahoma Press, 2016), 208–10; Lawrence M. Hauptman, *Conspiracy of Interests: Iroquois Dispossession and the Rise of New York State* (Syracuse: Syracuse University Press, 1999), 191–220; John Ross et al. to the Seneca Delegation, Apr. 14, 1834, *PCJR*, 1:284–86.

27. Louise Barry, "The Fort Leavenworth-Fort Gibson Military Road and the Founding of Fort Scott," *Kansas Historical Quarterly* 9, no. 2 (May 1942): 115–29.

28. Frederick Douglass, "Let the Negro Alone," in *The Frederick Douglass Papers*, ed. John W. Blassingame and John R. McKivigan (New Haven: Yale University Press, 1991), 4:206.

29. George Rollie Adams, *General William S. Harney: Prince of Dragoons* (Lincoln: University of Nebraska Press, 2001), 120–32.

30. Lewis Cass to Jonathan Jennings, John W. Davis, and Marks Crume, July 14, 1832, *CSE*, 2:876; John Ross to Lewis Cass, Feb. 14, 1833, *PCJR*, 1:262.

31. Memorial of Creeks, Feb. 3, 1830, PM, Protection of Indians, SEN21A-H3, NA; Big Kettle, Seneca White, and Thomson Harris to Andrew Jackson, Jan. 11, 1831, *PAJ*; Memorial of the Chickasaw Chiefs to the President of the United States, Nov. 22, 1832, LR, OIA, reel 136, frame 276, M-234, NA; *Georgia Journal* (Milledgeville, Ga.), May 11, 1824, 2.

32. Memorial of Inhabitants of Luzerne County, Pennsylvania, Feb. 14, 1831, PM, Protection of Indians, SEN21A-H3, NA; Memorial of Inhabitants of Chesterville, Maine, Feb. 15, 1831, PM, Protection of Indians, SEN21A-H3, NA; Memorial of the Inhabitants of Lafayette, New York, Jan. 7, 1830, PM, Protection of Indians, SEN21A-H3, NA; Memorial of Inhabitants of Lincoln County, Maine, Feb. 19, 1831, PM, Protection of Indians, SEN21A-H3, NA.

33. On rebuilding and survival, see David Treuer, *The Heartbeat of Wounded Knee: Native America from 1890 to the Present* (New York: Penguin, 2019). "A poem composed by a Choctaw of P.P. Pitchlynn's party while emigrating last winter to the West," [1832], 4026.8176, PPP.

ILLUSTRATION AND
MAP CREDITS

All maps by Claudio Saunt.

57 and 58   Memorial of the Cherokees, Dec. 1829, Committee of the Whole House, Petitions, "Various Subjects," HR21A-H1.1, NA.

78   *The Liberator* (Boston, Mass.), Apr. 23, 1831.

101   Robert Mills, *Guide to the National Executive Offices and the Capitol of the United States* (Washington, 1841), 15.

105   RG 77, Civil Works Map File, I.R. 50, NACP.

129 and 130   Gustave de Beaumont, "Voyage en Amérique," General Collection, Beinecke Rare Book and Manuscript Library, Yale University.

134   CGLR, box 3, NA.

161   Black Hawk and Major Ridge, copies after Charles Bird King, in Thomas L. McKenney and James Hall, *History of the Indian Tribes of North America* (Philadelphia, 1838–44), 1:212, 3:176.

180   RG 49, Old Map File, Alabama 11, NACP.

188   "Joseph D. Beers," Alice Curtis Desmond-Hamilton Fish Library, Garrison, N.Y. Photograph by Ross Corsair.

191   New York and Mississippi Land Company Stock Certificate, 1835, box 39, folder 1059, LPC.

193   Based on Joshua Stevens, NASA Earth Observatory images, https://earthobservatory.nasa.gov/images/92321/black-belt-prairie.

194   *Columbus Enquirer* (Columbus, Ga.), Apr. 24, 1835, 3.

209   Indenture, May 7, 1839, LR, OIA, box 180, RG 75, NA.

210   Numismatics Collection, Division of Work and Indus-
      try, National Museum of American History, Smithsonian
      Institution.

211   Based on "Cotton Lands for Sale," 1836, box 1, NYMS.

215   J.D. Beers to Elbert Herring, Mar. 4, 1836, Stocks 1836, box 1074,
      RG 75, NA.

261   Photo by Claudio Saunt.

273   Based on J.T. Pardee and C.F. Park, Jr., *Gold Deposits of the
      Southern Piedmont*, Geological Survey Professional Paper 213
      (U.S. Department of the Interior, n.d.), plate 7.

277   Based on *Army and Navy Chronicle* 7, no. 1 (July 5, 1838), 124;
      Sarah H. Hill, "Cherokee Removal: Forts Along the Georgia
      Trail of Tears" (National Parks Service and the Georgia Depart-
      ment of Natural Resources, Historic Preservation Program,
      2005); Benjamin C. Nance, "The Trail of Tears in Tennessee: A
      Study of the Routes Used during the Cherokee Removal of 1838"
      (Tennessee Department of Environment and Conservation,
      Division of Archaeology, 2001).

280   Based on National Parks Service, and Matthew T. Gregg and
      David M. Wishart, "The Price of Cherokee Removal," *Explora-
      tions in Economic History* 49, no. 4 (Oct. 1, 2012): table 4, p. 431.

287   Based on National Wetlands Inventory, U.S. Fish and Wildlife
      Service, Department of the Interior. Quotation from Stanley
      F. Horn, "Tennessee Volunteers in the Seminole Campaign of
      1836: The Diary of Henry Hollingsworth," *Tennessee Historical
      Quarterly* 2, no. 1 (Mar. 1943):63.

289   "Night ascension and Encampment," September 1840, Records
      of the Adjutant General's Office, RG 94, Miscellaneous File no.
      284, item 7, box 27, NA.

309   Based on U.S. Bureau of the Census, *Historical Statistics of the
      United States, 1789–1945* (U.S. Department of Commerce, 1949).

310 Based on U.S. Census of 1850, Steven Ruggles, Sarah Flood, Ronald Goeken, Josiah Grover, Erin Meyer, Jose Pacas, and Matthew Sobek, IPUMS USA: Version 8.0 [dataset] (Minneapolis, Minn.: IPUMS, 2018).

313 Based on U.S. Census of 1850, Steven Ruggles, Sarah Flood, Ronald Goeken, Josiah Grover, Erin Meyer, Jose Pacas, and Matthew Sobek, IPUMS USA: Version 8.0 [dataset] (Minneapolis, Minn.: IPUMS, 2018).

316 Based on "Indians Removed West of the Mississippi," 20th Cong., 1st sess., H.Doc. 233; and "Indians Removed to West of the Mississippi," 25th Cong., 3rd sess., H.Doc. 147.

319 Based on Claudio Saunt, "The Invasion of America," eHistory. org; Steven Manson, Jonathan Schroeder, David Van Riper, and Steven Ruggles, IPUMS National Historical Geographic Information System: Version 13.0 [Database] (Minneapolis: University of Minnesota, 2018); Newberry Library, *Atlas of Historical County Boundaries*, https://publications.newberry .org/ ahcbp/index.html; Douglas H. Ubelaker, "North American Indian Population Size: Changing Perspectives," in *Disease and Demography in the Americas*, ed. John W. Verano and Douglas H. Ubelaker (Washington, D.C.: Smithsonian Institution Press, 1992), 173; 25th Cong., 2nd sess., H.Doc. 59; 32nd Cong., 1st sess., S.Exec.Doc. 1, pt. 1, map following p. 304.

INDEX

Page numbers in *italics* indicate illustrations.